SECOND EDITION

Fundamentals of Research
in Criminology
and Criminal Justice

SECOND EDITION

Fundamentals of Research
in Criminology
and Criminal Justice

Ronet Bachman
University of Delaware

Russell K. Schutt
University of Massachusetts Boston

Los Angeles | London | New Delhi
Singapore | Washington DC

Los Angeles | London | New Delhi
Singapore | Washington DC

FOR INFORMATION:

SAGE Publications, Inc.
2455 Teller Road
Thousand Oaks, California 91320
E-mail: order@sagepub.com

SAGE Publications Ltd.
1 Oliver's Yard
55 City Road
London EC1Y 1SP
United Kingdom

SAGE Publications India Pvt. Ltd.
B 1/I 1 Mohan Cooperative Industrial Area
Mathura Road, New Delhi 110 044
India

SAGE Publications Asia-Pacific Pte. Ltd.
33 Pekin Street #02-01
Far East Square
Singapore 048763

Acquisitions Editor: Jerry Westby

Editorial Assistant: Erim Sarbuland

Production Editor: Karen Wiley

Copy Editor: Teresa Herlinger

Permissions Editor: Karen Ehrmann

Typesetter: C&M Digitals (P) Ltd.

Proofreader: Susan Schon

Indexer: Sheila Bodell

Cover Designer: Gail Buschman

Marketing Manager: Erica DeLuca

Copyright © 2012 by SAGE Publications, Inc.

Printed in the United States of America

Library of Congress Cataloging-in-Publication Data

Bachman, Ronet.

Fundamentals of research in criminology and criminal justice / Ronet Bachman, Russell K. Schutt. — 2nd ed.

p. cm
Includes bibliographical references and index.

ISBN 978-1-4129-9176-6 (pbk.)

1. Criminology—Research. 2. Criminal justice, Administration of—Research. I. Schutt, Russell K. II. Title.

HV6024.5.B32 2011 364.072—dc22 2010046433

This book is printed on acid-free paper.

11 12 13 14 15 10 9 8 7 6 5 4 3 2 1

Brief Contents

Student Study Site

The companion Student Study Site for *Fundamentals of Research in Criminology and Criminal Justice* can be found at **www.sagepub.com/bachmanfrccj2e.**

Visit the Student Study Site to enhance your understanding of the chapter content and to discover additional resources that will take your learning one step further. You can enhance your understanding of the chapters by using the comprehensive study material, which includes interactive exercises, e-flashcards, web exercises, practice self-tests, and more. You will also find special features, such as Learning From Journal Articles, which incorporate Sage's online journal collection.

Detailed Contents

4 Conceptualization and Measurement   79

5 Sampling 103

6 Causation and Research Design 131

8 Qualitative Methods and Data Analysis   195

10 Evaluation and Policy Analysis 255

11   Quantitative Data Analysis   283

12   Reporting Research Results   313

On Student Study Site, **www.sagepub.com/bachmanfrccj2e**

About the Authors

Ronet Bachman, PhD, is Professor and Chair of the Department of Sociology and Criminal Justice at the University of Delaware. She is coauthor of *Statistical Methods for Crime and Criminal Justice* (3rd ed.), and coeditor of *Explaining Crime and Criminology: Essays in Contemporary Criminal Theory*. In addition, she is author of *Death and Violence on the Reservation;* coauthor of *Stress, Culture, and Aggression in the United States;* coauthor of *Murder American Style;* and coauthor of *Violence: The Enduring Problem* as well as numerous articles and papers that examine the epidemiology and etiology of violence, with a particular emphasis on women, the elderly, and minority populations. She is currently the Co-PI of a National Institute of Justice–funded study to examine the trajectories of drug-involved offenders 10 years after release from prison using a mixed-method design.

Russell K. Schutt, PhD, is Professor of Sociology at the University of Massachusetts, Boston, and Lecturer on Sociology in the Department of Psychiatry (Beth Israel-Deaconess Medical Center) at the Harvard Medical School. He completed his BA, MA, and PhD (1977) degrees at the University of Illinois at Chicago and was a postdoctoral fellow in the Sociology of Social Control Training Program at Yale University (1977–1979). He is the author or coauthor of *Investigating Human Behavior*, as well as Sage research methods texts for sociology, social work, and criminology/criminal justice. He is also the author of *Homelessness, Housing, and Mental Illness*, as well as other books and numerous articles on homelessness, service preferences and satisfaction, mental health, cognitive functioning, service systems and organizations, law, and teaching research methods. His funded research experience includes a National Cancer Institute–funded study of community health workers and recruitment for cancer clinical trials; a large translational research project for the Massachusetts Department of Public Health's Women's Health Network; a National Institute of Mental Health–funded study of housing alternatives for homeless persons diagnosed with severe mental illness; and evaluations of service programs in the Massachusetts Department of Public Health, the Massachusetts Department of Mental Health, and the Veterans Administration.

Preface

If you are looking for a comprehensive yet accessible introduction to research methods, this is the book for you. After years of teaching courses in research methods, we have found that the best forum for learning is to link the teaching of key topics to contemporary research in the discipline. We have avoided the "recipe book" approach to research methods by combining discussions of research techniques along with practical research examples from the field. In this way, students not only learn how to conduct research, but they also learn why it is important to do so. In the second edition of *Fundamentals of Research in Criminology and Criminal Justice,* we have retained our unique method of "instruction by example" that is used in our more comprehensive text, *The Practice of Research in Criminology and Criminal Justice.* We believe this approach not only increases students' understanding of complex research methods, but also conveys to students the vital role that research plays in our discipline.

The purpose of this book is to introduce students to the basics of scientific methods of research and show how they are actually used. Each chapter in this book combines instruction in research methods with investigations of key research questions in our field: What are the causes of violent crime? What is the best police response to intimate partner violence? How do gang members perceive their world? Are boot camps effective in reducing recidivism? Do community police officers perceive their roles as different from regular patrol officers? These and many other research questions are explored through the text in tandem with a discussion of research methods. These substantive examples will help you see how research methods are used in practice.

By the end of the course, students will not only have the ability to conduct research, but they will also be more adept consumers of knowledge claims about "truth" that bombard us on a daily basis. We are careful to describe the benefits and liabilities of each major approach to research and emphasize why employing a combination of them is often preferable to a single-method approach. Students will come to appreciate why the results of particular research studies must always be interpreted within the context of prior research and through the lens of social and criminological theory. Extensive exercises are provided at the end of each chapter that allow students to engage in different research tasks both individually and within groups.

ORGANIZATION OF THE BOOK

The way this book is organized reflects our beliefs in making research methods interesting, teaching students how to critique research, and viewing specific research techniques as parts of an integrated research strategy. Our concern with ethical issues in all types of research is underscored by the fact that we have a new chapter devoted exclusively to research ethics in addition to sections on ethics in every methodology chapter. The first two chapters introduce the why and how of research in general. Chapter 1 shows how research has helped us understand the magnitude of and the factors related to youth violence. Chapter 2 illustrates the basic stages of research with a series of experiments on the police response to intimate partner violence. Chapter 3 is a new chapter that highlights issues of research ethics by taking you inside Philip Zimbardo's prison experiment and Stanley Milgram's research on obedience to authority. It also introduces you to different research philosophies. Chapters 4 and 5 discuss how to evaluate the way researchers design their measures and draw their samples. Chapter 6 explores issues related to making causal connections and provides a summary of the strengths and limitations of various research designs in making causal conclusions. It offers a detailed discussion of how true experimental designs are the gold standard when making causal inferences.

Chapters 7 and 8 present the other important methods of data collection: surveys and qualitative methods (including participant observation, intensive interviews, and focus groups). Chapter 9 examines methodologies that rely on existing content and includes a discussion of secondary data analysis, historical and comparative research, content analysis, and crime mapping, along with a discussion of triangulation methods. Chapter 10 covers evaluation research and policy analysis and highlights the different alternatives to evaluation along with a discussion of the most appropriate methods to use for each evaluation question (e.g., process versus impact). In this chapter, you will see how various methods have been used to investigate the effects of several programs and policies, including problem-oriented policing and boot camps. You will also see why "evidence-based" policy is increasingly in demand and how meta-analyses help policy makers summarize the findings of a large body of research.

In Chapter 11, we work through an analysis of survey data on self-reported delinquency to see how these statistics are used to answer actual research questions. We finish up in Chapter 12 with an overview of the process of and techniques for reporting research results along with some ethical problems in writing.

The substantive studies in each of these chapters show how each methodology has been used to improve our understanding of criminal justice–related issues, including the factors related to violence, how question wording affects estimates of victimization in surveys, how gang members perceive their world, how community police officers describe their role in comparison to regular patrol officers, the perceptions of jurors who have participated in a death penalty case, the effects of inmates' classification on institutional misconduct in prison, and the effects of poverty on homicide in a cross-national comparison, to name just a few of the examples provided.

DISTINCTIVE FEATURES OF THE BOOK

The most distinctive feature of this text compared with others in the field is the integration into each chapter of in-depth substantive examples from real criminal justice–related research. Examples from the literature are not simply dropped here and there to keep students' attention. Rather, each chapter presents a particular research method in the context of a substantive research story. As such, this book's success is due in no small measure to the availability in the research literature of so many excellent examples. The following points are additional strengths of this edition:

Expanded coverage of ethical issues. We have added a new chapter on research ethics (Chapter 3) that includes up-to-date information on institutional review boards. You will learn about issues in ethical practice through research examples from Philip Zimbardo's prison experiment and through Stanley Milgram's research investigations of obedience to authority. However, because we believe that every step in the research process raises ethical concerns, every chapter still reviews the relevant ethical issues in the context of each method of data collection, data analysis, and reporting including a new discussion of plagiarism in the chapter on reporting results (Chapter 13). The end-of-chapter "Making Research Ethical" exercises also remain in all chapters.

Streamlined introduction to research. We have incorporated a discussion of how victimization and offending are measured into the research story line of Chapter 1. It highlights the major sources of data including the Federal Bureau of Investigation's Uniform Crime Reporting Program and National Incident-Based Reporting System, the National Crime Victimization Survey, and various surveys that measure offending behavior. We have also moved the discussion of validity and generalizability from Chapter 1 to Chapter 2 and updated the discussion to introduce the concept of "authenticity." We changed the discussion of these concepts to revolve around the research presented in the chapter on arrest and intimate partner assault, which we believe will increase the understanding of these difficult concepts. A case study of a literature review on the deterrence value of arrest in cases of intimate partner assault has also been added to Chapter 2 to illustrate guidelines for effective literature searches.

Examples of criminological research as they occur in real-world settings. We include interesting studies taken from the literature on a variety of topics including the causes and correlates of violence, the efficacy of arrest for intimate partner assault, the perceptions of police officers regarding community policing, and an investigation into the lives of gang members, to name just a few. These real-world research examples illustrate the exigencies and complexities that shape the application of research methods.

Updated discussion of causation that includes more field experiments and other unique methods. The discussion of causation has been incorporated with several new field experiments from the literature, including research examining the impact of a criminal record on finding a job, the specialization of offending patterns in recidivists, the impact of drug courts on recidivism, and the impact of the Youth Criminal Justice Act in Canada.

Expanded discussion of increasingly utilized methods such as systematic observation and crime mapping. We have expanded the discussion of systematic observation and crime mapping within Chapters 9 and 10. We have also added a series of photos and video clips that can be utilized on the Student Study Site and used for coding exercises. These examples of systematic observation were obtained by Peter K. B. St. Jean (2007) for his research published in *Pockets of Crime: Broken Windows, Collective Efficacy, and the Criminal Point of View.*

New discussion of evidence-based policy and meta-analysis in the evaluation chapter. Because of the increasing demand for systematic reviews upon which to base policy decisions, the evaluation chapter now includes a discussion of evidence-based policy and meta-analysis. This section highlights a study examining the effectiveness of school-based anti-bullying programs.

Streamlined reporting results chapter. Chapter 12 now focuses exclusively on reporting results. We have expanded the section on participatory action research (PAR) and included a researcher's narrative of the PAR process that resurrected a college program in prison and evaluated its outcomes. We have also incorporated a discussion of plagiarism into the ethics section of this chapter.

End-of-chapter exercise with new "How to Use Excel" appendix on the Student Study Site. In addition to individual and group projects, each chapter includes exercises to give you experience in data analysis using IBM® SPSS® Statistics, the Statistical Package for the Social Sciences, or Excel. In addition, real data sets are provided to enhance your learning experience, including subsets of the National Crime Victimization Survey, a state-level file containing crime rates and other variables that measure structural characteristics of each state, such as the poverty rate, the divorce rate, and so on. Each chapter also provides updated end-of-chapter web exercises.

Aids to effective study. Lists of main points and key terms provide quick summaries at the end of each chapter. In addition, key terms are highlighted in boldface type when first introduced and defined in text. Definitions for these also can be found in the glossary at the end of the book. The instructor's manual includes more exercises that have been specially designed for collaborative group work inside and outside the classroom. Appendix A, "Conducting Literature Reviews and Finding Information," provides up-to-date information about using the Internet. The Student Study Site also provides invaluable tools for learning.

We are excited to introduce our unique approach to learning research methods in this *Fundamentals* book. If we have communicated the excitement of research and the importance of evaluating carefully the methods we use in research, then we have succeeded in representing what social scientists interested in issues related to criminal justice and criminology do. We think it conveys the latest developments in research methodology in a comprehensive yet very accessible manner.

We hope you enjoy learning how to investigate research questions related to criminal justice and criminology and will perhaps be inspired to do some research of your own along the way. We guarantee that the knowledge you develop about research methods will serve you well throughout your education, in your career, and in your community.

SUPPLEMENTS

Companion Student Study Site (http://www.sagepub.com/bachmanfrccj2e)

This web-based Student Study Site provides a variety of additional resources to enhance students' understanding of the book content and take their learning one step further. The site includes self-study quizzes, e-flashcards, a new "Learning From SAGE Journal Articles" feature, web exercises, real crime data including a subset of the National Crime Victimization Survey data and the General Social Survey, and appendices on how to use SPSS and Excel. It also contains interactive exercises with criminal justice and criminology tracks specifically designed to help students get into the latest research in the field.

Instructor Resources Site

A password-protected instructor resources site is available with this text. It offers a variety of resources to supplement the book material, including lecture outlines, PowerPoint® slides, test questions with answers, and student project ideas. The site also contains articles on teaching criminal justice research methods, film and software resources, and web resources.

A Note About Using IBM® SPSS® Statistics and HyperRESEARCH

To carry out the SPSS exercises at the end of each chapter and in Appendix D, you must have SPSS installed on your computer. The Student Study Site includes several subsets of data, including data from the National Crime Victimization Survey and the Uniform Crime Reports. Appendix D on the study site will also get you up and running with SPSS for Windows; you can then spend as much time as you like exploring the data sets provided, or even use your own data. You can also carry out analyses of the General Social Survey (GSS) at the University of California Berkeley website: http://sda.berkeley.edu:7502/archive.htm.

Appendix E on the study site contains a detailed discussion of what it is like to do qualitative research with the statistical software package HyperRESEARCH. In this appendix, you will learn how to begin a simple project in HyperRESEARCH by creating and managing data and ideas, coding, linking, modeling, and asking questions about your narrative data.

ACKNOWLEDGMENTS

We must first acknowledge our gratitude to Jerry Westby, whose hard work and guidance on this project are unrivaled. He has been more than an editor; he is an ideas man, a tenacious fact finder, a motivator, a therapist, and—most important—a friend. We are also indebted to Leah Mori for her attention to detail in marshalling the text through production, and to Teresa Herlinger for her meticulous copyediting and insightful suggestions for improvements. And finally, this text has been made more "user-friendly" by the herculean efforts of graduate assistant extraordinaire, Erin Kerrison, whose meticulous reading of the text has made it much more accessible to those without a social research background.

Gratitude also goes to all the reviewers of our *Research Methods* books who have helped make this *Fundamentals* version what it is, including Ira Sommers, California State University, Los Angeles; Kristy Holtfreter, Florida State University; Amy Craddock, Indiana State University; James R. Maupin, New Mexico State University; William Wells, Southern Illinois University Carbondale; Gennifer Furst, The College of New Jersey; Lori Guevara, Fayetteville State University; Frank Cormier, University of Manitoba; Michael J. DeValve, Fayetteville State University; Brian Colwell, Stanford University; Susan B. Haire, University of Georgia; Lisa Anne Zilney, Montclair State University; and Stephen M. Haas, Marshall University. Reviewers of previous editions included Cathy Couglan, Texas Christian University; Lucy Hochstein, Radford University; Mark Winton, University of Central Florida; Stephen Haas, Marshall University; Hank J. Brightman, Saint Peter's College; Eric Metchick, Salem State College; Kristen Kuehnle, Salem State College; Wilson R. Palacios, University of South Florida; and Phyllis B. Gerstenfeld, California State University–Stanislaus. Andre Rosay also provided an extensive and invaluable review of the first edition of this text. We also thank Lindsay R. Reed and Hanna S. Scott for their diligence and hard work in writing the instructor's manual, Ann Dupuis and Sharlene Hesse-Biber for the appendix on HyperRESEARCH software, Margarita Poteyava for writing the appendix on how to use Excel, and Kathryn Stoeckert as well as Heather Albertson and Peggy Plass for additional interactive exercises.

We continue to be indebted to the many students we have had an opportunity to teach and mentor, at both the undergraduate and graduate levels. In many respects, this book could not have been written without these ongoing reciprocal teaching and learning experiences. You inspire us to become better teachers!

Ronet is indebted to her colleagues in the Department of Sociology and Criminal Justice at the University of Delaware who are unwavering sources of support and inspire her by their exemplary dedication to mentorship, teaching, and the research process. Ronet is also indebted to an amazing circle of friends who endured graduate school with her and continue to be there for guidance, support, therapy, and laughter: Dianne Carmody, Gerry King, Peggy Plass, and Barbara Wauchope. You are the most amazing women in the world, and I am so blessed to have you in my life. She also thanks Alex Alvarez and Michelle Meloy, her other kindred spirits, for their support, guidance, and especially their humor; her mother, Jan, who remains her hero; and her father, Ron, for his steadfast critical eye in all matters of life.

Most important, Ronet would like to thank her husband, Raymond Paternoster, and their son, John, and Russ would like to thank his wife, Elizabeth Schneider Schutt, and daughter, Julia. They have provided love, support, patience, and remarkable joy in our lives.

CHAPTER 1

Science, Society, and Criminological Research

In this chapter, you will learn how the methods of social science research go beyond stories in the popular media to help us answer questions like "What are the causes of youth violence?" We will examine the motivations for research using youth violence as a theme. We will also explore the differences between quantitative and qualitative research methods. By the chapter's end, you should appreciate how the methods of social science can help us understand and answer research questions in criminology and criminal justice.

WHAT DO WE HAVE IN MIND?

When we were revising this manuscript in the spring of 2010, an unemployed middle-aged man in Eastern China entered a kindergarten and stabbed 28 children and three adults, killing five people. It had been the third school stabbing in China in less than a month. The characteristics of these mass killings in China appear to be very different from school killings in the United States, which largely involve guns and have other students as the offenders. For example, on April 16, 2007, Cho Seung Hui killed 32 students, faculty, and staff and left about 30 others injured on the campus of Virginia Tech in Blacksburg. Cho was armed with two semiautomatic handguns that he had legally purchased and was wearing a vestful of ammunition. As the police were closing in on the scene, he killed himself. The shooting rampage is now the deadliest in U.S. history. Less than a year later, on February 14, 2008, Steven Kazmierczak, who was described as "an outstanding student," entered a large oceanography class that was in session at Northern Illinois University and opened fire using a shotgun and three handguns, which he had smuggled into the room using a guitar case. A total of 24 people were shot, 6 of whom died, including Kazmierczak, who shot himself before police arrived.

Prior to these incidents of mass murder, on April 20, 1999, Eric Harris and Dylan Klebold turned Columbine High School, in suburban Colorado, into the scene of the deadliest high school shooting in American history. After killing 12 students and a teacher, the youths shot themselves in the head. In the end, 15 people were left dead and 28 were injured. When the bloodbath was over, police found the school in Littleton littered with bombs and other booby traps. Harris and Klebold were not typical terrorists. There have been many myths about the two, such as that they were social outcasts at their school (they weren't) and that they were affiliated with a group known as the Trenchcoat Mafia (they weren't) (Cullen 2009). But even before the killings, signs of trouble were still evident to many. Harris's webpages were filled with images of fire, skulls, devils, and weapons, and included recipes for and sketches of pipe bombs. The two young men also wrote poetry about death for their English class and made a video about guns for a video class.

Whenever such a tragedy occurs, it causes a media frenzy. Headlines such as "The School Violence Crisis" and "School Crime Epidemic" were plastered across national news-papers and weekly news journals after the Columbine shooting. From a statistical stand-point, these headlines seemed a little late, particularly because the juvenile arrest rate for murder had been declining in the late 1990s. In addition, the thousands of other shootings that occurred in less privileged communities during the same time rarely made the national news. For example, there were no such declarations when an 11-year-old boy was shot and killed in Chicago because he had allegedly shorted an 18-year-old on drug money. And where were such declarations the night two teenagers were shot outside a Baltimore nightclub when guns turned an argument into the final solution?

Many factors influence our beliefs about social phenomena, but the media play a large role in how we perceive both problems and solutions. What are your perceptions of vio-lence committed by youth, and how did you acquire such perceptions? What do you believe are the causes of youth violence? Many factors have been blamed for youth vio-lence in American society, including the easy availability of guns, the use of weapons in movies and television, the moral decay of our nation, poor parenting, unaware teachers, school and class size, racial prejudice, teenage alienation, unsupervised Internet access, anti-Semitism, rap and rock music, and the Goth culture. When trying to make sense out of the Littleton incident, then-President Bill Clinton talked about hate, prejudice, commu-nity policing, conflict resolution, parental responsibility, and violence in the culture. Charlton Heston, spokesman for the National Rifle Association, blamed the absence of armed security guards in schools, even though one was present in Littleton. Heston also blamed the parents and the school for allowing kids to wear black.

You probably have your own ideas about what factors may be related to violence in general and youth violence in particular. However, the factors you believe are important in explaining a phenomenon may not always be the ones supported by empirical research.

REASONING ABOUT THE SOCIAL WORLD

Case Study: Exploring Youth Violence

The story of just one murderous youth raises many questions. Take a few minutes to read each of the following questions and jot down your answers. Don't overthink or worry too much about the questions. This is not a test; there are no wrong answers.

- How would you describe Eric Harris?
- Why do you think Eric Harris wanted to kill other students?

- Was Eric Harris typical of other teenage murderers?
- How have you learned about youth violence?

Now let us consider the possible answers to one of these questions. The information about Eric Harris is somewhat inconsistent (Duggan, Shear, & Fisher 1999). He was the 18-year-old son of white, middle-class professionals. He had an older brother who attended the University of Colorado. Harris apparently thought of himself as a white supremacist, but he also loved music by antiracist rock bands. On his webpage, he quoted from KMFDM, a German rock band whose song "Waste" includes these lyrics: "What I don't say I don't do. What I don't do I don't like. What I don't like I waste." Online, Harris referred to himself as "Darkness."

Do you have enough information now to understand why Eric went on a shooting rampage in his school?

A year before the shootings at Columbine High School, Harris was arrested on a felony count of breaking into a car. A juvenile court put him on probation, required him to perform community service and take criminal justice classes, and sent him to a school counseling program. He was described by one of his probation officers as a "very bright young man who is likely to succeed in life."

Now can you construct an adequate description of Eric Harris? Can you explain the reason for his murderous rampage? Or do you feel you need to know more about him, about his friends and the family in which he grew up? And how about his experiences in school and with the criminal justice system? We have attempted to investigate just one person's experiences, and already our investigation is spawning more and more questions.

Questions and Answers

When questions concern not just one person but many people or general social processes, the number of possible answers quickly multiplies. For example, when a Gallup Poll (2007) asked American adults, "In your opinion, what is the single most important thing that could be done to prevent another incidence of school shootings by students, like the recent incident at Virginia Tech?" respondents offered many different opinions. The majority of respondents considered the most important preventive factor to fall within the category of increased student supervision (28%). About 1 in 5 respondents believed increased school security was the answer, 13% thought we needed tougher gun control laws, 12% thought more counseling for students would do the trick, 8% believed better upbringing by parents was the answer, while 9% believed that nothing could be done to prevent school shootings (10% had no opinion).

We cannot avoid asking questions about the actions and attitudes of others. We all try to make sense of the complexities of our social world, our position in it, in which we have quite a personal stake. In fact, the more that you begin to "think like a social scientist," the more questions will come to mind.

But why does each question have so many possible answers? Surely our individual perspectives play a role. One person may see a homicide offender as a victim of circumstance, while another person may see the same individual as inherently evil. Answers to questions we ask in the criminological sciences vary because individual life experiences and circumstances vary. The study of perceptions about the best prevention strategies conducted by the Gallup Poll (2007), summarized in Exhibit 1.1, gives some idea of how opinions about

Exhibit 1.1	Responses to the Question, *In your opinion, what is the single most important thing that could be done to prevent another incidence of school shootings by students, like the recent incident at Virginia Tech?* (Gallup Polls, 2007)

What Single Factor Would Be the Best Prevention?	
More Monitoring of Students	28%
Enhanced Security	20%
Change Gun Laws	13%
More Counseling for Students	12%
Better Upbringing	8%
Nothing Can be Done	9%
No Opinion	10%

the causes and cures for school violence vary. Despite respondents' answers regarding the most effective school violence prevention strategies, the overwhelming majority of all respondents (82%) believed that no matter what schools did, they would not be able to prevent school shootings in the future.

Everyday Errors in Reasoning

People give different answers to research questions for yet another reason: It is simply too easy to make errors in logic, particularly when we are analyzing the social world in which we ourselves are conscious participants. We can call some of these *everyday errors,* because they occur so frequently.

For evidence of everyday errors, just listen to your conversations or the conversations of others for one day. At some point in the day, it is inevitable that you or someone you are talking with will say something like, "Well, I knew a person who did X, and then Y happened." From this one piece of information, you draw a conclusion about the likelihood of Y. Four general errors in everyday reasoning can be made: overgeneralization, selective or inaccurate observation, illogical reasoning, and resistance to change.

Overgeneralization

Overgeneralization, an error in reasoning, occurs when we conclude that what we have observed or what we know to be true for some cases is true for all cases. We are always drawing conclusions about people and social processes from our own interactions with them, but sometimes we forget that our experiences are limited. The social (and natural) world is, after all, a complex place. We have the ability (and inclination) to interact with just a small fraction of the individuals who live in the world, especially in a limited span of time.

Selective or Inaccurate Observation

Selective observation is choosing to look only at things that align with our preferences or beliefs. When we are inclined to criticize individuals or institutions, it is all too easy to notice their every failing. We are also more inclined to see the failings of others who are "not like us." If we are convinced in advance that all kids who are violent are unlikely to be rehabilitated and will go on to commit violent offenses in adulthood, we will probably find many cases confirming our beliefs. But what about other youths who have become productive and stable citizens after engaging in violence as adolescents? If we acknowledge only the instances that confirm our predispositions, we are victims of our own selective observation. Exhibit 1.2 depicts the difference between overgeneralization and selective observation.

Our observations also can simply be inaccurate. If a woman says she is *hungry* and we think she said she is *hunted,* we have made an inaccurate observation. If we think five people are standing on a street corner when there are actually seven, we have also made an inaccurate observation. Such errors occur often in casual conversation and in everyday observation of the world around us. In fact, our perceptions do not provide a direct window to the world around us, for what we think we have sensed is not necessarily what we have seen (or heard, smelled, felt, or tasted). Even when our senses are functioning fully, our minds have to interpret what we have sensed (Humphrey 1992).

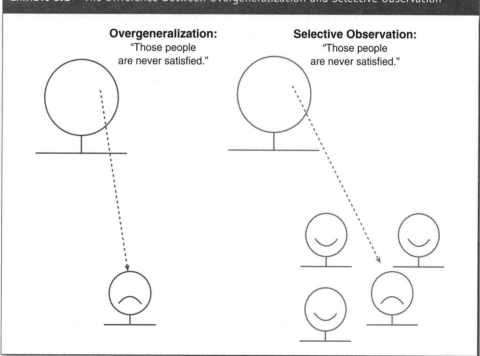

Exhibit 1.2   The Difference Between Overgeneralization and Selective Observation

Illogical Reasoning

When we prematurely jump to conclusions or argue on the basis of invalid assumptions, we are using illogical reasoning. For example, it is not reasonable to propose that depictions of violence in media such as television and movies cause violence if evidence indicates that the majority of those who watch such programs do not become violent. However, it is also illogical to assume that media depictions of gratuitous violence have no effect on individuals. Of course, logic that seems valid to one person can seem twisted or unsound to another; the problem emerges when our reasoning stems from different assumptions rather than a failure to "think straight."

Resistance to Change

Resistance to change, the reluctance to change our ideas in light of new information, may occur for several reasons:

- *Ego-based commitments.* We all learn to greet with some skepticism the claims by leaders of companies, schools, agencies, and so on that people in their organization are happy, that revenues are growing, that services are being delivered in the best possible way, and so forth. We know how tempting it is to make statements about the social world that conform to our own needs rather than to the observable facts. It also can be difficult to admit that we were wrong once we have staked out a position on an issue.
- *Excessive devotion to tradition.* Some degree of devotion to tradition is necessary for the predictable functioning of society. Social life can be richer and more meaningful if it is allowed to flow along the paths charted by those who have preceded us. But too much devotion to tradition can stifle adaptation to changing circumstances. When we distort our observations or alter our reasoning so that we can maintain beliefs that "were good enough for my grandfather, so they're good enough for me," we hinder our ability to accept new findings and develop new knowledge.
- *Uncritical agreement with authority.* If we lack the courage to critically evaluate the ideas of those in positions of authority, we will have little basis for complaint if they exercise their authority over us in ways we do not like. And if we do not allow new discoveries to call our beliefs into question, our understanding of the social world will remain limited. People often accept the beliefs of those in positions of authority without question.

Now take just a minute to reexamine the beliefs about youth violence that you recorded earlier. Did you settle on a simple explanation even though the reality was far more complex? Were your beliefs influenced by your own ego and feelings about your similarities to or differences from individuals prone to violence? Are your beliefs perhaps based on depictions of violence in the media or fiction? Did you weigh carefully the opinions of authority figures, including politicians, teachers, and even your parents, or just accept or reject those opinions? Could knowledge of research methods help to improve your own understanding of the factors related to violent behavior? By now, you can see some of the challenges faced by social scientists who study issues related to crime and the criminal justice system.

You do not have to be a scientist or use sophisticated research techniques to recognize and avoid these four errors in reasoning. If you recognize these errors for what they are and make a conscious effort to avoid them, you can improve your own reasoning. Simply stated, refrain from stereotyping people, avoid jumping to conclusions, and look at the big picture. These are the same errors that the methods of social science are designed to help us avoid.

HOW THE SCIENTIFIC APPROACH IS DIFFERENT

The scientific approach to answering questions about the social world is designed to greatly reduce these potential sources of error in everyday reasoning. Science relies on systematic methods to answer questions, and it does so in a way that allows others to inspect and evaluate its methods. In the realm of social research, these methods are not so unusual. After all, they involve asking questions, observing social groups, and counting people, which we often do in our everyday lives. However, social scientists develop, refine, apply, and report their understanding of the social world more systematically, or specifically, than Joanna Q. Public.

- Social science research methods can reduce the likelihood of overgeneralization by using systematic procedures for selecting individuals or groups to study that are representative of the individuals or groups that we wish to generalize.
- Social science methods can reduce the risk of selective or inaccurate observation by requiring that we measure and sample phenomena systematically.
- To avoid illogical reasoning, social researchers use explicit criteria for identifying causes and for determining if these criteria are met in a particular instance.
- Scientific methods lessen the tendency to develop answers about the social world from ego-based commitments, excessive devotion to tradition, or unquestioning respect for authority.

Science A set of logical, systematic, documented methods for investigating nature and natural processes; the knowledge produced by these investigations.

Social science The use of scientific methods to investigate individuals, societies, and social processes, including questions related to criminology and criminal justice; the knowledge produced by these investigations.

Why We Do Criminological Research

Like you, social scientists read and hear stories about incidents of violence committed by youth, observe this violence occasionally in their lives, and try to make sense of what they see. For most, that is the end of it. But for some social scientists, the problem of youth violence has become a major research focus. The motivations for selecting this particular research focus, as with any social science topic, can be any one or some combination of the following:

Policy motivations. Many social service agencies and elected officials seek better assessments and descriptions of youth violence so they can identify needs and allocate responsibility among agencies that could meet these needs. For example, federal agencies such as the U.S. Department of Justice and the Centers for Disease Control and Prevention want to identify the magnitude of youth violence, and many state and local officials use social research to guide development of their social service budgets. Programs designed to rehabilitate young offenders often use research to learn more about the needs of their clientele. These policy guidance and program management needs have resulted in numerous research projects.

Academic motivations. Young offenders have been a logical focus for researchers interested in a number of questions, ranging from how an individual's connection to parents and peers influences his or her behavior to how the social conditions under which the person lives, such as poverty, affect his or her behavior. For example, social scientists have long been concerned with the impact that social disorganization has on individual behavior. In the 1920s, researchers at the University of Chicago were interested in the effects that residential mobility and immigration had on levels of crime and delinquency in urban neighborhoods. Today, researchers are exploring similar questions concerning the impact of disintegrating economic bases in central cities and their relationship to crime and violence. Other researchers have focused on individual-level explanations such as neurological damage. Those who study social policy also have sought to determine whether correctional programs such as boot camps and other forms of shock incarceration serve to decrease the probability of juveniles reoffending in the future.

Personal motivations. Many who conduct research on youth violence feel that doing so can help to prevent it or ameliorate the consequences of this violence when it occurs. Some social scientists first volunteered with at-risk youth in such organizations as Big Brothers Big Sisters, and only later began to develop a research agenda based on their experiences.

Social Criminological Research in Action

Youth violence always has been a popular topic of social science research. However, the sharp increase in this violence in the United States that began in the late 1980s was unprecedented. Predictably, whenever a phenomenon is perceived as an epidemic, numerous explanations emerge to explain it. Unfortunately, most of these explanations are based on the media and popular culture, not on empirical research. Despite the anecdotal information floating around in the mass media about the factors that may have contributed to increases in youth violence, social scientists interested in this phenomenon have amassed a substantial body of findings that have refined knowledge about the problem and shaped social policy (Tonry & Moore 1998). These studies fall into the four categories of purposes for social scientific research:

Descriptive research. Defining and describing social phenomena of interest are part of almost any research investigation, but **descriptive research** is the primary focus of many studies of youth crime and violence. Some of the central questions used in these studies were "How many people are victims of youth violence?" "How many youth are offenders?" "What are the most common crimes committed by youthful offenders?" and "How many of the different youth are arrested and incarcerated each year for crime?" Measurement (see Chapter 4) and sampling (see Chapter 5) are central concerns in descriptive research.

Exploratory research. **Exploratory research** seeks to find out how people get along in the setting under question, what meanings they give to their actions, and what issues concern them. The goal is to answer the question, "What is going on here?" and to investigate social phenomena without expectations. This purpose is associated with the use of methods that capture large amounts of relatively unstructured information. For example, researchers investigating the emergence of youth gangs in the 1980s were encountering a phenomenon of which they had no direct experience. Thus, an early goal was to find out what it was like to be a gang member and how gang members made sense of their situation. Exploratory research like this frequently involves qualitative methods (see Chapter 8).

Explanatory research. Many people consider explanation to be the premier goal of any science. **Explanatory research** seeks to identify causes and effects of social phenomena, to predict how one phenomenon will change or vary in response to variation in some other phenomenon. Researchers adopted explanation as a principal goal when they began to ask such questions as "Why do people become offenders?" and "Does the unemployment rate influence the frequency of youth crime?" Methods with which to identify causes and effects are the focus of Chapter 6.

Evaluation research. **Evaluation research** seeks to determine the effects of a social program or other types of intervention. It is a type of explanatory research because it deals with cause and effect. However, evaluation research differs from other forms of explanatory research because it considers the implementation and outcomes of social policies and programs. These issues may not be relevant in other types of explanatory research. The increase of youth violence in the 1980s spawned many new government programs and, with them, evaluation research to assess the impact of these programs. Some of these studies are reviewed in Chapter 10, which covers evaluation research.

We will now summarize one study in each of these four areas to give you a feel for the projects motivated by those different concerns.

Description: How Prevalent Is Youth Violence?

Police reports. One of the most long-term sources of information on lethal violence in the United States is the Federal Bureau of Investigation's (FBI) Supplementary Homicide Reports (SHR). James Fox and Marianne Zawitz have been providing analyses of these homicide data for the Bureau of Justice Statistics for many years, including the most recent data available, for 2005 (Fox & Zawitz 2009). Homicide data indicate that for those under the age of 24, vulnerability to murder increased dramatically during the mid-1980s through about 1994 when rates began a steady decline. After 2000, homicide victimization rates for this age group leveled off, but have recently exhibited a slow increasing trend (Fox & Zawitz 2009). What accounted for this unprecedented rise in youth violence during the late 1980s and early 1990s? To answer this question, explanatory research is necessary. Based on their in-depth descriptive analysis of youth violence during this time, Cook and Laub (1998) contend that the increasing homicide rates began with the introduction of crack cocaine and the street-level conflict linked to its exchange. However, the primary factor, they believe, was adolescents' increased access to guns: "All of the increase in homicide rates was with guns, and it appears to be changing access [to] and use of guns, rather than a change in the character of the youths, that best accounts for their increased involvement in lethal violence" (p. 60).

Collecting data that measures the prevalence of nonlethal forms of violence such as robbery and assaults is a bit more complicated. How do we know how many young people are the victims of assault each year? People who report their victimizations to police represent one source for these calculations. The FBI compiles these numbers in its Uniform Crime Reporting system, which is slowly being replaced by the National Incident-Based Reporting System (NIBRS). Both of these data sources rely on state, county, and city law enforcement agencies across the United States to voluntarily participate in the reporting program. Can you imagine why relying on these data sources may be problematic for estimating prevalence rates of violent victimizations? If victimizations are never reported to police, they are not counted. This is especially problematic for victimizations between intimate partners and other offenses like rape in which only a fraction of incidents are ever reported to police.

Surveys. Instead, most social scientists believe the best way to determine the magnitude of violent victimization is through random sample surveys. While we will discuss survey methodology in greater detail in Chapter 7, this basically means randomly selecting individuals in the population of interest and asking them about their victimization experiences. The only ongoing annual survey to do this is the National Crime Victimization Survey (NCVS), which is sponsored by the U.S. Department of Justice's Bureau of Justice Statistics. Among other questions, the NCVS asks questions like "Has anyone attacked or threatened you with a weapon, for instance, a gun or knife; by something thrown, such as a rock or bottle, include any grabbing, punching, or choking?" Estimates indicate that youth aged 12 to 24 have the highest rates of violent victimization. Despite the recent increases observed in homicide rates for this age group in some locations, their victimization trends have generally declined since the peak of the early 1990s mentioned earlier.

The Youth Risk Behavior Survey (YRBS) is another large research survey that estimates the magnitude of youth violence (along with other risk-taking behavior such as taking drugs and smoking) and has been conducted every 2 years in the United States since 1990. To measure the extent of youth violence, students are asked the following questions: "During the past 30 days, on how many days did you carry a weapon such as a gun, knife, or club?" "During the past 12 months, how many times were you in a physical fight?" "During the past 12 months, how many times were you in a physical fight in which you were injured and had to be seen by a doctor or nurse?" "During the past 30 days, how many times did you carry a weapon such as a gun, knife, or club on school property?" "During the past 12 months, how many times were you in a physical fight on school property?" and "During the past 12 months, how many times did someone threaten or injure you with a gun, knife, or club on school property?"

Of course, another way to measure violence would be to ask respondents about their offending behaviors. Some surveys do this, including the National Youth Survey (NYS) and the Rochester Youth Development Study (RYDS). The RYDS sample consists of 1,000 students who were in the seventh and eighth grades in the Rochester, New York, public schools during the spring semester of the 1988 school year. This project has interviewed the original respondents at 12 different times, including the last interview that took place in 1997 when respondents were in their early twenties (Thornberry et al. 2008). (We will discuss longitudinal research of this kind in Chapter 6.) As you can imagine, respondents are typically more reluctant to reveal offending behavior compared to their victimization experiences. However, these surveys have proved to be very useful in examining the factors related to violent offending and other delinquency. We should also point out that although this discussion has been specific to violence, the measures we have discussed in this section, along with their strengths and weaknesses, apply to measuring all types of crime.

Exploration: How Do Schools Respond to Gun Violence?

Research that is exploratory in nature is generally concerned with uncovering detailed information about a given phenomenon, learning as much as possible about particular people or events. Asmussen and Creswell (1995) were interested in the responses to school shooting incidents. Because school shootings are relatively rare and empirical literature that addressed the topic was lacking at the time, Asmussen and Creswell performed an in-depth qualitative case study of a shooting incident that occurred at a large public university. The incident took place on an early Monday morning when a male graduate student entered a senior-level actuarial science class armed with a vintage Korean War semiautomatic military rifle loaded with a 30-round clip of .30-caliber ammunition. Twenty of the 34 students in the class were already there, and most of them were quietly reading the students' newspaper while the instructor was en route to class. The gunman pointed the rifle at the students, swept it across the room, and pulled the trigger. The gun jammed. Trying to unlock the rifle, he hit the butt of it on a desk and quickly tried firing it again. Again it did not fire. By this time, most students had realized what was happening and had dropped to the floor, overturned their desks, and tried to hide behind them. After about 20 seconds, one of the students shoved a desk into the gunman, and students ran past him out into the hall and out of the building. The gunman hastily left the room and went out of the building to his parked car, which he had left running. He was captured by police within the hour.

Asmussen and Creswell (1995) were surprised to find that, instead of seeking safety after leaving the classroom, all the students had stood together just outside the building. Although a few were openly emotional and crying, many were kidding about the incident, as if it had posed no real danger. This denial response is noted by the mental health literature, which finds that feelings of fear and anger usually follow an initial response of denial and disbelief. The researchers found that many other people, in addition to the students who witnessed the incident, were traumatized by what had occurred. In fact, three distinct groups of people sought counseling services during the weeks following the event. The first group had some direct involvement with the assailant, either by seeing him the day of the gun incident or because they had known him personally. The second group comprised the "silent connection"—individuals who were indirectly involved and yet emotionally traumatized. Many members of this group were parents. The third group included people who had previously experienced a trauma and whose fears were reactivated by this incident.

Because the assailant's future was in the hands of the criminal justice system, the importance of information from this system became critical to feelings of safety. Two combined debriefing sessions by mental health counselors, the campus police chief, and two county attorneys were held for all those interested.

Another phenomenon observed on the campus was an increase in the number of professors and staff members who were concerned with disruptive students or students who exhibited aberrant behavior in class. To address their concerns, the Student Judiciary Office advised departments on various methods of dealing with students who exhibited abnormal behavior in class. In addition, plainclothes police officers were sent to sit outside classrooms and offices whenever faculty and staff indicated concerns.

Explanation: What Factors Are Related to Youth Delinquency and Violence?

What are some of the factors related to youth violence? Using the South Carolina YRBS, MacDonald et al. (2005) examined the efficacy of *general strain theory* (GST) (Agnew 1992) and Gottfredson and Hirschi's (1990) *general theory of crime* in predicting youth violence. GST generally maintains that strain, such as disjunction between expectations and aspirations (e.g., wanting a good job but not being able to get one), increases the likelihood that individuals will experience negative emotions, which in turn increases the likelihood of antisocial or violent behavior. These negative emotions include anger, anxiety, dissatisfaction, and so on. The general theory of crime claims that a lack of self-control, which is primarily formed by the relationship children have with their parents or guardians, is the motivating factor for all crime. Individuals with low self-control, the theory predicts, will be more likely to pursue immediate gratification, be impulsive, prefer simple tasks, engage in risky behavior, have volatile tempers, and so on.

To measure violent behavior, the YRBS asks respondents how many times in the past 30 days they carried a weapon and how many times they were in a physical fight. To measure life satisfaction, MacDonald et al. (2005) used six questions that asked respondents to report on general satisfaction or the degree to which they felt "terrible" or "delighted" about family life, friendships, school, self, residential location, and overall life. To measure self-control, the authors used the indicators of smoking and sexual behavior to represent risky behaviors that are not illegal, since they "reflect impulsivity and short-run hedonism" (p. 1502). Consistent with the general theory of crime, MacDonald et al. found that high school students who reported more impulsive behaviors, indicative of low self-control, also reported greater participation in violent behavior.

Evaluation: Do Violence Prevention Programs in Schools Work?

To reduce violence and create a safer atmosphere at schools across the country, literally thousands of schools have adopted some form of violence prevention training for both students and teachers (Powell, Muir-McClain, & Halasyamani 1995). For students, these programs generally provide cognitive-behavioral and social skills training on various topics using a variety of methods. Such programs are commonly referred to as *conflict resolution* and *peer mediation training*. Many of these prevention programs are designed to improve interpersonal problem-solving skills among children and adolescents by training children in cognitive processing, such as identifying the interpersonal problem and generating non-aggressive solutions. However, there is limited evidence that such programs are actually effective in reducing violence.

Grossman et al. (1997) assessed the efficacy of one such program for children in elementary school called "The Second Step: A Violence Prevention Curriculum." The program involved 30 lessons, each lasting about 35 minutes, taught once or twice a week. Each lesson consisted of a photograph accompanied by a social scenario that formed the basis for discussion, role playing, and conceptual activities. Lessons were arranged in three units:

1. Empathy training, in which students identified their own feelings and those of others;

2. Impulse control, in which students were presented with a problem-solving strategy and behavioral skills for affecting solutions (e.g., apologizing or dealing with peer pressure); and

3. Anger management, in which students were presented with a coping strategy and behavioral skills for tense situations.

Twelve elementary schools in King County, Washington, were similarly paired according to three criteria: the school district, the proportion of students receiving free or reduced-cost lunch, and the proportion of minority enrollment. One school in each pair was randomly assigned either to participate in the Second Step program (experimental groups) or not to participate in the violence prevention training (control groups). Random assignment was necessary so the researchers could be more confident that any differences observed in aggression and violent behavior between the two groups after the program could be attributed to the program alone and not to some other factor. Violent and aggressive behavior was measured in three ways: teacher ratings of each child's behavior; parent ratings; and direct observation of students by trained observers in the classroom, playground, and cafeteria. Measures of aggression were taken at three time periods: before the start of the curriculum (baseline), 2 weeks after the conclusion of the curriculum, and 6 months after the curriculum.

To determine the effectiveness of the Second Step program, researchers examined the change in aggression between scores measured at baseline and those from the second and third periods of data collection. Grossman et al. (1997) found encouraging results: Observed physically aggressive behavior decreased significantly more among children who engaged in the curriculum than among children in the control group who were not exposed to the Second Step program. Moreover, prosocial behavior increased significantly among children in the Second Step program compared with the control group. Grossman and colleagues concluded, "This violence prevention curriculum appears to lead to modest reductions in levels of aggressive behavior and increases in neutral/prosocial behavior in school" (p. 1608).

STRENGTHS AND LIMITATIONS OF SOCIAL RESEARCH

These case studies are only four of the hundreds of studies investigating youth violence, but they illustrate some of the questions criminological research can address, several different methods social scientists studying these issues can use, and ways criminological research can inform public policy. Notice how each of the four studies was designed to reduce the errors common in everyday reasoning:

- The clear definition of the population of interest in each study and the selection of a broad, representative sample of that population in two studies increased the researchers' ability to draw conclusions without overgeneralizing findings to groups to which they did not apply.
- The use of surveys in which each respondent was asked the same set of questions reduced the risk of selective or inaccurate observation.
- The risk of illogical reasoning was reduced by carefully describing each stage of the research, clearly presenting the findings, and carefully testing the basis for cause-and-effect conclusions.
- Resistance to change was reduced by using an experimental design that randomly assigned classes to an experimental treatment (the Second Step program) and a control group to fairly evaluate the efficacy of the program.

Nevertheless, it would be misleading to suggest that simply engaging in criminological research will result in the unveiling of absolute truths! Research always has its flaws and limitations (as does any human endeavor), and findings are always subject to differing interpretations. Social research allows us to consider and reveal more, to observe with fewer distortions, and to describe more clearly to others the basis for our opinions, but it will not settle all arguments. Other people will always have differing opinions, and some opposition will come from other social scientists who have conducted their own studies and drawn different conclusions. For example, we must ask ourselves if programs similar to Second Step also reduce levels of aggression among students. Only a handful of studies have used randomized controlled designs to examine these programs, and the results of these studies have been mixed. Like the Grossman et al. (1997) study, some researchers have found a reduction in aggressive behavior by children exposed to such social skills training programs, whereas others have not. Until more scientific research is conducted to evaluate these programs, it is difficult to determine whether these programs should be more widely implemented.

But even in areas of research that are fraught with controversy, where social scientists differ in their interpretations of the evidence, the quest for new and more sophisticated research has value. What is most important for improving understanding of the social world and issues in criminology is not the results of any one particular study but the accumulation of evidence from different studies of related issues. By designing new studies that focus on the weak points or controversial conclusions of prior research, social scientists contribute to a body of findings that gradually expands our knowledge about the social world and resolves some of the disagreements about it.

Whether you plan to conduct your own research projects, read others' research reports, or just think about and act in the social world, knowing about research methods has many benefits. This knowledge will give you greater confidence in your own opinions; improve your ability to evaluate others' opinions; and encourage you to refine your questions, answers, and methods of inquiry about the social world.

Of course, the methods of social science, as careful as they may be, cannot answer all questions of interest to criminologists. Should we do unto others as we would have them do unto us? Does anyone deserve the fate he or she receives? Are humans inherently good or evil? These are all very important questions that have been asked throughout history, but we must turn to religion or philosophy to answer questions about values. Social research on the consequences of forgiveness or the sources of interpersonal conflict may help us understand and implement our values, but even the best research cannot tell us which values should guide our lives.

TYPES OF RESEARCH METHODS

As you will see in this book, the data we utilize in criminological research are derived from many different sources, and the research methods we employ in criminology and criminal justice are very diverse.

An experimental approach is used in criminological research, particularly when the efficacy of a program or policy is being evaluated. As we will see in Chapter 6, true experiments must have three aspects: two groups (one receiving the treatment or intervention and the other receiving no treatment or another form thereof), random assignment to these two groups, and an assessment of change in the outcome variable after the treatment or policy has been received. Quasi-experimental designs, experiments that lack one of these three ingredients, also are used in our discipline. Chapter 10 focuses exclusively on research designs used in evaluation research.

Asking people questions on surveys or questionnaires is another popular method used by criminological researchers and is probably the most versatile. Most concepts about individuals can be defined in such a way that measurement with one or more questions becomes an option. These surveys can be self-administered by respondents (e.g., through the mail) or can be read by an interviewer (e.g., through a telephone survey).

Although in principle, survey questions can be a straightforward and efficient means to measure individual characteristics, facts about events, level of knowledge, and opinions of any sort, in practice, survey questions can result in misleading or inappropriate answers.

All questions proposed for a survey must be screened carefully for their adherence to basic guidelines and then tested and revised until the researcher feels some confidence that they will be clear to the intended respondents (Fowler 1995). Some variables may prove to be inappropriate for measurement with any type of question. We have to recognize that memories and perceptions of events and even honesty may be limited. Specific guidelines for writing questions and developing surveys are presented in Chapter 7.

In other cases, a researcher may want to directly participate in the activity being observed. Included in this type of research design is **participant observation**, which involves developing a sustained relationship with a person or group and observing them while they go about their normal activities. In other instances, the subject matter of interest may not be amenable to a survey, or perhaps we want more detailed and in-depth information than questions with fixed formats can answer. In these cases, we turn to research techniques such as intensive interviewing. These methods are preferred when we seek in-depth information on an individual's feelings, experiences, and perceptions. Chapter 8 shows how these methods and other field research techniques can uncover aspects of the social world that we are likely to miss in experiments and surveys.

Secondary data analysis (Riedel 2000), which is the reanalysis of already existing data, is another method used by researchers. These data usually come from one of two places: from official sources such as local or federal agencies (e.g., rates of crime reported to police, information on incarcerated offenders from state correctional authorities, adjudication data from the courts), or from surveys sponsored by government agencies or conducted by other researchers. Most of the data collected by government agencies and a great deal of survey data collected by independent researchers are made available to the public through the Inter-University Consortium for Political and Social Research (ICPSR), which is located at the University of Michigan. When documents from the past, such as correspondence, newspaper accounts, and trial transcripts, are analyzed, the research is generally termed *historical events research*.

Another type of indirect measurement is called **content analysis**. In this type of study, a researcher studies representations of the research topic in such media forms as news articles, TV shows, and radio talk shows. An investigation of the drinking climate on campuses might include a measurement of the amount of space devoted to ads for alcoholic beverages in a sample of issues of the student newspaper. Campus publications also might be coded to indicate the number of times that statements discouraging substance abuse appear. Content analysis techniques also can be applied to legal opinions, historical documents, novels, songs, or other cultural productions.

With the emergence of increasingly advanced computer technology, crime mapping also has become a popular method for examining the relationship between criminal behavior and other geographical space. Chapter 8 covers each of these methodologies and illustrates the importance of these unobtrusive research techniques in describing criminology and criminal justice.

Quantitative and Qualitative Methods

In general, research methods can be divided into two somewhat different domains called quantitative research methods and qualitative research methods. Did you notice the difference between the types of data used in the case studies discussed at the beginning of the chapter? The data collected in the Youth Risk Behavior Survey were counts of the responses students gave on the survey. These data were numerical, so we say that this study used quantitative methods. MacDonald et al. (2005) looked at the extent to which impulsivity and life satisfaction affected students' participation in violence; they examined this relationship with statistical methods. This, too, represents quantitative methods. In contrast, Asmussen and Creswell's (1995) exploratory study used in-depth interviews with people who had experienced the attempted school shooting. This methodology was designed to capture the social reality of the participants as they experienced it, in their own words rather than in predetermined categories. Because they focused on the participants' words rather than counts and numbers, we say that this study used qualitative methods.

Quantitative methods Methods such as surveys and experiments that record variation in social life in terms of categories that vary in amount. Data that are treated as quantitative are either numbers or attributes that can be ordered in terms of magnitude.

Qualitative methods Methods such as participant observation, intensive interviewing, and focus groups that are designed to capture social life as participants experience it, rather than in categories predetermined by the researcher. Data that are treated as qualitative are mostly written or spoken words, or observations that do not have a direct numerical interpretation.

The distinction between quantitative and qualitative methods involves more than just the type of data collected. Quantitative methods are most often used when the research agendas are exploratory, explanatory, descriptive, or evaluative. Exploratory research agendas most commonly use qualitative methods, although researchers also use these methods for descriptive and evaluative purposes. The goals of quantitative and qualitative researchers also may differ. Whereas quantitative researchers generally adopt the goal of developing an understanding that correctly reflects what is actually happening in the real world, some qualitative researchers instead emphasize the goal of developing a broader, more "authentic" understanding of a social process or social setting (Gubrium & Holstein 1997).

We do not want to place too much emphasis on the distinction between qualitative and quantitative methods because social scientists are increasingly combining these methods to enrich their research. For example, "qualitative knowing" about social settings can be essential for understanding patterns in quantitative data (Campbell & Russo 1999: 141). Qualitative data can be converted to quantitative data—for example, when we count the frequency of particular words or phrases in a text or measure the time elapsed between different behaviors that we have observed. Surveys that collect primarily quantitative data also may include questions that require written responses, all of which can be used in a qualitative, textual analysis. Researchers using quantitative methods may engage in some exploration in order to find unexpected patterns in their data. Qualitative researchers may test explicit explanations of social phenomena using textual or observational data. Combining methodologies to answer a research question is called triangulation. The term suggests that a researcher can get a clearer picture of the social reality being studied by viewing it from several different perspectives. Each will have its drawbacks and limitations in a specific research application, but all can benefit from a combination of one or more other methods (Brewer & Hunter 1989; Sechrest & Sidani 1995).

Triangulation The use of multiple methods to study one research question. Also used to mean the use of two or more different measures of the same variable.

As you will see in the chapters that follow, the distinction between quantitative and qualitative data is not always sharp. We'll examine "mixed method" possibilities in each of the chapters that review specific methods of data collection.

SOCIAL RESEARCH GOALS

A scientist seeks to develop an accurate understanding of empirical reality, the reality we encounter firsthand, by conducting research that leads to valid knowledge about the world. But when is knowledge valid? In general, we have reached the goal of validity when our statements or conclusions about empirical reality are correct. If you look out your window and observe that it is raining, this is probably a valid observation, if your eyes and ears are to be trusted. However, if you pick up the newspaper and read that the majority of Americans favor the death penalty, this may be of questionable validity because it is probably based on a social survey. In fact, you will see in Chapter 7 that attitudes toward the death penalty vary substantially depending on the wording of the questions asked.

To some of you, the goal of validity may sound a bit far-fetched. After all, how can we really be sure our understandings of phenomena are correct when we can perceive the world only through the filter of our own senses? Hopefully, this concern will remind you to be skeptical about new discoveries!

This book is about validity more than anything else, about how to conduct research that leads to valid interpretations of the social world. We will refer to validity repeatedly, and we ask you to register it in your brain now as the central goal of all the research conducted in our field. The goal of research conducted by social scientists investigating issues related to criminology and criminal justice is not to come up with conclusions that people will like or conclusions that suit their personal preferences. The goal is to determine the most valid answers through empirical research methods.

We must be concerned with three aspects of validity: **measurement validity**, **generalizability**, and **causal validity** (also known as **internal validity**). Each of these three aspects of validity is essential: Conclusions based on invalid measures, invalid generalizations, or invalid causal inferences will themselves be invalid. We will also be concerned with the goal of **authenticity**, a concern with reflecting fairly the perspectives of participants in a setting that we study.

Imagine that we survey a sample of 250 high school seniors and ask them two questions: "Do you have friends who have taken illegal drugs in the past 6 months?" (the measure of peer behavior) and "Have you taken illegal drugs in the past 6 months?" (respondents' behavior). We then compare the frequency of illegal drug use between students who have friends who have used illegal drugs and those whose friends have not used illegal drugs. We find that students who have friends who have used illegal drugs in the last 6 months are more likely to have used drugs themselves, and we conclude that drug use is, in part, due to the influence of peers.

But did our questions indeed tell us the frequency with which the students and their peers took illegal drugs? If they did, we achieved measurement validity. Do our results hold true of the larger adolescent population to which our conclusion referred? If so, our conclusion would satisfy the criterion for generalizability. Did the likelihood of students taking drugs actually increase if they had friends who also took drugs? If so, our conclusion is causally valid.

Measurement Validity

Measurement validity is our first concern in establishing the validity of research results, because without having measured what we think we measured, we really don't know what we're talking about.

Problems with measurement validity can occur for many reasons. In the study by MacDonald et al. (2005) highlighted earlier, were they really measuring impulsivity and self-control by using smoking and sexual behavior? The bottom line is that we cannot just *assume* that measures are valid.

Measurement validity exists when a measure actually measures what we think it does.

Generalizability

The generalizability of a study is the extent to which it can be used to inform us about persons, places, or events that were not studied. MacDonald and his colleagues (2005) relied on responses from 5,545 students in the South Carolina Youth Risk Behavior Survey and then generalized what they found with those individuals to the entire U.S. high school population. Were they correct to do so? Were their generalizations valid? Chapter 5 on sampling will give you the tools you need to answer questions like these.

Generalizability has two aspects. Sample generalizability refers to the ability to generalize from a sample, or subset, of a larger population to that population itself. This is the most common meaning of generalizability. Cross-population generalizability refers to the ability to generalize from findings about one group, population, or setting to other groups, populations, or settings. Cross-population generalizability can also be referred to as external validity.

Sample generalizability exists when a conclusion based on a sample, or subset, of a larger population holds true for that population.

Cross-population generalizability (external validity) exists when findings about one group, population, or setting hold true for other groups, populations, or settings.

Causal Validity

Causal validity, also known as internal validity, refers to the truthfulness of an assertion that A causes B and is the focus of Chapter 6. Most research seeks to determine what causes what, so social scientists frequently must be concerned with causal validity. You will learn in Chapter 2 that Sherman and Berk (1984) were concerned with the effect of arrest on the likelihood of recidivism by people accused of domestic violence. To test their causal hypothesis, they designed an experiment in which some accused persons were arrested and others were not.

Chapter 6 will give you much more understanding of how some features of a research design can help us evaluate causal propositions. However, you will also learn that the solutions are neither easy nor perfect: We always have to consider critically the validity of causal statements that we hear or read.

Causal validity (internal validity) exists when a conclusion that A leads to or results in B is correct.

Authenticity

The goal of authenticity is to fairly reflect the perspectives of the participants in a study setting and is stressed by researchers who focus attention on the subjective dimension of the social world. An authentic understanding of a social process or social setting is one that reflects fairly the various perspectives of participants in that setting (Gubrium & Holstein 1997). Authenticity is one of several different standards proposed by some as uniquely suited to qualitative research; it reflects a belief that those who study the social world should focus first and foremost on how participants view that social world, not on developing a unique social scientists' interpretation of that world. Rather than expecting social scientists to be able to provide a valid mirror of reality, this perspective emphasizes how our recognition of participants' own reality can help us as researchers to uncover a more nuanced truth (Kvale 2002).

Authenticity exists when the understanding of a social process or social setting is one that reflects fairly the various perspectives of participants in that setting.

CONCLUSION

We hope this first chapter has given you an idea of what to expect in the rest of this book. Our aim is to introduce you to social research methods by describing what social scientists have learned about issues in criminology and criminal justice as well as how they tackled systematic challenges in conducting their research. For many students, the substance of social science inevitably is more interesting than the research methods used to bring those findings to light. However, in this volume, you will see that the research methods not only demand interest and merit, but are also fundamental to our understanding of criminology and criminal justice. We have focused attention on research on youth violence and delinquency in this chapter; in subsequent chapters, we will introduce research examples from other areas.

Chapter 2 continues to build the foundation for our study of social research by reviewing the types of problems that criminologists study, the role of theory, the major steps in the research process, and other sources of information that may be used in social research. We stress the importance of considering scientific standards in social research and review generally accepted ethical guidelines. Throughout the chapter, we use several studies of domestic violence to illustrate the research process.

KEY TERMS

Causal validity (internal validity)

Content analysis

Crime mapping

Descriptive research

Evaluation research

Experimental approach

Explanatory research

Exploratory research

External validity

Generalizability

Illogical reasoning

Inaccurate observation

Intensive interviewing

Measurement validity

Overgeneralization

Participant observation

Qualitative methods

Quantitative methods

Questionnaire

Resistance to change

Science

Secondary data analysis

Selective observation

Social science

Survey

Validity

HIGHLIGHTS

- Criminological research cannot resolve value questions or provide answers that will convince everyone and remain settled for all time.

- All empirically based methods of investigation are based on either direct experience or others' statements.

- Four common errors in reasoning are overgeneralization, selective or inaccurate observation, illogical reasoning, and resistance to change. Illogical reasoning is due to the complexity of the social world, self-interest, and human subjectivity. Resistance to change may be due to unquestioning acceptance of tradition or of those in positions of authority, or to self-interested resistance to admitting the need to change one's beliefs.

- Social science is the use of logical, systematic, documented methods to investigate individuals, societies, and social processes, as well as the knowledge produced by these investigations.

- Criminological research can be motivated by policy guidance and program management needs, academic concerns, and charitable impulses.

- Criminological research can be descriptive, exploratory, explanatory, or evaluative, or some combination of these.

- Quantitative methods record variation in social life in terms of categories that vary in amount. Qualitative methods are designed to capture social life as participants experience it, rather than in categories predetermined by the researcher.

- Triangulation is the use of multiple research methods to study a single research question.

- Valid knowledge is the central concern of scientific research. The three components of validity are measurement validity, generalizability (both from the sample to the population from which it was selected and from the sample to other populations), and causal (internal) validity.

EXERCISES

Discussing Research

1. What criminological topic or issue would you focus on if you could design a research project without any concern for costs? What are your motives for studying this topic? List at least four of your beliefs about this phenomenon. Try to identify the sources of each belief—for example, television, newspaper, parental influence.

2. Develop four research questions related to a topic or issue, one for each of the four types of research (descriptive, exploratory, explanatory, and evaluative). Be specific.

3. Find a report of social science research in an article in a daily newspaper. What are the motives for the research? How much information is provided about the research design? What were the major findings? What additional evidence would you like to see in the article to increase your understanding of the findings in the research conclusions?

4. Find a CNN blog discussing some topic about crime. How do your opinions on the subject differ?

Finding Research on the Web

1. You have been asked to prepare a brief presentation on a criminological topic or issue of interest to you. Go to the Bureau of Justice Statistics (BJS) website at www.ojp.usdoj.gov/bjs. Browse the BJS publications for a topic that interests you. Write a short outline for a 5- to 10-minute presentation regarding your topic, including statistics and other relevant information.

2. Go to the Federal Bureau of Investigation (FBI) website at www.fbi.gov. Explore the types of programs and initiatives sponsored by the FBI. Discuss at least three of these programs or initiatives in terms of their purposes and goals. For each program or initiative examined, do you believe the program or initiative is effective? What are the major weaknesses? What changes would you propose the FBI make to more effectively meet the goals of the program or initiative?

3. Go to the website of a major newspaper and find an article discussing the causes of violence. What conclusions does the article draw, and what research methods does the author discuss to back up his or her claims?

Critiquing Research

1. Find a story about a criminological issue in the popular press (e.g., newspaper or periodical like *Time* magazine). Does the article provide a scientific basis for claims made in the story? If rates of crime are reported, does the article discuss how these rates were actually obtained?

2. Read an article in a recent issue of a major criminological journal or on the study site for this book (www.sagepub.com/bachmanfrccj2e). Identify the type of research conducted for each study. Are the research questions clearly stated? Can you identify the purpose of the research (e.g., description, explanation, exploration, evaluation)?

Making Research Ethical

Throughout the book, we will be discussing the ethical challenges that arise in research on crime and criminal justice. At the end of each chapter, we will ask you to consider some questions about ethical issues related to that chapter's focus. Chapter 3 is devoted to issues of ethics in research, but we will begin here with some questions for you to ponder.

1. You have now learned about Asmussen and Creswell's (1995) qualitative study of a school shooting incident. We think it provided important information for policy makers about the social dynamics in these tragedies. But what would *you* do if you were conducting a similar study in a high school and you learned that another student was planning to bring a gun to school to kill some other students? What if he was only thinking about it? Or just talking with his friends about how "neat" it would be? Can you suggest some guidelines for researchers?

2. Grossman et al. (1997) found that the Second Step program reduced aggressive behavior in schools and increased prosocial behavior. If you were David Grossman, would you announce your findings in a press conference and encourage schools to adopt this program? If you were a school principal who heard about this research, would you agree to let another researcher replicate (repeat) the Grossman et al. study in your school, with some classrooms assigned to receive the Second Step program randomly (on the basis of the toss of a coin) and others not allowed to receive the program for the duration of the study?

Developing a Research Proposal

1. What topic would you focus on if you could design a social research project without any concern for costs? What are your motives for studying this topic?

2. Develop four questions that you might investigate about the topic you just selected. Each question should reflect a different research motive: description, exploration, explanation, or evaluation. Be specific.

3. Which question most interests you? Would you prefer to attempt to answer that question using quantitative or qualitative methods? Why?

Performing Data Analysis in SPSS or Excel

The SPSS exercises at the end of each chapter use the data sets included on the companion website. In NCVS.assault.por (an SPSS export file that can be brought into most versions of SPSS or Excel), a sample of assault incidents from the National Crime Victimization Survey, variable V2089, identifies the metropolitan statistical area (MSA) status (urban, suburban, or rural) of each assault incident included in the data set.

1. Create a bar chart of V2089 using the graph procedure to show the percentage of assault incidents occurring in urban, suburban, and rural areas. Be sure to select "options," and indicate that you want to leave out the missing values.

2. Do a frequency distribution of V3010, which is the age of the victim in years. In the Statistics box, ask for the mean and the median. How would you describe the typical assault victim? What accounts for the difference between the mean and the median?

3. Do a frequency distribution for the victim and offender relationship in assault victimizations using the two variables V4239 and V4243. Do the results surprise you?

Student Study Site

The companion Student Study Site for *Fundamentals of Research in Criminology and Criminal Justice* can be found at www.sagepub.com/bachmanfrccj2e.

Visit the Student Study Site to enhance your understanding of the chapter content and to discover additional resources that will take your learning one step further. You can enhance your understanding of the chapters by using the comprehensive study material, which includes interactive exercises, e-flashcards, web exercises, practice self-tests, and more. You will also find special features, such as Learning From Journal Articles, which incorporates Sage's online journal collection.

CHAPTER 2

The Process and Problems of Criminological Research

In this chapter, you will see that many criminological researchers rely on criminological theory to guide their research. In criminology, as in any other science, theory plays an important role as a basis for formulating research questions and later understanding the larger implications of one's research results. Scientists' own personal interests and motivations also shape their research. In this chapter, we will explore several aspects of the origins of research, and we will also highlight how previous research sparks new questions, methods, and perspectives. We will use the Minneapolis experiment and the SARP research to illustrate the three main research strategies: deductive, inductive, and descriptive research. In all three, theory and data are inextricably linked. The chapter concludes with scientific and ethical guidelines that should be adhered to no matter what research strategy is used, and an illustration of how those guidelines were implemented in the Minneapolis experiment. By the chapter's end, you should be ready to formulate a criminological research question, design a general strategy for answering this question, and critique previous studies that have addressed this question.

WHAT DO WE HAVE IN MIND?

When the bloodied and bruised face of pop star Rihanna was splashed across television screens in 2009, the reality of intimate partner assault was once again brought to the forefront of public consciousness. In June 2009, R&B singer Chris Brown pleaded guilty to assaulting her. Intimate partner violence (violence between spouses or intimates), sometimes referred to as domestic violence, is a major problem in our society. Every year, police respond to between 2 million and 8 million complaints of assault by a spouse or lover (Sherman 1992). Moreover, it is estimated from victimization surveys that many of these assaults are never reported to police (Bachman 2000; Tjaden & Thoennes 2000). Domestic violence is not just a frequent crime, it is also costly in terms of the injuries suffered by the parties involved and also in terms of shattered families. The management of this social problem is an important policy question. For over 30 years, the criminal justice system has attempted to effectively respond to intimate partner violence and other domestic assaults in a way that best protects victims and punishes offenders.

But what is the proper police response?

In 1981, the Police Foundation and the Minneapolis Police Department began an experiment to determine whether immediately arresting accused spouse abusers on the spot would deter future offending incidents. For misdemeanor cases, the experimental course of action involved the random assignment of police to respond by either arresting the suspect or giving the suspect a simple warning. The experimental treatment, then, was whether the suspect was arrested, and the researchers wanted to know whether arrest was better than not arresting the suspect in reducing recidivism. The study's results, which were widely publicized, indicated that arrest did have a deterrent effect. Partly as a result of the reported results of this experiment, the percentage of urban police departments that made arrest the preferred response to complaints of domestic violence rose from 10% in 1984 to 90% in 1988 (Sherman 1992: 14). Six other cities later carried out studies like the Minneapolis Domestic Violence Experiment (collectively, this was called the Spouse Assault Replication Program [SARP]), but from city to city, the results were mixed (Buzawa & Buzawa 1996; Hirschel, Hutchison, & Dean 1992; Pate & Hamilton 1992; Sherman 1992; Sherman & Berk 1984). In some cities (and for some people), arrest did seem to prevent future incidents of domestic assault; in other cities, it seemed only to make matters worse, contributing to additional assault; and in still other cities, arrest seemed to have no discernible effect. After these replications of the original Minneapolis experiment, people still wondered, "Just what is the effect of arrest in reducing domestic violence cases, and how should the police respond to such cases?" The answer simply was not clear. The Minneapolis experiment, the studies modeled after it, and the related controversies provide many examples for a systematic overview of the social research process.

CRIMINOLOGICAL RESEARCH QUESTIONS

The first concern in criminological research, indeed in any research, is deciding what to study. That is, how does one go about selecting an issue, problem, or question to address? A criminological research question is a question about some aspect of crime or deviance that the researcher seeks to answer through the collection and analysis of firsthand, verifiable, empirical data. The types of questions that can be asked are virtually limitless. For example, "Are children who are violent more likely than nonviolent children to use violence as adults?" "Does the race of a victim who is killed influence whether someone is sentenced to death rather than life imprisonment?" "Why do some kinds of neighborhoods have more crime than others? Is it due to the kinds of people who live there or characteristics of the neighborhood itself?" "Does community policing reduce the crime rate?" "Has the U.S. government's war on drugs done anything to reduce the use of illegal drugs?" So many research questions are possible in criminology that it is more of a challenge to specify what does *not* qualify as a social research question than to specify what does.

That being said, specifying which research question to ask as well as pursuing its answer are no easy tasks. In fact, formulating a good research question can be surprisingly difficult.

We can break the process into three stages: identifying one or more questions for study, refining the questions, and then evaluating the questions.

Identifying Criminological Research Questions

Formulating a research question is often an intensely personal process in addition to being a scientific or professional one. Curiosity about the social world may emerge from your "personal troubles," as Mills (1959) put it, or personal experiences. Examples of these troubles or experiences could range from how you feel about injustices raised against you in your past or present, to an awareness you may have that crime is not randomly distributed within a city but that there seem to be "good" or safe parts of town and "bad" or unsafe areas. Can you think of other possible research questions that flow from your own experience in the world?

The experience of others is another fruitful source of research questions. Knowing a relative who was abused by a spouse, seeing a TV special about violence, or reading a gang member's autobiography can stimulate questions about general criminological processes. Can you draft a research question based on a relative's experiences, a TV show, or a book?

Other researchers may also pose interesting questions for you to study. Most research articles end with some suggestions for additional research that highlight unresolved issues. Any issue of a journal in your field is likely to have comments that point toward unresolved issues.

The primary source of research questions for many criminologists is criminological theory. As you will soon learn, criminological theory provides an explanation as to why crime occurs, or why it occurs in some places and under some conditions but not others. Theory, then, is a very rich source of research ideas. Some researchers spend much of their careers conducting research intended to refine an answer to one central question. For example, you may find *rational choice theory* to be a useful approach to understanding diverse forms of social behavior, like crime, because you think people do seem to make decisions on the basis of personal cost–benefit calculations. So you may ask whether rational choice theory can explain why some people commit crimes and others do not, or why some people decide to quit committing crimes while others continue their criminal ways.

Some research questions arise from a very pragmatic rationale concerning their research design. You may focus on a research question posed by someone else because doing so would be to your professional or financial advantage. For instance, some criminologists conduct research on specific questions posed by a funding source in what is termed a *request for proposals* (RFP). (Sometimes the acronym RFA is used, meaning request for applications.) Or you may learn that the public defenders in your city are curious as to whether they are more successful in getting their clients acquitted of a criminal charge than private lawyers.

Refining Criminological Research Questions

As you have no doubt guessed, coming up with interesting criminological questions for research is less problematic than focusing on a problem of manageable size. We are often interested in much more than we can reasonably investigate with our limited time and resources (or the limited resources of a funding agency). Researchers may worry about staking a research project (and thereby a grant) on a narrowly-defined problem, so they commit to addressing several research questions at once, and often in a jumbled fashion. It may also seem risky to focus on a research question that may lead to results discrepant with our own cherished assumptions about the social world.

The best way to avoid these problems is to develop the research question one bit at a time with a step-by-step strategy. Do not keep hoping that the perfect research question will just spring forth from your pen. Instead, develop a list of possible research questions as you go along. Narrow your list to the most interesting, most workable candidates. Repeat this process as long as it helps to improve your research questions. Keep in mind that the research on which you are currently working will likely generate additional research questions for you to answer.

Evaluating Criminological Research Questions

In the third stage of selecting a criminological research question, you evaluate the best candidate against the criteria for good social research questions: feasibility given the time and resources available, social importance, and scientific relevance (King, Keohane, & Verba 1994).

The research question in the Minneapolis Domestic Violence Experiment, "Does the formal sanction of police arrest versus nonarrest inhibit domestic violence?" certainly meets the criteria of social importance and scientific relevance, but it would not be a feasible question for a student project because it would require you to try to get the cooperation of a police department.

Feasibility

You must be able to conduct any study within the time frame and with the resources you have. If time is limited, questions that involve long-term change—for example, "If a state has recently changed its law so that it now permits capital punishment for those convicted of murder, does it eventually see a reduction in the homicide rate over time?"—may not be feasible. This is an interesting and important question, but one that requires years of data collection and research. Another issue is the people, groups, or files that you can expect to gain access to. Although experienced researchers may be granted access to police or correctional department files to do their research, less seasoned and less well-known researchers or students may not be granted such access.

Social Importance

Criminological research is not a simple undertaking, so you must focus on a substantive area that you feel is important and that is either important to the discipline or for public policy. You also need to feel personally motivated to carry out the study; there is little point in trying to answer a question that does not interest you.

In addition, you should consider whether the research question is important to other people. Will an answer to the research question make a difference for society? Again, the

Minneapolis Domestic Violence Experiment is an exemplary case. If that study showed that a certain type of police response to domestic violence reduced the risk of subsequent victimization, a great deal of future violence could be prevented. But clearly, criminology and criminal justice researchers are far from lacking important research questions.

Scientific Relevance

Every research question in criminology should be grounded in the existing empirical literature. By *grounded,* we mean the research we do must be informed by what others before us have done on the topic. Whether you formulate a research question because you have been stimulated by an academic article or because you want to investigate a current public policy problem, or are motivated by questions regarding your own personal experiences, you must turn to existing criminological literature to find out what has already been learned about this question. (Appendix A explains how to find information about previous research, using both printed and computer-based resources.)

For example, the Minneapolis experiment was built on a substantial body of contradictory theorizing about the impact of punishment on criminality (Sherman & Berk 1984). Deterrence theory predicted that, because it was a more severe penalty, arresting people would better deter them from repeat offenses than not arresting them. Labeling theory, on the other hand, predicted that arrest would make repeat offenses more likely because it would stigmatize offenders. Studies among adults and nonexperimental research had not yielded consistent findings about the effects of arrest on recidivism in domestic violence cases. Clearly, the Minneapolis researchers had good reason to perform another study. Prior research and theory also helped them develop the most effective research design.

THE ROLE OF CRIMINOLOGICAL THEORY

We have already pointed out that criminological theory can be a rich source of research questions. What deserves more attention at this point is the larger role of theory in research. Criminological theories serve many purposes:

- They help us explain or understand things like why some people commit crimes or commit more crimes than others; why some people quit and others continue; and what the expected effect of good families, harsh punishment, or other factors might be on crime.
- They help us make predictions about the criminological world: "What would be the expected effect on the homicide rate if we employed capital punishment rather than life imprisonment?" "What would be the effect on the rate of property crimes if unemployment were to substantially increase?"
- They help us organize and make sense of empirical findings in a discipline.
- They help guide future research.
- They help guide public policy: "What should we do to reduce the level of domestic violence?"

Social scientists such as criminologists, who connect their work to theories in their discipline, can generate better ideas about what to look for in a study and develop conclusions with more implications for other research. Building and evaluating theory are therefore among the most important objectives of a social science like criminology.

Theory A logically interrelated set of propositions about empirical reality. Examples of criminological theories include social learning, routine activities, labeling, general strain, and social disorganization theory.

For centuries, scholars have been interested in developing theories about crime and criminals. Sometimes these theories involve very fanciful ideas that are not well developed or organized, whereas at other times they strike us as being very compelling and well organized. Theories usually contain what are called theoretical constructs. In criminology, these theoretical constructs describe what is important to look at to understand, explain, predict, and "do something about" crime. Some criminological theories reflect a substantial body of research and the thinking of many social scientists; others are formulated in the course of one investigation. A few have been widely accepted, at least for a time; others are the subject of vigorous controversy, with frequent changes and refinements in response to criticism and new research.

We can use the studies of the police response to domestic assault to illustrate the value of theory for social research. Even in this very concrete and practical matter, we must draw on social theories to understand how people act and what should be done about those actions. Consider three action options that police officers have when they confront a domestic assault suspect (Sherman & Berk 1984: 263). Fellow officers might encourage separation to achieve short-term peace, police trainers might prefer mediation to resolve the underlying dispute, and feminist groups may advocate arrest to protect the victim from further harm. None of these recommendations is really a theory, but each suggests a different perspective on crime and legal sanctions. Remember that social theories do not provide the answers to research questions. Instead, social theories suggest the areas on which we should focus and the propositions that we should consider for a test. That is, theories suggest testable hypotheses about phenomena, and research verifies whether those hypotheses are true. In fact, one of the most important requirements of theory is that it be testable, or what philosophers of science call falsifiable; theoretical statements must be capable of being proven wrong. If a body of thought cannot be empirically tested, it is more likely philosophy than theory.

The original Minneapolis experiment (Sherman & Berk 1984) was actually a test of predictions derived from two alternative theories concerning the impact of punishment on crime, deterrence theory, and labeling theory:

Deterrence theory presumes that human beings are at least marginally rational beings who are responsive to the expected costs and benefits of their actions. Committing a crime nets certain benefits for offenders; therefore, if we want to inhibit crime, there must be a compensating cost that outweighs the potential benefits associated with the offense. One cost is the criminal sanction (arrest, conviction, punishment). Deterrence theory expects punishment to inhibit crime in two ways: (1) General deterrence occurs when people see that crime results in undesirable punishments for others, that "crime doesn't pay." Those who are punished serve as examples for those who have not yet committed an offense but might be thinking of what awaits them should they engage in similarly punishable acts. (2) Specific deterrence occurs when persons who are punished decide not to commit another offense so they can avoid further punishment (Lempert & Sanders 1986: 86–87). Deterrence theory leads to the prediction that arresting spouse abusers will reduce the likelihood of their reoffending when compared with a less serious sanction (not being arrested but being warned or counseled).

Labeling theory distinguishes between primary deviance (the acts of individuals that lead to public sanctions) and secondary deviance (the deviance that occurs in response to public sanction) (Hagan 1994: 33). Arrest or some other public sanction for misdeeds labels the offender as deviant in the eyes of others. Once the offender is labeled, others will treat the offender as a deviant, and he or she is then more likely to act in a way that is consistent with the deviant label. Ironically, the act of punishment stimulates more of the very behavior that it was intended to eliminate (Tannenbaum 1938). This theory suggests that persons arrested for intimate partner violence are more likely to reoffend than those who are caught but not punished because the formal sanction of arrest is more stigmatizing than being warned or counseled. This prediction about the effect of formal legal sanctions is the reverse of the deterrence theory prediction.

Exhibit 2.1 summarizes how these general theories relate to the question of whether to arrest spouse abusers.

Does either deterrence theory or labeling theory make sense to you as an explanation for the impact of punishment? Do they seem consistent with your observations of social life? More than a decade after Sherman and Berk's (1984) study, Paternoster et al. (1997) decided to study punishment of domestic violence from a different perspective. They

Exhibit 2.1 Two Social Theories and Their Predictions About the Effect of Arrest for Intimate Partner Assault		
	Rational Choice Theory	**Symbolic Interactionism**
Theoretical assumption	People's behavior is shaped by calculations of the costs and benefits of their actions.	People give symbolic meanings to objects, behaviors, and other people.
Criminological component	Deterrence theory: People break the law if the benefits of doing so outweigh the costs.	Labeling theory: People label offenders as deviant, promoting further deviance.
Prediction (effect of arrest for domestic assault)	Abusing spouse, having seen the costs of abuse (namely, arrest), decides not to abuse again.	Abusing spouse, having been labeled as "an abuser," abuses more often.

turned to a social psychological theory called *procedural justice theory,* which explains law-abiding behavior as resulting from a sense of duty or morality (Tyler 1990). People obey the law from a sense of obligation that flows from seeing legal authorities as moral and legitimate. From this perspective, individuals who are arrested seem less likely to reoffend if they are treated fairly, irrespective of the outcome of their case, because fair treatment will enhance their view of legal authorities as moral and legitimate. Procedural justice theory expands our view of the punishment process by focusing attention on how police act and how authorities treat subjects, rather than just on the legal decisions they make. Thus, it gives us a sense of the larger importance of the research question.

Are you now less certain about the likely effect of arrest for intimate partner violence? Will arrest decrease recidivism because abusers do not wish to suffer from legal sanctions again? Will it increase recidivism because abusers feel stigmatized by being arrested and thus are more likely to act like criminals? Or will arrest reduce abuse only if the abusers feel they have been treated fairly by the legal authorities? By posing such questions, social theory makes us much more sensitive to the possibilities and so helps us to design better research. Before, during, and after a research investigation, we need to keep thinking theoretically.

SOCIAL RESEARCH STRATEGIES

All social research, including criminological research, is the effort to connect theory and empirical data. As Exhibit 2.2 shows, theory and data have a two-way, mutually reinforcing relationship. Research that begins with a theory implying that certain data should be found involves *deductive reasoning,* which moves from general ideas (theory) to specific reality (data). In contrast, *inductive reasoning* moves from the specific to the general.

Both deductive reasoning and inductive reasoning are essential to criminologists. We cannot test an idea fairly unless we use deductive reasoning, stating our expectations in advance and then designing a way to test the validity of our claims. A theory that has not survived these kinds of tests can be regarded only as very tentative. Yet theories, no matter how cherished, cannot always make useful predictions for every social situation or research problem that we seek to investigate. We may find unexpected patterns in the data we collect, called serendipitous findings or anomalous findings. In either situation, we should reason inductively, making whatever theoretical sense we can of our unanticipated findings. Then, if the new findings seem sufficiently important, we can return to deductive reasoning and plan a new study to formally test our new ideas.

The Research Circle

This process of conducting research, moving from theory to data and back again, or from data to theory and back again, can be characterized as a research circle. Exhibit 2.3 depicts this circle. Note that it mirrors the relationship between theory and data shown in Exhibit 2.2 and that it comprises three main research strategies: deductive research, inductive research, and descriptive research.

Exhibit 2.2 The Links Between Theory and Data

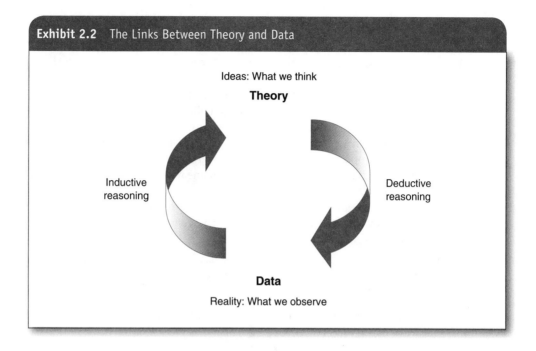

Exhibit 2.3 The Research Circle

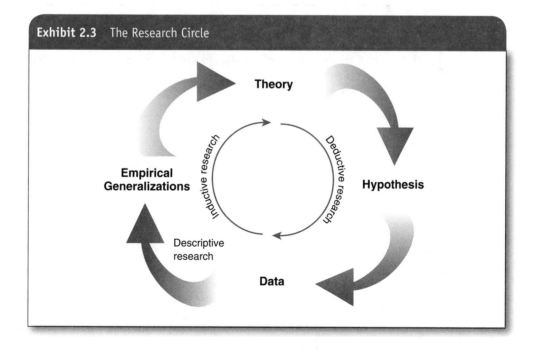

Deductive Research

As Exhibit 2.3 shows, deductive research proceeds from theorizing to data collection and then back to theorizing. In essence, a specific expectation is deduced from a general premise and then tested.

Notice that a theory leads first to a hypothesis, which is a specific implication deduced from the more general theory. Researchers actually test a hypothesis, not the complete theory itself, because theories usually contain many hypotheses. A hypothesis proposes a relationship between two or more theoretical constructs or variables. A variable is a characteristic or property that can vary. A constant is a characteristic or a property that cannot vary. For example, if we were to conduct some research in a male adult penitentiary, the theoretical construct "type of crime committed" would be a variable because persons will have been incarcerated for different offenses (one person for armed robbery, another for rape, etc.). However, the theoretical construct "gender" would be a constant because every inmate in the penitentiary would be male.

Hypothesis A tentative statement about empirical reality, involving a relationship between two or more variables

Example of a hypothesis: The higher the level of residential mobility in a community, the higher its rate of crime will be.

Variable A characteristic or property that can vary (take on different values or attributes)

Constant A characteristic or property that does not vary but takes on only one value

---

Variables are of critical importance in research because, in a hypothesis, variation in one variable is proposed to predict, influence, or cause variation in the other variable. The proposed influence is the independent variable; its effect or consequence is the dependent variable. After the researchers formulate one or more hypotheses and develop research procedures, they collect data with which to test the hypothesis.

Independent variable A variable that is hypothesized to cause, or lead to, variation in the dependent variable

Example of an independent variable: Residential mobility (residents moving in and out of the community)

Dependent variable A variable that is hypothesized to vary depending on or under the influence of the independent variable

Example of a dependent variable: The rate of crime in a community per 1,000 residents

---

Hypotheses can be worded in several different ways, and identifying the independent and dependent variables is sometimes difficult. When in doubt, try to rephrase the hypothesis as an if–then statement: "If the independent variable increases (or decreases), then the dependent variable increases (or decreases)." Exhibit 2.4 presents several hypotheses with their independent and dependent variables and their if–then equivalents.

Exhibit 2.4 Examples of Hypotheses

Original Hypothesis	Independent Variable	Dependent Variable	If–Then Hypothesis
1. The greater the social disorganization in a community, the higher the rate of crime.	Social disorganization	Crime rate	If social disorganization is higher, then the crime rate is higher.
2. As one's self-control gets stronger, the fewer delinquent acts one commits.	Self-control	Self-reported delinquency	If self-control is higher, then the number of delinquent acts is lower.
3. As the unemployment rate in a community decreases, the community rate of property crime decreases.	Unemployment rate	Rate of property crime	If the unemployment rate is lower, then the rate of property crime is lower.
4. As the discrepancy between one's aspirations and expectations increases, one's level of strain increases.	Discrepancy between one's aspirations and expectations	Strain	If the discrepancy between one's aspirations and expectations is high, then the level of strain is high.
5. Crime is lower in those communities where the police patrol on foot.	Presence of foot patrols	Crime	If a community has police foot patrols, then the level of crime is lower.

Inductive Research

In contrast to deductive research, inductive research begins at the bottom of the research circle and then works upward (see Exhibit 2.3). The inductive researcher begins with specific data, which are then used to develop (induce) a general explanation (a theory) to account for the data. The patterns in the data are then summarized in one or more empirical generalizations.

The motive for inductive research is exploration. In Chapter 1, you read about an exploratory study of individuals' responses to an incident involving a school shooting (Asmussen & Creswell 1995). The incident took place at a public university where a gunman tried to shoot the students in his class. Fortunately, the gun jammed and all the students escaped uninjured. Because there was very little previous work in this area, Asmussen and Creswell conducted in-depth interviews with the students and tried to classify typical responses to the situation. Although the researchers did not develop a theory from their work, they did develop a classification scheme, or *taxonomy,* of different responses to traumatic events.

In strictly inductive research, researchers already know what they have found when they start theorizing, or attempting to explain what accounts for these findings. The result can be new insights and provocative questions. But the adequacy of an explanation formulated after the fact is necessarily less certain than an explanation presented prior to the collection of data. Every phenomenon can always be explained in some way. Inductive explanations are thus more trustworthy if they are tested subsequently with deductive research.

DOMESTIC VIOLENCE AND THE RESEARCH CIRCLE

The Sherman and Berk (1984) study of domestic violence is a classic example of how the research circle works. In an attempt to determine ways to prevent the recurrence of intimate partner violence, the researchers repeatedly linked theory and data, developing both hypotheses and empirical generalizations.

Phase 1: Deductive Research

The first phase of Sherman and Berk's (1984) study was designed to test a hypothesis. According to deterrence theory, punishment will reduce recidivism, or repeated offending. From this theory, Sherman and Berk deduced a specific hypothesis: "Arrest for spouse abuse reduces the risk of repeat offenses." In this hypothesis, arrest is the independent variable, and variation in the risk of repeat offenses is the dependent variable (hypothesized to depend on arrest).

Sherman and Berk (1984) tested their hypothesis by setting up an experiment in which the police responded to complaints of spouse abuse in one of two ways: by arresting the offender or by separating the offender and victim and then leaving the scene. When the researchers examined their data (police records for the persons in their experiment), they found that of those arrested for assaulting their spouse, only 13% repeated the offense, compared with a 26% recidivism rate for those who were separated from their spouse by the police without any arrest. This pattern in the data, or empirical generalization, was consistent with the hypothesis that the researchers deduced from deterrence theory. The theory thus received support from the experiment (see Exhibit 2.5).

In designing their study, Sherman and Berk (1984) anticipated an important question: "How valid is the connection between theory and data?" The three dimensions of validity—measurement validity, generalizability, and causal validity—had to be taken into consideration.

Determining whether spouses were assaulted after the initial police intervention was the key measurement concern. Official records of subsequent assaults by the suspect would provide one measure. But most spousal assaults are not reported to the police, so research assistants also sought out the victims for interviews every 2 weeks during a

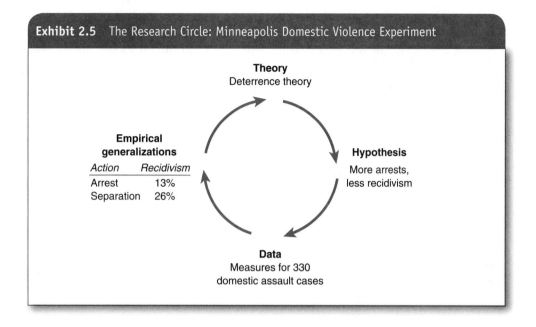

Exhibit 2.5 The Research Circle: Minneapolis Domestic Violence Experiment

Theory
Deterrence theory

Hypothesis
More arrests,
less recidivism

**Empirical
generalizations**

Action	*Recidivism*
Arrest	13%
Separation	26%

Data
Measures for 330
domestic assault cases

6-month follow-up period. Although fewer than half the victims completed all the follow-up interviews, the availability of the self-report measure allowed the researchers to provide information on the validity of the official data. In general, the two measures yielded comparable results, although some discrepancies troubled critics.

The generalizability of the study's results was the researchers' greatest concern. Minneapolis is no more a typical U.S. city than any other, and we cannot assume that police policies that are effective in Minneapolis will be equally effective in cities with very different political histories, criminal justice agencies, and population characteristics. Sherman and Berk (1984) warned readers, "External validity will have to wait for replications" (p. 269)—that is, for repetitions of the study using the same research methods to answer the same research question.

Finally, Sherman and Berk's (1984) claims about the causal validity of their results rested primarily on the experimental design they used. The 330 misdemeanor domestic assault cases in the study were handled by the police in one of three ways: an arrest, an order that the offending spouse leave the house for eight hours, or some type of verbal advice by the police officers. The officers were not allowed to choose which treatment to apply (except in extreme cases, such as when severe injury had occurred or when the spouse had demanded that an arrest be made). Instead, the treatments were carried out by police in random order, according to the color of the next report form on a pad that had been prepared by the researchers.

By insisting on the random assignment of cases to treatments, the researchers tried to ensure that police officers would not arrest just the toughest spouses or the spouses who seemed most obnoxious or the spouses they encountered late in the day. In other words, the random assignment procedure made it unlikely that arrested spouse abusers would differ, on average, from the other spouse abusers except for the fact that they were arrested (although, because of chance factors, the possibility of other differences cannot completely be ruled out). The researchers' conclusion that arrest caused a lower incidence of repeat offenses therefore seems valid.

Phase 2: Deductive Research

There still were doubts concerning the generalizability of their results, so Sherman, Berk, and new collaborators began to journey around the research circle again, with funding from the National Institute of Justice for replications (repetitions). The Minneapolis experiment was recreated in six more cities. These replications used the same basic research approach but with some improvements. The random assignment process was tightened up in most of the cities so that police officers would be less likely to replace the assigned treatment with a treatment of their own choice. In addition, data were collected about repeat violence against other victims as well as against the original complainant. Some replications also examined different aspects of the arrest process, to see whether professional counseling helped and whether the length of time spent in jail after arrest mattered at all.

By the time results were reported from five of the cities in the new study, a problem was apparent. In three cities—Omaha, Nebraska; Charlotte, North Carolina; and Milwaukee, Wisconsin—researchers were finding long-term increases in domestic violence incidents among arrestees. But in Colorado Springs, Colorado, and Dade County, Florida, the predicted deterrent effects seemed to be occurring (Sherman et al. 1992).

Researchers had now traveled around the research circle twice in an attempt to answer the original research question, first in Minneapolis and then in six other cities. However, rather than leading to more confidence in deterrence theory, the research results were calling it into question. Deterrence theory now seemed inadequate to explain empirical reality, at least as the researchers had measured this reality. So the researchers began to reanalyze the follow-up data from several cities to try to explain the discrepant results, thereby starting the research circle once again (Berk et al. 1992; Pate & Hamilton 1992; Sherman et al. 1992).

Phase 3: Inductive Research

At this point, the researchers' approach became more inductive, and they began trying to make sense of the differing patterns in the data collected in the different cities. Could systematic differences in the samples or in the implementation of arrest policies explain the differing outcomes? Or was the problem an inadequacy in the theoretical basis of their research? Was deterrence theory really the best way to explain the patterns in the data they were collecting?

Sherman et al. (1992) now turned to *control theory* (Toby 1957), yet another broad explanation for social behavior. It predicts that having a stake in conformity (resulting from inclusion in social networks at work or in the community) decreases a person's likelihood of committing crimes. The implication is that people who are employed and married are more likely to be deterred by the threat of arrest than those without such stakes in conformity. This is because an arrest for domestic violence could jeopardize one's job and one's marriage, thus making arrest more costly for the employed and married. This, indeed, is what a reexamination of the data revealed: Individuals who were married and employed were deterred from repeat offenses by arrest, but individuals who were unmarried and unemployed were actually more likely to commit repeat offenses if they were arrested. This was an important theoretical insight. It suggested that one powerful way that formal sanctions work is that they can potentially trigger informal sanctions or costs (e.g., loss of respect from friends and family).

Now the researchers had circumnavigated the research circle almost three times, a process perhaps better described as a spiral (see Exhibit 2.6). The first two times, the researchers had traveled around the research circle in a deductive, hypothesis-testing way: They started with theory and then deduced and tested hypotheses. The third time they went around the circle in a more inductive, exploratory way: They started with empirical generalizations from the data they had already obtained and then turned to a new theory to account for the unexpected patterns in the data. At this point, their belief was that deterrence theory makes correct predictions given certain conditions and that another theory, control theory, may specify what these conditions are.

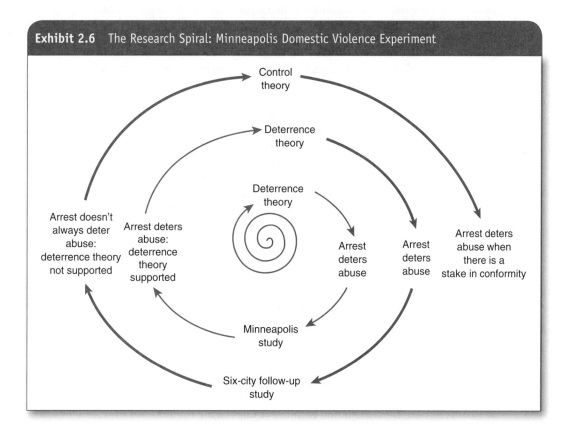

Exhibit 2.6   The Research Spiral: Minneapolis Domestic Violence Experiment

After two-and-one-half cycles through the research circle, the picture became more complex but also conceptually richer. The researchers came closer to understanding how to inhibit domestic violence, but they cautioned us that their initial question, the research problem, was still not completely answered. Employment status and marital status alone do not measure the strength of social attachments; they also are related to how much people earn and the social standing of victims in court. So perhaps social ties are not really what make arrest an effective deterrent to domestic violence. More research was still needed (Berk et al. 1992).

Phase 4: Deductive Research

In 1997, Paternoster et al. reexamined data from one of the replication sites in Milwaukee to test hypotheses derived from yet another theory, procedural justice theory. As explained earlier, procedural justice theory predicts that people will comply with the law out of a sense of duty and obligation if they are treated fairly by legal authorities. In the Milwaukee sample, arrest had a *criminogenic* effect: Those who were arrested were subsequently more likely to abuse their spouses than those who were simply warned or were temporarily separated from their spouse. Paternoster et al. (1997) thought that this effect might have been due to the way subjects were treated when they were arrested rather than simply to the fact that they were arrested. One of their hypotheses spells out the reasoning:

> Among those persons arrested for spouse assault, those who perceive themselves as being treated in a procedurally unfair manner will be more likely to commit acts of spouse assault in the future than those arrested persons who perceive themselves as being treated in a procedurally fair manner. (p. 173)

To carry out this study, Paternoster et al. (1997) reexamined data collected earlier in Milwaukee, where the findings had seemed anomalous. However, this reanalysis of the data qualifies as deductive research because the hypotheses were derived from theory and then tested with the data, rather than being induced by the data.

The procedural justice hypotheses were supported: Persons who were arrested in the Milwaukee experiment became more likely to reoffend only if they perceived that they had been treated unfairly by the police. Otherwise, their rate of rearrest was similar to that for the persons who were not arrested. Thus, another element was added to our understanding of the effects of the police response to domestic violence.

Clearly our understanding of effective responses to domestic violence will never truly be complete, but research to date has greatly improved our understanding of this social problem. The future should yield an even better understanding, even though at times it may be hard to make sense out of conflicting findings from different studies. Science is an ongoing enterprise in which findings accumulate and eventually yield greater understanding, or even radical revisions in our understanding. Needless to say, researchers do not need to worry about running out of work to do.

Adding Exploration to the Mix

While researchers were grappling with the results of the randomized experiments, other researchers were engaged in inductive research by interviewing victims and offenders in depth and then developing an explanation for what was found. Because qualitative research is often exploratory and, hence, inductive, researchers often ask questions like "What is going on here?" "How do people interpret these experiences?" or "Why do people do what they do?" Rather than testing a hypothesis, the researchers are trying to make sense of some social phenomenon.

A Qualitative Exploration of the Response to Domestic Violence

Bennett, Goodman, and Dutton (1999) used this approach to investigate one of the problems that emerge when police arrest domestic batterers: The victims often decide not to press charges. Bennett et al. did not set out to test hypotheses with qualitative interviews—there was another, hypothesis-testing component in their research—but sought, inductively, to "add the voice of the victim to the discussion" and present "themes that emerged from [the] interviews" (p. 762).

Research assistants interviewed 49 victims of domestic violence in one court; Lauren Bennett also worked in the same court as a victim advocate. The researchers were able to draw from their qualitative data four reasons why victims became reluctant to press charges: Some were confused by the court procedures, others were frustrated by the delay, some were paralyzed by fear of retribution, and others did not want to send the batterer to jail.

Explanations developed inductively from qualitative research can feel authentic because we have heard what people have to say "in their own words" and we have tried to see the social world "as they see it." One victim interviewed by Bennett et al. (1999) felt that she "was doing time instead of the defendant"; another expressed her fear by saying that she would like "to keep him out of jail if that's what it takes to keep my kids safe" (pp. 768–769). Explanations derived from qualitative research will be richer and more finely textured than those resulting from quantitative research, but they are likely to be based on fewer cases and from a limited area. We cannot assume that the people studied in this setting are like others or that other researchers would develop explanations similar to ours to make sense of what was observed or heard. Because we do not initially set up a test of a hypothesis according to some specific rules, another researcher cannot come along and conduct exactly the same test. However, by examining the results of both qualitative and quantitative research, we get a more detailed and nuanced picture of reality compared to using one set of methods alone.

GUIDELINES FOR CRIMINOLOGISTS

The guidelines followed by social researchers fall into two categories: those that help keep research scientific and those that help keep research ethical. Both types of guidelines are essential for a field of inquiry that seeks empirical generalizations about human society. To point out their value, we use examples from the domestic violence research.

Scientific Guidelines

The following nine guidelines are applicable to any type of scientific research, but they are particularly useful to criminologists and to those who read about criminology and criminal justice. Adherence to these guidelines will reduce the temptation "to project on what is observed whatever [they] want the world to be for [their] own private purposes" (Hoover 1980: 131).

1. *Test ideas against empirical reality without becoming too personally invested in a particular outcome.* This testing approach is reflected in the research process and is implicit in the goal of validity. Empirical testing requires a neutral and open-minded approach: Scientists are personally disinterested in the outcome and not swayed by the popularity or the social status of those who would prefer other outcomes. This does not mean that the researchers are not personally involved or interested in the research—they must be; rather, the point is that they cannot have so much invested in a research project personally or professionally that they try in subtle or not-so-subtle ways to affect the outcome.

2. *Plan and carry out investigations systematically.* Social researchers have little hope of conducting a careful test of their ideas if they do not think through in advance how they should go about the test and then proceed accordingly. But a systematic approach is not always easy. For example, Sherman and Berk (1984) needed to ensure that spouse abusers were assigned to be either arrested or not on a random basis, rather than on the basis of the police officers' personal preferences. So the researchers devised an elaborate procedure using randomly sequenced report sheets in different colors. But the researchers found that police officers did not always follow this systematic procedure. Subsequently, in some replications of the study, the researchers ensured compliance with their research procedures by requiring police officers to call in to a central number to receive the experimentally determined treatment.

3. *Document all procedures, and disclose them publicly.* Social researchers who disclose the methods on which their conclusions rest allow others to evaluate for themselves the likely soundness of these conclusions. Such disclosure is a key feature of science. Again, Sherman and Berk (1984) provide a compelling example. In their research report, after describing the formal research plan, they described at length the apparent slippage from this plan, which occurred primarily because some police officers avoided implementing the random assignment procedure.

4. *Clarify assumptions.* No investigation is complete unto itself; whatever the researcher's method, the research rests on some background assumptions. Research to determine whether arrest has a deterrent effect assumes that potential law violators think rationally, that they calculate potential costs and benefits prior to committing crimes. When a researcher conducts an election poll, the assumption is that people actually vote for the candidate they say they will vote for. By definition, research assumptions are not tested, so we do not know whether they are correct. By taking the time to think about and to disclose their assumptions, researchers provide important information for those who seek to evaluate the validity of their conclusions.

5. *Specify the meaning of all terms.* Words often have multiple or unclear meanings. Strain, differential association, social disorganization, subculture of violence, problem-oriented policing, and so on can mean different things to different people. Thus, the terms used in scientific research must be defined explicitly and used consistently.

6. *Maintain a skeptical stance toward current knowledge.* Scientists may feel very confident about interpretations of the social or natural world that have been supported by repeated investigations, but the results of any particular investigation must be examined critically. A general skepticism about current knowledge stimulates researchers to improve the validity of current research results and expand the frontier of knowledge.

7. *Replicate research and accumulate knowledge.* No one study can be viewed as definitive in itself; usually at least some plausible threats to the validity of the conclusions exist. In addition, no conclusion can be understood adequately apart from the larger body of knowledge to which the study is related. Scientific investigations may begin with a half-baked or off-the-wall idea, but a search of the literature for other relevant work must be conducted in short order. The other side of the coin is that the results of scientific research must be published, to serve as a foundation for others who seek to replicate or extend the research.

8. *Maintain an interest in theory.* Theories organize the knowledge accumulated by numerous investigations into a coherent whole and serve as a guide to future inquiries. Even though much research is purely descriptive, this research can still serve as a basis for others to evaluate different theories. The Minneapolis Domestic Violence Experiment was devised initially as a test of the competing predictions of deterrence and labeling theory, but the researchers extended their attention to control theory to help them explain unanticipated findings. These theoretical connections make the research much more relevant to other criminologists working to understand different types of crime and social control.

9. *Search for regularities or patterns.* Science is concerned with classes rather than with individuals (except inasmuch as individuals are representatives of a class). Scientists assume that the natural world has some underlying order of relationships, and that every event and individual is not so unique that general principles cannot be discerned (Grinnell 1992: 27–29). The goal of elaborating individual cases is to understand social patterns that characterize many individuals.

These general guidelines are only ideals for social research. No particular investigation will follow every guideline exactly. Real investigations by criminologists do not always include much attention to theory, specific definitions of all terms, and so forth. However, any study that strays far from these guidelines cannot be considered scientific.

CONCLUSION

Criminological researchers can find many questions to study, but not all questions are equally worthy. Those that warrant the expense and effort of social research are feasible, socially important, and scientifically relevant. The simplicity of the research circle presented in this chapter belies the complexity of the social research process. In the following chapters, we will focus on particular aspects of that process. Ethical issues also should be considered when evaluating research. As Chapter 3 will show, ethical issues in research are no less complex than the other issues researchers confront. It is inexcusable to jump into research involving people without paying attention to how our work can and does impact their lives.

KEY TERMS

Anomalous finding	Empirical generalization	Replication
Constant	Falsifiable statement	Research circle
Criminological research question	Hypothesis	Serendipitous finding
Deductive reasoning	Independent variable	Theoretical construct
Deductive research	Inductive reasoning	Theory
Dependent variable	Inductive research	Variable

HIGHLIGHTS

- Research questions should be feasible (within the time and resources available), socially important, and scientifically relevant.

- Building criminological theory is a major objective of criminological research. Investigate relevant theories before starting criminological projects, and draw out the theoretical implications of research findings.

- The type of reasoning in most criminological research can be described as primarily deductive or inductive. Research based on deductive reasoning proceeds from general ideas, deduces specific expectations from these ideas, and then tests the ideas with empirical data. Research based on inductive reasoning begins with specific data and then develops general ideas or theories to explain patterns in the data.

- It may be possible to explain unanticipated research findings after the fact, but such explanations have less credibility than those that have been tested with data collected for the purpose of the study.

- The scientific process can be represented as circular, with connections from theory to hypotheses to data to empirical generalizations. Research investigations may begin at different points along the research circle and travel along different portions of it. Deductive research begins at the point of theory; inductive research begins with data but ends with theory. Descriptive research begins with data and ends with empirical generalizations.

- Replications of a study are essential to establish its generalizability in other situations. An ongoing line of research stemming from a particular question should include a series of studies that, collectively, travel around the research circle multiple times.

- Criminologists, like all social scientists, should structure their research so that their own ideas can be proved wrong, should disclose their methods for others to critique, and should recognize the possibility of error. Nine specific guidelines are recommended.

EXERCISES

Discussing Research

1. State a problem for research related to a criminological topic or issue of interest to you. Write down as many questions as you can about this topic.

   a. Considering your interest, opportunities, and findings from past research, which of your research questions does not seem feasible or interesting?
   b. Pick out one question that seems feasible and that your other coursework suggests has been the focus of prior research or theorizing. Write this research question in one sentence. Elaborate on your question in a single paragraph. List at least three reasons why it is a good research question to investigate.
   c. Ultimately, how would you characterize this research effort? Does it contribute to the discipline, policy, or society at large?

Finding Research on the Web

1. Search the scholarly literature on your topic of interest. Refer to Appendix A for guidance on conducting the search, if necessary.

   a. Copy at least 10 citations to recent articles reporting research relevant to your research question.
   b. Look up at least three of these articles. Write a brief description of each article, and evaluate its relevance to your research question. What additions or changes to your thoughts about the research question are suggested by these sources?
   c. Would you characterize the findings of these articles as largely consistent or inconsistent? How would you explain discrepant findings?
   d. How well did the authors summarize their work in their abstracts for the articles you consulted? What important points would you have missed if you had relied on only the abstracts?

2. You have been assigned to write a paper on domestic violence and the law. To start, you would like to find out what the American Bar Association's stance is on the issue. Go to the American Bar Association Commission on Domestic Violence's website at http://new.abanet. org/domesticviolence/Pages/default.aspx. What is the American Bar Association's definition of domestic violence? How does it suggest one can identify a person as a victim of domestic violence?

3. Go to the Bureau of Justice Statistics (BJS) website at www.ojp.usdoj.gov/bjs. Go to "Publications." Browse the list of publications for topics related to domestic violence. List the titles of all publications focusing on violence between intimate partners. Choose the most recent publication. How does the BJS define "intimate partners"? What are some of the characteristics of intimate partner violence? What trends are identified in the report? Based on the data presented, what might you induce from the findings about police reporting of violence exhibited in particular kinds of relationships (married, divorced, by age of victim, etc.)?

Critiquing Research

1. Using one of the research articles you consulted in the last section, identify and look up one of the cited articles or websites. Compare the cited source to what was said about it in the original article or website. Was the discussion in the cited source accurate?

2. Using the same research article you focused on for the last exercise, identify the stages of the research project corresponding to the points on the research circle. Did the research cover all four stages? Identify the theories and hypotheses underlying the study. What data were collected or utilized for the study? What were the findings (empirical generalizations)?

Making Research Ethical

1. Review the ethical guidelines adopted by the American Sociological Association (1997: 63). Indicate whether you think each guideline was followed in the Sherman and Berk (1984) research on the policy response to domestic violence. If you find it hard to give a simple "yes" or "no" answer for each guideline, indicate the issues that make this evaluation difficult.

2. Concern with how research results are used is one of the hallmarks of ethical researchers, but deciding what form that concern should take is often difficult. You learned in this chapter about the controversy that occurred after Sherman and Berk (1984) encouraged police departments to adopt a pro-arrest policy in domestic abuse cases, based on findings from their Minneapolis study. Do you agree with the researchers' decision to suggest policy changes to police departments based on their study, in an effort to minimize domestic abuse? Several replication studies failed to confirm the Minneapolis findings. Does this influence your evaluation of what the researchers should have done after the Minneapolis study was completed? In one paragraph, propose a policy that researchers should follow about how much publicity is warranted and at what point in the research it should occur.

Developing a Research Proposal

The next exercises are very critical first steps in writing a research proposal.

1. State a problem for research. If you have not already identified a problem for study, or if you need to evaluate whether your research problem is doable, a few suggestions should help to get the ball rolling and keep it on course:

    a. Jot down a few questions you have had about some issue. Now take stock of your interests and your opportunities. Which of your research questions no longer seem feasible or interesting?

    b. Write out your research question in one sentence, and elaborate on it in one paragraph. List at least three reasons why it is a good research question for you to investigate.

2. Search the literature (and the web) on the research question you identified. Refer to Appendix A for guidance on conducting the search. Copy down at least 10 citations to articles and 5 websites reporting research that seems highly relevant to your research question. Inspect the article bibliographies and the links in the websites and identify at least one more relevant article and website from each source. What additions or changes to your thoughts about the research question are suggested by the sources?

3. Propose at least two hypotheses that pertain to your research question. Justify these hypotheses in terms of the literature you have read.

4. Which standards for the protection of human subjects might pose the most difficulty for researchers on your proposed topic? Explain your answers and suggest appropriate protection procedures for human subjects.

Performing Data Analysis in SPSS or Excel

Browse the variables in YOUTH.por on the Student Study Site. This is a survey of high school youth regarding attitudes toward delinquency and delinquent behavior.

1. From these variables (excluding sex of respondent), write two hypotheses about levels of delinquency (DELINQ1) among high school youth.

2. Create a bar chart for at least one of the variables you hypothesize to be associated with levels of delinquency.

3. Compare the distribution of your chosen variable across gender groups. Select all males (SEX = 1) and request a bar chart of your chosen variable; then select all females (SEX = 2) and generate the bar chart again.

4. Compare the distributions between the two bar charts and formulate a hypothesis as to the relationship between the two variables. Is there a relationship between SEX and your chosen variable?

5. From these results, what do you hypothesize is the relationship between gender and level of delinquency?

Student Study Site

The companion Student Study Site for *Fundamentals of Research in Criminology and Criminal Justice* can be found at www.sagepub.com/bachmanfrccj2e.

Visit the Student Study Site to enhance your understanding of the chapter content and to discover additional resources that will take your learning one step further. You can enhance your understanding of the chapters by using the comprehensive study material, which includes interactive exercises, e-flashcards, web exercises, practice self-tests, and more. You will also find special features, such as Learning From Journal Articles, which incorporates Sage's online journal collection.

Research Ethics and Philosophies

The primary focus of this chapter is on research ethics. While each methods chapter in this book provides a discussion of ethical issues devoted specifically to a particular method (e.g., experimental design, survey), this chapter will highlight the general ethical considerations everyone should consider before beginning his or her research. Every researcher needs to consider how to practice his or her discipline ethically. Whenever we interact with other people as social scientists, we must place great importance on the concerns and emotional needs that shape their responses to our actions. It is here that ethical research practice begins, with the recognition that our research procedures involve people who deserve respect. At the end of the chapter, we conclude with a brief discussion of different social research philosophies that will set the stage for the remainder of the book.

WHAT DO WE HAVE IN MIND?

Consider the following scenario: One day as you are drinking coffee and reading the newspaper during your summer in California, you notice a small ad recruiting college students for a study at Stanford University. You go to the campus and complete an application. The ad read as follows:

> Male college students needed for psychological study of prison life. $80 per day for 1–2 weeks beginning Aug. 14. For further information & applications, come to Room 248, Jordan Hall, Stanford U. (Zimbardo 1973: 38)

After you arrive at the university, you are given an information form with more details about the research (Zimbardo 1973).

Prison Life Study: General Information

Purpose: A simulated prison will be established somewhere in the vicinity of Palo Alto, Stanford [sic], to study a number of problems of psychological and sociological relevance. Paid volunteers will be randomly assigned to play the roles of either prisoners and guards [sic] for the duration of the study. This time period will vary somewhat from about five days to two weeks for any one volunteer—depending upon several factors, such as the "sentence" for the prisoner or the work effectiveness of the guards. Payment will be $80 a day for performing various activities and work associated with the operation of our prison. Each volunteer must enter a contractual arrangement with the principal investigator (Dr. P. G. Zimbardo) agreeing to participate for the full duration of the study. It is obviously essential that no prisoner can leave once jailed, except through established procedures. In addition, guards must report for their 8-hour work shifts promptly and regularly since surveillance by the guards will be around-the-clock—three work shifts will be rotated or guards will be assigned a regular shift—day, evening, or early morning. Failure to fulfill this contract will result in a partial loss of salary accumulated—according to a prearranged schedule to be agreed upon. Food and accommodations for the prisoners will be provided which will meet minimal standard nutrition, health, and sanitation requirements. A warden and several prison staff will be housed in adjacent cell blocks, meals and bedding also provided for them. Medical and psychiatric facilities will be accessible should any of the participants desire or require such services. All participants will agree to having their behavior observed and to be interviewed and perhaps also taking psychological tests. Films of parts of the study will be taken, participants agreeing to allow them to be shown, assuming their content has information of scientific value.

[The information form then summarizes two of the "problems to be studied" and provides a few more details.]

Thanks for your interest in this study. We hope it will be possible for you to participate and to share your experiences with us.

Philip G. Zimbardo, PhD
Professor of Social Psychology
Stanford University

Source: Zimbardo (1973).

First, you are asked to complete a long questionnaire about your family background, physical and mental health history, and prior criminal involvement. Next, you are interviewed by someone, and then you finally sign a consent form. A few days later, you are informed that you and 20 other young men have been selected to participate in the experiment. You return to the university to complete a battery of "psychological tests" and are told you will be picked up for the study the next day (Haney, Banks, & Zimbardo 1973: 73).

The next morning, you hear a siren just before a squad car stops in front of your house. A police officer charges you with assault and battery, warns you of your constitutional rights, searches and handcuffs you, and drives you off to the police station. After fingerprinting and a short stay in a detention cell, you are blindfolded and driven to the "Stanford County Prison." Upon arrival, your blindfold is removed and you are stripped naked, skin-searched, deloused, and issued a uniform (a loosely fitting smock with an ID number printed on it), bedding, soap, and a towel. You don't recognize anyone, but you notice that the other "prisoners" and the "guards" are college-age, apparently almost all middle-class white men (except for one Asian) like you (Haney et al. 1973; Zimbardo et al. 1973).

The prison warden welcomes you:

> As you probably know, I'm your warden. All of you have shown that you are unable to function outside in the real world for one reason or another—that somehow you lack the responsibility of good citizens of this great country. We of this prison, your correctional staff, are going to help you learn what your responsibilities as citizens of this country are. . . . If you follow all of these rules and keep your hands clean, repent for your misdeeds and show a proper attitude of penitence, you and I will get along just fine. (Zimbardo et al. 1973: 38)

Among other behavioral restrictions, the rules stipulate that prisoners must remain silent during rest periods, during meals, and after lights out. They must address each other only by their assigned ID numbers, they are to address guards as "Mr. Correctional Officer," and everyone is warned that punishment will follow any rule violation (Zimbardo et al. 1973).

You look around and can tell that you are in the basement of a building. You are led down a corridor to a small cell (6' x 9') with three cots, where you are locked behind a steel-barred black door with two other prisoners (Exhibit 3.1). Located across the hall, there is a small solitary confinement room (2' x 2' x 7') for those who misbehave. There is little privacy, since you realize that the uniformed guards, behind the mirrored lenses of their sunglasses, can always observe the prisoners. After you go to sleep, you are awakened by a whistle summoning you and the others for a roll call periodically through the night.

The next morning, you and the other eight prisoners must stand in line outside your cells and recite the rules until you remember all 17 of them. Prisoners must chant, "It's a wonderful day, Mr. Correctional Officer." Two prisoners who get out of line are put in the solitary confinement unit. After a bit, the prisoners in Cell 1 decide to resist: They barricade their cell door and call on the prisoners in other cells to join in their resistance. The guards respond by pulling the beds out from the other cells and spraying several of the inmates with a fire extinguisher. The guards succeed in enforcing control and become more authoritarian, while the prisoners become increasingly docile. Punishments are regularly meted out for infractions of rules and sometimes for

Exhibit 3.1 Prisoner in His Cell

Source: From *The Lucifer Effect*, by Philip Zimbardo © 2008, p. 155. Reprinted with permission.

seemingly no reason at all; punishments include doing push-ups, being stripped naked, having legs chained, and being repeatedly wakened during the night. If this were you, would you join in the resistance? How would you react to this deprivation of your liberty by these authoritarian guards? How would you respond given that you signed a consent form allowing you to be subjected to this kind of treatment?

By the fifth day of the actual Stanford Prison Experiment, five student prisoners had to be released due to evident extreme stress (Zimbardo 2008). On the sixth day, Philip Zimbardo terminated the experiment. A prisoner subsequently reported,

> The way we were made to degrade ourselves really brought us down and that's why we all sat docile towards the end of the experiment. (Haney et al. 1973: 88)

One guard later recounted his experience:

> I was surprised at myself. . . . I made them call each other names and clean the toilets out with their bare hands. I practically considered the prisoners cattle, and I kept thinking: "I have to watch out for them in case they try something."
> (Zimbardo et al. 1973: 174)

Exhibit 3.2 gives some idea of the difference in how the prisoners and guards behaved. What is most striking about this result is that all the guards and prisoners had been screened before the study began to ensure that they were physically and mentally healthy. The roles of guard and prisoner had been assigned randomly, by the toss of a coin, so the two groups were very similar when the study began. Something about the "situation" appears to have led to the deterioration of the prisoners' mental states and the different behavior of the guards. Being a guard or a prisoner, with rules and physical arrangements reinforcing distinctive roles, changed their behavior.

Are you surprised by the outcome of the experiment? By the guard's report of his unexpected, abusive behavior? By the prisoners' ultimate submissiveness and the considerable psychic distress some felt? (We leave it to you to assess how you would have responded if you had been an actual research participant.)

Of course, our purpose in introducing this small "experiment" is not to focus attention on the prediction of behavior in prisons but to introduce the topic of research ethics. We will refer to Philip Zimbardo's Stanford Prison Experiment throughout this chapter, since it is fair to say that this research ultimately had a profound influence on the way that social scientists think about research ethics as well as on the way that criminologists understand behavior in prisons. We will also refer to Stanley Milgram's (1963) experiments on obedience to authority, since that research also pertains to criminal justice issues and has stimulated much debate about research ethics.

HISTORICAL BACKGROUND

Formal procedures regarding the protection of research participants emerged only after the revelation of several very questionable and damaging research practices. A defining event

Exhibit 3.2   Chart of Guard and Prisoner Behavior

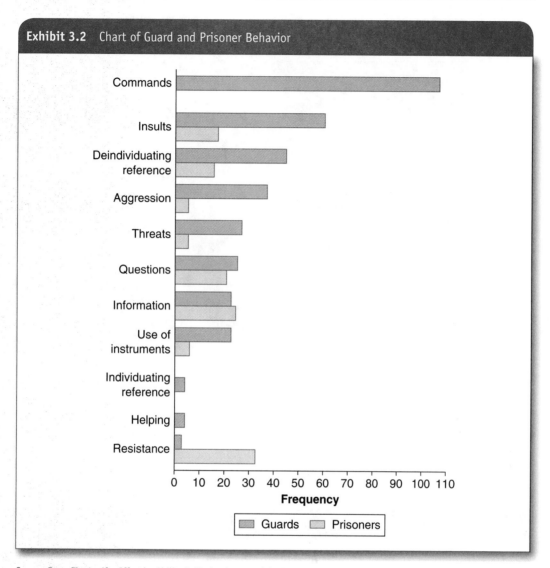

Source: From *The Lucifer Effect* by Philip G. Zimbardo, copyright © 2007 by Philip G. Zimbardo, Inc. Used by permission of Random House Inc.

occurred in 1946, when the Nuremberg War Crime Trials exposed horrific medical experiments conducted by Nazi doctors and others in the name of "science." In the 1970s, Americans were shocked to learn that researchers funded by the U.S. Public Health Service had followed 399 low-income African American men with syphilis in the 1930s, collecting data to study the "natural" course of the illness (Exhibit 3.3). Many participants were not informed of their illness and were denied treatment until 1972, even though a cure (penicillin) was developed in the 1950s.

Exhibit 3.3 Tuskegee Syphilis Experiment

Source: Tuskegee Syphilis Study Administrative Records. Records of the Centers for Disease Control and Prevention. National Archives—Southeast Region (Atlanta).

Horrible violations of human rights similar to these resulted, in the United States, in the creation of a National Commission for the Protection of Human Subjects of Biomedical and Behavioral Research. The commission's 1979 **Belmont Report** (from the Department of Health, Education, and Welfare) established three basic ethical principles for the protection of human subjects (Exhibit 3.4):

Exhibit 3.4 Belmont Report Principles

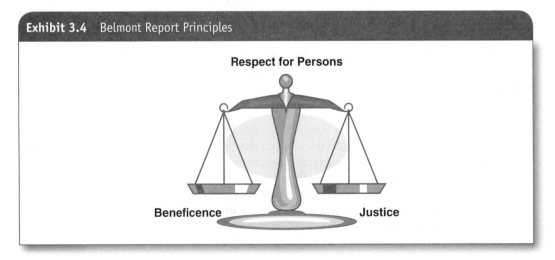

- **Respect for persons:** Treating persons as autonomous agents and protecting those with diminished autonomy
- **Beneficence:** Minimizing possible harms and maximizing benefits
- **Justice:** Distributing benefits and risks of research fairly

The Department of Health and Human Services and the Food and Drug Administration then translated these principles into specific regulations that were adopted in 1991 as the **Federal Policy for the Protection of Human Subjects.** This policy has shaped the course of social science research ever since. This section introduces these regulations.

Federal regulations require that every institution, including universities that seek federal funding for biomedical or behavioral research on human subjects, have an **institutional review board (IRB)** to review research proposals. IRBs at universities and other agencies adopt a review process that is principally guided by federally regulated ethical standards but can be expanded by the IRB itself (Sieber 1992). To promote adequate review of ethical issues, the regulations require that IRBs include members with diverse backgrounds. The **Office for Protection From Research Risks in the National Institutes of Health** monitors IRBs, with the exception of research involving drugs (which is the responsibility of the federal Food and Drug Administration).

The Academy of Criminal Justice Sciences (ACJS) and the American Society of Criminology (ASC), like most professional social science organizations, have adopted ethical guidelines for practicing criminologists that are more specific than the federal regulations. The ACJS Code of Ethics also establishes procedures for investigating and resolving complaints concerning the ethical conduct of the organization's members. The Code of Ethics of the ACJS (2000) is available on the ACJS Web site (www.acjs.org). The ASC follows the American Sociological Association's code (ASA 1999).

ETHICAL PRINCIPLES

Achieving Valid Results

A commitment to achieving valid results is the necessary starting point for ethical research practice. Simply put, we have no business asking people to answer questions, submit to observations, or participate in experimental procedures if we are simply seeking to verify our preexisting prejudices or convince others to take action on behalf of our personal interests. It is the pursuit of objective knowledge about human behavior—the goal of validity—that motivates and justifies our investigations and gives us some claim to the right to influence others to participate in our research. If we approach our research projects objectively, setting aside our personal predilections in the service of learning a bit more about human behavior, we can honestly represent our actions as potentially contributing to the advancement of knowledge.

The details in Zimbardo's articles and his recent book (2008) on the prison experiment make a compelling case for his commitment to achieving valid results—to learning how and why a prison-like situation influences behavior. In Zimbardo's (2009) own words,

> Social-psychological studies were showing that human nature was more pliable than previously imagined and more responsive to situational pressures than we cared to acknowledge. . . . Missing from the body of social-science research at the time was the direct confrontation . . . of good people pitted against the forces inherent in bad situations. . . . I decided that what was needed was to create a situation in a controlled experimental setting in which we could array on one side a host of variables, such as . . . coercive rules, power differentials, anonymity. . . . On the other side, we lined up a collection of the "best and brightest" of young college men. . . . I wanted to know who wins—good people or an evil situation—when they were brought into direct confrontation.

Zimbardo (Haney et al. 1973) devised his experiment so the situation would seem realistic to the participants and still allow careful measurement of important variables and observation of behavior at all times. Questionnaires and rating scales, interviews with participants as the research proceeded and after it was over, ongoing video and audio recording, and documented logs maintained by the guards all ensured that very little would escape the researcher's gaze.

Zimbardo's (Haney et al. 1973) attention to validity is also apparent in his design of the physical conditions and organizational procedures for the experiment. The "prison" was constructed in a basement without any windows so that participants were denied a sense of time and place. Their isolation was reinforced by the practice of placing paper bags over their heads when they moved around "the facility," meals were bland, and conditions were generally demeaning. This was a very different "situation" from what the participants were used to—suffice it to say that it was no college dorm experience.

However, not all social scientists agree that Zimbardo's approach achieved valid results. British psychologists Stephen Reicher and S. Alexander Haslam (2006) argue that guard behavior was not so consistent and that it was determined by the instructions Zimbardo gave the guards at the start of the experiment, rather than by becoming a guard in itself. For example, in another experiment, when guards were trained to respect prisoners, their behavior was less malicious (Lovibond, Mithiran, & Adams 1979).

In response to such criticism, Zimbardo (2007) has pointed to several replications of his basic experiment that support his conclusions—as well as to the evidence of patterns of abuse in the real world of prisons, including the behavior of guards who tormented prisoners at Abu Ghraib during the war in Iraq.

Do you agree with Zimbardo's assumption that the effects of being a prisoner or guard could fruitfully be studied in a mock prison, with "pretend" prisoners? Do you find merit in the criticisms? Will your evaluation of the ethics of Zimbardo's experiment be influenced by your answers to these questions? Should our ethical judgments differ when we are confident a study's results provide valid information about important social processes?

As you attempt to answer such questions, bear in mind that both Zimbardo and his critics support their conflicting ethical arguments with assertions about the validity (or invalidity) of the experimental results. It is hard to justify *any* risk for human subjects, or *any* expenditure of time and resources, if our findings tell us nothing about the reality of crime and punishment.

Honesty and Openness

The scientific concern with validity requires that scientists openly disclose their methods and honestly present their findings. In contrast, research distorted by political or personal pressures to find particular outcomes or to achieve the most marketable results is unlikely to be carried out in an honest and open fashion. To assess the validity of a researcher's conclusions and the ethics of his or her procedures, you need to know exactly how the research was conducted. This means that articles or other reports must include a detailed methodology section, perhaps supplemented by appendices containing the research instruments or websites or an address where more information can be obtained.

Philip Zimbardo's research reports seemed to present an honest and forthright account of the methods used in the Stanford experiment. His initial article (Haney et al. 1973) contained a detailed description of study procedures, including the physical aspects of the prison, the instructions to participants, the uniforms used, the induction procedure, and the specific data collection methods and measures. Many more details, including forms and pictures, are available on Zimbardo's website (www.prisonexperiment.org) and in his recent book (Zimbardo 2008).

The act of publication itself is a vital element in maintaining openness and honesty. It allows others to review and question study procedures and generate an open dialogue with the researcher. Although Zimbardo disagreed sharply with his critics about many aspects of his experiment, their mutual commitment to public discourse in publications resulted in a more comprehensive presentation of study procedures and a more thoughtful discourse about research ethics (Savin 1973; Zimbardo 1973). Almost 40 years later, this commentary continues to inform debates about research ethics (Reicher & Haslam 2006; Zimbardo 2007).

Openness about research procedures and results goes hand in hand with honesty in research design. Openness is also essential if researchers are to learn from the work of others. In spite of this need for openness, some researchers may hesitate to disclose their procedures or results to prevent others from building on their ideas and taking some of the credit. Scientists are like other people in their desire to be first. Enforcing standards of honesty and encouraging openness about research are the best solutions to this problem.

Protecting Research Participants

The ACJS code's standards concerning the treatment of human subjects include federal regulations and ethical guidelines emphasized by most professional social science organizations:

- Research should expose participants to no more than minimal risk of personal harm. (#16)
- Researchers should fully disclose the purposes of their research. (#13)
- Participation in research should be voluntary, and therefore subjects must give their informed consent to participate in the research. (#16)
- Confidentiality must be maintained for individual research participants unless it is voluntarily and explicitly waived. (#14, #18, #19)

Philip Zimbardo (2008) himself decided that his Stanford Prison Experiment was unethical because it violated the first two of these principles: First, participants "did suffer considerable anguish . . . and [the experiment] resulted in such extreme stress and emotional turmoil that five of the sample of initially healthy young prisoners had to be released early" (pp. 233–234). Second, Zimbardo's research team did not disclose in advance the nature of the arrest or booking procedures at police headquarters nor did they disclose to the participants' parents how bad the situation had become when they came to a visiting night. Nonetheless, Zimbardo (Zimbardo et al. 1973; Zimbardo 2008) argued that there was no long-lasting harm to participants and that there were some long-term social benefits from this research. In particular, **debriefing** participants—discussing their experiences and revealing the logic behind the experiment—and follow-up interviews enabled the participants to recover from the experience without lasting harm (Zimbardo 2007). Also, the experience led several participants in the experiment, including Zimbardo, to dedicate their careers to investigating and improving prison conditions. As a result, publicity about the experiment has also helped focus attention on problems in prison management.

Do you agree with Zimbardo's conclusion that his experiment was not ethical? Do you think it should have been prevented from happening in the first place? Are you relieved to learn that current standards in the United States for the protection of human subjects in research would not allow his experiment to be conducted?

In contrast to Zimbardo, Stanley Milgram (1963) believed that his controversial experiments on obedience to authority were entirely ethical, so debate about this study persists today. His experiments raise most of the relevant issues we want to highlight here.

Milgram had recruited community members to participate in his experiment at Yale University. His research was prompted by the ability of Germany's Nazi regime of the 1930s and 1940s to enlist the participation of ordinary citizens in unconscionable acts of terror and genocide. Milgram set out to identify through laboratory experiments the conditions under which ordinary citizens will be obedient to authority figures' instructions to inflict pain on others. He operationalized this obedience by asking subjects to deliver electric shocks (fake, of course) to students supposedly learning a memory task. Subjects ("teachers") were told to administer a shock to the learner each time he gave a wrong response and to incrementally raise the voltage with each incorrect response. They were told to increase the shocks over time and many did so, even after the "students," behind a partition, began to cry out in (simulated) pain (Exhibit 3.5). The participants became very tense, and some resisted as the shocks increased to the (supposedly) lethal range, but many still complied with the authority in that situation and increased the shocks. Like Zimbardo, Milgram debriefed participants afterward and followed up later to check on their well-being. It seemed that none had suffered long-term harm (Milgram 1974).

As we discuss how the ACJS Code of Ethics standards apply to Milgram's experiments, you will begin to realize that there is no simple answer to the question, "What *is* (or *isn't*) ethical research practice?" The issues are just too complicated and the relevant principles too subject to different interpretations. But we do promise that by the end of this chapter, you will be aware of the major issues in research ethics and be able to make informed, defensible decisions about the ethical conduct of social science research.

Exhibit 3.5 Diagram of Milgram's Experiment

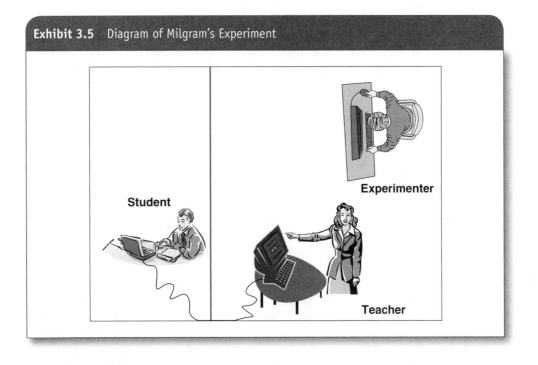

Avoid Harming Research Participants

Although this standard may seem straightforward, it can be difficult to interpret in specific cases and harder yet to define in a way that is agreeable to all social scientists. Does it mean that subjects should not be harmed at all, psychologically or physically? That they should feel no anxiety or distress whatsoever during the study or even after their involvement ends? Should the possibility of *any* harm, no matter how remote, deter research?

Before we address these questions with respect to Milgram's experiments, a verbatim transcript of one session will give you an idea of what participants experienced (Milgram 1965):

150 volts delivered.	You want me to keep going?
165 volts delivered.	That guy is hollering in there. There's a lot of them here. He's liable to have a heart condition. You want me to go on?
180 volts delivered.	He can't stand it! I'm not going to kill that man in there! You hear him hollering? He's hollering. He can't stand it. . . . I mean who is going to take responsibility if anything happens to that gentleman?

[The experimenter accepts responsibility.] All right.

195 volts delivered.   You see he's hollering. Hear that? Gee, I don't know. *[The experimenter says: "The experiment requires that you go on."]* I know it does, sir, but I mean—Hugh—he don't know what he's in for. He's up to 195 volts.

210 volts delivered.

225 volts delivered.

240 volts delivered. (p. 67)

This experimental manipulation generated "extraordinary tension" (Milgram 1963):

Subjects were observed to sweat, tremble, stutter, bite their lips, groan and dig their fingernails into their flesh. . . . Full-blown, uncontrollable seizures were observed for 3 subjects. [O]ne . . . seizure [was] so violently convulsive that it was necessary to call a halt to the experiment [for that individual]. (p. 375)

An observer (behind a one-way mirror) reported, "I observed a mature and initially poised businessman enter the laboratory smiling and confident. Within 20 minutes he was reduced to a twitching, stuttering wreck, who was rapidly approaching a point of nervous collapse" (p. 377).

Psychologist Diana Baumrind (1964) disagreed sharply with Milgram's approach, concluding that the emotional disturbance subjects experienced was "potentially harmful because it could easily affect an alteration in the subject's self-image or ability to trust adult authorities in the future" (p. 422). Stanley Milgram (1964) quickly countered, "As the experiment progressed there was no indication of injurious effects in the subjects; and as the subjects themselves strongly endorsed the experiment, the judgment I made was to continue the experiment" (p. 849).

When Milgram (1964) surveyed the subjects in a follow-up, 83.7% endorsed the statement that they were "very glad" or "glad" "to have been in the experiment," 15.1% were "neither sorry nor glad," and just 1.3% were "sorry" or "very sorry" to have participated (p. 849). Interviews by a psychiatrist a year later found no evidence "of any traumatic reactions" (p. 197). Subsequently, Milgram (1974) argued that "the central moral justification for allowing my experiment is that it was judged acceptable by those who took part in it" (p. 21).

Milgram (1964) also attempted to minimize harm to subjects with post-experimental procedures "to assure that the subject would leave the laboratory in a state of well being" (p. 374). A friendly reconciliation was arranged between the subject and the victim, and an effort was made to reduce any tensions that arose as a result of the experiment. In some cases, the "dehoaxing" (or "debriefing") discussion was extensive, and all subjects were promised (and later received) a comprehensive report (p. 849).

In a later article, Baumrind (1985) dismissed the value of the self-reported "lack of harm" of subjects who had been willing to participate in the experiment—and noted that 16% did *not* endorse the statement that they were "glad" they had participated in the experiment (p. 168). Baumrind also argued that research indicates most students who have participated in a deception experiment report a decreased trust in authorities as a result—a tangible harm in itself.

Many social scientists, ethicists, and others concluded that Milgram's procedures had not harmed the subjects and so were justified for the knowledge they produced, but others sided with Baumrind's criticisms (Miller 1986). What is your opinion at this point? Does Milgram's debriefing process relieve your concerns? Are you as persuaded by the subjects' own endorsement of the procedures as was Milgram?

Would you ban such experiments because of the potential for harm to subjects? Does the fact that Zimbardo's and Milgram's experiments seemed to yield significant insights into the effect of a social situation on human behavior—insights that could be used to improve prisons or perhaps lessen the likelihood of another holocaust—make any difference (Reynolds 1979)? Do you believe that this benefit outweighs the foreseeable risks?

Obtain Informed Consent

The requirement of informed consent is also more difficult to define than it first appears. To be informed consent, it must be given by the persons who are competent to consent, can consent voluntarily, are fully informed about the research, and comprehend what they have been told (Reynolds 1979). Still, even well-intentioned researchers may not foresee all the potential problems and may not point them out in advance to potential participants (Baumrind 1985). In Zimbardo's prison-simulation study, all the participants signed consent forms, but they were not "fully informed" in advance about potential risks. The researchers themselves did not realize that the study participants would experience so much stress so quickly, that some prisoners would have to be released for severe negative reactions within the first few days, or that even those who were not severely stressed would soon be begging to be released from the mock prison. But on the other hand, are you concerned that real harm "could result from *not doing* research on destructive obedience" and other troubling human behavior (Miller 1986:138, italics original)?

Obtaining informed consent creates additional challenges for researchers. The language of the consent form must be clear and understandable to the research participants yet sufficiently long and detailed to explain what will actually happen in the research. Examples A (Exhibit 3.6) and B (Exhibit 3.7) illustrate two different approaches to these trade-offs.

Consent form A was approved by the University of Delaware IRB for in-depth interviews with former inmates about their experiences after release from prison. Consent form B is the one used by Philip Zimbardo. It is brief and to the point, leaving out many of the details that current standards for the protection of human subjects require. Zimbardo's consent form also released the researchers from any liability for problems arising out of the research (Such a statement is no longer allowed.).

As in Milgram's (1963) study, experimental researchers whose research design requires some type of subject deception try to minimize disclosure of experimental details by withholding some information before the experiment begins but then debrief subjects at the end. In the debriefing, the researcher explains to the subjects what happened in the experiment and why, and then addresses participants' concerns or questions. A carefully

Exhibit 3.6 Consent Form A

INFORMED CONSENT

ROADS DIVERGE: LONG-TERM PATTERNS OF RELAPSE, RECIDIVISM, AND DESISTANCE FOR A RE-ENTRY COHORT (National Institute of Justice, 2008-IJ-CX-0017)

PURPOSE: You are one of approximately 300 people being asked to participate in a research project conducted by the Center for Drug and Alcohol Studies at the University of Delaware. You were part of the original study of offenders in Delaware leaving prison in the 1990s, and we want to find out how things in your life have changed since that time. The overall purpose of this research is to help us understand what factors lead to changes in criminal activity and drug use over time.

PROCEDURES: If you agree to take part in this study, you will be asked to complete a survey, which will last approximately 60 to 90 minutes. We will ask you to provide us with some contact information so that we can locate you again if we are able to do another follow up study in the future. You will be asked about your employment, family history, criminal involvement, health history, drug use, and how these have changed over time. We will use this information, as well as information that you have previously provided or which is publicly available. We will not ask you for the names of anyone, or the specific dates or specific places of any of your activities. The interviews will be tape-recorded, but you will not be identified by name on the tape. The tapes will be stored in a locked cabinet until they can be transcribed to an electronic word processor. After the tapes have been transcribed and checked for accuracy they will be destroyed. Anonymous transcribed data will be kept indefinitely – no audio data will be kept.

RISKS: There are some risks to participating in this study. You may experience distress or discomfort when asked questions about your drug use, criminal history, and other experiences. Should this occur, you may choose not to answer such questions. If emotional distress occurs, our staff will make referrals to services you may need, including counseling, and drug abuse treatment and support services.

The risk that confidentiality could be broken is a concern, but it is very unlikely to occur. You will not be identified on the audiotape of the interview. We request that you not mention names of other people or places, but if this happens, those names will be deleted from the audiotape prior to transcription. All study materials are kept in locked file cabinets. Only three members of [the] research team will have access to study materials.

BENEFITS: You will have the opportunity to participate in an important research project, which may lead to the better understanding of what factors both help and prevent an individual's recovery from drug use and criminal activity.

COMPENSATION: You will receive $100 to compensate you for your time and travel costs for this interview.

CONFIDENTIALITY: Your records will be kept confidential. They will be kept under lock and key and will not be shared with anyone without your written permission. Your name will not appear on any data file or research report.

A Privacy Certificate has been approved by the U.S. Department of Justice. The data will be protected from being revealed to non-research interests by court subpoena in any federal, state, or local civil, criminal, administrative, legislative or other proceedings.

You should understand that a Privacy Certificate does not prevent you or a member of your family from voluntarily releasing information about yourself or your involvement in this research. If you give anyone written consent to receive research information, then we may not use the Certificate to withhold that information.

The Privacy Certificate does not prevent research staff from voluntary disclosures to authorities if we learn that you intend to harm yourself or someone else. These incidents would be reported as required by state and federal law. However, we will not ask you questions about these areas.

Because this research is paid for by the National Institute of Justice, staff of this research office may review copies of your records, but they also are required to keep that information confidential.

RIGHT TO QUIT THE STUDY: Participation in this research project is voluntary and you have the right to leave the study at any time. The researchers and their assistants have the right to remove you from this study if needed.

You may ask and will receive answers to any questions concerning this study. If you have any questions about this study, you may contact Ronet Bachman or Daniel O'Connell at (302) 831-6107. If you have any questions about your rights as a research participant you may contact the Chairperson of the University of Delaware's Human Subjects Review Board at (302) 831-2136.

CONSENT TO BE INTERVIEWED

I have read and understand this form (or it has been read to me), and I agree to participate in the in-depth interview portion of this research project.

_____

Participant Signature   Date

_____

Signature of Witness/Interviewer   Date

CONSENT TO BE CONTACTED IN FUTURE

I have read and understand this form (or it has been read to me), and I agree to be recontacted in the future as part of this research project.

_____

Participant Signature   Date

_____

Signature of Witness/Interviewer   Date

Ronet Bachman, PhD
Principal Investigator
University of Delaware
Telephone: (302) 831-6107

Exhibit 3.7 Consent Form B

CONSENT

Prison Life Study
Dr. Zimbardo
August 1971

_____

(date) (name of volunteer)

I, _____, the undersigned, hereby consent to participate as a volunteer in a prison life study research project to be conducted by the Stanford University Psychology Department.

The nature of the research project has been fully explained to me, including, without limitation, the fact that paid volunteers will be randomly assigned to the roles of either "prisoners" or "guards" for the duration of the study. I understand that participation in the research project will involve a loss of privacy, that I will be expected to participate for the full duration of the study, that I will only be released from participation for reasons of health deemed adequate by the medical advisers to the research project or for other reasons deemed appropriate by Dr. Philip Zimbardo, Principal Investigator of the project, and that I will be expected to follow directions from staff members of the project or from other participants in the research project.

I am submitting myself for participation in this research project with full knowledge and understanding of the nature of the research project and of what will be expected of me. I specifically release the Principal Investigator and the staff members of the research project, Stanford University, its agents and employees, and the Federal Government, its agents and employees, from any liability to me arising in any way out of my participation in the project.

_____

(signature of volunteer)

Witness: _____

If volunteer is a minor:

_____

(signature of person authorized to consent for volunteer)

Witness: _____

_____

(relationship to volunteer)

designed debriefing procedure can help the research participants learn from the experimental research and grapple constructively with feelings elicited by the realization that they were deceived (Sieber 1992). However, even though debriefing can be viewed as a substitute, in some cases, for securing fully informed consent prior to the experiment, debriefed subjects who disclose the nature of the experiment to other participants can contaminate subsequent results (Adair, Dushenko, & Lindsay 1985). Unfortunately, if the debriefing process is delayed, the ability to lessen any harm resulting from the deception may also be compromised.

If you were to serve on your university's IRB, would you allow this type of research to be conducted? Can students who are asked to participate in research by their professor be considered able to give informed consent? Do you consider "informed consent" to be meaningful if the true purpose or nature of an experimental manipulation is not revealed?

The process and even possibility of obtaining informed consent must take into account the capacity of prospective participants to give informed consent. For example, children cannot legally give consent to participate in research. Instead, minors must in most circumstances be given the opportunity to give or withhold their *assent* or compliance to participate in research, usually by a verbal response to an explanation of the research. In addition, a child's legal guardian typically must grant additional written informed consent to have the child participate in research (Sieber 1992). There are also special protections for other populations that are likely to be vulnerable to coercion—prisoners, pregnant women, mentally disabled persons, and educationally or economically disadvantaged persons. Would you allow research on prisoners, whose ability to give "informed consent" can be questioned? If so, what special protections do you think would be appropriate?

Avoid Deception in Research, Except in Limited Circumstances

Deception occurs when subjects are misled about research procedures in an effort to determine how they would react to the treatment if they were not research subjects. In other words, researchers deceive their subjects when they believe that knowledge of the experimental premise may actually change the subjects' behavior. Deception is a critical component of many experiments, in part because of the difficulty of simulating real-world stresses and dilemmas in a laboratory setting. The goal is to get subjects "to accept as true what is false or to give a false impression" (Korn 1997: 4). In Milgram's (1963) experiment, for example, deception seemed necessary because the subjects could not be permitted to administer real electric shocks to the "student," yet it would not have made sense to order the subjects to do something that they didn't find to be so troubling. Milgram (1992) insisted that the deception was absolutely essential. The results of many other experiments would be worthless if subjects understood what was really happening to them while the experiment was in progress. The real question is this: Is that sufficient justification to allow the use of deception?

There are many examples of research efforts that employ placebos, ruses, or guises to ensure that participants' behavior is genuine. For example, Piliavin and Piliavin (1972) staged fake seizures on subway trains to study helpfulness. Would you vote to allow such deceptive practices in research if you were a member of your university's IRB? What about less dramatic instances of deception in laboratory experiments with students like yourself? Do you react differently to the debriefing by Milgram compared to that by Zimbardo?

What scientific or educational or applied "value" would make deception justifiable, even if there is some potential for harm? Who determines whether a nondeceptive intervention is "equally effective" (Miller 1986: 103)? Diana Baumrind (1985) suggested that personal "introspection" would have been sufficient to test Milgram's hypothesis and has argued subsequently that intentional deception in research violates the ethical principles of self-determination, protection of others, and maintenance of trust between people and so can never be justified. How much risk, discomfort, or unpleasantness might be seen as affecting willingness to participate? When should a post-experimental "attempt to correct any misconception" due to deception be deemed sufficient?

Can you see why an IRB, representing a range of perspectives, is an important tool for making reasonable, ethical research decisions when confronted with such ambiguity?

Maintain Privacy and Confidentiality

Maintaining privacy and confidentiality is another key ethical standard for protecting research participants, and the researcher's commitment to that standard should be included in the informed consent agreement (Sieber 1992). Procedures to protect each subject's privacy, such as locking records and creating special identifying codes, must be created to minimize the risk of access by unauthorized persons. However, statements about confidentiality should be realistic: In some cases, laws allow research records to be subpoenaed and may require reporting child abuse; a researcher may feel compelled to release information if a health- or life-threatening situation arises and participants need to be alerted. Also, the standard of confidentiality does not apply to observation in public places and information available in public records.

There are two exceptions to some of these constraints: The National Institute of Justice can issue a "**Privacy Certificate**," and the National Institutes of Health can issue a "**Certificate of Confidentiality.**" Both of these documents protect researchers from being legally required to disclose confidential information. Researchers who are focusing on high-risk populations or behaviors, such as crime, substance abuse, sexual activity, or genetic information, can request such a certificate. Suspicions of child abuse or neglect must still be reported, as well as instances where respondents may immediately harm themselves or others. In some states, researchers also may be required to report crimes such as elder abuse (Arwood & Panicker 2007).

The Health Insurance Portability and Accountability Act (HIPAA) passed by Congress in 1996 created much more stringent regulations for the protection of health care data. As implemented by the U.S. Department of Health and Human Services in 2000 (and revised in 2002), the HIPAA Final Privacy Rule applies to oral, written, and electronic information that "relates to the past, present, or future physical or mental health or condition of an individual." The HIPAA rule requires that researchers have valid authorization for any use or disclosure of "protected health information" (PHI) from a health care provider. Waivers of authorization can be granted in special circumstances (Cava, Cushman, & Goodman 2007).

The Uses of Research

Although many scientists believe that personal values should be left outside the laboratory, some feel that it is proper—even necessary—for scientists to concern themselves with the way their research is used. Philip Zimbardo made it clear that he was concerned about the phenomenon of situational influence on behavior precisely because of its implications for people's welfare. As you have already learned, his first article (Haney et al. 1973) highlighted abuses in the treatment of prisoners. In his more comprehensive book, Zimbardo (2007) used his findings to explain the atrocities committed at Abu Ghraib. He also urged reforms in prison policy.

It is also impossible to ignore the very practical implications of Milgram's investigations, which Milgram (1974) took pains to emphasize. His research highlighted the extent of obedience to authority and identified multiple factors that could be manipulated to lessen blind obedience (such as encouraging dissent by just one group member, removing the subject from direct contact with the authority figure, and increasing the contact between the subject and the victim).

The evaluation research by Lawrence Sherman and Richard Berk (1984) on the police response to domestic violence provides an interesting cautionary tale about the uses of science. As you will recall from Chapter 2, the results of this field experiment indicated that those who were arrested were less likely to subsequently commit violent acts against their partners. Sherman (1992) explicitly cautioned police departments not to adopt mandatory arrest policies based solely on the results of the Minneapolis experiment, but the results were publicized in the mass media and encouraged many jurisdictions to change their policies (Binder & Meeker 1993; Lempert 1989). Although we now know that the original finding of a deterrent effect of arrest did not hold up in other cities where the experiment was repeated, Sherman (1992) later suggested that implementing mandatory arrest policies might have prevented some subsequent cases of spouse abuse. JoAnn Miller's (2003) analysis of victims' experiences and perceptions concerning their safety after the mandatory arrest experiment in Dade County, Florida, found that victims reported less violence if their abuser had been arrested (or assigned to a police-based counseling program called "Safe Streets") (Exhibit 3.8). Should this Dade County finding be publicized in the popular press so it could be used to improve police policies? What about the results of the other replication studies where arrest led to increased domestic assault? The answers to such questions are never easy.

Social scientists who conduct research on behalf of specific organizations may face additional difficulties when the organization, instead of the researcher, controls the final report and the publicity it receives. If organizational leaders decide that particular research results are unwelcome, the researcher's desire to have findings used appropriately and reported fully can conflict with contractual obligations. Researchers can often anticipate such dilemmas in advance and resolve them when the contract for research is negotiated—or simply decline a particular research opportunity altogether. But other times, such problems come up only after a report has been drafted, or the problems are ignored by a researcher who needs a job or needs to maintain particular professional relationships. These possibilities cannot be avoided entirely, but because of them, it is always important to acknowledge the source of research funding in reports and to consider carefully the sources of funding for research reports written by others.

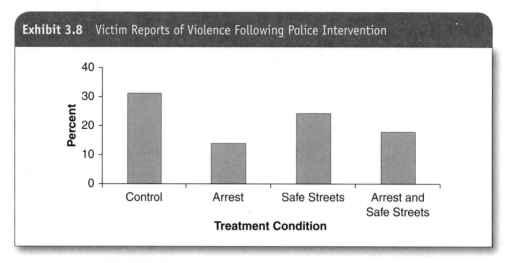

Exhibit 3.8 Victim Reports of Violence Following Police Intervention

Source: Adapted from Miller (2003: 704).

The withholding of a beneficial treatment from some subjects also is a cause for ethical concern. Recall that the Sherman and Berk (1984) experiment required the random assignment of subjects to treatment conditions and thus had the potential of causing harm to the victims of domestic violence whose batterers were not arrested. The justification for the study design, however, is quite persuasive: The researchers didn't know prior to the experiment which response to a domestic violence complaint would be most likely to deter future incidents (Sherman 1992). The experiment provided clear evidence about the value of arrest, so it can be argued that the benefits outweighed the risks.

In later chapters, we will continue to highlight the ethical dilemmas faced by research that utilizes particular types of methods. Before we begin our examination of various research methods, however, we first want to introduce you to the primary philosophies.

SOCIAL RESEARCH PHILOSOPHIES

What influences the decision to choose one research strategy over another? The motive for conducting research is critical: An explanatory or evaluative motive generally leads a researcher to use quantitative methods, whereas an exploratory motive often results in the use of qualitative methods. Of course, a descriptive motive means choosing a descriptive research strategy.

Positivism and Postpositivism

A researcher's philosophical perspective on reality and on the appropriate role of the researcher also will shape his or her choice of methodological preferences. Researchers with a philosophy of positivism believe that there is an objective reality that exists apart from the perceptions of those who observe it; the goal of science is to better understand this reality.

> Whatever nature "really" is, we assume that it presents itself in precisely the same way to the same human observer standing at different points in time and space. . . . We assume that it also presents itself in precisely the same way across different human observers standing at the same point in time and space. (Wallace 1983: 461)

This philosophy is traditionally associated with science (Weber 1949), with the expectation that there are universal laws of human behavior, and with the belief that scientists must be objective and unbiased to see reality clearly.

Postpositivism is a philosophy of reality that is closely related to positivism. Postpositivists believe that there is an external, objective reality, but are very sensitive to the complexity of this reality and the limitations of the scientists who study it. Social scientists, in particular, recognize the biases they bring to their research as they are social beings themselves (Guba & Lincoln 1994: 109–111). As a result, they do not think scientists can ever be sure that their methods allow them to perceive objective reality. Rather, the goal of science can only be to achieve intersubjective agreement among scientists about the nature of reality (Wallace 1983: 461). For example, postpositivists may worry that researchers' predispositions may bias them in favor of deterrence theory. Therefore, they will remain somewhat skeptical of results that support predictions based on deterrence until a number of researchers feel that they have found supportive evidence. The postpositivist retains much more confidence in the ability of the community of social researchers to develop an unbiased account of reality than in the ability of any individual social scientist to do so (Campbell & Russo 1999: 144).

Positivist Research Guidelines

To achieve an accurate understanding of the social world, a researcher operating within the positivist or postpositivist tradition must adhere to some basic guidelines about how to conduct research:

1. *Test ideas against empirical reality without becoming too personally invested in a particular outcome.* This guideline requires a commitment to "testing," as opposed to just reacting to events as they happen or looking for what we want to or expect to see (Kincaid 1996: 51–54).

2. *Plan and carry out investigations systematically.* Social researchers have little hope of conducting a careful test of their ideas if they do not fully think through in advance how they should go about the test and then proceed accordingly.

3. *Document all procedures and disclose them publicly.* Social researchers should disclose the methods on which their conclusions are based so that others can evaluate for themselves the likely soundness of these conclusions (Kincaid 1996).

4. *Clarify assumptions.* No investigation is complete in itself. Whatever the researcher's method(s), the effort rests on some background assumptions. For example, research to determine whether arrest has a deterrent effect assumes that potential law violators think rationally and that they calculate potential costs and benefits prior to committing crimes.

5. *Specify the meaning of all terms.* Words often have multiple or unclear meanings. "Recidivism," "self-control," "poverty," "overcrowded," and so on can mean different things to different people. In scientific research, all terms must be defined explicitly and used consistently.

6. *Maintain a skeptical stance toward current knowledge.* The results of any particular investigation must be examined critically, although confidence about interpretations of the social or natural world increases after repeated investigations yield similar results.

7. *Replicate research and build social theory.* No one study is definitive by itself. We cannot fully understand a single study's results apart from the larger body of knowledge to which it is related, and we cannot place much confidence in these results until the study has been replicated.

8. *Search for regularities or patterns.* Positivist and postpositivist scientists assume that the natural world has some underlying order of relationships, so that unique events and individuals can be understood at least in part in terms of general principles (Grinnell 1992: 27–29).

Real investigations by social scientists do not always include much attention to theory, specific definitions of all terms, and so forth. However, all social researchers should be compelled to study these guidelines and to consider the consequences of not following any with which they do not agree.

A Positivist Research Goal: Advancing Knowledge

The goal of the traditional positivist scientific approach is to advance scientific knowledge. This goal is achieved when research results are published in academic journals or presented at academic conferences.

The positivist approach regards value considerations to be beyond the scope of science. In Max Weber's (1949) words, "An empirical science cannot tell anyone what he should do—but rather what he can do—and under certain circumstances—what he wishes to do" (p. 54). The idea is that developing valid knowledge about how society *is* organized, or how we live our lives, does not tell us how society *should* be organized or how we *should* live our lives. The determination of empirical facts should be a separate process from the evaluation of these facts as satisfactory or unsatisfactory (p. 11).

Intersubjective agreement An agreement by different observers on what is happening in the natural or social world

Positivism The belief, shared by most scientists, that there is a reality that exists quite apart from our own perception of it, although our knowledge of this reality may never be complete

Postpositivism The belief that there is an empirical reality but that our understanding of it is limited by its complexity and by the biases and other limitations of researchers

Interpretivism and Constructivism

Qualitative research is often guided by a philosophy of interpretivism. Interpretive social scientists believe that reality is socially constructed and that the goal of social scientists is to understand what meanings people give to reality, not to determine how reality works apart from these interpretations. This philosophy rejects the positivist belief that there is a concrete, objective reality that scientific methods help us to understand (Lynch & Bogen 1997); instead, interpretivists believe that scientists construct an image of reality based on their own preferences and prejudices and their interactions with others.

Here is the basic argument: The empirical data we collect all come to us through our own senses and must be interpreted with our own minds. This suggests that we can never be sure that we have understood reality properly, or that we ever can, or that our own understandings can really be judged more valid than someone else's.

> Searching for universally applicable social laws can distract from learning what people know and how they understand their lives. The interpretive social researcher examines meanings that have been socially constructed. . . . There is not one reality out there to be measured; objects and events are understood by different people differently, and those perceptions are the reality—or realities—that social science should focus on. (Rubin & Rubin 1995: 35)

The paradigm of constructivism extends interpretivist philosophy by emphasizing the importance of exploring how different stakeholders in a social setting construct their beliefs (Guba & Lincoln 1989: 44–45). It gives particular attention to the different goals of researchers and other participants in a research setting and seeks to develop a consensus among participants about how to understand the focus of inquiry. The constructivist research report will highlight different views of the social program or other issue and explain how a consensus can be reached among participants.

Interpretivism The belief that reality is socially constructed and that the goal of social scientists is to understand what meanings people give to that reality. Max Weber termed the goal of interpretivist research ***verstehen***, or "understanding."

Constructivism A perspective that emphasizes how different stakeholders in social settings construct their beliefs

---

Constructivist inquiry uses an interactive research process, in which a researcher begins an evaluation in some social setting by identifying the different interest groups in that setting. The researcher goes on to learn what each group thinks, and then gradually tries to develop a shared perspective on the problem being evaluated (Guba & Lincoln 1989: 42).

Interpretivist/Constructivist Research Guidelines

Researchers guided by an interpretivist philosophy reject some of the guidelines to which positivist researchers seek to adhere. In fact, there is a wide variety of specific approaches that can be termed "interpretivist," and each has some guidelines that it highlights. For those working within the constructivist perspective, Guba and Lincoln (1989) suggest four key steps for researchers, each of which may be repeated many times in a given study:

1. Identify stakeholders and solicit their "claims, concerns, and issues."

2. Introduce the claims, concerns, and issues of each stakeholder group to the other stakeholder groups and ask for their reactions.

3. Focus further information collection on claims, concerns, and issues about which there is disagreement among stakeholder groups.

4. Negotiate with stakeholder groups about the information collected, and attempt to reach consensus on the issues about which there is disagreement (p. 42).

An Interpretivist or Constructivist Research Goal: Creating Change

Some social researchers with an interpretivist or constructivist orientation often reject explicitly the traditional positivist distinction between facts and values (Sjoberg & Nett 1968). Bellah et al. (1985) have instead proposed a model of "social science as public philosophy." In this model, social scientists focus explicit attention on achieving a more just society.

Whyte (1991) proposed a more activist approach to research called participatory action research. As the name implies, this approach encourages social researchers to get "out of the academic rut" and bring values into the research process (p. 285).

In participatory action research, the researcher involves as active participants some members of the setting studied. Both the organizational members and the researcher are assumed to want to develop valid conclusions, to bring unique insights, and to desire change, but Whyte (1991) believes these objectives are more likely to be obtained if the researcher collaborates actively with the persons studied.

An Integrated Philosophy

It is tempting to think of positivism and postpositivism as representing an opposing research philosophy to interpretivism and constructivism. Then it seems that we should choose the one philosophy that seems closest to our own preferences and condemn the other as "unscientific," "uncaring," or perhaps just "unrealistic." But there are good reasons to prefer a research philosophy that integrates some of the differences between these philosophies (Smith 1991).

And what about the important positivist distinction between facts and values in social research? Here, too, there is evidence that neither the "value-free" presumption of positivists nor the constructivist critique of this position is entirely correct. For example, Savelsberg, King, and Cleveland (2002) examined influences on the focus and findings of published criminal justice scholarship. They found that criminal justice research was more likely to be oriented to topics and theories suggested by the state when it was funded by government agencies. This reflects a political influence on scholarship. However, government funding did not have any bearing on the researchers' conclusions about the criminal justice processes they examined. This suggests that scientific procedures can insulate the research.

Which philosophy makes the most sense to you? Do you agree with positivists and postpositivists that scientific methods can help us understand the social world as it is, not just as we would like to think it is? Does the interpretivist focus on meanings sound like a good idea? Whatever your answers to these questions, you would probably agree that developing a valid understanding of the social world is not an easy task for social scientists.

CONCLUSION

The extent to which ethical issues present methodological challenges for researchers varies dramatically with the type of research design. Survey research, in particular, creates few ethical problems. In fact, researchers from Michigan's Institute for Social Research Survey Center interviewed a representative national sample of adults and found that 68 % of those who had participated in a survey were somewhat or very interested in participating in another; the more times respondents had been interviewed, the more willing they were to participate again. Presumably, they would have felt differently if they had been treated unethically (Reynolds 1979). On the other hand, some experimental studies in the social sciences that have put people in uncomfortable or embarrassing situations have generated vociferous complaints and years of debate about ethics (Reynolds 1979; Sjoberg 1967).

The evaluation of ethical issues in a research project should be based on a realistic assessment of the overall potential for harm and benefit to research subjects rather than an apparent inconsistency between any particular aspect of a research plan and a specific ethical guideline. For example, full disclosure of "what is really going on" in an experimental study is unnecessary if subjects are unlikely to be harmed. Nevertheless, researchers should make every effort to foresee all possible risks and to weigh the possible benefits of the research against these risks. They should consult with individuals with different perspectives to develop a realistic risk–benefit assessment, and they should try to maximize the benefits to, as well as minimize the risks for, subjects of the research (Sieber 1992).

Ultimately, these decisions about ethical procedures are not just up to you, as a researcher, to make. Your university's IRB sets the human subjects' protection standards for your institution and will require researchers—even, in most cases, students—to submit their research proposal to the IRB for review. So we leave you with the instruction to review the human subjects guidelines of the ACJS or other professional association in your field, consult your university's procedures for the conduct of research with human subjects, and then proceed accordingly.

KEY TERMS

Belmont Report

Beneficence

Certificate of Confidentiality

Code of Ethics

Constructivism

Debriefing

Federal Policy for the
Protection of Human
Subjects

Institutional review board (IRB)

Interpretivism

Intersubjective agreement

Nuremberg War Crime Trials

Office for Protection From
Research Risks in the
National Institutes of
Health

Participatory action research

Philip Zimbardo's Stanford
Prison Experiment

Positivism

Postpositivism

Privacy Certificate

Respect for persons

Stanley Milgram's experiments
on obedience to authority

Verstehen

HIGHLIGHTS

- Philip Zimbardo's prison-simulation study and Stanley Milgram's obedience experiments led to intensive debate about the extent to which deception could be tolerated in social science research and how harm to subjects should be evaluated.

- Egregious violations of human rights by researchers, including scientists in Nazi Germany and researchers in the Tuskegee syphilis study, led to the adoption of federal ethical standards for research on human subjects.

- The 1979 Belmont Report, developed by a national commission, established three basic ethical standards for the protection of human subjects: respect for persons, beneficence, and justice.

- The Department of Health and Human Services adopted in 1991 a Federal Policy for the Protection of Human Subjects. This policy requires that every institution seeking federal funding for biomedical or behavioral research on human subjects have an institutional review board (IRB) to exercise oversight.

- The ACJS standards for the protection of human subjects require avoiding harm, obtaining informed consent, avoiding deception except in limited circumstances, and maintaining privacy and confidentiality.

- Scientific research should maintain high standards for validity and be conducted and reported in an honest and open fashion.

- Effective debriefing of subjects after an experiment can help reduce the risk of harm resulting from the use of deception in the experiment.

- Positivism is the belief that there is a reality quite apart from one's own perception of it that is amenable to observation.

- Intersubjective agreement is an agreement by different observers on what is happening in the natural or social world.

- Postpositivism is the belief that there is an empirical reality but that our understanding of it is limited by its complexity and by the biases and other limitations of researchers.

- Interpretivism is the belief that reality is socially constructed, and the goal of social science should be to understand what meanings people give to that reality.

- The constructivist paradigm emphasizes the importance of exploring and representing the ways in which different stakeholders in a social setting construct their beliefs. Constructivists interact with research subjects to gradually develop a shared perspective on the issue being studied.

EXERCISES

Discussing research

1. What policy would you recommend that researchers such as Sherman and Berk follow in reporting the results of their research? Should social scientists try to correct misinformation in the popular press about their research, or should they just focus on what is published in academic journals? Should researchers speak to audiences like at police conventions in order to influence policies related to their research results?

2. Now go to this book's study site at www.sagepub.com/bachmanfrccj2e and choose the Learning From Journal Articles option. Read one article based on research involving human subjects. What ethical issues did the research pose, and how were they resolved? Does it seem that subjects were appropriately protected?

3. Outline your own research philosophy. You can base your outline primarily on your reactions to the points you have read in this chapter, but try also to think seriously about which perspective seems the most reasonable to you.

4. Researchers should consider their research philosophy as well as their theoretical stance prior to designing a research project. The "Theories and Philosophies" lesson on the text's study site will help you think about the options. To use these lessons, choose one of the four "Theories and Philosophies" exercises from the opening menu for the Interactive Exercises. Follow the instructions for entering your answers and responding to the program's comments.

Finding Research on the Web

1. The Collaborative Institutional Training Initiative (CITI) offers an extensive online training course in the basics of human subjects protections issues. Go to the public access CITI site at www.citiprogram.org/rcrpage.asp?affiliation = 100 and complete the course in social and behavioral research. Write a short summary of what you have learned.

2. Philip Zimbardo provides extensive documentation about the Stanford Prison Experiment at www.prisonexperiment.org. Read several documents that you find on this website, and write a short report about them.

3. Read the entire ACJS Code of Ethics at www.acjs.org. Discuss the meaning of each research standard.

4. There are many interesting websites that discuss philosophy of science issues. Read the summaries of positivism and interpretivism at www.misq.org/archivist/vol/no28/issue1/ EdCommentsV28N1.pdf. What do these summaries add to your understanding of these philosophical alternatives?

Critiquing Research

1. Investigate the standards and operations of your university's IRB. Interview one IRB member and one researcher whose research has been reviewed by the IRB (after receiving the appropriate permissions!). How well do typical IRB meetings work to identify the ethical issues in proposed research? Do researchers feel that their proposals are treated fairly? Why or why not?

2. Continue the debate between positivism and interpretivism with an in-class discussion. Be sure to review the guidelines for these research philosophies and the associated goals. You might also consider whether an integrated philosophy is preferable.

3. How do you evaluate the current ACJS ethical code? Is it too strict, too lenient, or just about right? Are the enforcement provisions adequate? What provisions could be strengthened?

Making Research Ethical

1. Should criminologists be permitted to conduct replications of Zimbardo's prison simulation? Of Milgram's obedience experiments? Can you justify such research as permissible within the current ACJS ethical standards? If not, do you believe that these standards should be altered so as to permit this type of research?

2. Why does unethical research occur? Is it inherent in science? Does it reflect "human nature"? What makes ethical research more or less likely?

3. Does debriefing solve the problem of subject deception? How much must researchers reveal after the experiment is over as well as before it begins?

Developing a Research Proposal

Now it's time to consider the potential ethical issues in your proposed study and the research philosophy that will guide your research. The following exercises involve very critical "Decisions in Research."

1. List the elements in your research plans that an IRB might consider to be relevant to the protection of human subjects. Rate each element from 1 to 5, where 1 indicates no more than a minor ethical issue and 5 indicates a major ethical problem that probably cannot be resolved.

2. Write one page for the application to the IRB that explains how you will ensure that your research adheres to each relevant ASA standard.

3. Draft a consent form to be administered to your subjects when they enroll in your research. Use underlining and margin notes to indicate where each standard for informed consent statements is met.

Performing Data Analysis in SPSS or Excel

1. Access HOMICIDE.por. Obtain a pie chart for *MURCON*, which is a variable that gives the disposition of a homicide case according to three values: (1) no conviction, (2) a murder conviction, or (3) some other felony conviction. What do you conclude about this sample of homicide cases after analyzing the pie chart for this variable?

2. Using these same data, ask for a bar chart to be made for the variable giving the number of prior arrests the homicide defendant had (*PRIARR*). What do you conclude about the criminal history for this sample of homicide defendants?

3. Access YOUTH.por. Ask for a frequency distribution for the variable *V63*, which provides information on how often respondents' parents know where they are when they are away from home, using the following response options: 1 = never, 2 = sometimes, 3 = usually, 4 = always. You can also ask for a bar chart to be included in the output. What do you conclude about parents' knowledge of the whereabouts of their children from this sample of adolescents?

Student Study Site

The companion Student Study Site for *Fundamentals of Research in Criminology and Criminal Justice* can be found at www.sagepub.com/bachmanfrccj2e.

Visit the Student Study Site to enhance your understanding of the chapter content and to discover additional resources that will take your learning one step further. You can enhance your understanding of the chapters by using the comprehensive study material, which includes interactive exercises, e-flashcards, web exercises, practice self-tests, and more. You will also find special features, such as Learning From Journal Articles, which incorporates Sage's online journal collection.

CHAPTER 4

Conceptualization and Measurement

Every time you begin to review or design research, you will have to answer two questions: (1) What do the main concepts mean in this research? and (2) How are the main concepts measured? Both questions must be answered to evaluate the validity of any research. For example, to investigate the impact of community policing on the crime rate, you may conceptualize "community policing" strategies as those which involve active, ongoing contact between police and community members. You might measure the presence of community policing with the use of foot patrols, police–community crime-prevention meetings, and support for resident-initiated crime control (such as Neighborhood Watch programs). We cannot make sense of a research study until we know how the concepts were defined and measured, nor can we begin our own research until we have defined our concepts clearly and constructed valid measures of them.

In this chapter, we first address the issue of conceptualization, or defining your main terms. We then describe measurement sources, such as available data, questions, observations, and less direct and obtrusive measures. Next, we discuss the level of measurement reflected in different measures. The final topic is how to assess the validity and reliability of these measures. By chapter's end, you should have a good understanding of measurement, the first of the three legs on which a research project's validity rests.

WHAT DO WE HAVE IN MIND?

A June 2009 editorial in the *New York Times* noted that binge drinking by young adults not attending college had significantly declined over a 27-year period, while binge drinking by the same-age cohorts who were attending college had not. This evidence, drawn from the National Survey on Drug Use and Health, appeared to indicate that it was something about attending college that increased the likelihood of binge drinking behavior. Many programs have been initiated to attempt to curtail binge drinking on college campuses. For example, in another *New York Times* article, Johnson (1997) reported that five U.S. colleges had participated in a pilot program to ban alcohol in their fraternities. Moreover, the article claimed that substance-free housing would soon become the norm on U.S. campuses. But what do these concepts really mean? Some of these concepts—*alcohol, colleges, campuses,* and *pilot program*—are widely understood and commonly used. However, do we all have the same idea in mind when we hear these terms? For example, are junior colleges classified within the term *college?* Does the concept of *on campus* extend to fraternity houses that are not physically on college property? Does *substance-free housing* mean banning tobacco products as well as alcohol?

CONCEPTS

Concepts such as *substance-free housing* require an explicit definition before they are used in research because we cannot be certain that all readers will share the same definition. It is even more important to define concepts that are somewhat abstract or unfamiliar. When we refer to concepts such as *poverty,* or *social control,* or *strain,* we cannot be certain that others know exactly what we mean.

Clarifying the meaning of such concepts does not just benefit those unfamiliar with them; even experts often disagree about their meaning. We need not avoid using these concepts. We just have to specify clearly what we mean when we use them, and we must expect others to do the same.

Concept A mental image that summarizes a set of similar observations, feelings, or ideas

Conceptualization The process of specifying what we mean by a term. In deductive research, conceptualization helps to translate portions of an abstract theory into testable hypotheses involving specific variables. In inductive research, conceptualization is an important part of the process used to make sense of related observations.

Defining Youth Gangs

Do you have a clear image in mind when you hear the term *youth gangs?* Although this is a very ordinary term, social scientists' attempts to define precisely the concept "youth gang" have not yet succeeded: "Neither gang researchers nor law enforcement agencies can agree on a common definition . . . and a concerted national effort . . . failed to reach a consensus" (Howell 2003: 75). Exhibit 4.1 lists a few of the many alternative definitions of youth gangs.

As you can see, there are many different ideas about what constitutes a "gang." What is the basis of this conceptual difficulty? Howell (2003) suggests that defining the term *youth gangs* has been difficult for four reasons:

- Youth gangs are not particularly cohesive.
- Individual gangs change their focus over time.
- Many have a "hodgepodge of features," with diverse members and unclear rules.
- There are many incorrect but popular "myths" about youth gangs. (pp. 27–28)

Exhibit 4.1   Alternative Definitions of Youth Gangs

- The term gang tends to designate collectivities that are marginal members of mainstream society, loosely organized, and without a clear, social purpose. (Ball & Curry 1995: 227)
- The gang is an interstitial group (between childhood and maturity) originally formed spontaneously, and then integrated through conflict. (Thrasher 1927: 18)
- [A gang is] any denotable adolescent group of youngsters who a) are generally perceived as a distinct aggregation by others in the neighborhood, b) recognize themselves as a denotable group (almost invariably with a group name), and c) have been involved in a sufficient number of delinquent incidents to call forth a consistently negative response from neighborhood residents and/or law enforcement agencies. (Klein 1971: 13)
- A youth gang is a self-formed association of peers united by mutual interests with identifiable leadership and internal organization who act collectively or as individuals to achieve specific purposes, including the conduct of illegal activity and control of a particular territory, facility, or enterprise. (Miller 1992: 21)
- [A gang is] an age-graded peer group that exhibits some permanence, engages in criminal activity, and has some symbolic representation of membership. (Decker & Van Winkle 1996: 31)
- [A gang is] a self-identified group of kids who act corporately, at least sometimes, and violently, at least sometimes. (Kennedy, Piehl, & Braga 1996: 158)
- A Criminal Street Gang is any ongoing organization, association, or group of three or more persons, whether formal or informal, having as one of its primary activities the commission of . . . criminal acts. (Street Terrorism Enforcement and Prevention Act of 1988, California Penal Code sec. 186.22[f])

Source: Based on Howell (2003: 76).

In addition, youth gangs are only one type of social group, and it is important to define youth gangs in a way that distinguishes them from these other types of groups—for example, childhood play groups, youth subculture groups, delinquent groups, and adult criminal organizations. Whenever you define a concept, you need to consider whether the concept is unidimensional or multidimensional. If it is multidimensional, your job of conceptualization is not complete until you have specified the related subconcepts that belong under the umbrella of the larger concept. And finally, the concept you define must capture an idea that is distinctly separate from related ideas.

CONCEPTS AND VARIABLES

After defining the concepts in a theory, we can identify variables corresponding to the concepts and develop procedures to measure them. Recall that a variable is a characteristic or property that can vary (e.g., religion, socioeconomic status, self-esteem scale). This is an important step. Consider the concept of social control, which Donald Black (1984) defines as "all of the processes by which people define and respond to deviant behavior." What variables do you think represent this conceptualization of social control? The proportion of persons arrested in a community? The average length of sentences for crimes? Types of bystander reactions to public intoxication? Some combination of these?

Although we must proceed carefully to specify what we mean by a concept like social control, some concepts are represented well by the specific variables in the study and therefore define themselves. We may define binge drinking as heavy episodic drinking and measure it, as a variable, by asking people how many drinks they consumed in succession during some period (see Wechsler et al. 1994). That is pretty straightforward.

Be aware that not every concept in a study is represented by a variable. For example, if the term *tolerance of drinking* is defined as the absence of rules against drinking in a fraternity, it brings to mind a phenomenon that varies across different fraternities at different colleges. But if we study social life at only those fraternities that prohibit drinking, tolerance of drinking would not be a variable: In this hypothetical study, all the fraternities in the sample have the same level of tolerance, and thus tolerance of drinking is a constant and not a variable. Of course, the concept of tolerance of drinking would still be important for understanding social life in the "dry" fraternities.

HOW WILL WE KNOW WHEN WE'VE FOUND IT?

After we have defined our concepts in the abstract—that is, after conceptualizing—and after we have specified the specific variables we want to measure, we must develop our measurement procedures. The goal is to devise operations that actually measure the concepts we intend to measure—in other words, to achieve measurement validity.

Operationalization The process of specifying the operations that will indicate the value of a variable for each case

---

Exhibit 4.2 represents the operationalization process in three studies. The first researcher defines her concept (binge drinking) and chooses one variable (frequency of heavy episodic drinking) to represent it. This variable is then measured with responses to a single question, or indicator: "How often within the past 2 weeks did you consume five or more drinks containing alcohol in a row?" The second researcher defines his concept, poverty, as having two aspects or dimensions, subjective poverty and absolute poverty. Subjective poverty is measured with responses to a survey question: "Do you consider yourself to be poor?" Absolute poverty is measured by comparing family income to the poverty threshold. The third researcher decides that her concept, social class, can be indicated with three measured variables: income, education, and occupational prestige.

Good conceptualization and operationalization can prevent confusion later in the research process. For example, a researcher may find that substance abusers who join a self-help group are less likely to drink again than those who receive hospital-based substance abuse treatment. But what is it about these treatment alternatives that is associated with successful abstinence? Level of peer support? Beliefs about the causes of alcoholism? Financial investment in the treatment? If the researcher had considered such

Exhibit 4.2 Concepts, Variables, and Indicators

Concept	Variable	Indicator
Binge drinking	Frequency of heavy episodic drinking	"How often within the past 2 weeks did you consume five or more drinks containing alcohol in a row?"
Poverty	Subjective poverty Absolute poverty	"Would you consider yourself to be poor?" Family income vs. poverty threshold
Social class	Income Education Occupational prestige	Income + education + prestige

aspects of the concept of substance abuse treatment before collecting her data, she might have been able to measure different elements of treatment and then identify which, if any, were associated with differences in abstinence rates. Because she did not measure these variables, she will not contribute as much as she might have to our understanding of substance abuse treatment.

Social researchers have many options for operationalizing their concepts. Measures can be based on activities as diverse as asking people questions, reading judicial opinions, observing social interactions, coding words in books, checking census data, enumerating the contents of trash receptacles, or drawing urine and blood samples. We focus here on the operations of using published data, asking questions, observing behavior, and using unobtrusive means of measuring people's behavior and attitudes.

Using Available Data

Government reports are rich and readily accessible sources of criminal justice data, as are data sets available from nonprofit advocacy groups, university researchers, and some private businesses. For example, law enforcement and health statistics provide several community-level indicators of substance abuse (Gruenewald et al. 1997). Statistics on arrests for the sale and possession of drugs, drunk driving arrests, and liquor law violations (such as sales to minors) can usually be obtained on an annual basis, and often quarterly, from local police departments or state crime information centers.

Still, indicators like these cannot be compared across communities or over time without reviewing carefully how they were constructed in each community (Gruenewald et al. 1997). We also cannot assume that available data are accurate, even when they appear to measure the concept in which we are interested in a way that is consistent across communities.

Government statistics that are generated through a central agency like the U.S. Bureau of the Census are usually of high quality, but caution is still warranted when using official data. Data accuracy is more of an issue for data collected by local levels of government. For example, the Uniform Crime Reports (UCR) program administered by the Federal Bureau of Investigation imposes standard classification criteria, with explicit guidelines and regular training at the local level, but data are still inconsistent for many crimes. Different jurisdictions vary in their definition of terms such as "more than necessary force" and even in the classification of offenses as aggravated or simple assaults (Mosher, Miethe, & Phillips 2002: 66). The new National Incident-Based Reporting System (NIBRS), mentioned in Chapter 1, corrects some of the problems with the UCR, but it requires much more training and documentation and has not yet been adapted by all jurisdictions (Mosher et al.).

Constructing Questions

Asking people questions is the most common and probably the most versatile operation for measuring social variables. "Overall, how satisfied are you with the police in your community?" "How would you rate your current level of safety?" Most concepts about individuals are measured with these sorts of questions.

Questions can be designed with or without explicit response choices. The question that follows is considered a closed-ended (fixed-choice) question because respondents are offered explicit responses to choose from. It has been selected from the Core Alcohol and Drug Survey distributed by the Core Institute (Presley, Meilman, & Lyerla 1994), Southern Illinois University.

> Compared with other campuses with which you are familiar, this campus's use of alcohol is . . . (*Mark one*)
> _____ Greater than for other campuses
> _____ Less than for other campuses
> _____ About the same as for other campuses

Response choices should be mutually exclusive and exhaustive, so that every respondent can find one, and only one, choice that applies to him or her (unless the question is of the "Check all that apply" format). To make response choices exhaustive, researchers may need to offer at least one option with room for ambiguity. For example, a questionnaire asking college students to indicate their school status should not use freshman, sophomore, junior, senior, and graduate student as the only response choices. Most campuses also have students in a "special" category, so you might add "Other (please specify)" to the five fixed responses to this question. If respondents do not find a response option that corresponds to their answer to the question, they may skip the question entirely or choose a response option that does not indicate what they are really thinking.

Most surveys of a large number of people primarily contain fixed-choice questions, which are easy to process with computers and analyze with statistics. With fixed-choice questions, respondents are also more likely to answer the question that the researcher really wants them to answer. Including response choices reduces ambiguity and makes it easier for respondents to answer. However, fixed-response choices may obscure what people really think if the choices do not match the range of possible responses to the question; many studies show that some respondents will choose response choices that do not apply to them simply to give some sort of answer (Peterson 2000: 39). We will discuss question wording and response options in greater detail in Chapter 7.

Open-ended questions—questions without explicit response choices, to which respondents write in their answers—are preferable when the range of responses cannot adequately be anticipated. By this we mean questions that have not previously been used in surveys and questions that are asked of new groups. Open-ended questions can also lessen confusion about the meaning of responses involving complex concepts. The question below is an open-ended version of the earlier fixed-choice question:

How would you say alcohol use on this campus compares to that on other campuses?

Making Observations

Observations can be used to measure characteristics of individuals, events, and places. The observations may be the primary form of measurement in a study, or they may supplement measures obtained through questioning.

Robert J. Sampson and Stephen W. Raudenbush (1999) and Peter St. Jean (2007) used direct observation (and other techniques) in their studies of neighborhood disorder and crime. Teams drove in "a sport utility vehicle at a rate of five miles per hour down every street" in a sample of Chicago neighborhoods. On both sides of the vehicle, video cameras recorded activities while a trained observer completed a log for each block—a very careful method of observing phenomena termed systematic social observation (SSO) (Reiss 1971). Sampson and Raudenbush's research resulted in 23,816 observer logs containing information about building conditions and land use, while the videotapes were coded to measure features of streets, buildings, businesses, and social interaction on 15,141 blocks. Direct observation is often the method of choice for measuring behavior in natural settings, as long as it is possible to make the requisite observations.

Collecting Unobtrusive Measures

Unobtrusive measures allow us to collect data about individuals or groups without their direct knowledge or participation. In their classic book (now revised), Webb et al. (2000 [1966]) identified four types of unobtrusive measures: physical trace evidence, archives (available data), simple observation, and contrived observation (using hidden recording hardware or manipulation to elicit a response). We will focus attention in this section on physical trace evidence and archives.

The physical traces of past behavior are one type of unobtrusive measure that is most useful when the behavior of interest cannot directly be observed (perhaps because it is hidden or it occurred in the past) and has not been recorded in a source of available data. To measure the prevalence of drinking in college dorms or fraternity houses, we might count the number of empty bottles of alcoholic beverages in the surrounding dumpsters. However, you can probably see that care must be taken to develop trace measures that are useful for comparative purposes. For instance, comparison of the number of empty bottles in dumpsters outside different dorms can be misleading; at the very least, you would need to take into account the number of residents in the dorms, the time since the last trash collection, and the accessibility of each dumpster to passersby.

Unobtrusive measures can also be created from such diverse forms of media as newspaper archives or magazine articles, TV or radio talk shows, legal opinions, historical documents, journals, personal letters, or e-mail messages. An investigation of the drinking climate on campuses might include a count of the amount of space devoted to ads for alcoholic beverages in a sample of issues of the student newspaper. Campus publications also might be coded to indicate the number of times that statements discouraging substance abuse appear. With this tool, you could measure the frequency of articles reporting substance abuse–related crimes, the degree of approval of drinking expressed in TV shows or songs, or the relationship between region of the country and amount of space devoted in the print media to alcohol consumption.

Combining Measurement Operations

Using available data, asking questions, making observations, and using unobtrusive indicators are interrelated measurement tools, each of which may include or be supplemented by the others. From people's answers to survey questions, the U.S. Bureau of the Census develops widely consulted reports containing available data on people, firms, and geographic units in the United States. Data from employee surveys may be supplemented by information available in company records. Interviewers may record observations about those whom they question. Researchers may use insights gleaned from questioning participants to make sense of the social interaction they have observed. Unobtrusive indicators can be used to evaluate the honesty of survey responses.

Questioning can be a particularly poor approach for measuring behaviors that are very socially desirable, such as voting or attending church, or that are socially stigmatized or illegal, such as abusing alcohol or drugs. Triangulation, the use of two or more different measures of the same variable, as defined in Chapter 1, can strengthen measurement considerably (Brewer & Hunter 1989: 17). When we achieve similar results with different measures of the same variable, particularly when they are based on such different methods as survey questions and field-based observations, we can be more confident in the validity of each measure. If results diverge with different measures, it may indicate that one or more of these measures are influenced by more measurement error than is tolerable. Divergence between measures could also indicate that they actually operationalize different concepts. An interesting example of this interpretation of divergent results comes from research on crime. Official crime statistics only indicate those crimes that are reported to and recorded by the police; when surveys are used to measure crimes with self-reports of victims, many "personal annoyances" are included as if they were crimes (Levine 1976).

HOW MUCH INFORMATION DO WE REALLY HAVE?

Whether we collect information through observations, questions, available data, or using unobtrusive measures, the data that result from our particular procedures may vary in mathematical precision. We express this level of precision as the variable's level of measurement. A variable's level of measurement also has important implications for the types of statistics that can be used with the variable, as you will learn in Chapter 11. There are four levels of measurement: nominal, ordinal, interval, and ratio. Exhibit 4.3 depicts the differences among these four levels.

Level of measurement The mathematical precision with which the values of a variable can be expressed. The nominal level of measurement, which is qualitative, has no mathematical interpretation; the quantitative levels of measurement (ordinal, interval, and ratio) are progressively more precise mathematically.

Exhibit 4.3   Levels of Measurement

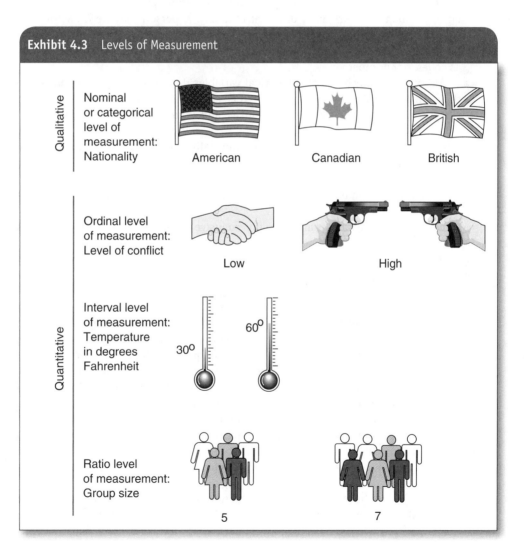

Nominal Level of Measurement

The nominal level of measurement (also called the categorical or qualitative level) identifies variables whose values have no mathematical interpretation; they only vary in kind or quality but not in amount. In fact, it is conventional to refer to the values of nominal variables as "attributes" instead of values. Gender is one example. The variable "gender" has two attributes (or categories or qualities): male and female. We might indicate male with the value 1 and female with the value 2, but these numbers do not tell us anything about the difference between male and female except that they are different. Female is not one unit more of "gender" than male, nor is it twice as much "gender." Ethnicity, occupation, religious affiliation, and region of the country are also measured at the nominal level. A person may be Spanish or Portuguese, but one ethnic group does not represent more ethnicity than another, just a different ethnicity. A person may be a doctor (arbitrarily valued as 4) or a truck driver (valued as 1), but one does not represent three units more occupation than the other. The values assigned to nominal variables should be thought of as codes, not numbers.

Although the attributes of categorical variables do not have a mathematical meaning, they must be assigned to cases with great care. The attributes we use to measure, or categorize, cases must be mutually exclusive and exhaustive:

- A variable's attributes or values are mutually exclusive attributes if every case can have only one attribute.
- A variable's attributes or values are exhaustive attributes when every case can be classified into one of the categories.

When a variable's attributes are mutually exclusive and exhaustive, every case corresponds to one, and only one, attribute.

Ordinal Level of Measurement

The first of the three quantitative levels is the ordinal level of measurement. At this level, the numbers assigned to cases specify only the order of the cases, permitting greater-than and less-than distinctions. For example, the Core Alcohol and Drug Survey (Presley et al. 1994) measures substance abuse with a series of questions that permit ordinal distinctions (see Exhibit 4.4). You can determine with these categories whether one respondent consumes approximately the same amount of alcohol or more or less than another respondent, but you don't know exactly how much more or less.

The properties of variables measured at the ordinal level are illustrated in Exhibit 4.3 by the contrast between the level of conflict in two groups. The first group, symbolized by two people shaking hands, has a low level of conflict. The second group, symbolized by two persons pointing guns at each other, has a higher level of conflict. To measure conflict, we could put the groups "in order" by assigning the number 1 to the low-conflict group and the number 2 to the group using guns. The numbers thus indicate the relative position or order of the cases. Although a low level of conflict is represented by the number 1, it is not mathematically two less units of conflict than the high level of conflict, which is represented by the number 3.

Exhibit 4.4 Example of Ordinal Measures: Core Alcohol and Drug Survey

Within the last year, about how often have you used . . . (mark one for each line)	Did Not Use	Once a Year	6 Times a Year	Once a Month	Twice a Month	Once a Week	3 Times a Week	5 Times a Week	Every Day
a. Tobacco (smoke, chew, snuff)									
b. Alcohol (beer, wine, liquor)									
c. Marijuana (pot, hash, hash oil)									
d. Cocaine (crack, rock, freebase)									
e. Amphetamines (diet pills, speed)									
f. Sedatives (downers, ludes)									
g. Hallucinogens (LSD, PCP)									
h. Opiates (heroin, smack, horse)									
i. Inhalants (glue, solvents, gas)									
j. Designer drugs (ecstasy, MDMA)									
k. Steroids									
l. Other illegal drugs									

Source: Core Institute. 1994. "Core Alcohol and Drug Survey: Long Form." Carbondale, IL: Author. (Available online at www.core.siuc.edu/pdfs/longform.pdf)

As with nominal variables, the different values of a variable measured at the ordinal level must be mutually exclusive and exhaustive. They must cover the range of observed values and allow each case to be assigned no more than one value.

Interval Level of Measurement

The numbers indicating the values of a variable at the interval level of measurement represent fixed measurement units (e.g., the change in value from one unit to the next is equal and incremental) but have no absolute, or fixed, zero point. This level of measurement is represented in Exhibit 4.3 by the difference between two Fahrenheit temperatures. Although 60 degrees is 30 degrees hotter than 30 degrees, 60 in this case is not twice as hot as 30. Why not? Because heat does not "begin" at 0 degrees on the Fahrenheit scale. The numbers can therefore be added and subtracted, but ratios between them (2 to 1, or "twice as much") are not meaningful.

Sometimes social scientists create indexes by combining responses to a series of questions measured at the ordinal level. An index of this sort could be created with responses to the Core Institute's (Presley et al. 1994) questions about friends' disapproval of substance use (see Exhibit 4.5). The survey has 13 questions on the topic, all of which have the same three response choices. If "Do not disapprove" is valued at 1, "Disapprove" is valued at 2, and "Strongly disapprove" is valued at 3, the summed index of disapproval would range from 12 to 36. Many social scientists would consider scores on an index like this to reflect an interval-level measure. So a score of 20 could be treated as if it were four more units than a score of 16.

Ratio Level of Measurement

The numbers indicating the values of a variable at the ratio level of measurement represent fixed measuring units and an absolute zero point (meaning absolutely no amount of whatever the variable measures or represents). On a ratio scale, 10 is two points higher than 8 and is also two times greater than 5. Ratio numbers can be added and subtracted, and because the numbers begin at an absolute zero point, they can be multiplied and divided (so ratios can be formed between the numbers).

For example, people's ages can be represented by values ranging from 0 years (or some fraction of a year) to 120 or more. A person who is 30 years old is 15 years older than someone who is 15 years old (30 – 15 = 15) and is twice as old as that person (30/15 = 2). Of course, the numbers also are mutually exclusive and exhaustive, so that every case can be assigned one and only one value.

Exhibit 4.3 displays an example of a variable measured at the ratio level. The number of people in the first group is 5, and the number in the second group is 7. The ratio of the two groups' sizes is then 1.4, a number that mirrors the relationship between the sizes of the groups. Note that there does not actually have to be any group with a size of 0; what is important is that the numbering scheme begins at an absolute zero—in this case, the absence of any people.

| Exhibit 4.5 | Ordinal-Level Variables Can Be Added to Create an Index With Interval-Level Properties: Core Alcohol and Drug Survey | | | |

How do you think your close friends feel (or would feel) about you . . . (mark one for each line)	Do Not Disapprove	Disapprove	Strongly Disapprove
a. Trying marijuana once or twice			
b. Smoking marijuana occasionally			
c. Smoking marijuana regularly			
d. Trying cocaine once or twice			
e. Taking cocaine regularly			
f. Trying LSD once or twice			
g. Taking LSD regularly			
h. Trying amphetamines once or twice			
i. Taking amphetamines regularly			
j. Taking one or two drinks of an alcoholic beverage (beer, wine, liquor) nearly every day			
k. Taking four or five drinks nearly every day			
l. Having five or more drinks in one sitting			
m. Taking steroids for bodybuilding or improved athletic performance			

Source: Core Institute. 1994. "Core Alcohol and Drug Survey: Long Form." Carbondale, IL: Author. (Available at www.core .siuc.edu/pdfs/longform.pdf)

Comparison of Levels of Measurement

Exhibit 4.6 summarizes the types of comparisons that can be made with different levels of measurement, as well as the mathematical operations that are legitimate. All four levels of measurement allow researchers to assign different values to different cases. All three quantitative measures allow researchers to rank cases in order.

Researchers *choose* levels of measurement in the process of operationalizing the variables; the level of measurement is not inherent in the variable itself. Many variables can be measured at different levels, with different procedures. For example, the Core Alcohol

Exhibit 4.6   Properties of Measurement Levels

Examples of Comparison Statements	Appropriate Math Operations	Relevant Level of Measurement			
		Nominal	Ordinal	Interval	Ratio
A is equal to (not equal to) *B*	= (≠)	✓	✓	✓	✓
A is greater than (less than) *B*	> (<)		✓	✓	✓
A is three more than (less than) *B*	+ (−)			✓	✓
A is twice (half) as large as *B*	× (/)				✓

and Drug Survey (Presley et al. 1994) identifies binge drinking by asking students, "Think back over the last two weeks. How many times have you had five or more drinks at a sitting?" You might be ready to classify this as a ratio-level measure, but you must first examine the fixed-response options given to respondents. This is a *closed-ended question,* and students are asked to indicate their answer by checking None, Once, Twice, 3 to 5 times, 6 to 9 times, or 10 or more times. Use of these categories makes the level of measurement ordinal. The distance between any two cases cannot be clearly determined. A student with a response in the "6 to 9 times" category could have binged just one more time than a student who responded 3 to 5 times, or he or she could have binged four more times. With these response categories, you cannot mathematically distinguish the number of times a student binged, only the relative amount of binging behavior.

Usually, it is a good idea to measure variables at the highest level of measurement possible, if doing so does not distort the meaning of the concept that is to be measured. For example, measure age in years, if possible, rather than in categories. You can always combine the responses into categories that compare teenagers to young adults, but it is impossible to obtain the actual age in years when the question is asked in the first place using just an ordinal response format.

Be aware, however, that other considerations may preclude measurement at a high level. For example, many people are very reluctant to report their exact incomes, even in anonymous questionnaires. So asking respondents to report their income in mutually exclusive and exhaustive categories (such as under $10,000, $10,000–19,999, $20,000–29,999, etc.) will result in more responses, and thus more valid data, than asking respondents for their income in dollars.

DID WE MEASURE WHAT WE WANTED TO MEASURE?

Do the operations developed to measure our concepts actually do so—are they valid? If we have weighed our measurement options, carefully constructed our questions and observational procedures, and carefully selected indicators from the available data, we should be on the right track. We cannot have much confidence in a measure until we have empirically evaluated its validity. In addition, we must also evaluate its reliability (consistency).

Measurement Validity

As mentioned in Chapter 1, we can consider measurement validity the first concern in establishing the validity of research results, because without having measured what we think we measured, we really do not know what we are talking about.

As an example of measurement validity, consider the following two-part question: "How prevalent is youth violence and delinquency in the United States; how many juveniles are involved in delinquency?" Data on the extent of juvenile delinquency come from two primary sources: official statistics and unofficial statistics. Official statistics are based on the aggregate records of juvenile offenders and offenses processed by agencies of the criminal justice system: police, courts, and corrections. One primary source of official statistics on juvenile delinquency is the UCR, mentioned earlier in this chapter. Unofficial statistics are data produced by people or agencies outside the criminal justice system such as victimization surveys and self-report studies. The validity of official statistics for measuring the extent of juvenile delinquency is hotly debated among criminologists. Although some researchers believe official reports are a valid measure of serious delinquency, others contend that UCR data is lacking for the same reasons highlighted earlier but also because the data may say more about the behavior of the police than about delinquency. These criminologists think the police may over-supervise certain groups of people or certain types of crimes.

Unquestionably, official reports underestimate the actual amount of delinquency because a great deal of delinquent behavior never comes to the attention of police (Mosher et al. 2002). Sometimes delinquent acts are committed and not observed, or they are observed and not reported. There is also evidence that the UCRs often reflect the political climate and police policies as much as they do criminal activity. The HBO series *The Wire* highlighted this problem in almost every episode. The extent to which measures indicate what they are intended to measure can be assessed with one or more of four basic approaches: face validation, content validation, criterion validation, and construct validation.

Face Validity

Researchers apply the term face validity to the confidence gained from careful inspection of a concept to see if it is appropriate "on its face." More precisely, we can say that a measure has face validity if it obviously pertains to the concept being measured more than to other concepts (Brewer & Hunter 1989: 131). For example, if college students' alcohol consumption is what we are trying to measure, asking for students' favorite color seems unlikely on its face to tell us much about their drinking patterns. A measure with greater face validity would be a count of how many drinks they had consumed in the past week.

Although every measure should be inspected in this way, face validation on its own is not the gold standard of measurement validity. The question "How much beer or wine did you have to drink last week?" may look valid on its face as a measure of frequency of drinking, but people who drink heavily tend to underreport the amount they drink. So the question would be an invalid measure in a study that includes heavy drinkers.

Content Validity

Content validity establishes that the measure covers the full range of the concept's meaning. To determine that range of meaning, the researcher may solicit the opinions of experts and review literature that identifies the different aspects of the concept. An example of a measure that covers a wide range of meaning is the Michigan Alcoholism Screening Test (MAST). The MAST includes 24 questions representing the following subscales: recognition of alcohol problems by self and others; legal, social, and work problems; help seeking; marital and family difficulties; and liver pathology (Skinner & Sheu 1982). Many experts familiar with the direct consequences of substance abuse agree that these dimensions capture the full range of possibilities. Thus, the MAST is believed to be valid from the standpoint of content validity.

Criterion Validity

Consider the following scenario: When people drink an alcoholic beverage, the alcohol is absorbed into their bloodstream and then gradually metabolized (broken down into other chemicals) in their liver (National Institute of Alcohol Abuse and Alcoholism [NIAAA] 1997). The alcohol that remains in their blood at any point, unmetabolized, impairs both thinking and behavior (NIAAA 1994). As more alcohol is ingested, cognitive and behavioral consequences multiply. These biological processes can be identified with direct measures of alcohol concentration in the blood, urine, or breath. Questions about alcohol consumption, on the other hand, can be viewed as attempts to measure indirectly what biochemical tests measure directly.

Criterion validity is established when the scores obtained on one measure can accurately be compared to those obtained with a more direct or already validated measure of the same phenomenon (the criterion). A measure of blood-alcohol concentration or a urine test could serve as the criterion for validating a self-report measure of drinking, as long as the questions we ask about drinking refer to the same period. Observations of substance use by friends or relatives could also, in some circumstances, serve as a criterion for validating self-report substance use measures.

An attempt at criterion validation is well worth the effort because it greatly increases confidence that the measure is actually measuring the concept of interest—criterion validity basically offers evidence. However, often no other variable might reasonably be considered a criterion for individual feelings or beliefs or other subjective states. Even with variables for which a reasonable criterion exists, the researcher may not be able to gain access to the criterion, as would be the case with a tax return or employer document as criterion for self-reported income.

Construct Validity

Measurement validity also can be established by showing that a measure is related to a variety of other measures as specified in a theory. This validation approach, known as construct validity, is commonly used in social research when no clear criterion exists for validation purposes. For example, in one study of the validity of the Addiction Severity Index (ASI), A. Thomas McLellan et al. (1985) compared subject scores on the ASI to a number of indicators that they felt from prior research should be related to substance abuse: medical problems, employment problems, legal problems, family problems, and psychiatric problems. They could not use a criterion-validation approach because they did not have a more direct measure of abuse, such as laboratory test scores or observer reports. However, their extensive research on the subject had given them confidence that these sorts of other problems were all related to substance abuse, and thus their measures seemed to be valid from the standpoint of construct validity. Indeed, the researchers found that individuals with higher ASI ratings tended to have more problems in each of these areas, giving us more confidence in the ASI's validity as a measure.

The distinction between criterion and construct validation is not always clear. Opinions can differ about whether a particular indicator is indeed a criterion for the concept that is to be measured. For example, if you need to validate a question-based measure of sales ability for applicants to a sales position, few would object to using actual sales performance as a criterion. But what if you want to validate a question-based measure of the amount of social support that people receive from their friends? Should you just ask people about the social support they have received? Could friends' reports of the amount of support they provided serve as a criterion? Even if you could observe people in the act of counseling or otherwise supporting their friends, can an observer be sure that the interaction is indeed supportive? There isn't really a criterion here, just a combination of related concepts that could be used in a construct-validation strategy.

What construct and criterion validation have in common is the comparison of scores on one measure to scores on other measures that are predicted to be related. It is not so important that researchers agree that a particular comparison measure is a criterion rather than a related construct. But it is very important to think critically about the quality of the comparison measure and whether it actually represents a different measure of the same phenomenon. For example, it is only a weak indication of measurement validity to find that scores on a new self-report measure of alcohol use are associated with scores on a previously used self-report measure of alcohol use.

Reliability

Reliability means that a measurement procedure yields consistent scores as long as the phenomenon being measured is not changing. If a measure is reliable, it is affected less by random error, or chance variation, than if it is unreliable. For example, if we gave students a survey with the same questions asking them about their alcohol consumption, the measure would be reliable if the same students gave approximately the same answers 6 months later (assuming their drinking patterns had not changed much). Reliability is a prerequisite for measurement validity; we cannot really measure a phenomenon if the measure we are using gives inconsistent results.

Reliability A measure is reliable when it yields consistent scores or observations of a given phenomenon on different occasions. Reliability is a prerequisite for measurement validity.

There are four possible methods for measuring the reliability of a measure: test–retest reliability, inter-item reliability, alternate-forms reliability, and inter-observer reliability.

Test–Retest Reliability

When researchers measure a phenomenon that does not change between two points separated by an interval of time, the degree to which the two measurements yield comparable, if not identical, values is the test–retest reliability of the measure. If you take a test of your math ability and then retake the test 2 months later, the test is performing reliably if you receive a similar score both times, presuming that nothing happened during the 2 months to change your math ability. Of course, if events between the test and the retest have changed the variable being measured, then the difference between the test and retest scores should reflect that change.

Inter-Item Reliability (Internal Consistency)

When researchers use multiple items to measure a single concept, they are concerned with inter-item reliability (or internal consistency). For example, if we are to have confidence that a set of questions (such as those in Exhibit 4.7) reliably measures attitudes toward violence, the answers to the questions should be highly associated with one another. The stronger the association among the individual items, and the more items that are included, the higher is the reliability of the index.

Exhibit 4.7   Questions Used in the Violent Defensive Values Index

Would you approve of a man punching a stranger who had hit the man's child after the child accidentally damaged the stranger's car?

_____ No (0)
_____ I don't know or not sure (1)
_____ Yes (2)

Would you approve of a man punching a stranger who was beating up a woman and the man saw it?

_____ No (0)
_____ I don't know or not sure (1)
_____ Yes (2)

Would you approve of a man punching a stranger who had broken into the man's house?

_____ No (0)
_____ I don't know or not sure (1)
_____ Yes (2)

Source: Cao, L., A. Adams and V. J. Jensen. 1997. "A Test of the Black Subculture of Violence Thesis: A Research Note." *Criminology* 35(2): 367–79. Reprinted with permission.

Alternate-Forms Reliability

Researchers are testing alternate-forms reliability when they compare subjects' answers to slightly different versions of survey questions (Litwin 1995: 13–21). A researcher may reverse the order of the response choices in an index or modify the question wording in minor ways and then readminister that index to subjects. If the two sets of responses are not too different, alternate-forms reliability is established.

A related test of reliability is the split-halves reliability approach. A survey sample is divided in two by flipping a coin or using some other random assignment method. These two halves of the sample are then administered the two forms of the questions. If the responses of the two halves are about the same, the measure's reliability is established.

Intra-observer and Inter-observer Reliability

When ratings by an observer, rather than ratings by the subjects themselves, are being assessed at two or more points in time, test–retest reliability is termed intra-observer reliability or intra-rater reliability. Let's say a researcher observes a gradeschool cafeteria for signs of bullying behavior on multiple days. If his observations captured the same degree of bullying on every Friday, it can be said that his observations were reliable. When researchers use more than one observer to rate the same persons, events, or places, inter-observer reliability is their goal. If observers are using the same instrument to rate the same thing, their ratings should be very similar. In this case, the researcher interested in cafeteria bullying would use more than one observer. If the measurement of bullying is similar across the observers, we can have much more confidence that the ratings reflect the actual degree of bullying behavior.

Can We Achieve Both Reliability and Validity?

Exhibit 4.8 illustrates the differences between reliability and validity. The reliability and validity of measures in any study must be tested after the fact to assess the quality of the information obtained. But then if it turns out that a measure cannot be considered reliable and valid, little can be done to save the study. Thus, it is supremely important to select in the first place measures that are likely to be reliable and valid. In studies that use interviewers or observers, careful training is often essential to achieving a consistent approach. In most cases, however, the best strategy is to use measures that have been used before and whose reliability and validity have been established in other contexts. However, know that the selection of "tried and true" measures still does not absolve researchers from the responsibility of testing the reliability and validity of the measure in their own studies.

It may be possible to improve the reliability and validity of measures in a study that already has been conducted if multiple measures were used. For example, in a study of housing for homeless mentally ill persons, residents' substance abuse was assessed with several different sets of direct questions as well as with reports from subjects' case managers and others (Goldfinger et al. 1996). It was discovered that the observational reports were often inconsistent with self-reports, and that different self-report measures were not always in agreement and were thus unreliable. A more reliable measure of substance abuse was initial reports of lifetime substance abuse problems. This measure was extremely accurate in identifying all those who subsequently abused substances during the project.

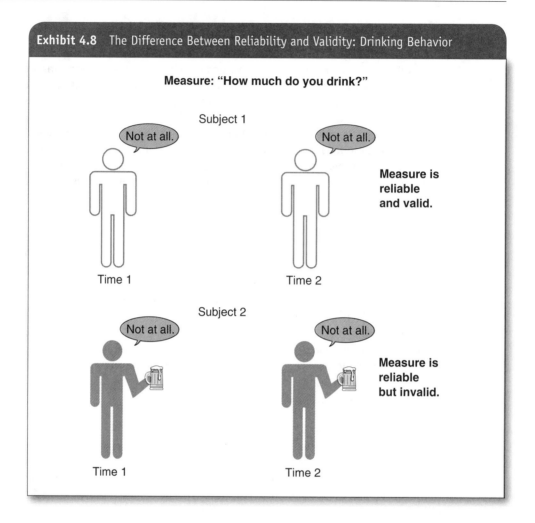

Exhibit 4.8 The Difference Between Reliability and Validity: Drinking Behavior

CONCLUSION

Always remember that measurement validity is a necessity for social research. Gathering data without careful conceptualization or conscientious efforts to operationalize key concepts often is a wasted effort.

The difficulties of achieving valid measurement vary with the concept being operationalized and the circumstances of the particular study. The examples in this chapter of difficulties in achieving valid measures of substance abuse should sensitize you to the need for caution, particularly when the concepts you wish to measure are socially stigmatized or illegal.

Careful planning ahead is the key to achieving valid measurement in your own research; careful evaluation is the key to sound decisions about the validity of measures in others' research. Statistical tests can help to determine whether a given measure is valid after data have been collected, but if it appears after the fact that a measure is invalid, little can be done to correct the situation. If you cannot tell how key concepts were operationalized when you read a research report, do not trust the findings. If a researcher does not indicate the results of tests used to establish the reliability and validity of key measures, always remain skeptical!

KEY TERMS

Alternate-forms reliability	Inter-item reliability	Operation
Closed-ended question	Inter-observer reliability	Operationalization
Concept	Interval level of measurement	Ordinal level of measurement
Conceptualization	Intra-observer reliability (intra-rater reliability)	Ratio level of measurement
Construct validity		Reliability
Content validity	Level of measurement	Split-halves reliability
Criterion validity	Measurement validity	
Exhaustive attributes	Mutually exclusive attributes	Systematic social observation
Face validity	Nominal level of measurement	Test–retest reliability
Indicator	Open-ended questions	Unobtrusive measures

HIGHLIGHTS

- Conceptualization plays a critical role in research. In deductive research, conceptualization guides the operationalization of specific variables; in inductive research, it guides efforts to make sense of related observations.

- Concepts are operationalized in research by one or more indicators, or measures, which may derive from observation, self-report, available records or statistics, books and other written documents, clinical indicators, discarded materials, or some combination of these.

- The validity of measures should always be tested. There are four basic approaches: face validation, content validation, criterion validation, and construct validation. Criterion validation provides the strongest evidence of measurement validity, but there often is no criterion to use in validating social science measures.

- Measurement reliability is a prerequisite for measurement validity, although reliable measures are not necessarily valid. Reliability can be assessed through test–retest procedures, in terms of inter-item consistency, through a comparison of responses to alternate forms of the test, or in terms of consistency among observers.

- Level of measurement indicates the type of information obtained about a variable and the type of statistics that can be used to describe its variation. The four levels of measurement can be ordered by complexity of the mathematical operations they permit: nominal (least complex), ordinal, interval, and ratio (most complex). The measurement level of a variable is determined by how the variable is operationalized.

EXERCISES

Discussing Research

1. Pick one important, frequently used concept such as "crime," "juries," "community policing," "racism," or some other concept suggested by your instructor. Then find five uses of it in newspapers, magazines, or journals. Is the concept defined clearly in each article? How similar are the definitions? Write up what you have found in a short report.

2. How would you define "rape"? Write a brief definition. Based on this conceptualization, what circumstances constitute rape? Describe a method of measurement that would be valid for a study of rape (as you define it). Now go to the Rape Victim Advocates' website at www.RapeVictimAdvocates.org. Go to "Myths & Facts." In a group, discuss some facts about rape that you were previously unaware of or some myths you believed. Rewrite your definition of rape based on your new knowledge. What additional circumstances constitute rape based on your new conceptualization?

3. Do you and your classmates share the same beliefs about the meanings of important concepts? First, divide your class into several groups, with each group having at least six students. Then assign each group a concept from the following list: promiscuity, hazing, academic success, stress, social support, mental illness, social norms, drug abuse. In each group, each student should independently write a brief definition of his or her concept and some different examples supporting it. Finally, all students who have worked on the same concept should meet together, compare their definitions and examples, and try to reach agreement on the meaning of the concept. Discuss what you learned from this effort.

4. Propose an open-ended question to measure one of the concepts you discussed in the preceding exercises. Compare your approach to those adopted by other students.

Finding Research on the Web

1. Are important concepts in criminological research always defined clearly? Are they defined consistently? Search the literature for six articles that focus on "violent crime," "domestic violence," or some other concept suggested by your instructor. Is the concept defined clearly in each article? How similar are the definitions? Write what you have found in a short report.

2. How would you define "alcoholism"? Write a brief definition. Based on this conceptualization, describe a method of measurement that would be valid for a study of alcoholism (as you define it). Now go to the National Council on Alcohol and Drug Dependence (NCADD) website (www.ncadd.org/facts/defalc.html) and read its official "Definition of Alcoholism." What is the definition of alcoholism used by NCADD? How is alcoholism conceptualized? How does this compare to your definition?

3. How would you define a "hate crime"? Write a brief definition. Now go to the Bureau of Justice Statistics (BJS) website (http://bjs.ojp.usdoj.gov/) and find a publication that presents statistics on victimizations perceived to be motivated by hate. How does BJS define a hate crime? How do they actually measure the extent to which a victimization is motivated by hate? How does this compare to your definition of a hate crime?

4. What are some of the research questions you could attempt to answer with available statistical data? Visit your library and ask for an introduction to the government documents collection. Inspect the volumes from the Federal Bureau of Investigation (FBI) Uniform Crime Report (UCR) or the *Sourcebook for Criminal Justice Statistics*, both of which report statistics on crimes by offender characteristics. List 10 questions you could explore with such data.

Critiquing Research

1. Develop a plan for evaluating the validity of a measure. Your instructor will give you a copy of a questionnaire actually used in a study. Choose one question and define the concept that you believe it is intended to measure. Then develop a construct-validation strategy involving other measures in the questionnaire that you think should be related to the question of interest—that is, it measures what you think it does.

2. Compare two different measures of substance abuse. A site maintained by the National Institute on Alcoholism and Alcohol Abuse (http://silk.nih.gov/silk/niaaa1/publication/instable. htm) provides many of the most popular measures. Pick two of them. What concept of substance abuse is reflected in each measure? Is either measure multidimensional? What do you think the relative advantages of each measure might be? What evidence is provided about their reliability and validity? What other test of validity would you suggest?

Making Research Ethical

1. In order to measure disorder in Chicago neighborhoods, Sampson and Raudenbush (1999) recorded the street scene with video cameras in a van with darkened windows. Do you judge this measurement procedure to be ethical? Refer to each of the ethical guidelines in Chapter 3. How could the guidelines about "anonymity/confidentiality" and "informed consent" be interpreted to permit this type of observational procedure?

2. Both some Department of Homeland Security practices and inadvertent releases of web-searching records have raised new concerns about the use of unobtrusive measures of behavior and attitudes. If all identifying information is removed, do you think criminologists should be able to study who is stopped by police for traffic violations? Or what types of books are checked out in libraries in different communities? Or the extent of use of pornography in different cities by analyzing store purchases? Or how much alcohol different types of people use by linking credit card records to store purchases?

Developing a Research Proposal

At this point, you can begin the processes of conceptualization and operationalization. You will need to assume that your primary research method will be conducting a survey.

1. List at least 10 variables that will be measured in your research. No more than two of these should be socio-demographic indicators like race or age. The inclusion of each variable should be justified in terms of theory or prior research that suggests it would be an appropriate independent or dependent variable, or will have some relation to either of these.

2. Write a conceptual definition for each variable. Whenever possible, this definition should come from the existing literature, either a book you have read for a course or the research literature that you have been searching. Ask two class members for feedback on your definitions.

3. Develop measurement operations for each variable. Several measures should be single questions and indexes that were used in prior research (Search the web and the journal literature in *Criminal Justice Abstracts, Soc Abstracts,* or *Psych Abstracts.*). Make up a few questions and one index yourself. Ask classmates to answer these questions and give you feedback on their clarity.

4. Propose tests of reliability and validity for four of the measures.

Performing Data Analysis in SPSS or Excel

HOMICIDE.por contains a sample of homicide defendants from a sample of 33 U.S. counties for the year 1988.

1. Obtain a frequency distribution for the variables INTIMATE, NUMVICT, and PRIMTIME. At what levels (nominal or categorical, ordinal, interval, ratio) are each of these variables measured?

2. What conclusions do you make about the victim–offender relationship, number of victims, and length of sentence received based on these frequency distributions?

Student Study Site

The companion Student Study Site for *Fundamentals of Research in Criminology and Criminal Justice* can be found at www.sagepub.com/bachmanfrccj2e.

Visit the Student Study Site to enhance your understanding of the chapter content and to discover additional resources that will take your learning one step further. You can enhance your understanding of the chapters by using the comprehensive study material, which includes interactive exercises, e-flashcards, web exercises, practice self-tests, and more. You will also find special features, such as Learning From Journal Articles, which incorporates Sage's online journal collection.

CHAPTER 5

Sampling

In this chapter, we first review the rationale for using sampling in social research and consider two alternatives. We then turn to the topic of specific sampling methods and when they are most appropriate, using a variety of examples from the criminological research literature. We also briefly introduce the concept of a sampling distribution and explain how it helps in estimating our degree of confidence in statistical generalizations. By the chapter's end, you should know which questions you need to ask to evaluate the generalizability of a study as well as what choices you need to make to design a sampling strategy.

WHAT DO WE HAVE IN MIND?

As a Supreme Court Justice nominee, Elena Kagan was required to sit before a series of congressional Supreme Court confirmation hearings. While most of us in the criminal justice world realize the influence that the Supreme Court has on policy and practice, many Americans may not. In fact, CNN conducted an online survey asking readers to answer the following question: "Do U.S. Supreme Court rulings affect your life?" As of July 14, 2009, a total of 74% of the 140,509 responders said "Yes" and 26% responded "No." Do these percentages necessarily reflect the percentage of all U.S. residents? How about all people who log on to CNN.com? Unfortunately, even with such a huge number of respondents, we cannot generalize these findings to any larger population. If we cannot have confidence in their generalizability, their validity is suspect. In reality, of course, we have no idea whether these opinions are widely shared or unique to those who took the time to answer the online poll.

SAMPLE PLANNING

You have encountered the problem of generalizability in each of the studies you have read about in this book. For example, MacDonald et al. (2005) generalized their sample-based explanation of adolescent aggression and violence to the population of high school students in the United States; Powell, Muir-McClain, and Halasyamani (1995) generalized their evaluation findings of violence prevention programs from an elementary school in

King County, Washington, to all public elementary schools; and Sherman and Berk (1984) and others (Berk et al. 1992; Garner, Fagan, and Maxwell 1995; Hirschel et al. 1992; Pate & Hamilton 1992; Sherman 1992) tried to determine the generalizability of findings from the original study of domestic violence in Minneapolis (see Chapter 2). As sampling is very common in social research, whether we are designing a sampling strategy or evaluating the generalizability of someone else's findings, we have to understand how and why researchers decide to sample.

Define Sample Components and the Population

Let's say that we are designing a study of a topic that involves a lot of people (or other entities such as high schools or cities). We do not have the time or resources to study the entire population—all the elements in which we are interested—so we resolve to study a sample, or subset, of this population.

Population The entire set of elements (e.g., individuals, cities, states, countries, prisons, schools) in which we are interested

Sample A subset of elements from the larger population

In many studies, we sample directly from the elements in the population of interest. We may survey a sample of the entire population of students in a school, based on a list obtained from the registrar's office. This list, from which the elements of the population are selected, is termed the sampling frame. The students who are selected and interviewed from that list are the elements.

We may collect our data directly from the elements in our sample. Some studies are not so simple, however. The entities we can easily reach to gather information are not the same as the entities about whom we really want information. So we may collect information about the elements from another set of entities called the sampling units. For example, if we interview mothers to learn about their families, the families are the elements and the mothers are the sampling units. If we survey prison wardens to learn about prisons, the prisons are the elements and the wardens are the sampling units.

A *single-stage sample* is a study in which individual people are sampled and are the focus of the study; the sampling units are the same as the elements (information is gathered about students *from* students). However, if a sample is selected in two or more stages, the units selected—let's say groups and individuals—at each stage within the groups are sampling units, but it may be that only one sampling unit is the study's element (see Exhibit 5.1). For example, a researcher might sample families for a survey about household theft victimizations and then interview only one adult representative of the family, such as a parent (a sample), to obtain information about any victimizations. The families are the primary sampling units (and are the elements in the study), and the parents are secondary sampling units (but they are not the primary elements, because they act as one person providing information about the entire family).

Exhibit 5.1   Sample Components in a Two-Stage Study

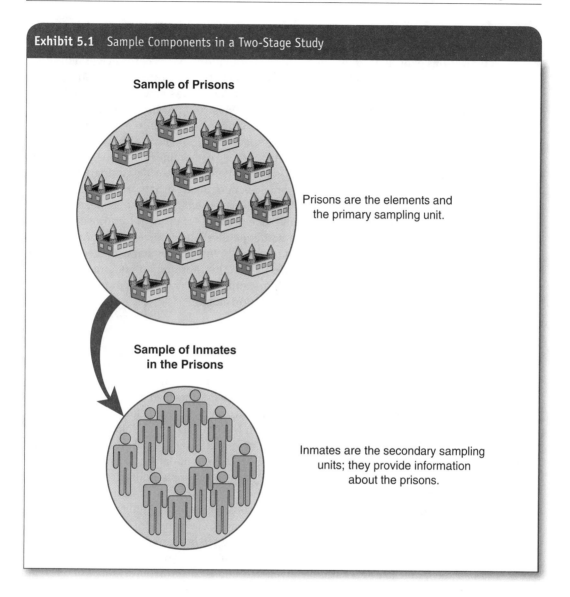

Sample of Prisons

Prisons are the elements and
the primary sampling unit.

Sample of Inmates
in the Prisons

Inmates are the secondary sampling
units; they provide information
about the prisons.

One key issue with selecting or evaluating sample components is understanding exactly what population they represent. In a survey of adult Americans, the general population may be reasonably construed as all residents of the United States who are at least 21 years old. But always be alert to ways in which the population may have been narrowed by the sample-selection procedures. Perhaps only English-speaking adult residents of the continental United States were actually sampled. The population for a study is the aggregation of elements that we actually focus on and sample from, not a larger aggregation that we really wish we could have studied.

Some populations cannot easily be identified by a simple criterion such as a geographic boundary or an organizational membership. Let us say you were interested in victimizations experienced by the homeless population. In this case, a clear definition of the homeless population is difficult, but quite necessary. In research, anyone reading the study should be able to determine what population was actually examined. However, studies of homeless persons in the early 1980s "did not propose definitions, did not use screening questions to be sure that the people they interviewed were indeed homeless, and did not make major efforts to cover the universe of homeless people" (Burt 1996: 15). For example, some studies relied on homeless persons in only one shelter. The result was "a collection of studies that could not be compared" (p. 15). According to Burt, several studies of homeless persons in urban areas addressed the problem by employing a more explicit definition of the population: People are homeless if they have no home or permanent place to stay of their own (renting or owning) and no regular arrangement to stay at someone else's place. Even this more explicit definition still leaves some questions unanswered: What is a regular arrangement? How permanent does a permanent place have to be? The more complete and explicit the definition of the population from which a sample is selected, the more precise our generalizations from a sample to that population can be.

Evaluate Generalizability

After clearly defining the population we will sample, we need to determine the scope of the generalizations we will seek to make from our sample. Let us say we are interested in the extent to which high school youth are fearful of being attacked or harmed at school or going to and from their schools. It would be easy to go down to the local high school and hand out a survey asking students to report their level of fear in these situations. But what if my local high school were located in a remote and rural area of Alaska? Would this sample reflect levels of fear perceived by suburban youth in California or urban youth in New York City? Obviously not. Often, regardless of the sample utilized, researchers will assert that "this percentage of high school students are fearful" or "freshman students are more fearful than seniors," as if their study results represented all high school students. Many social researchers and criminologists (and most everyone else, for that matter) are eager to draw conclusions about all individuals they are interested in, not just their samples. Generalizations make their work (and opinions) sound more important. If every high school student were like every other one, generalizations based on observations of one high school student would be valid. This, however, is not the case.

As noted in Chapter 1, generalizability has two aspects. Sample generalizability refers to the ability to generalize from a sample, or subset, of a larger population to that population itself (e.g., using those Alaskan students' survey results to speak more generally about rural students' perceptions of fear). This is the most common meaning of generalizability. Cross-population generalizability refers to the ability to generalize from findings about one group, population, or setting to other groups, populations, or settings (see Exhibit 5.2). In this book, we use the term external validity to refer only to cross-population generalizability, not to sample generalizability.

Exhibit 5.2 Sample and Cross-Population Generalizability

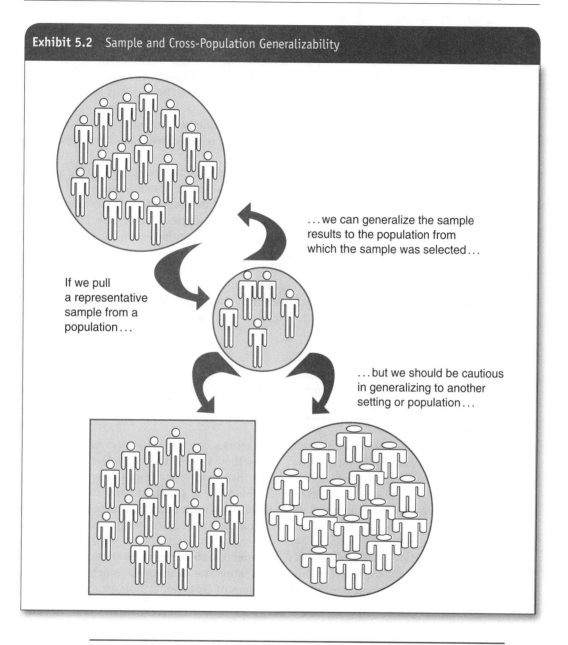

If we pull a representative sample from a population . . .

. . . we can generalize the sample results to the population from which the sample was selected . . .

. . . but we should be cautious in generalizing to another setting or population . . .

Sample generalizability Exists when a conclusion based on a sample, or subset, of a larger population holds true for that population

Cross-population generalizability Exists when findings about one group, population, or setting hold true for other groups, populations, or settings. This is also called *external validity*.

Generalizability is a key concern in research design, so this chapter focuses primarily on the problem of sample generalizability. We rarely have the resources to study the entire population that is of interest to us. For this reason, we have to select cases to study that will allow our findings to be generalized to the population of interest. We can never be sure that our propositions will hold under all conditions, so we should be cautious in generalizing to populations that we did not actually sample.

When designing our research studies, we must ask whether findings from a sample may be generalized to the population from which the sample was drawn. Social research methods provide many tools to address this concern.

Sample generalizability depends on sample quality, which is determined by the amount of sampling error. Sampling error can generally be defined as the difference between the characteristics of a sample and the characteristics of the population from which it was selected. The larger the sampling error, the less representative is the sample, and thus the less generalizable are the findings. To assess sample quality when you are planning or evaluating a study, ask yourself these questions:

- From what population were the cases selected?
- What method was used to select cases from this population?
- Do the cases that are/were studied represent, in the aggregate, the population from which they were selected?

Sampling error Any difference between the characteristics of a sample and the characteristics of the population from which it was drawn. The larger the sampling error, the less representative the sample is of the population.

In reality, researchers often project their theories onto groups or populations much larger than, or simply different from, those they have actually studied. The target population consists of a set of elements larger than or different from the population that was sampled, and to which the researcher would like to generalize any study findings. When we generalize findings to target populations, we must be somewhat speculative and carefully consider the claim that the findings can be applied to other groups, geographic areas, cultures, or times.

Because the validity of cross-population generalizations cannot be tested empirically, except by conducting more research in other settings, we do not focus much attention on this problem here. We will return to the problem of cross-population generalizability in Chapter 6, which addresses experimental research.

Assess Population Diversity

Sampling is unnecessary if all the units in the population are identical. Physicists do not need to select a representative sample of atomic particles to learn about basic physical processes. They can study a single atomic particle because it is identical to every other particle of its type. Similarly, biologists do not need to sample a particular type of plant to determine whether a given chemical has toxic effects on it. The idea is, "If you've seen one, you've seen 'em all."

What about people? Certainly all people are not identical—nor are animals, in many respects. Nonetheless, if we are studying physical or psychological processes that are the same among all people, sampling is not needed to achieve generalizable findings. Various types of psychologists including social psychologists often conduct experiments on college students to learn about processes that they think are identical for all individuals. They believe that most people will have the same reactions as the college students if they experience the same experimental conditions. Field researchers who observe group processes in a small community sometimes make the same assumption.

There is a potential problem with this assumption, however. There is no way to know whether the processes being studied are identical for all people. In fact, experiments can give different results depending on the type of people studied or the conditions for the experiment. Milgram's (1965) experiments on obedience to authority discussed in Chapter 3 illustrate this point very well. Recall that Milgram concluded that people are very obedient to authority. But were these results generalizable to all men, to men in the United States, or to men in New Haven? We can have confidence in these findings because similar results were obtained in many replications of the Milgram experiments when the experimental conditions and subjects were similar to those studied by Milgram.

Accurately generalizing the results of experiments and of participant observation is risky because such research often studies a small number of people who do not represent a particular population. Researchers may put aside concerns about generalizability when they observe the social dynamics of specific clubs; or college dorms; or a controlled experiment that tests the effect of, say, a violent movie on feelings for others. Nonetheless, we should still be cautious about generalizing the results of such studies.

The important point is that social scientists rarely can skirt the problem of demonstrating the generalizability of their findings. If a small sample has been studied in an experiment or field research project, the study should be replicated in different settings or, preferably, with a **representative sample** of the population for which the generalizations are sought (see Exhibit 5.3).

The people in our social world are just too diverse to be considered identical units. Social psychological experiments and small field studies have produced good social science, but they need to be replicated in other settings, with other subjects, to claim any generalizability. Even when we believe that we have uncovered basic social processes in a laboratory experiment or field observation, we must seek confirmation in other samples and other research.

Representative sample A sample that looks like the population from which it was selected in all respects that are potentially relevant to the study. The distribution of characteristics among the elements of a representative sample is the same as in the total population. In an unrepresentative sample, some characteristics are overrepresented or underrepresented and sampling error emerges.

Exhibit 5.3   Representative and Unrepresentative Samples

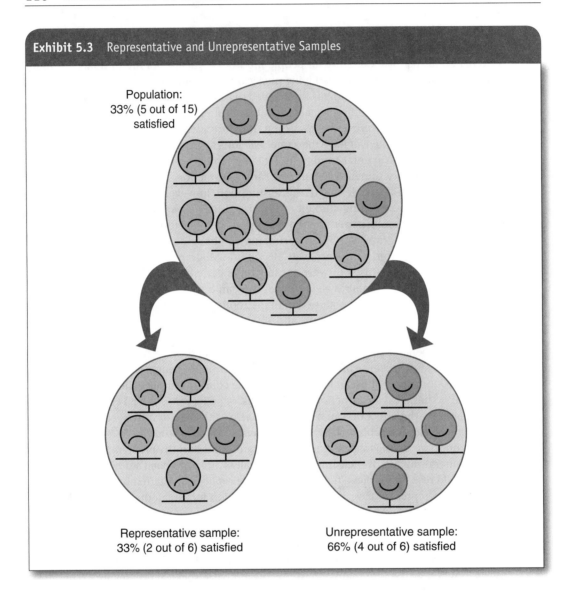

Population:
33% (5 out of 15) satisfied

Representative sample:
33% (2 out of 6) satisfied

Unrepresentative sample:
66% (4 out of 6) satisfied

Consider a Census

In some circumstances, researchers can bypass the issue of generalizability by conducting a census that studies the entire population of interest rather than drawing a sample. The federal government tries to do this every 10 years with the U.S. Census. A census can also involve studies of all the employees (or students) in small organizations (or universities), studies comparing all 50 states, or studies of the entire population of a particular type of organization in a particular area. However, in all these instances—except for the U.S. Census—the population studied is relatively small.

Social scientists do not often attempt to collect data from all the members of some large population simply because doing so is very expensive and time-consuming. Some social scientists do conduct research with data from the U.S. Census, but this data is collected by the government. Even if the population of interest for a survey is a small town of 20,000 or students in a university of 10,000, researchers will have to sample. The costs of surveying even thousands of individuals far exceed the budgets for most research projects.

SAMPLING METHODS

The most important distinction made about samples is whether they are based on a probability or a nonprobability sampling method. Sampling methods that allow us to know in advance how likely it is that any element of a population will be selected for the sample are probability sampling methods. Sampling methods that do not reveal the likelihood of selection in advance are nonprobability sampling methods.

Probability sampling methods rely on a random selection procedure. In principle, this is the same as flipping a coin to decide which person wins and which one loses. Heads and tails are equally likely to turn up in a coin toss, so both persons have an equal chance to win. That chance, or the probability of selection, is 1 out of 2, or .5.

Probability of selection The likelihood that an element will be selected from the population for inclusion in the sample. In a census of all the elements of a population, the probability that any particular element will be selected is 1.0 because everyone will be selected. If half the elements in the population will be sampled on the basis of chance (say, by tossing a coin), the probability of selection for each element is one-half, or 0.5. When the size of the desired sample as a proportion of the population decreases, so does the probability of selection.

Flipping a coin is a fair way to select 1 of 2 people because the selection process harbors no systematic bias. You might win or lose the coin toss, but you know that the outcome was due simply to chance, not to bias (unless your opponent tossed a two-headed coin!). For the same reason, rolling a six-sided die is a fair way to choose 1 of 6 possible outcomes (the odds of selection are 1 out of 6, or .17). Similarly, state lotteries use a random process to select winning numbers. Thus, the odds of winning a lottery, the probability of selection, are known even though they are very small (perhaps 1 out of 1 million) compared with the odds of winning a coin toss. As you can see, the fundamental strategy in probability sampling is the random selection of elements into the sample. When a sample is randomly selected from the population, every element has a known and independent chance of being selected into the sample.

Random selection The fundamental element of probability samples. The essential characteristic of random selection is that every element of the population has a known and independent chance of being selected into the sample.

There is a natural tendency to confuse the concept of probability, in which cases are selected only on the basis of chance, with a haphazard method of sampling. On first impression, leaving things up to chance seems to imply the absence of control over the sampling method. But to ensure that nothing but chance influences the selection of cases, the researcher must actually proceed very methodically and leave nothing to chance except the selection of the cases themselves. The researcher must carefully follow controlled procedures if a purely random process is to occur. In fact, when reading about sampling methods, do not assume that a random sample was obtained just because the researcher used a random selection method at some point in the sampling process. Look for these two particular problems: selecting elements from an incomplete list of the total population and failing to obtain an adequate response rate (say, only 45% of the people who were asked to participate actually agreed).

If the sampling frame, or list from which the elements of the population are selected, is incomplete, a sample selected randomly from the list will not be random. How can it be when the sampling frame fails to include every element in the population? Even for a simple population like a university's student body, the registrar's list is likely to be at least a bit out of date at any given time. For example, some students will have dropped out, but their status will not yet be officially recorded. Although you may judge the amount of error introduced in this particular situation to be negligible, the problems are greatly compounded for a larger population. The sampling frame for a city, state, or nation is always likely to be incomplete because of constant migration into and out of the area. Even unavoidable omissions from the sampling frame can bias a sample against particular groups within the population.

A very inclusive sampling frame may still yield systematic bias if many sample members cannot be contacted or refuse to participate. Nonresponse is a major hazard in survey research because individuals who do not respond to a survey are likely to differ systematically from those who take the time to participate. You should not assume that findings from a randomly selected sample will be generalizable to the population from which the sample was selected if the rate of nonresponse is considerable (certainly if it is much above 30%).

Probability Sampling Methods

Probability sampling methods require that the probability of selection is known and is not zero (so there is some chance of selecting each element). These methods randomly select elements and therefore have no systematic bias. Nothing but chance determines which elements are included in the sample. This feature of probability samples, sometimes referred to as random samples, makes them much more desirable than nonprobability samples when the goal is to generalize your findings to a larger population.

Even though a random sample has no systematic bias, it certainly will have some sampling error due to chance. The probability of selecting a head is .5 in a single toss of a coin, and in 20, 30, or however many tosses of a coin you like. Be aware, however, that it is perfectly possible to toss a coin twice and get a head both times. The random sample of the two sides of the coin is selected in an unbiased fashion, but it still is unrepresentative. Imagine randomly selecting a sample of 10 people from a population comprising 50 men and 50 women. Just by chance, it is possible that your sample of 10 people will include 7 women and only 3 men. Fortunately, we can determine mathematically the likely degree of sampling error in an estimate based on a random sample (as you will see later in this chapter), assuming that the sample's randomness has not been destroyed by a high rate of nonresponse or by poor control over the selection process.

In general, both the size of the sample and the homogeneity (sameness) of the population affect the degree of error due to chance; the proportion of the population that the sample represents does not. To elaborate, *the larger the sample, the more confidence we can have in the sample's representativeness of the population from which it was drawn.* If we randomly pick five people to represent the entire population of our city, our sample is unlikely to be very representative of the entire population in terms of age, gender, race, attitudes, and so on. But if we randomly pick 100 people, the odds of having a representative sample are much better; with a random sample of 1,000, the odds become very good indeed.

The more homogeneous the population, the more confidence we can have in the representativeness of a sample of any particular size. Let us say we plan to draw samples of 50 from each of two communities to estimate mean family income. One community is very diverse, with family incomes ranging from $12,000 to $85,000. In the more homogeneous community, family incomes are concentrated in a narrower range, from $41,000 to $64,000. The estimated average family income based on the sample from the homogeneous community is more likely to be representative than is the estimate based on the sample from the more heterogeneous community. With less variation, fewer cases are needed to represent the larger population.

The fraction of the total population that a sample contains does not affect the sample's representativeness, unless that fraction is large. We can regard any sampling fraction under 2% with about the same degree of confidence (Sudman 1976: 184). In fact, sample representativeness is not likely to increase much until the sampling fraction is quite a bit higher. Other things being equal, a sample of 1,000 from a population of 1 million (with a sampling fraction of 0.001, or 0.1%) is much better than a sample of 100 from a population of 10,000 (although the sampling fraction is 0.01, or 1%, which is 10 times higher). The size of a sample is what makes representativeness more likely, not the proportion of the whole that the sample represents.

Because they do not disproportionately select particular groups within the population, random samples that are successfully implemented avoid systematic bias. The Gallup Poll is a good example of the accuracy of random samples. For example, in 2008, the final Gallup prediction of 55% for Obama was within 2 percentage points of his winning total of 53%. The four most common methods for drawing random samples are simple random sampling, systematic random sampling, stratified random sampling, and cluster sampling.

Simple Random Sampling

Simple random sampling requires a procedure that generates numbers or identifies cases strictly on the basis of chance. As you know, flipping a coin and rolling a die can be used to identify cases strictly on the basis of chance, but these procedures are not very efficient tools for drawing a sample. A **random number table**, which can be found on many websites, simplifies the process considerably. The researcher numbers all the elements in the sampling frame and then uses a systematic procedure for picking corresponding numbers from the random number table. Alternatively, a researcher may use a lottery procedure. Each case number is written on a small card, and then the cards are mixed up and the sample selected from the cards.

When a large sample must be generated, these procedures are very cumbersome. Fortunately, a computer program can easily generate a random sample of any size. The researcher must first number all the elements to be sampled (the sampling frame) and then run the computer program to generate a random selection of the numbers within the desired range. The elements represented by these numbers are the sample.

Organizations that conduct phone surveys often draw random samples with another automated procedure called random digit dialing. A machine dials random numbers within the phone prefixes corresponding to the area in which the survey is to be conducted. Random digit dialing is particularly useful when a sampling frame is not available. The researcher simply replaces any inappropriate numbers (e.g., those no longer in service or for businesses) with the next randomly generated phone number.

The probability of selection in a true simple random sample is equal for each element. If a sample of 500 is selected from a population of 17,000 (i.e., a sampling frame of 17,000), then the probability of selection for each element is 500/17,000, or .03. Every element has an equal and independent chance of being selected, just like the odds in a toss of a coin (1/2) or a roll of a die (1/6). Simple random sampling can be done either with or without replacement sampling. In replacement sampling, each element is returned to the sampling frame from which it is selected so that it may be sampled again. In sampling without replacement, each element selected for the sample is then excluded from the sampling frame. In practice, it makes no difference whether sampled elements are replaced after selection, as long as the population is large and the sample is to contain only a small fraction of the population.

Systematic Random Sampling

Systematic random sampling is a variant of simple random sampling and is a little less time-consuming. When you systematically select a random sample, the first element is selected randomly from a list or from sequential files, and then every nth element is systematically selected thereafter. This is a convenient method for drawing a random sample when the population elements are arranged sequentially. It is particularly efficient when the elements are not actually printed (i.e., there is no sampling frame) but instead are represented by folders in filing cabinets.

Systematic random sampling requires three steps:

1. The total number of cases in the population is divided by the number of cases required for the sample. This division yields the sampling interval, the number of cases from one sampled case to another. If 50 cases are to be selected out of 1,000, the sampling interval is 20 (1,000/50 = 20); every 20th case is selected.

2. A number from 1 to 20 (the sampling interval) is selected randomly. This number identifies the first case to be sampled, counting from the first case on the list or in the files.

3. After the first case is selected, every *n*th case is selected for the sample, where *n* is the sampling interval. If the sampling interval is not a whole number, the size of the sampling interval is systematically varied to yield the proper number of cases for the sample. For example, if the sampling interval is 30.5, the sampling interval alternates between 30 and 31.

In almost all sampling situations, systematic random sampling yields what is essentially a simple random sample. The exception is a situation in which the sequence of elements is affected by periodicity—that is, the sequence varies in some regular, periodic pattern. The list or folder device from which the elements are selected must be truly random in order to avoid sampling bias. For example, we could not have a list of convicted felons sorted by offense type, age, or some other characteristic of the population. If the list is sorted in any meaningful way, this will introduce bias to the sampling process, and the resulting sample is not likely to be representative of the population.

Stratified Random Sampling

Although all probability sampling methods use random sampling, some add steps to the process to make sampling more efficient or easier. Samples are easier to collect when they require less time, money, or prior information.

Stratified random sampling uses information known about the total population prior to sampling to make the sampling process more efficient. First, all elements in the population (i.e., in the sampling frame) are differentiated on the basis of their value on some relevant characteristic. This sorting step forms the sampling strata. Next, elements are sampled randomly from within these strata. For example, race may be the basis for distinguishing individuals in some population of interest. Within each racial category selected for the strata, individuals are then sampled randomly.

Why is this method more efficient than drawing a simple random sample? Well, imagine that you plan to draw a sample of 500 from an ethnically diverse neighborhood. The neighborhood population is 15% African American, 10% Hispanic, 5% Asian, and 70% Caucasian. If you drew a simple random sample, you might end up with disproportionate numbers of each group. But if you created sampling strata based on race and ethnicity, you could randomly select cases from each stratum: 75 African Americans (15% of the sample), 50 Hispanics (10%), 25 Asians (5%), and 350 Caucasians (70%). By using proportionate stratified sampling you would eliminate any possibility of error in the sample's distribution of ethnicity. Each stratum would be represented exactly in proportion to its size in the population from which the sample was drawn (see Exhibit 5.4).

In disproportionate stratified sampling, the proportion of each stratum that is included in the sample is intentionally varied from what it is in the population. In the case of the sample stratified by ethnicity, you might select equal numbers of cases from each racial or ethnic group: 125 African Americans (25% of the sample), 125 Hispanics (25%), 125 Asians (25%), and 125 Caucasians (25%). In this type of sample, the probability of selection of every case is known but unequal between strata. You know what the proportions are in the population, so you can easily adjust your combined sample accordingly. For instance, if you want to combine the ethnic groups and estimate the average income of the total

Exhibit 5.4 Stratified Random Sampling

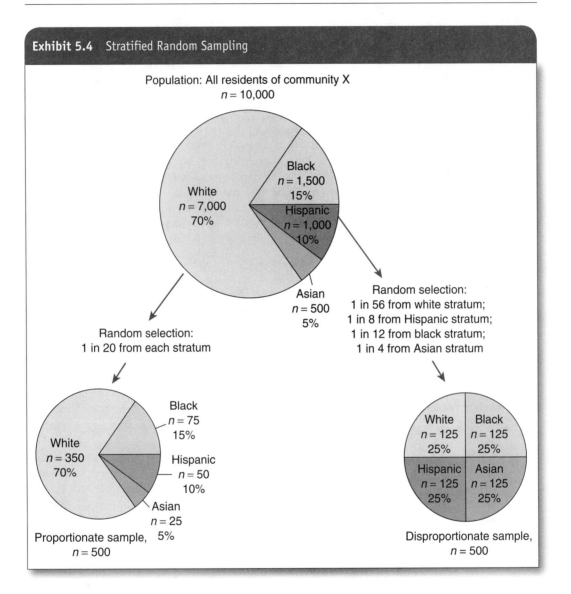

population, you would have to weight each case in the sample. The *weight* is a number you multiply by the value of each case based on the stratum it is in. For example, you would multiply the incomes of all African Americans in the sample by 0.6 (75/125), the incomes of all Hispanics by 0.4 (50/125), and so on. Weighting in this way reduces the influence of the oversampled strata and increases the influence of the undersampled strata to just what they would have been if pure probability sampling had been used.

Why would anyone select a sample that is so unrepresentative in the first place? The most common reason is to ensure that cases from smaller strata are included in the sample in sufficient numbers. Only then can separate statistical estimates and comparisons be made between strata (e.g., between African Americans and Caucasians). Remember that one determinant of sample quality is sample size. If few members of a particular group are in the population, they need to be oversampled. Such disproportionate sampling may also result in a more efficient sampling design if the costs of data collection differ markedly between strata or if the variability (heterogeneity) of the strata differs.

Cluster Sampling

Although stratified sampling requires more information than usual prior to sampling (about the size of strata in the population), **cluster sampling** requires less prior information. Specifically, cluster sampling can be useful when a sampling frame is not available, as is often the case for large populations spread across a wide geographic area or among many different organizations. In fact, if we wanted to obtain a sample from the entire U.S. population, there would be no list available. Yes, there are lists in telephone books of residents in various places who have telephones, lists of those who have registered to vote, lists of those who hold driver's licenses, and so on. However, all these lists are incomplete: Some people do not list their phone number or do not have a telephone, some people are not registered to vote, and so on. Using incomplete lists such as these would introduce selection bias into our sample.

In such cases, the sampling procedures become a little more complex, and we usually end up working toward the sample we want through a series of steps: First, researchers extract a random sample of groups or clusters of elements that are available and then randomly sample the individual elements of interest from within these selected clusters. So what is a cluster? A **cluster** is a naturally occurring, mixed aggregate of elements of the population, with each element appearing in one and only one cluster. Schools could serve as clusters for sampling students, blocks could serve as clusters for sampling city residents, counties could serve as clusters for sampling the general population, and businesses could serve as clusters for sampling employees.

In a cluster sample of city residents, for example, blocks could be the first-stage clusters. A research assistant could walk around each selected block and record the addresses of all occupied dwelling units. Or, in a cluster sample of students, a researcher could contact the schools selected in the first stage and make arrangements with the registrars or office staff to obtain lists of students at each school. Cluster samples often involve multiple stages (see Exhibit 5.5).

Many federal government–funded surveys use multistage cluster samples or even combinations of cluster and stratified probability sampling methods. The U.S. Justice Department's National Crime Victimization Survey (NCVS) is an excellent example of a cluster sample. In the NCVS, the first stage of clusters selected are referred to as primary sampling units (PSUs) and represent a sample of rural counties and large metropolitan areas. The second stage of sampling involves the selection of geographic districts within each of the PSUs that have been listed by the U.S. Bureau of the Census population census. Finally, a probability sample of residential dwelling units is selected from these geographic districts. These dwelling units, or addresses, represent the last stage of the multistage sampling.

Exhibit 5.5 Cluster Sampling

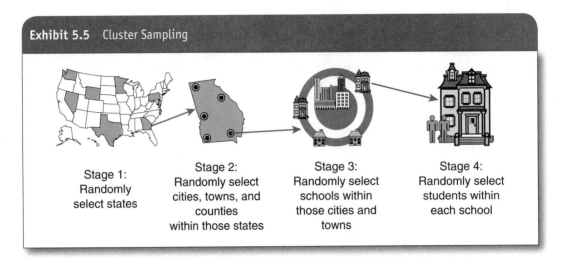

Stage 1:
Randomly
select states

Stage 2:
Randomly select
cities, towns, and
counties
within those states

Stage 3:
Randomly select
schools within
those cities and
towns

Stage 4:
Randomly select
students within
each school

Anyone who resides at a selected address who is 12 years of age or older and is a U.S. citizen is eligible for the NCVS sample. Approximately 50,500 housing units or other living quarters are designated for the NCVS each year and are selected in this manner.

How would we evaluate the NCVS sample, using the sample evaluation questions?

- *From what population were the cases selected?* The population was clearly defined for each cluster.
- *What method was used to select cases from this population?* The random selection method was carefully described.
- *Do the cases that were studied represent, in the aggregate, the population from which they were selected?* The unbiased selection procedures make us reasonably confident in the representativeness of the sample.

Nonprobability Sampling Methods

Unlike probability samples, when collecting a sample using nonprobability sampling techniques, elements within the population do not have a known probability of being selected into the sample. Thus, because the chance of any element being selected is unknown, we cannot be certain the selected sample actually represents our population. These methods are useful for several purposes, including those situations in which we do not have a population list, when we are exploring a research question that does not concern a large population, or when we are doing a preliminary or exploratory study. Suppose, for example, that we were interested in the crime of shoplifting and wanted to investigate the rationalization used by shoplifters. It would be hard to define a population in this case because we do not have a list of shoplifters from which to randomly select. There may be lists of convicted shoplifters, but of course they only represent those shoplifters who were actually caught.

There are four nonprobability sampling methods frequently used in criminological research: availability sampling, quota sampling, purposive sampling, and snowball sampling.

Availability Sampling

In availability sampling, elements are selected because they are available or easy to find. Consequently, this sampling method is also known as haphazard, accidental, or convenience sampling. News reporters often use passersby—availability samples—to inject a personal perspective into a news story and show what ordinary people may think of a given topic. Availability samples are also used by university professors and researchers all the time. Have you ever been asked to complete a questionnaire before leaving one of your classes? If so, you may have been selected for inclusion in an availability sample.

Even though they are not generalizable, availability samples are often appropriate in research—for example, when a field researcher is exploring a new setting and trying to get some sense of prevailing attitudes or when a survey researcher conducts a preliminary test of a questionnaire. There are a variety of ways to select elements for an availability sample: standing on street corners and talking to anyone walking by, asking questions of employees who come to pick up their paychecks at a personnel office, or distributing questionnaires to an available and captive audience such as a class or a group meeting. Availability samples are also frequently used in fieldwork studies when the researchers are interested in obtaining detailed information about a particular group.

How does the generalizability of survey responses from an availability sample compare to those obtained from probability samples? The difference is that in an availability sample, there is no clearly definable population from which the respondents were drawn, and no systematic technique was used to select the respondents. Consequently, there is not much likelihood that the sample is representative of any target population; the problem is that we can never be sure. Unfortunately, availability sampling often masquerades as a more rigorous form of research. Much like CNN's use of polling results, noted earlier in the chapter, popular magazines and Internet sites frequently survey their readers by asking them to fill out questionnaires. Follow-up articles then appear in the magazine or on the site, displaying the results under such titles as "What You Think About the Death Penalty for Teenagers." If the magazine's circulation is extensive, a large sample can be achieved in this way. The problem is that usually only a tiny fraction of readers fill out the questionnaire, and these respondents are probably unlike other readers who did not have the interest or time to participate. So the survey is based on an availability sample. Even though the follow-up article may be interesting, we have no basis for thinking that the results describe the readership as a whole, much less the larger population.

Quota Sampling

Quota sampling is intended to overcome availability sampling's biggest downfall: the likelihood that the sample will just consist of who or what is available, without any concern for its similarity to the population of interest. The distinguishing feature of a quota sample is that quotas are set to ensure that the sample represents certain characteristics in proportion to their prevalence in the population.

Quota samples are similar to stratified probability samples, but they are generally less rigorous and precise in their selection procedures. Quota sampling simply involves designating the population into proportions of some group that you want to be represented in your sample. Similar to stratified samples, in some cases these proportions may actually represent the true proportions observed in the population. At other times, these quotas may represent predetermined proportions of subsets of people you deliberately want to oversample.

The problem is that even when we know that a quota sample is representative of the particular characteristics for which quotas have been set, we have no way of knowing if the sample is representative in terms of any other characteristics. In Exhibit 5.6, for example, quotas have been set for gender only. Under the circumstances, it's no surprise that the sample is representative of the population only in terms of gender, not in terms of race. Interviewers are only human and guided by their own biases; they may avoid potential respondents with menacing dogs in the front yard, or they could seek out respondents who are physically attractive or who look like they would be easy to interview. Realistically, researchers can set quotas for only a small fraction of the characteristics relevant to a study, so a quota sample is really not much better than an availability sample (although following careful, consistent procedures for selecting cases within the quota limits always helps).

This last point leads to another limitation of quota sampling: You must know the characteristics of the entire population to set the right quotas. In most cases, researchers know what the population looks like in terms of no more than a few of the characteristics relevant to their concerns, and in some cases they have no such information on the entire population.

Exhibit 5.6 Quota Sampling

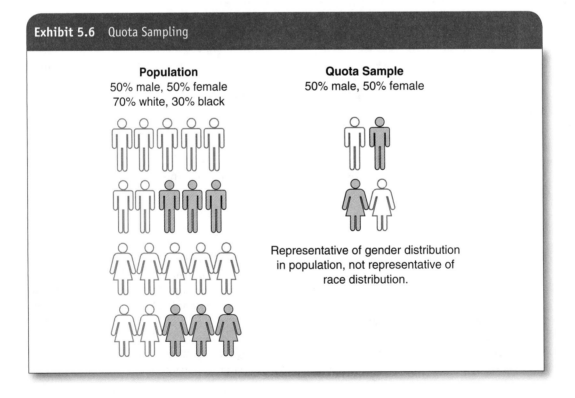

Population
50% male, 50% female
70% white, 30% black

Quota Sample
50% male, 50% female

Representative of gender distribution in population, not representative of race distribution.

Purposive or Judgment Sampling

In purposive sampling, each sample element is selected for a purpose, usually because of the unique position of the sample elements. It is sometimes referred to as *judgment sampling*, because the researcher uses his or her own judgment about whom to select into the sample, rather than drawing sample elements randomly. Purposive sampling may involve studying the entire population of some limited group (members of a street gang) or a subset of a population (juvenile parolees). A purposive sample may also be a key informant survey, which targets individuals who are particularly knowledgeable about the issues under investigation.

Rubin and Rubin (1995: 66) suggest three guidelines for selecting informants when designing any purposive sampling strategy. Informants should be

- Knowledgeable about the cultural arena or situation or experience being studied;
- Willing to talk; and
- Representative of the range of points of view.

Purposive sampling does not produce a sample that represents some larger population, but it can be exactly what is needed in a case study of an organization, community, or some other clearly defined and relatively limited group. For example, in their book *Crimes of the Middle Class*, Weisburd et al. (1991) examined a sample of white-collar criminal offenders convicted in seven federal judicial districts. These judicial districts were not randomly selected from an exhaustive list of all federal districts, but were instead deliberately selected by the researchers because they were thought to provide a suitable amount of geographical diversity. They were also selected because they were believed to have a substantial proportion of white-collar crime cases. The cost of such nonprobability sampling, you should realize by now, is generalizability; we do not know if their findings hold true for white-collar crime in other areas of the country.

Snowball Sampling

For snowball sampling, you identify one member of the population and speak to him or her, then ask that person to identify others in the population and speak to them, then ask them to identify others, and so on. The sample size thus increases with time as a snowball would, rolling down a slope. This technique is useful for hard-to-reach or hard-to-identify, interconnected populations where at least some members of the population know each other, such as drug dealers, prostitutes, practicing criminals, gang leaders, and informal organizational leaders.

St. Jean (2007) used snowball sampling for recruiting offenders in a Chicago neighborhood for interviews. After several years of participant observation (see Chapter 9) within a Chicago community, St. Jean wanted to understand the logic offenders used for setting up street drug dealing and staging robberies. He explained his sampling technique as follows:

> I was introduced to the offenders mainly through referrals from relatives, customers, friends, and acquaintances who, after several months (sometimes years), trusted me as someone whose only motive was to understand life in their neighbourhood. For instance, the first three drug dealers I interviewed were introduced by their close relatives. Toward the end of each interview, I asked for leads to other subjects, with the first three interviews resulting in eleven additional leads. (p. 26)

One problem with this technique is that the initial contacts may shape the entire sample and foreclose access to some members of the population of interest. Because Decker and Van Winkle (1996) wanted to interview members from several gangs, they had to restart the snowball sampling procedure many times to gain access to a large number of gangs. One problem, of course, was validating whether individuals claiming to be gang members— so-called wannabes—actually were legitimate members. Over 500 contacts were made before the final sample of 99 was complete.

More systematic versions of snowball sampling can also reduce the potential for bias. The most sophisticated version, *respondent-driven sampling*, gives financial incentives, also called gratuities, to respondents to recruit peers (Heckathorn 1997). Limitations on the number of incentives that any one respondent can receive increase the sample's diversity. Targeted incentives can steer the sample to include specific subgroups. When the sampling is repeated through several waves, with new respondents bringing in more peers, the composition of the sample converges on a more representative mix of characteristics. Exhibit 5.7 shows how the

Exhibit 5.7   Respondent-Driven Sampling—A Version of Snowball Sampling

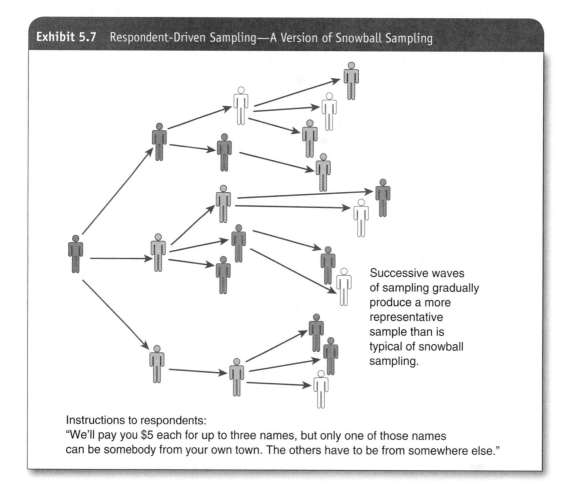

Successive waves of sampling gradually produce a more representative sample than is typical of snowball sampling.

Instructions to respondents:
"We'll pay you $5 each for up to three names, but only one of those names can be somebody from your own town. The others have to be from somewhere else."

sample spreads out through successive recruitment waves to an increasingly diverse pool (Heckathorn 1997: 178). As with all nonprobability sampling techniques, however, researchers using even the most systematic versions of snowball sampling cannot be confident that their sample is representative of the population of interest.

Lessons About Sample Quality

Some lessons are implicit in our evaluations of the samples in this chapter:

- We cannot evaluate the quality of a sample if we do not know what population it is supposed to represent. If the population is unspecified because the researchers were never clear about just what population they were trying to sample, then we can safely conclude that the sample itself is no good.
- We cannot evaluate the quality of a sample if we do not know exactly how cases in the sample were selected from the population. If the method was specified, we then need to know whether cases were selected in a systematic fashion or on the basis of chance. In any case, we know that a haphazard method of sampling (as in person-on-the-street interviews) undermines generalizability.
- Sample quality is determined by the sample actually obtained, not just by the sampling method itself. That is, findings are only as generalizable as the sample from which they are drawn. If many of the people (or other elements) selected for our sample do not respond or participate in the study, even though they have been selected for the sample, generalizability is compromised.
- We need to be aware that even researchers who obtain very good samples may talk about the implications of their findings for some group that is larger than or just different from the population they actually sampled. For example, findings from a representative sample of students in one university often are discussed as if they tell us about university students in general. Maybe they do; the problem is, we just don't know.

UNITS OF ANALYSIS AND ERRORS IN CAUSAL REASONING

In criminological research, we obtain samples from many different units, including individuals, groups, cities, prisons, countries, and so on. When we make generalizations from a sample to the population, it is very important to keep in mind the units under study, which are referred to as the units of analysis. These units of analysis are the level of social life on which the research question is focused, such as individuals, groups, or nations.

Individual and Group Units of Analysis

In most social science research, including criminological studies, the units of analysis are individuals. The researcher may collect survey data from individuals, analyze the data, and then report on how many individuals felt socially isolated and whether recidivism by individuals related to their feelings of social isolation. Data are collected from individuals, and the focus of analysis is on the individual.

In other instances, however, the units of analysis may instead be groups, such as families, schools, prisons, towns, states, or countries. In some studies, groups are the units of analysis but data are collected from individuals. For example, Sampson, Raudenbush, and Earls (1997) studied influences on violent crime in Chicago neighborhoods. Collective efficacy was one variable they hypothesized as an influence on the neighborhood crime rate. This variable was a characteristic of the neighborhood residents who were likely to help other residents and were trusted by them, so they measured this variable in a survey of individuals. The responses of individual residents about their perceptions of their neighbors' helpfulness and trustworthiness were averaged to create a collective efficacy score for each neighborhood. It was this neighborhood measure of collective efficacy that was used to explain variation in the rate of violent crime between neighborhoods. The data were collected from individuals and were about individuals, but they were combined or aggregated to describe neighborhoods. The units of analysis were thus groups (neighborhoods).

In a study such as that of Sampson and colleagues, we can distinguish the concept of **units of analysis** from the **units of observation**. Data were collected from individuals, the units of observation, and then the data were aggregated and analyzed at the group level. In some studies, the units of observation and the units of analysis are the same while in others they are not.

The Ecological Fallacy and Reductionism

Researchers should make sure that their conclusions reflect the units of analysis in their study. For example, a conclusion that crime increases as unemployment increases could imply that individuals who lose their jobs are more likely to commit a crime, that a community with a high unemployment rate is also likely to have a high crime rate, or both. Conclusions about processes at the individual level should be based on individual-level data; conclusions about group-level processes should be based on data collected about groups. In most cases, violation of this rule creates one more reason to suspect the validity of the causal conclusions.

A researcher who draws conclusions about individual-level processes from group-level data is constructing an **ecological fallacy** (see Exhibit 5.8). The conclusions may or may not be correct, but we must recognize that group-level data do not describe individual-level processes.

Bear in mind that conclusions about individual processes based on group-level data are not necessarily wrong. The data simply do not provide information about processes at the individual level. Suppose we find that communities with higher average incomes have lower crime rates. The only thing special about these communities may be that they have more individuals with higher incomes, who tend to commit fewer crimes. Even though we collected data at the group level and analyzed them at the group level, they reflect a causal process at the individual level (Sampson & Lauritsen 1994: 80–83).

When data about individuals are used to make inferences about group-level processes, a problem occurs that can be thought of as the mirror image of the ecological fallacy: the **reductionist fallacy** or **reductionism** (see Exhibit 5.8).

Exhibit 5.8   Errors in Causal Conclusions

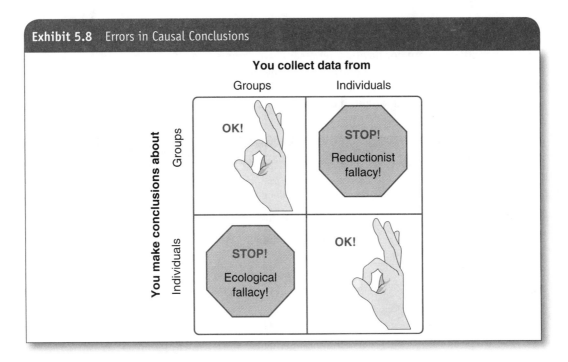

The solution to these problems is to know what the units of analysis and units of observation were in a study, and to take these into account when weighing the credibility of the researcher's conclusions. The goal is not to reject conclusions that refer to a level of analysis different from what was actually studied. Instead, the goal is to consider the likelihood that an ecological fallacy or a reductionist fallacy has been made when estimating the causal validity of the conclusions.

CONCLUSION

Sampling is the fundamental starting point in criminological research. Probability sampling methods allow researchers to use the laws of chance, or probability, to draw samples from populations and maintain a standard of representativeness that can be estimated with a high degree of confidence. A sample of just 1,000 or 1,500 individuals can easily be used to reliably estimate the characteristics of the population of a nation comprising millions of individuals.

The alternatives to random, or probability-based, sampling methods are almost always much less desirable, even though they typically are less expensive. Without a method of selecting cases likely to represent the population in which the researcher is interested, research findings will have to be carefully qualified. Unrepresentative samples may help researchers understand which aspects of a social phenomenon are important, but questions about the generalizability of this understanding are still left unanswered.

Social scientists often seek to generalize their conclusions from the population that they studied to some larger target population. The validity of generalizations of this type is necessarily uncertain, for having a representative sample of a particular population does not at all ensure that what we find will hold true in other populations. Nonetheless, the accumulation of findings from studies based on local or otherwise unrepresentative populations can provide important information about broader populations.

KEY TERMS

Availability sampling

Census

Cluster

Cluster sampling

Cross-population generalizability

Disproportionate stratified sampling

Ecological fallacy

External validity

Nonprobability sampling method

Nonresponse

Periodicity

Population

Probability of selection

Probability sampling method

Proportionate stratified sampling

Purposive sampling

Quota sampling

Random digit dialing

Random number table

Random selection

Reductionist fallacy (reductionism)

Replacement sampling

Representative sample

Sample

Sample generalizability

Sampling distribution

Sampling frame

Sampling interval

Sampling unit

Simple random sampling

Snowball sampling

Stratified random sampling

Systematic random sampling

Systematic sampling error

Target population

Units of analysis

Units of observation

HIGHLIGHTS

- Sampling is usually necessary except in two conditions: (1) when the elements that would be sampled are identical, which is almost never the case; and (2) when you have the option of conducting a complete census of a population.

- Nonresponse undermines sample quality: It is the obtained sample, not the desired sample, that determines sample quality.

- Probability sampling methods rely on a random selection procedure to ensure there is no systematic bias in the selection of elements. In a probability sample, the odds of selecting elements are independent, equal, and known, and the method of selection is carefully controlled.

- Simple random sampling and systematic random sampling are equivalent probability sampling methods in most situations. However, systematic random sampling is inappropriate for sampling from lists of elements that have a regular, periodic structure.

- Other types of random sampling include stratified random sampling, which uses prior information about a population to make sampling more efficient, and cluster sampling.

- Nonprobability sampling methods can be useful when random sampling is not possible, when a research question does not concern a larger population, and when a preliminary exploratory study is appropriate. However, the representativeness of nonprobability samples cannot be determined.

- The likely degree of error in an estimate of a population characteristic based on a probability sample decreases as the size of the sample increases. Sampling error also decreases if the population from which the sample was selected is homogeneous.

EXERCISES

Discussing Research

1. Assess two different polls offering opinions about the same heated topic related to crime—compare CNN.com with Slate.com, for example. What information does the article provide on the sample that was selected? What additional information do you need to determine whether the sample was a representative one? What do the responses tell you about the people who participate in pools on these websites?

2. Select a random sample using the table of random numbers, which typically can be found on many websites (http://stattrek.com/Tables/Random.aspx). Now find information on crime rates from some source such as the government documents section of your library or online at the Bureau of Justice Statistics or the FBI. Find a listing of crime rates (e.g., robbery or homicide) by some geographical units (e.g., states, cities) and number them. Then apply your selected random sample to the list and extract the sample. Compute the average crime rate from your sample. Now compute the average for the entire population list. How does the sample average compare to the corresponding figure for the entire population?

3. Draw a snowball sample of people who have some characteristic of interest that is not common (i.e., have been skydiving). Ask friends and relatives to locate a first contact, and then call or visit this person and ask for names of others. Stop when you have identified a sample of 10. Review the problems you encountered, and consider how you would proceed if you had to draw a larger sample.

4. All adult U.S. citizens are required to participate in the decennial census, but some do not. Some social scientists have argued for putting more resources into a large representative sample so that more resources are available to secure higher rates of response from hard-to-include groups. Do you think that the U.S. Census should shift to a probability-based sampling design? Why or why not?

Finding Research on the Web

1. What can you learn about sampling on the web? Conduct a search on "sampling" and "population" and select a few of these sites. List a few new points that you learn about sampling and how the inclusion of cell phone users will steer future research findings.

2. Go to the INFOMINE Scholarly Internet Resource Collections website at http://infomine.ucr.edu/. Search for five resources containing information on crime or victimization. Briefly describe your sources and list the websites where they can be found. How do these sources of information differ in their approaches to collecting information? Do they report the sampling information? What statistics do they present? Do they report the sampling method used in the studies from which they obtained these statistics? What sampling methods were used? Evaluate the sampling methods in terms of representativeness and generalizability. How would you improve on the sampling methods to increase the representativeness and generalizability of the data? If no sampling methods are mentioned, propose one that would have been appropriate to obtain the statistics.

Critiquing Research

1. Select five scholarly journal articles that describe criminological research using a sample drawn from some population. Identify the type of sample used in each study, and note any strong and weak points in how the sample was actually drawn. Did the researchers have a problem due to nonresponse? Considering the sample, how confident are you in the validity of generalizations about the population based on the sample? Do you need any additional information to evaluate the sample? Do you think a different sampling strategy would have been preferable? What larger population were the findings generalized to? Do you think these generalizations were warranted? Why or why not?

2. What are the advantages and disadvantages of probability-based sampling designs compared with nonprobability-based designs? Could any of the research described in this chapter with a nonprobability-based design have been conducted instead with a probability-based design? What are the difficulties that might have been encountered in an attempt to use random selection? How would you discuss the degree of confidence you can place in the results obtained from research using a nonprobability-based sampling design? Can you think of other examples where probability sampling is not an option for researchers?

Making Research Ethical

1. How much pressure is too much pressure to participate in a probability-based sample survey? Is it okay for the U.S. government to mandate that all citizens participate in the decennial census? Should companies be able to require employees to participate in survey research about work-related issues? Should students be required to participate in surveys about teacher performance? Should parents be required to consent to the participation of their high school–age students in a survey about substance abuse and health issues? Is it okay to give monetary incentives for participation in a survey of homeless shelter clients? Can monetary incentives be coercive? Explain your decisions.

2. Tjaden and Thoennes (2000) sampled adults with random digit dialing in order to study violent victimization. Do you believe that the researchers had any ethical obligation to take any action whatsoever when they learned that a respondent was currently being victimized? Are any of the ethical guidelines presented in Chapter 3 relevant to this situation? Teachers and medical personnel are required by law to report cases they believe to represent incidents of child abuse. Should researchers have the same obligation? How would this affect large-scale surveys using random digit dialing in which you want to preserve the anonymity of respondents?

Developing a Research Proposal

Consider the possibilities for sampling:

1. Propose a sampling design that would be appropriate if you were to survey students on your campus only. Define the population, identify the sampling frame(s), and specify the elements and any other units at different stages. Indicate the exact procedure for selecting people to be included in the sample.

2. Propose a different sampling design for conducting your survey in a larger population, such as your city, state, or the entire nation.

Performing Data Analysis in SPSS or Excel

Using the data set NCVS9205.ASSAULT.por, which contains a random sample of assault victimizations from the National Crime Victimization Survey from 1992 to 2005, the variable V2089 reports the location (urban, suburban, rural) of each assault incident.

1. Create a frequency distribution for this variable, and record the valid percentage for each category.

2. Select a random sample of approximately 5% of all cases. Create a second frequency distribution for the robbery location, and record the valid percentage for each category.

3. Select a random sample containing approximately 1% of all cases. Create a third frequency distribution, and record the valid percentage for each category.

4. Compare the three frequency distributions. How does sample size influence the results? Does the sample size affect the reliability or validity of where robbery is most likely to occur?

5. For those assault victims who were injured and lost time from work, describe the number of days of work lost (V4487). It is important to recode "don't know" and "residue" responses as missing for this analysis—you should include the values of 997 (don't know) and 998 (residue) as missing along with the values of 999, which are already specified as missing. Produce both a frequency distribution and a histogram for this variable. How would you describe the impact of assault victimizations on lost work productivity in America?

Student Study Site

The companion Student Study Site for *Fundamentals of Research in Criminology and Criminal Justice* can be found at www.sagepub.com/bachmanfrccj2e.

    Visit the Student Study Site to enhance your understanding of the chapter content and to discover additional resources that will take your learning one step further. You can enhance your understanding of the chapters by using the comprehensive study material, which includes interactive exercises, e-flashcards, web exercises, practice self-tests, and more. You will also find special features, such as Learning From Journal Articles, which incorporates Sage's online journal collection.

CHAPTER 6

Causation and Research Design

This chapter considers the meaning of causation and then reviews the criteria for achieving causally valid explanations, the ways in which experimental and quasi-experimental research designs seek to meet these criteria, and the difficulties that can sometimes result in drawing invalid conclusions. By the end of the chapter, you should have a good grasp of the meaning of causation and the logic of experimental design—and understand why the features of experiments are so well suited to testing causal hypotheses. In subsequent chapters, we will show how causal issues are handled in other research designs.

WHAT DO WE MEAN BY CAUSATION?

Identifying causes—figuring out why things happen—is the goal of most social science research. Unfortunately, valid explanations of the causes of social phenomena do not come easily. According to the National Crime Victimization Survey, violent crime victimization rates have been declining steadily since the 1990s (cited in Catalano 2006). However, not all cities or demographic groups (e.g., age groups and ethnicities) have experienced such drops (Ousey & Lee 2004). Moreover, in some cities, rates of violence have begun to increase tremendously. Is this recent rise in violence due to the release of hard-core convicts who had been imprisoned during the crime wave of the 1980s and early 1990s (Liptak 2004)? Is it simply a "crime-drop party is over" phenomenon (Lichtblau 2000: A2)? And why has the violent crime rate continued its downward trend in some cities like New York (Dewan 2004a: A25)? Is it because of Compstat, the city's computer program that identifies for police where crimes are clustering (Dewan 2004b: A1; Kaplan 2002: A3)? Or should credit be given to the "Safe Streets, Safe Cities" program, which increased the numbers of police officers (Rashbaum 2002)? To determine which of these possibilities could contribute to the increase or decline of serious crime, we must design our research strategies carefully.

CAUSAL EXPLANATION

A *cause* is an explanation for some characteristic, attitude, or behavior of groups, individuals, or other entities (such as families, organizations, or cities) or for events. Most social scientists seek causal explanations that reflect tests of the types of hypotheses with which you are familiar (recall Chapter 2). In these tests, the independent variable is the presumed cause, and the dependent variable is the potential effect. For example, does problem-oriented policing (independent variable) reduce violent crime (dependent variable)? Does experiencing abuse as a child (independent variable) increase the likelihood that the person will be a violent adult (dependent variable)?

A **causal effect** is said to occur if variation in the independent variable is followed by variation in the dependent variable, when all other things are equal (***ceteris paribus***), or when all other potentially influential conditions and factors are taken into consideration. For instance, we know that men are more likely than women to commit violent crimes, but is this because of a genetic predisposition? Different patterns of socialization to violence? Perhaps different levels of job frustration? We need to know whether men commit more crimes than women, *ceteris paribus*, that is, when all these other potential factors are taken into consideration.

We admit that you can legitimately argue that "all" other things can't literally be equal. We can't compare the same people at the same time in exactly the same circumstances; we can only manipulate the independent variable (King et al. 1994). However, you will see that we can design research to create conditions that are comparable indeed, so that we can confidently assert our conclusions *ceteris paribus*—other things being equal.

Causal effect When variation in one phenomenon, an independent variable, leads to or results, on average, in variation in another phenomenon, the dependent variable

Example: Individuals arrested for domestic assault tend to commit fewer subsequent assaults than do similar individuals who are accused in the same circumstances but not arrested.

Five criteria must be considered when deciding whether a causal connection exists. When a research design leaves one or more of the criteria unmet, we may have some important doubts about causal assertions the researcher may have made. The first three criteria are generally considered the necessary and most important bases for identifying a causal effect: empirical association, appropriate time order, and nonspuriousness. The other two criteria—identifying a causal mechanism and specifying the context in which the effect occurs—can also considerably strengthen causal explanations.

Research designs that allow us to establish these criteria require careful planning, implementation, and analysis. Many times, researchers have to leave one or more of the criteria unmet, leaving us with doubts about the validity of their causal conclusions. Consequently, some may even avoid making any causal assertions at all.

Exhibit 6.1 Association: Noise Intensity for Two Groups in an Experiment

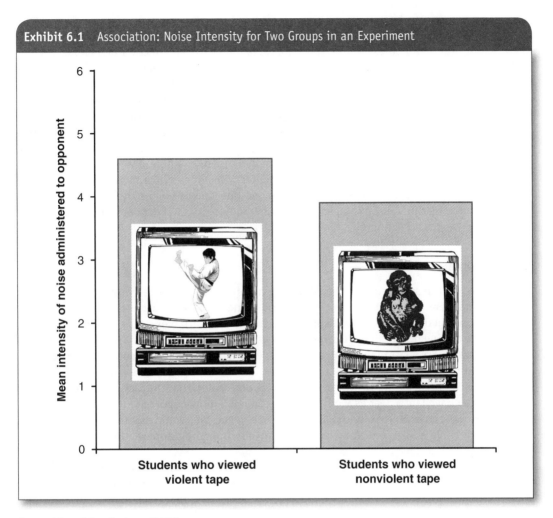

Source: Adapted from Bushman (1995).

Association

Exhibit 6.1 displays the association that Brad Bushman (1995) found between watching a violent videotape and aggressive behavior. Students who watched a violent videotape in his lab administered more intense noise to an opponent than those who watched a nonviolent videotape. Thus, variation in exposure to media violence is associated with a likelihood of exhibiting aggressive behavior. A change in the independent variable is associated with—correlated with—a change in the dependent variable. By contrast, if there is no association between two variables, there cannot be a causal relationship.

Time Order

Association is a necessary criterion for establishing a causal effect, but it is not sufficient on its own. We must also ensure that the variation in the independent variable came *before* variation in the dependent variable—the cause must come before the presumed effect. This is the criterion of time order. Bushman's (1995) experiment satisfied this criterion because he controlled the variation in the independent variable: All the students saw the movie excerpts (which varied in violent content) before their level of aggressiveness was measured. As you can imagine, we cannot be so sure about time order when we use a survey or some other observation done at one point in time. For example, if we find that neighborhoods with higher levels of disorder have higher crime rates, we can't be sure that the level of disorder came first, and that it led to more crime. Maybe higher crime rates made residents too fearful to keep things in order. Without longitudinal data or other clues to time order, we just don't know.

Nonspuriousness

Even when research establishes that two variables are associated and that variation in the independent variable precedes variation in the dependent variable, we cannot be sure we identified a causal relationship between the two variables. Have you heard the old adage among researchers, "Correlation does not prove causation"? It is meant to remind us that an association between two variables might be caused by something else. If we measure children's shoe sizes and their academic knowledge, for example, we will find a positive association. However, the association results from the fact that older children tend to have larger feet as well as more academic knowledge. As it turns out, shoe size does not cause increased knowledge or vice versa. We would say that the association between shoe size and knowledge is **spurious** (meaning apparently but not actually valid—that is, false).

Before we conclude that variation in an independent variable causes variation in a dependent variable, we must have reason to believe that the relationship is nonspurious. Nonspuriousness is a relationship between two variables that is not due to variation in a third variable (see Exhibit 6.2).

Mechanism

Confidence in a conclusion that two variables have a causal connection will be strengthened if a mechanism—some discernible means of creating a connection—can be identified (Cook & Campbell 1979: 35; Marini & Singer 1988). Many social scientists believe that a causal explanation is not adequate until a causal mechanism is identified—what process or mechanism actually is responsible for the relationship between the independent and dependent variables.

For instance, there seems to be an empirical association at the individual level between poverty and delinquency: Children who live in impoverished homes seem more likely to be involved in petty crime. But why? Some researchers have argued for a *mechanism* of low parent–child attachment, inadequate supervision of children, and erratic discipline as the

Exhibit 6.2 A Spurious Relationship

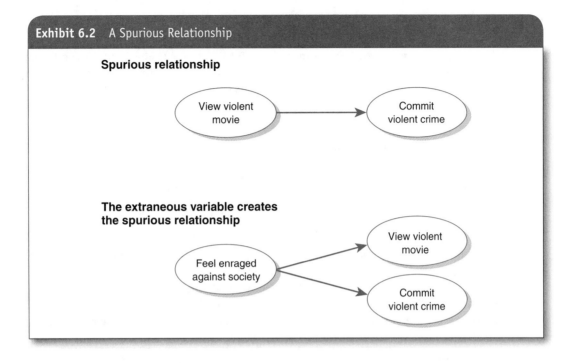

Spurious relationship

View violent movie → Commit violent crime

The extraneous variable creates the spurious relationship

Feel enraged against society → View violent movie

Feel enraged against society → Commit violent crime

means by which poverty and delinquency are connected (Sampson & Laub 1993). In this way, identifying some aspects of the process by which the independent variable influenced the variation in the dependent variable can increase confidence in our conclusion that there was a causal effect (Costner 1989).

Context

In the social world, it is virtually impossible to claim that one and only one independent variable is responsible for causing or affecting a dependent variable. Stated another way, no cause can be separated from the larger context in which it occurs. A cause is really only one of a set of interrelated factors required for the effect (Hage & Meeker 1988; Papineau 1978). When relationships among variables differ across geographic units like counties or across other social settings, or even between different types of individuals, researchers say there is a contextual effect. Identification of the context in which a causal relationship occurs can help us to understand that relationship.

In a classic study of children's aggressive behavior in response to media violence, Albert Bandura, Dorothea Ross, and Sheila Ross (1963) examined several contextual factors. For example, they found children reacted more aggressively after observing men committing violent acts than after observing women committing these same acts. Bandura and colleagues strengthened their conclusions by focusing on a few likely contextual factors.

WHY EXPERIMENT?

Experimental research provides the most powerful design for testing causal hypotheses because it allows us to confidently establish the first three criteria for causality—association, time order, and nonspuriousness. **True experiments** have at least three features that help us meet these criteria:

1. Two comparison groups—one receiving the experimental condition (e.g., treatment or intervention), termed the experimental group, and the other receiving no treatment/intervention or another form thereof, termed the control group

2. Random assignment to the two (or more) comparison groups

3. Assessment of change in the dependent variable for both groups after the experimental condition has been applied

We can determine whether an association exists between the independent and dependent variables in a true experiment because two or more groups differ in terms of their value on the independent variable. One group, the **experimental group,** receives some "treatment" that is a manipulation of the value of the independent variable. In a simple experiment, there may be one other group that does not receive the treatment; it is termed the **control group.**

Experimental group In an experiment, the group of subjects that receives the treatment or experimental manipulation

Control group A comparison group that receives no treatment

Let's consider the Bushman experiment in detail (see the simple diagram in Exhibit 6.3). Does watching a violent video lead to aggressive behavior? Imagine a simple experiment. Suppose you (like Brad Bushman) believe that watching violent movies leads people to be aggressive, commit crimes, and so on. But other people think that violent media has no effect and that it is people who are already predisposed to violence who seek out violent movies to watch. To test your research hypothesis ("Watching violent movies causes aggressive behavior"), you need to compare two randomly assigned groups of subjects, a control group and an experimental group.

First, it is crucial that the two groups be more or less equal at the beginning of the study. If you let students choose which group to be in, the more violent students may pick the violent movie, hoping, either consciously or unconsciously, to have their aggressive habits reinforced. If so, your two groups won't be equivalent at the beginning of the study. As such, any difference in their aggressiveness may be the result of that initial difference (a source of spuriousness), not whether they watched the violent video. You must randomly sort the students into the two different groups. You can do this by flipping a coin for each one of them, or by pulling names out of a hat, or by using a random number table as described in the previous chapter. In any case, the subjects themselves should not be free to choose, nor should you (the experimenter) be free to put them into whatever group you want.

Exhibit 6.3   Experimental Design Used in the Bushman (1995) Research

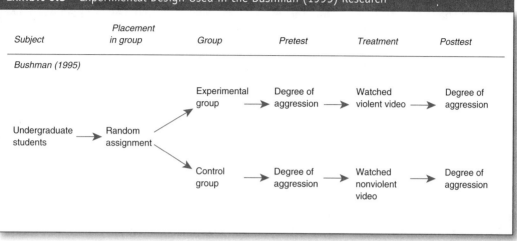

Note that the random assignment of subjects to experimental and comparison groups is not the same as random sampling of individuals from some larger population (see Exhibit 6.4). In fact, **random assignment (randomization)** does not help at all to ensure that the research subjects are representative of some larger population; instead, representativeness is the goal of random sampling. What random assignment does—create two (or more) equivalent groups—is useful for ensuring internal validity, not generalizability.

Next, people in the two groups will interact among themselves. Then, the control group will watch a video about gardening while the experimental group will watch a video featuring a lot of violence. Next, both groups will sit and interact again among themselves. At the end, the interactions within both groups before and after the videos will be coded and you will see whether either group increased in aggressiveness. Thus, you may establish *association.*

Matching is another procedure sometimes used to equate experimental and comparison groups, but by itself it is a poor substitute for randomization. Matching of individuals in a treatment group with those in a comparison group might involve pairing persons on the basis of similarity of gender, age, year in school, or some other characteristic. The basic problem is that, as a practical matter, individuals can be matched on only a few characteristics. Unmatched and unknown differences between the experimental and comparison groups may still influence outcomes.

These defining features of true experimental designs give us a great deal of confidence that we can meet the three basic criteria for identifying causes: association, time order, and nonspuriousness. However, we can strengthen our understanding of causal connections, and increase the likelihood of drawing causally valid conclusions, by also investigating causal mechanism and causal context.

Even after establishing the random assignment of experimental and control groups, you may find an association outside the experimental setting, but it won't establish time order. Perhaps aggressive people choose to watch violent videos, while nonaggressive people do not. So there would be an association, but *not* the causal relation for which we are looking. By controlling who watches the violent video, and when, we establish time order.

All true experiments have a posttest—that is, a measurement of the outcome in both groups after the experimental group has received the treatment. Many true experiments also have pretests that measure the dependent variable before the experimental intervention. A pretest is exactly the same as a posttest, just administered at a different time. Strictly speaking, though, a true experiment does not require a pretest. When researchers use random assignment, the groups' initial scores on the dependent variable (or observed effect or behavior) and on all other variables are very likely to be similar. Any difference in outcome between the experimental and comparison groups is therefore likely to be due to the intervention (or to other processes occurring during the experiment), and the likelihood of a difference just on the basis of chance can be calculated.

An Experiment in Action: Prison Classification and Inmate Behavior

There is wide variability in the criteria used to classify prisoners across the United States. Regardless of how these classifications are made, once these labels are assigned, they have the effect that all labels have: They attach various stigmas and expectations to prisoners. Bench and Allen (2003) state,

> An offender classified as maximum security instantly obtains an image of one who is hard to handle, disrespectful of authority, prone to fight with other inmates, and at a high risk for escape. In contrast, an offender classified as medium security is generally regarded as more manageable, less of an escape risk, and not requiring as much supervision as a maximum-security offender. (p. 371)

To examine whether prison classification actually affects inmate behavior, Bench and Allen (2003) obtained a random sample of 200 inmates admitted to the Utah State Prison who had been classified as maximum security following their initial assessment based on the following criteria: severity of current crime, expected length of incarceration, criminal violence history, escape history, prior institutional commitment, age, history of institutional adjustment, and substance abuse history.

From this group, inmates were randomly assigned to either an experimental group, in which inmates were reclassified to medium-security status, or to a control group, in which inmates retained their maximum-security status. The independent variable, then, was security classification. The dependent variable was the number of disciplinary infractions, or sanctions for violation of prison rules received by each group. The severity of infractions was weighted to control for the severity of the violations (e.g., possession of unauthorized food was weighted lower than assaulting another inmate). The primary hypothesis was that the experimental group, those reclassified as medium security, would have a lower number of disciplinary infractions compared with the control group, the inmates who retained their maximum-security classification. A diagram depicting the experiment is provided in Exhibit 6.5. Results indicated that inmates reclassified to medium security did not receive a lower number of infractions; both groups received about the same number of disciplinary infractions, regardless of security classification.

Exhibit 6.4 Random Sampling Versus Random Assignment

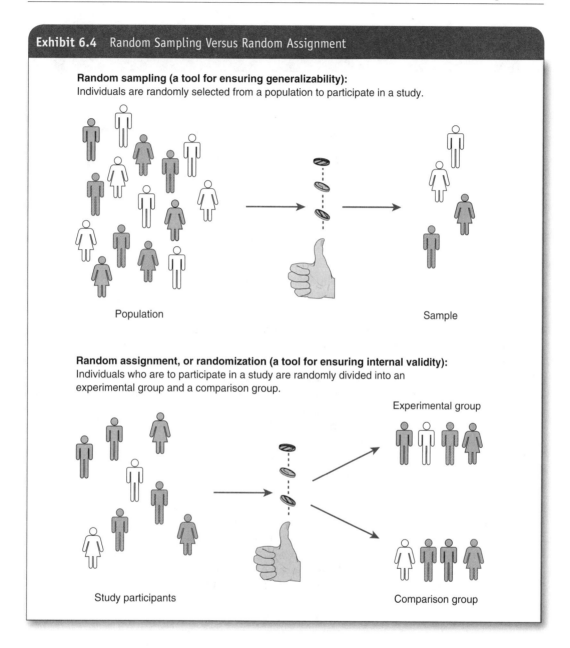

Random sampling (a tool for ensuring generalizability):
Individuals are randomly selected from a population to participate in a study.

Population

Sample

Random assignment, or randomization (a tool for ensuring internal validity):
Individuals who are to participate in a study are randomly divided into an
experimental group and a comparison group.

Experimental group

Study participants

Comparison group

Field Experiments: Determining the Effect
of Incarceration on Employment

As you have seen, social experiments are not always conducted in a laboratory or controlled environment. In fact, many experiments are conducted out in the real world.

Exhibit 6.5 Experiment Examining the Effect of Prison Classification on Inmate Behavior (Bench & Allen 2003)

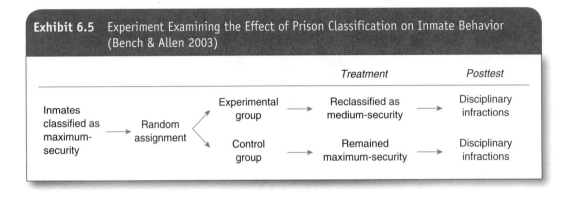

Whenever studies utilize the conditions of an experimental method in a real-world setting, they are termed field experiments. All of the studies examining the effects of arrest on future intimate partner assaults discussed in Chapter 2 were field experiments.

One recent innovative field experiment was conducted by Pager (2007) to determine the effects of incarceration on the likelihood of obtaining employment. This is an extremely important research question because the prison population in the United States has vastly increased over the past 30 years. In addition to the laws barring ex-offenders in some states from obtaining employment in certain sectors, reentering offenders also face other obstacles in finding a job, particularly from the stigma attached to having a record. How could we determine the effects of a formal criminal record on the likelihood of getting a job? Well, we could examine employer attitudes about hiring ex-offenders through a survey, but as you now know, this would not help us isolate a causal relationship between having a record and getting a job. We could interview offenders reentering the community to find out their own experiences, but this would tell us only about a few individuals' experiences. The best way to determine the effects of a criminal record on employment chances would be to conduct a field experiment, which is what Pager did.

Pager (2007) designed a field experiment in which pairs of applicants, one who had a criminal record and one who did not, applied for real jobs. Her study used two male teams of applicants, one composed of two African Americans and one composed of two whites. These individuals were actually college students in Milwaukee, Wisconsin, whom Pager refers to as "testers." The testers were matched on the basis of age, physical appearance, and general style of self-presentation, and all were assigned fictitious résumés that reflected equivalent levels of education (all had a high school education) and equivalent levels of steady work experience. However, one tester within each team was randomly assigned to have a criminal record and the other was not. The fictitious criminal record consisted of a felony drug conviction and 18 months of served prison time. This assignment rotated each week of the study (e.g., one individual played the job applicant with a record one week, and the other did so the next week) as a check against unobserved differences between team members. Same-race testers (one with a criminal record and one without) applied for the same job, one day apart. The African American team applied for a total of 200 jobs, and the white team applied for a total of 150 jobs.

The primary outcome of the study was the proportion of applications that elicited either callbacks from employers or on-the-spot job offers. The testers went through intensive training to become familiar with their assumed profiles and to respond similarly to potential interview questions. As such, the only difference between the two testers on each race team was that one had a criminal record and the other didn't. Because there was random assignment to these two conditions and the other characteristics of the testers were essentially the same, the differences observed in the percentage of callbacks between team members can be assumed to be related to the criminal record only and not to other factors.

The results of Pager's (2007) field experiment were stark. White testers with a criminal record were one-half to one-third less likely to receive a callback from employers, and the effect was even more pronounced for African American applicants. Pager concludes, "Mere contact with the criminal justice system in the absence of any transformative or selective effects severely limits subsequent job prospects. The mark of a criminal record indeed represents a powerful barrier to employment" (p. 145). With such a powerful randomly assigned field experiment, the internal (causal) validity of these findings is strong. The implications of these findings in light of the hundreds of thousands of offenders who attempt to reenter society from prison each year are troubling indeed.

WHAT IF A TRUE EXPERIMENT ISN'T POSSIBLE?

Often, testing a hypothesis with a true experimental design is not feasible. A true experiment may be too costly or take too long to carry out, it may not be ethical to randomly assign subjects to the different conditions, or it may be too late to do so. Researchers may instead use "quasi-experimental" designs that retain several components of experimental design but differ in important details.

In a **quasi-experimental design**, a comparison group is predetermined to be comparable to the treatment group in critical ways, such as being eligible for the same services or being in the same school cohort (Rossi & Freeman 1989: 313). These research designs are only "quasi"-experimental because subjects are not randomly assigned to the comparison and experimental groups. As a result, we cannot be as confident in the comparability of the groups as in true experimental designs. Nonetheless, in order to term a research design "quasi-experimental," we have to be sure that the comparison groups meet specific criteria.

We will discuss here the two major types of quasi-experimental designs, as well as one type—ex post facto (after the fact) control group design—that is often mistakenly termed quasi-experimental (Other types can be found in Cook & Campbell 1979, and Mohr 1992.).

- Nonequivalent control group designs—These designs have experimental and comparison groups that are designated before the treatment occurs but are not created by random assignment.

- Before-and-after designs—This type has a pretest and posttest but no comparison group. In other words, the subjects exposed to the treatment served, at an earlier time, as their own control group.
- Ex post facto control group designs—These designs use nonrandomized control groups designated after the fact.

These designs are weaker than true experiments in establishing the nonspuriousness of an observed association—that it does not result from the influence of some third, uncontrolled variable. On the other hand, because these quasi-experiments do not require the high degree of control necessary in order to achieve random assignment, they can be conducted using more natural procedures in more natural settings, so we may be able to achieve a more complete understanding of causal context. In identifying the mechanism of a causal effect, though, quasi-experiments are neither better nor worse than experiments.

Nonequivalent Control Group Designs

In this type of quasi-experimental design, a comparison group is selected to be as comparable as possible to the treatment group. Two selection methods can be used:

1. *Individual matching*—Individual cases in the treatment group are matched with similar individuals in the comparison group. This can sometimes create a comparison group that is very similar to the experimental group.

2. *Aggregate matching*—In most situations when random assignment is not possible, this second method of matching makes more sense: identifying a comparison group that matches the treatment group in the aggregate rather than trying to match individual cases. This means finding a comparison group that has similar distributions on key variables: the same average age, the same percentage female, and so on.

Case Study: The Effectiveness of Drug Courts

Listwan et al.'s (2003) study of the effectiveness of a drug court on recidivism illustrates a quasi-experimental nonequivalent control group design. Their quasi-experimental design is diagrammed in Exhibit 6.6. Reflecting the priority that policy makers place on controlling drug use and drug-related crime, drug courts have become extremely popular in the United States. They emerged as an alternative to correctional prison and jail-based responses to addicted offenders and generally rely on community-based treatment models. The assumption behind the drug court movement is that drug users and their drug-related crimes will increasingly clog the courts and fill our jails and prisons if their addictions are not remedied. Although drug court programs vary tremendously across jurisdictions, they generally integrate alcohol and drug treatment services with justice system case processing. In addition, they are designed to decrease case-processing time, alleviate the demand of drug-related cases on the court, and decrease jail and prison commitments to

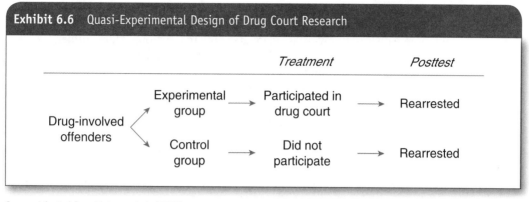

Exhibit 6.6   Quasi-Experimental Design of Drug Court Research

Source: Adapted from Listwan et al. (2003).

drug-related offenders, all of which are supposed to decrease the cost of controlling drug offenders.

Listwan and her colleagues (2003) examined whether participants in the Hamilton County Drug Court program in Cincinnati, Ohio, had lower rates of recidivism for both drug-related and other offenses. Exhibit 6.6 illustrates that there were two groups compared: those who participated in the drug court (experimental group) and those who were eligible but did not receive the drug court treatment services or the additional court supervision (control group). Importantly, the offenders were not randomly assigned to these groups. The researchers simply stated, "Members of [the control group] . . . either refused drug treatment or were refused by the drug court team" (p. 396).

Unfortunately, many evaluations of this nature do not have the ability to employ random assignment, thereby diluting the ability to determine the causal relationship between the treatment and the results. The researchers did examine the potential differences between the two groups and determined that they did not significantly differ in terms of age, race, education, or prior arrest for a drug-related offense, but the experimental group had a higher number of women and people with other prior records not related to drugs. Arrest and incarceration records for the participants were collected for up to 4 years after the program, but results were mixed. While participation in the program decreased the probability that offenders would be rearrested for drug-related offenses, it did not decrease the likelihood that they would be rearrested for other offenses.

Before-and-After Designs

The common feature of before-and-after designs is the absence of a comparison group: All cases are exposed to the experimental treatment. The basis for comparison is instead provided by the pretreatment measures in the experimental group. These designs are thus useful for studies of interventions that are experienced by virtually every case in some population.

The simplest type of before-and-after design is the fixed-sample panel design. In a panel design, the same individuals are studied over time; the research may entail one pretest and one posttest. However, this type of before-and-after design does not qualify as a quasi-experimental design because comparing subjects with themselves at just one earlier point in time does not provide an adequate comparison group. Many influences other than the experimental treatment may affect a subject following the pretest—for instance, basic life experiences for a young subject.

A more powerful way to ensure that the independent variable actually affected the dependent variable when using a before-and-after design is by using a multiple group before-and-after design. In this design, before-and-after comparisons are made of the same variables between different groups. Another type of before-and-after design involves multiple pretest and posttest observations of the same group. Repeated measures panel designs include several pretest and posttest observations, allowing the researcher to study the process by which an intervention or treatment has an impact over time; hence, they are better than a simple before-and-after study.

Time series designs include many (preferably 30 or more) such observations in both pretest and posttest periods. They are particularly useful for studying the impact of new laws or social programs that affect large numbers of people and that are readily assessed by some ongoing measurement. For example, we might use a time series design to study the impact of a new seat belt law on the severity of injuries in automobile accidents, using a monthly state government report on insurance claims. Specific statistical methods are required to analyze time series data, but the basic idea is simple: Identify a trend in the dependent variable up to the date of the intervention, and then control for outside influences and project the trend into the postintervention period. This *projected* trend is then compared to the *actual* trend of the dependent variable after the intervention. A substantial disparity between the actual and projected trend is evidence that the intervention or event had an impact (Rossi & Freeman 1989).

How well do these before-and-after designs meet the five criteria for establishing causality? The before–after comparison enables us to determine whether an *association* exists between the intervention and the dependent variable (because we can determine whether there was a change after the intervention). They also clarify whether the change in the dependent variable occurred after the intervention, so *time order* is not a problem. However, there is no control group so we cannot rule out the influence of extraneous factors as the actual cause of the change we observe; *spuriousness* may be a problem. Some other event may have occurred during the study that resulted in a change in posttest scores. Overall, the longitudinal nature (the measurement of a phenomenon over a long period of time) of before-and-after designs can help to identify causal mechanisms, while the loosening of randomization requirements makes it easier to conduct studies in natural settings, where we learn about the influence of contextual factors.

Case Study: The Effects of the Youth Criminal Justice Act

Carrington and Schulenberg's (2008) study of the effect of the Youth Criminal Justice Act (YCJA) of 2002 in Canada on police discretion with apprehended young offenders illustrates a *time series design*. This design typically includes many pretest and posttest observations that allow the researcher to study the process by which an intervention or a treatment has an impact over time.

One of the major objectives of the YCJA, which came into effect in 2003 in Canada, was to reduce the number of referrals to youth court. The YCJA generally requires police officers who are thinking of charging a minor with a crime to first consider extralegal judicial measures such as giving the youth an informal warning.

To study the effects of the YCJA, Carrington and Schulenberg (2008) examined the number of juveniles who were apprehended and charged from January 1, 1986, through December 31, 2006. The Canadian Uniform Crime Reporting Survey records the number of minors who were charged, as well as the number who were "chargeable" but not charged. The researchers note, "A change in the charge ratio, or proportion of chargeable youth who were charged, is an indication of a change in the use of police discretion with apprehended youth" (p. 355). To control for the actual crime rate of youth, the researchers also examined per capita ratios. Exhibit 6.7 displays the annual rates per 100,000 young persons who were (a) apprehended (i.e., chargeable), (b) charged, and (c) not charged. This clearly shows that the YCJA may have had the intended effect. Of course, the study design leaves open the possibility that something else in 2003 may have happened to effect this change in formal charges against juveniles. However, because there was no known event that could have had such a national impact, the conclusion that this effect is attributable

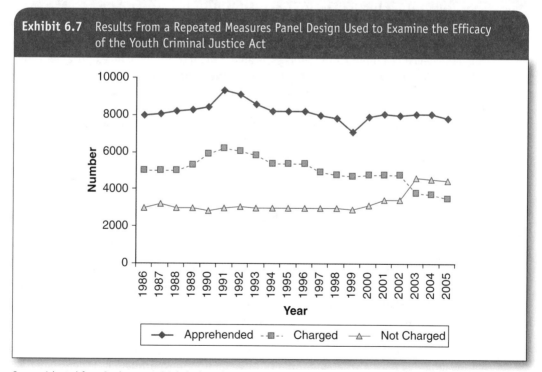

Exhibit 6.7   Results From a Repeated Measures Panel Design Used to Examine the Efficacy of the Youth Criminal Justice Act

Source: Adapted from Carrington and Schulenberg (2008).

to the YCJA is more plausible. As you can see, this time series design is particularly useful for studying the impact of new laws or social programs that affect everyone and can be readily assessed by ongoing measurement.

Ex Post Facto Control Group Designs

The ex post facto control group design appears to be very similar to the nonequivalent control group design and is often confused with it, but it does not meet as well the criteria for quasi-experimental designs. Like nonequivalent control group designs, this design has experimental and comparison groups that are not created by random assignment. However, unlike the groups in nonequivalent control group designs, the groups in ex post facto designs are designated after the treatment has occurred. The problem with this is that if the treatment takes any time at all, people with particular characteristics may select themselves for the treatment or avoid it. Of course, this makes it difficult to determine whether an association between group membership and outcome is spurious. However, the particulars will vary from study to study; in some circumstances, we may conclude that the treatment and control groups are so similar that causal effects can be tested (Rossi & Freeman 1989: 343–344).

Case Study: Does an Arrest Increase Delinquency?

David P. Farrington's (1977) classic study of how arrest sometimes increases delinquency, called the deviance amplification process, is an excellent example of an ex post facto control group design (Exhibit 6.8). Farrington tested the hypothesis that juveniles who were publicly labeled as deviant through being convicted of a delinquent act would increase their deviant behavior compared with those who were not so labeled. Using secondary data from the Cambridge Study of Delinquent Development, Farrington measured outcomes of 400 London working-class youths from age 8 to 18. Results indicated that youth who were labeled as delinquent (through conviction) subsequently committed more delinquent acts than similar youth who were not labeled in this way.

WHAT ARE THE THREATS TO INTERNAL VALIDITY AND GENERALIZABILITY IN EXPERIMENTS?

Like any research design, experimental designs must be evaluated for their ability to yield valid conclusions. True experiments are particularly well suited to producing valid conclusions about causality (internal validity), but they are less likely to fare well in achieving generalizability. Quasi-experiments may provide more generalizable results than true experiments, but they are more prone to problems of internal invalidity (although some design schemes allow the researcher to rule out almost as many potential sources of internal invalidity as does a true experiment). In general, nonexperimental designs (such as survey research and participant observation) permit less certainty about internal validity.

Exhibit 6.8   Ex Post Facto Control Group Design: Farrington's (1977) Test of Deviance Amplification

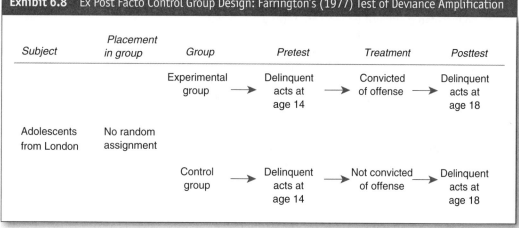

Causal (Internal) Validity

An experiment's ability to yield valid conclusions about causal effects is determined by the comparability of its experimental and comparison groups. First, of course, a comparison group must be created. Second, this comparison group must be so similar to the experimental group that it will show what the experimental group would be like if it did not receive the experimental treatment—that is, if the independent variable was not varied. For example, the only difference between the two groups in Bushman's (1995) study was that one group watched a violent movie and the other group did not.

There are five basic sources of internal invalidity:

1. *Selection bias*—When characteristics of the experimental and comparison group subjects differ

2. *Endogenous change*—When the subjects develop or change during the experiment as part of an ongoing process independent of the experimental treatment

3. *External events/history effects*—When something occurs during the experiment, other than the treatment, that influences outcome scores

4. *Contamination*—When either the experimental group or the comparison group is aware of the other group and is influenced in the posttest as a result (Mohr 1992)

5. *Treatment misidentification*—When variation in the independent variable (the treatment) is associated with variation in the observed outcome, but the change occurs through a process that the researcher has not identified

Selection Bias

You may already realize that the composition of the experimental and comparison groups in a true experiment is unlikely to be affected by their difference. If it were affected, it would cause selection bias. Random assignment equates the groups' characteristics, though with some possibility for error due to chance. The likelihood of difference due to chance can be identified with appropriate statistics.

Even when the random assignment plan works, the groups can differ over time because of differential attrition, or what can be thought of as *deselection*—that is, the groups become different because for various reasons some subjects drop out of groups. This is not a likely problem for a laboratory experiment that occurs in one session, but for experiments in which subjects must participate over time, differential attrition may become a problem.

When subjects are not randomly assigned to treatment and comparison groups, as in nonequivalent control group designs, there is a serious threat of selection bias. Even if the researcher selects a comparison group that matches the treatment group on important variables, there is no guarantee that the groups were similar initially in terms of the dependent variable or another characteristic that ultimately influences posttest scores.

Endogenous Change

The type of problem considered an endogenous change occurs when natural developments in the subjects, independent of the experimental treatment, account for some or all of the observed change between pretest and posttest. Endogenous change includes three specific threats to internal validity:

1. *Testing.* Taking the pretest can in itself influence posttest scores. Subjects may learn something or be sensitized to an issue by the pretest and, as a result, respond differently when they are asked the same questions in the posttest.

2. *Maturation.* Changes in outcomes scores during experiments that involve a lengthy treatment period may be due to maturation. Subjects may age or gain experience in school or grow in knowledge, all as part of a natural maturational experience, and thus respond differently on the posttest from the way they responded on the pretest.

3. *Regression.* People experience cyclical or episodic changes that result in different posttest scores, a phenomenon known as a regression effect. Subjects who are chosen for a study because they received very low scores on a test may show improvement in the posttest, on average, simply because some of the low scorers had been having a bad day. It is hard, in many cases, to know whether a phenomenon is subject to naturally occurring fluctuations, so the possibility of regression effects should be considered whenever subjects are selected because of their initial extremely high or low values on the outcome variable (Mohr 1992: 56, 71–79).

Testing, maturation, and regression effects are generally not a problem in true experiments. Both the experimental group and the comparison group take the pretest, and they are both subject to maturation and regression effects, so even if these possibilities lead to a change in posttest scores, the comparison between the experimental and control groups will not be affected because the groups started off with similar characteristics. Of course, in experiments with no pretest, testing effects themselves are not a problem. However, in most before-and-after designs without a comparison group, endogenous change effects could occur and lead to an invalid conclusion that there had been an effect of the independent variable.

External Events

External events, sometimes referred to as the history effect during the experiment—things that happen outside the experiment—can also change the subjects' outcome scores. An example of this is a newsworthy event that is relevant to the focus of an experiment to which subjects are exposed. What if researchers were evaluating the effectiveness of a mandatory arrest policy in decreasing incidents of intimate partner assault, and an event such as the murder trial of O. J. Simpson occurred during the experiment? This would clearly be a historical event that might compromise the results. This trial saw a momentous amount of media coverage, and as a result intimate partner assault and homicide were given a tremendous amount of attention. Because of this increased awareness, many victims of intimate partner violence reported their victimizations during this time—police agencies and women's shelters were flooded with calls. If a researcher had been using calls to police in a particular jurisdiction as an indicator of the incidence of intimate partner assault, this historical event would have seriously jeopardized the internal validity of his or her results. Why? Because the increase in police calls would have had more to do with the trial than with any recent change in arrest policies.

Contamination

Contamination occurs in an experiment when the comparison group is in some way affected by, or affects, the treatment group. This problem basically arises from failure to adequately control the conditions of the experiment. When comparison group members become aware that they are being denied some advantage, they may increase their efforts to compensate, creating a problem called compensatory rivalry, or the John Henry effect (Cook & Campbell 1979: 55). On the other hand, control group members may become demoralized if they feel that they have been left out of some valuable treatment and may perform worse than they would have outside the experiment. The treatment may seem, in comparison, to have a more beneficial effect than it actually did. Both compensatory rivalry and demoralization can thus distort the impact of the experimental treatment.

The danger of contamination can be minimized if the experiment is conducted in a laboratory, if members of the experimental group and the comparison group have no contact while the study is in progress, and if the treatment is relatively brief. To the degree that these conditions are not met, the likelihood of contamination will increase.

Treatment Misidentification

Treatment misidentification occurs when subjects experience a "treatment" that wasn't intended by the researcher. Treatment misidentification has at least three sources:

1. *Expectancies of experimental staff.* Change among experimental subjects may be due to the positive expectancies of the experimental staff who are delivering the

treatment rather than due to the treatment itself. This type of treatment misidentification can occur even in randomized experiments when well-trained staff convey their enthusiasm for an experimental program to the subjects in subtle ways, and because social programs are delivered by human beings, these expectancy effects can be very difficult to control in field experiments. However, in some experiments concerning the effects of treatments such as medical drugs, double-blind procedures can be used. Staff will deliver the treatments without knowing which subjects are getting the treatment and which are receiving a placebo—something that looks like the treatment but has no effect. In fact, the prison experiment discussed earlier in this chapter used a double-blind procedure to randomly assign inmates to a security classification category. In the experiment, only the executive director of the corrections department and the director of classification were aware of the research. Correctional staff, other individuals who worked with the inmates, and the inmates themselves were unaware of the study. In this way, any expectancies that the staff may have had were unlikely to affect inmate behavior.

2. *Placebo effect.* Treatment misidentification may occur when subjects receive a treatment that they consider likely to be beneficial, and then improve because of that expectation rather than the treatment itself. In medical research, the placebo is often a chemically inert substance that looks like the experimental drug but actually has no medical effect. Research indicates that the placebo effect produces positive health effects in two-thirds of patients suffering from relatively mild medical problems (Goleman 1993). Placebo effects can also occur in social science research. The only way to reduce this threat to internal validity is to treat the comparison group with something similar.

3. *Hawthorne effect.* Members of the treatment group may change in terms of the dependent variable because their participation in the study makes them feel special. This problem can occur when treatment group members compare their situation to that of the control group members who are not receiving the treatment. In this case, this is a type of contamination effect. However, experimental group members could feel special simply because they are in the experiment. The Hawthorne effect is named after a famous productivity experiment at the Hawthorne electric plant outside Chicago. Workers were moved to a special room for a study of the effects of lighting intensity and other work conditions on their productivity. After this move, the workers began to increase their output no matter what change was made in their working conditions, even when the conditions became worse. The researchers concluded that the workers felt they should work harder because they were part of a special experiment.

Generalizability

The need for generalizable findings can be thought of as the Achilles heel of the true experimental design. The design components that are essential for a true experiment and minimize the threats to causal (internal) validity also make it more difficult to achieve sample generalizability, or the ability to apply the findings to a clearly defined, larger population.

Sample Generalizability

Subjects who can be recruited for a laboratory experiment, randomly assigned to a group, and kept under carefully controlled conditions for the study's duration are often not a representative sample of any large population of interest. In fact, most are recruited from college populations. Can they be expected to react to the experimental treatment in the same way as members of the larger population who are not students or may never have gone to college? The more artificial the experimental arrangements, the greater the problem can be (Campbell & Stanley 1996).

Not only do the characteristics of the subjects themselves determine the generalizability of the experimental results, but the generalizability of the treatment and of the setting for the experiment also must be considered (Cook & Campbell 1979). Field experiments are likely to yield findings that are more generalizable to broader populations than are laboratory experiments using subjects who must volunteer. When random selection is not feasible, the researchers may be able to increase generalizability by selecting several sites for conducting the experiments that offer obvious contrasts in the key variables of the population. The follow-up studies to Sherman and Berk's (1984) work, for example (see Chapter 2), were conducted in cities that differed from Minneapolis, the original site, in social class and ethnic composition. As a result, although the findings are not statistically generalizable to a larger population, they do give some indication of the study's general applicability (Cook & Campbell 1979).

External Validity (Cross-Population Generalizability)

Researchers are often interested in determining whether the treatment effects identified in an experiment hold true for subgroups of subjects or across different populations. Of course, determining that a relationship between the treatment and the outcome variable holds true for certain subgroups does not establish that the same relationship also holds for these subgroups in the larger population, but it does suggest that the relationship might have external validity (see Chapters 1 and 5).

External validity The applicability of a treatment effect (or noneffect) across subgroups within an experiment or across different populations and settings

Example of external validity: Sherman and Berk (1984) found that arrest reduced repeat offenses for employed subjects but not for unemployed subjects. The effect of arrest thus varied with employment status, so a conclusion that arrest deters recidivism would not be externally valid.

Interaction of Testing and Treatment

A variation of the problem of external validity occurs when the experimental treatment is effective only when particular conditions created by the experiment occur. For example, if subjects have had a pretest, it may sensitize them to a particular issue, so when they are exposed to the treatment, their reaction is different from what it would have been if they had not taken the pretest. In other words, testing and treatment interact to produce the outcome.

Suppose you were interested in the effects of a diversity training film on prejudicial attitudes. After answering questions in a pretest about their attitudes on various topics related to diversity (e.g., racial or sexual prejudice), the subjects generally became more sensitive to the issue of prejudice without seeing the training film. On the posttest, then, their attitudes may be different from pretest attitudes simply because they have become sensitized to the issue of diversity through pretesting. In this situation, the treatment may actually have an effect, but it would be difficult to determine how *much* of the effect was attributable to the sensitizing pretest and how much was due to seeing the film.

This possibility can be tested with what is called the Solomon four-group design. In this version of a true experimental design, subjects are randomly assigned to at least two experimental groups and at least two comparison groups. One experimental group and one comparison group will have a pretest, and the other two groups will not have a pretest (see Exhibit 6.9). If testing and treatment do interact, the difference in outcome scores between the experimental and comparison groups will differ between the subjects who took the pretest and those who did not.

Ultimately, the external validity of experimental results will increase with the success of replications taking place at different times and places, using different forms of the treatment. As indicated by the replications of the Sherman and Berk (1984) study of arrest for domestic violence, the result may be a more detailed, nuanced understanding of the hypothesized effect.

The Element of Time in Research

Nonexperimental research designs can be either cross-sectional or longitudinal. In a cross-sectional research design, all data are collected at one point in time. Identifying the time order of effects—what happened first, second, and so on—is critical for developing a causal analysis, but can be an insurmountable problem with a cross-sectional design. In longitudinal research designs, data are collected at two or more points in time, so identification of the time order of effects can be quite straightforward. You can think of an experiment as a type of longitudinal design because subjects are observed at two or more points in time.

Exhibit 6.9   Solomon Four-Group Design Testing the Interaction of Pretesting and Treatment

Experimental group	R	O1	X	O2
Comparison group	R	O1		O2
Experimental group	R		X	O2
Comparison group	R			O2

Note: R = random assignment; O = observation (pretest or posttest); X = experimental treatment.

Much of the research you have encountered so far in this text has been cross-sectional. Although each survey and interview takes some time to carry out, if it measures the actions, attitudes, and characteristics of respondents at only one time, it is considered cross-sectional. The name comes from the idea that a snapshot from a cross-section of the population is obtained at one point in time.

In contrast, longitudinal research collects data at two or more points in time and, as such, data can be ordered in time. By measuring the value of cases on an independent variable and a dependent variable at different times, the researcher can determine whether variation in the independent variable precedes variation in the dependent variable.

In some longitudinal designs, the same sample (or panel) is followed over time; in other designs, sample members are rotated or completely replaced. The population from which the sample is selected may be defined broadly, as when a longitudinal survey of the general population is conducted, or the population may be defined narrowly, as when members of a specific age group are sampled at multiple points in time. The frequency of follow-up measurement can vary, ranging from a before-and-after design with just one follow-up to studies in which various indicators are measured every month for many years.

Collecting data at two or more points in time rather than at one time can prove difficult for a number of reasons: lack of long-term funding, participant attrition, and so on. Quite frequently, researchers cannot or are simply unwilling to delay completion of a study for even 1 year in order to collect follow-up data. But think of the many research questions that really should involve a much longer follow-up period: Does community-oriented policing decrease rates of violent crime? What is the impact of job training in prison on recidivism rates? How effective are batterer treatment programs for individuals convicted of intimate partner assault? Do parenting programs for young mothers and fathers reduce the likelihood of their children becoming delinquent? It is safe to say that we will never have enough longitudinal data to answer many important research questions. Nonetheless, the value of longitudinal data is so great that every effort should be made to develop longitudinal research designs when they are appropriate for the research question being asked. The following discussion of the three major types of longitudinal designs will give you a sense of the possibilities (see Exhibit 6.10).

Repeated Cross-Sectional Designs

Studies that use a **repeated cross-sectional design**, also known as **trend studies**, have become fixtures of the political arena around election time. Particularly in presidential election years, we accustom ourselves to reading weekly, even daily, reports on the percentage of the population that supports each candidate. Similar polls are conducted to track sentiment on many other social issues. For example, a 1993 poll reported that 52% of adult Americans supported a ban on the possession of handguns, compared with 41% in a similar poll conducted in 1991. According to pollster Louis Harris, this increase indicated a "sea change" in public attitudes (cited in Barringer 1993: A14). Another researcher said, "It shows that people are responding to their experience [of an increase in handgun-related killings]" (cited in Barringer 1993: A14).

Exhibit 6.10   Three Types of Longitudinal Design

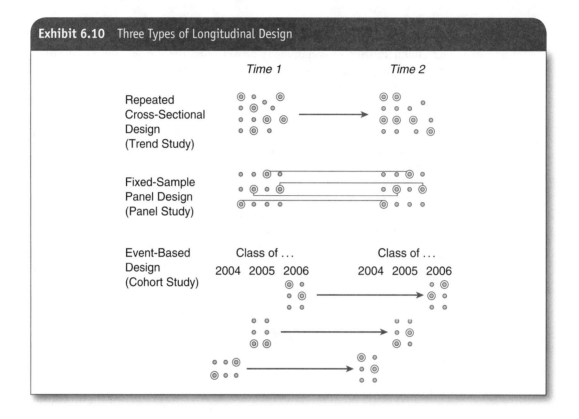

Repeated cross-sectional design (trend study) A type of longitudinal study in which data are collected at two or more points in time from different samples of the same population

---

Repeated cross-sectional surveys are conducted as follows:

1. A sample is drawn from a population at Time 1, and data are collected from the sample.

2. As time passes, some people leave the population and others enter it.

3. At Time 2, a different sample is drawn from this population.

Fixed-Sample Panel Designs

Panel designs allow us to identify changes in individuals, groups, or whatever we are studying. This is the process for conducting fixed-sample panel designs:

1. A sample (called a panel) is drawn from a population at Time 1, and data are collected from the sample.

2. As time passes, some panel members become unavailable for follow-up, and the population changes.

3. At Time 2, data are collected from the same people as at Time 1 (the panel), except for those people who cannot be located.

Because a panel design follows the same individuals, it is better than a repeated cross-sectional design for testing causal hypotheses. For example, Sampson and Laub (1990) used a fixed-sample panel design to investigate the effect of childhood deviance on adult crime. They studied a sample of white males in Boston when the subjects were between 10 and 17 years old and then followed up when the subjects were in their adult years. Data were collected from multiple sources, including the subjects themselves and criminal justice records. The researchers found that children who had been committed to a correctional school for persistent delinquency were much more likely than other children in the study to commit crimes as adults: 61% were arrested between the ages of 25 and 32, compared with 14% of those who had not been in correctional schools as juveniles (p. 614). In this study, juvenile delinquency unquestionably occurred before adult criminality. If the researchers had used a cross-sectional design to study the past of adults, the juvenile delinquency measure might have been biased by memory lapses, by self-serving recollections about behavior as juveniles, or by loss of agency records. The problem, of course, is that tracking people for years is extremely expensive, and many people in the original sample drop out for various reasons. Panel designs are also a challenge to implement successfully, and often are not even attempted, because of two major difficulties:

1. *Expense and attrition.* It can be difficult, and very expensive, to keep track of individuals over a long period, and inevitably the proportion of panel members who can be located for follow-up will decline over time. Panel studies often lose more than one quarter of their members through attrition (Miller 1991: 170), and because those who are lost are often dissimilar to those who remain in the panel, the sample's characteristics begin to change and internal validity is compromised.

2. *Subject fatigue.* Panel members may grow weary of repeated interviews and drop out of the study, or they may become so used to answering the standard questions in the survey that they start giving stock answers rather than actually thinking about their current feelings or actions (Campbell 1992). This is called the problem of subject fatigue. Fortunately, subjects do not often seem to become fatigued in this way, particularly if the research staff have maintained positive relations with them.

Event-Based Designs

In an event-based design, often called a *cohort study*, the follow-up samples (at one or more times) are selected from the same cohort, people who all have experienced a similar event or a common starting point. Examples include the following:

- *Birth cohorts:* those who share a common period of birth (those born in the 1940s, 1950s, 1960s, etc.);
- *Seniority cohorts:* those who have worked at the same place for about 5 years, about 10 years, and so on; and
- *School cohorts:* freshmen, sophomores, juniors, and seniors.

HOW DO EXPERIMENTERS PROTECT THEIR SUBJECTS?

Social science experiments often raise difficult ethical issues. You have already read in Chapter 3 about Philip Zimbardo's (2004) Stanford Prison Experiment. This experiment was actually ended after only 6 days, rather than after the planned 2 weeks, because of the psychological harm that seemed to result from the unexpectedly sadistic behavior of some of the "guards." Although Zimbardo's follow-up research convinced him that there had been no lasting harm to subjects, concern about the potential for harm would preclude many such experiments today.

In spite of the ethical standard of disclosure and "informed consent" by subjects, deception is an essential part of many experimental designs. As a result, contentious debate continues about the interpretation of this standard. Experimental evaluation of social programs also poses ethical dilemmas because they require researchers to withhold possibly beneficial treatment from some of the subjects just on the basis of chance (Boruch 1997). In this section, we will give special attention to the problems of deception and the distribution of benefits in experimental research.

Deception

Deception is used in social experiments to create more "realistic" treatments, often within the confines of a laboratory. You learned in Chapter 3 about Stanley Milgram's (1965) use of deception in his classic study of obedience to authority. Volunteers were recruited for what they were told was a study of the learning process, not a study of "obedience to authority." The experimenter told the volunteers that they were administering electric shocks to a "student" in the next room, when there were actually neither students nor shocks. Subjects seemed to believe the deception.

Whether or not you believe that you could be deceived in this way, you are not likely to be invited to participate in an experiment such as Milgram's. Current federal regulations preclude deception in research that might trigger such upsetting feelings. However, deception is still routine in many college laboratories. The question that must always be answered is, "Is there sufficient justification to allow the use of deception?"

Selective Distribution of Benefits

Field experiments conducted to evaluate social programs also can involve issues of informed consent (Hunt 1985). One ethical issue that is somewhat unique to field experiments is the **distribution of benefits**: How much are subjects harmed by the way treatments are distributed in the experiment? For example, Sherman and Berk's (1984) experiment, and its successors, required police to make arrests in domestic violence cases largely on the basis of a random process. When arrests were not made, did the subjects' abused spouses suffer? Price, Van Ryn, and Vinokur (1992) randomly assigned unemployed individuals who had volunteered for job-search help to an intensive program. Were the unemployed volunteers assigned to the comparison group at a big disadvantage?

Is it ethical to give some potentially advantageous or disadvantageous treatment to people on a random basis? For example, in the drug court field experiment, is it ethical to randomly assign those who wanted extra help with their drug problem to the comparison group that did not receive extra treatment? Random distribution of benefits is justified when the researchers do not know whether some treatment actually is beneficial—and, of course, it is the goal of the experiment to find out. Chance is as reasonable a basis for distributing the treatment as any other. Also, if insufficient resources are available to fully fund a benefit for every eligible person, distribution of the benefit on the basis of chance to equally needy persons is ethically defensible (Boruch 1997).

CONCLUSION

True experiments play two critical roles in criminological research. First, they are the best research design for testing causal hypotheses. Even when conditions preclude the use of a true experimental design, many research designs can be improved by adding experimental components. Second, true experiments provide a comparison point for evaluating the ability of the other research designs to achieve causally valid results.

In spite of their obvious strengths, true experiments are used infrequently to study many research problems related to criminology and criminal justice. There are three basic reasons for this:

1. The experiments required to test many important hypotheses require more resources than most social scientists can access.

2. Most research problems of interest to social scientists simply are not amenable to experimental designs, for reasons ranging from ethical considerations to the limited possibilities for randomly assigning people to different conditions in the real world.

3. The requirements of experimental design usually preclude large-scale studies and so limit generalizability to a degree that is unacceptable to many social scientists.

When a true experimental design is not feasible, researchers may instead use a quasi-experimental design, including nonequivalent control group designs, before-and-after designs, and ex post facto control group designs. As the studies highlighted in this chapter show, researchers examining issues related to criminology and criminal justice have been very creative in developing experimental research projects in the real world that can appropriately meet the demands of causal inference.

KEY TERMS

Association

Before-and-after designs

Causal effect

Ceteris paribus

Cohort study

Compensatory rivalry

Context

Contextual effect

Control group

Cross-sectional research design

Debriefing

Differential attrition

Distribution of benefits

Double-blind procedures

Endogenous change

Event-based design

Ex post facto control group design

Expectancies

Experimental group

Extraneous variable

Fixed-sample panel design

Hawthorne effect

History effect

Longitudinal research design

Matching

Mechanism

Nonequivalent control group designs

Nonspuriousness

Placebo effect

Posttest

Pretest

Quasi-experimental design

Random assignment

Regression effect

Repeated measures panel design

Selection bias

Solomon four-group design

Spurious relationship

Time order

Time series design

Treatment misidentification

True experiment

HIGHLIGHTS

- A causal explanation relies on a comparison. The value of cases on the dependent variable is measured after they have been exposed to variation on an independent variable. This measurement is compared to what the value of cases on the dependent variable would have been if they had not been exposed to the variation in the independent variable. The validity of causal conclusions rests on how closely the comparison group comes to the ideal counterfactual.

- Three criteria are generally viewed as necessary for identifying a causal relationship: association between the variables, proper time order, and nonspuriousness of the association. In addition, the basis for concluding that a causal relationship exists is strengthened by identification of a causal mechanism and the context for the relationship.

- Association between two variables is in itself insufficient evidence of a causal relationship. This point is commonly made with the expression, "Correlation does not prove causation."

- Experiments use random assignment to make comparison groups as similar as possible at the outset of an experiment in order to reduce the risk of spurious effects due to extraneous variables.

- Nonexperimental designs use statistical controls to reduce the risk of spuriousness. A variable is controlled when it is held constant so that the association between the independent and dependent variables can be assessed without being influenced by the control variable.

- Longitudinal designs are usually preferable to cross-sectional designs for establishing the time order of effects. Longitudinal designs vary in terms of whether the same people are measured at different times, how the population of interests is defined, and how frequently follow-up measurements are taken. Fixed-sample panel designs provide the strongest test for the time order of effects, but they can be difficult to carry out successfully because of their expense as well as subject attrition and fatigue.

- Ethical and practical constraints often prevent the use of experimental designs.

EXERCISES

Discussing Research

1. Review articles in several newspapers, copying down all causal assertions. These might include assertions that the presence of community policing was related positively to decreasing rates of violence, claims that the stock market declined because of uncertainty in the Middle East, or explanations about why a murder was committed. Inspect the articles carefully, noting all evidence used to support the causal assertions. Which criteria for establishing causality are met? What other potentially important influences on the reported outcome have been overlooked?

2. Select several research articles in professional journals that assert, or imply, that they have identified a causal relationship between two or more variables. Is each of the criteria for establishing the existence of a causal relationship met? Find a study in which subjects were assigned randomly to experimental and comparison groups to reduce the risk of spurious influences on the supposedly causal relationship. How convinced are you by the study?

3. The web-based interactive exercises contain lessons on causation and experimental design. Try them out at this point.

Finding Research on the Web

1. Read an original article describing a social experiment. (Social psychology "readers," collections of such articles for undergraduates, are a good place to find interesting studies.) Critique the article, focusing on the extent to which experimental conditions were controlled and the causal mechanism was identified. Based on the study's control over conditions and identification of the causal mechanism, how confident were you in the causal conclusions?

2. Go to the website of the Community Policing Consortium at www.communitypolicing.org. What causal assertions are made on the site? Pick one of these assertions and propose a research design with which to test this assertion. Be specific.

3. Go to SocioSite at www.sociosite.net. Choose "Subject Areas." Then choose "Crime" or "Criminology." Find an example of research that has been done using experimental methods.

Explain the experiment. Choose at least five of the key terms for this chapter (listed above) that are relevant to and incorporated in the research experiment you have located on the web. Explain how each of the five key terms you have chosen plays a role in the research example you have found.

Critiquing Research

1. Go to this book's Study Site, www.sagepub.com/bachmanfrccj2e, and choose two research articles that include some attention to causality (as indicated by a check in that column of the article matrix). Describe the approach taken in each article to establish causality. How do the approaches differ from each other? Which approach seems stronger to you?

2. Select a true experiment, perhaps from the *Journal of Experimental Criminology* or from sources suggested in class. Diagram the experiment using the exhibits in this chapter as a model. Discuss the extent to which experimental conditions were controlled and the causal mechanism was identified. How confident can you be in the causal conclusions from the study, based on review of the threats to internal validity discussed in this chapter: selection bias, endogenous change, external events, contamination, and treatment misidentification? How generalizable do you think the study's results are to the population from which the cases were selected? How generalizable are they to specific subgroups in the study? How thoroughly do the researchers discuss these issues?

3. Repeat #2 above with a quasi-experiment.

4. Go to the Disaster Center website, www.disastercenter.com/crime. Select links to state crime reports and compare the recent crime rates in two states. Report on the prevalence of the crimes you have examined. Propose a causal explanation for variation in crime between states, over time, or both. What research design would you propose to test this explanation? Elaborate.

5. Go to Crime Stoppers USA's (CSUSA) website at www.crimestopusa.com. Check out "About Us" and then "What is Crime Stoppers?" How is CSUSA "fighting crime"? What does CSUSA's approach assume about the cause of crime? Do you think CSUSA's approach to fighting crime is based on valid conclusions about causality? Explain.

Making Research Ethical

1. Under what conditions do you think that randomized assignment of subjects to a specific treatment is ethical in criminal justice research? Was it ethical for Sherman and Berk (1984) and the researchers who conducted the replication studies to randomly assign individuals accused of domestic violence to an arrest or nonarrest treatment? What about in a laboratory study with students like yourself? Do you think it would be ethical to assign students randomly to different groups, with some receiving stressful stimuli, like loud noises?

2. Critique the ethics of one of the experiments presented in this chapter, or some other experiment you have read about. What specific rules do you think should guide researchers' decisions about subject deception and the selective distribution of benefits?

3. Bushman (1995) tested the impact of watching a violent video on students' level of aggressiveness. He found that watching the violent video increased aggressiveness. Do you

consider it ethical to expose subjects to an intervention that might increase their aggressiveness? Are there any situations in which you would not approve of such research? Any types of subjects you would exclude from such research? Any limits you would draw on the type of intervention that could be tested? Would you impose any requirements for debriefing?

Developing a Research Proposal

How will you try to establish the causal effects you hypothesize?

1. Identify at least one hypothesis involving what you expect is a causal relationship.
2. Identify key variables that should be controlled in your survey design in order to decrease the possibility of arriving at a spurious conclusion about the hypothesized causal effect. Draw on relevant research literature and social theory to identify these variables.
3. Add a longitudinal component to your research design. Explain why you decided to use this particular longitudinal design.
4. Review the criteria for establishing a causal effect and discuss your ability to satisfy each one.

Performing Data Analysis in SPSS or Excel

We can use the GSS2004 mini data to learn how causal hypotheses can be evaluated with non-experimental data.

1. Specify four hypotheses in which CAPPUN is the dependent variable and the independent variable is also measured with a question in the GSS2004. The independent variables should have no more than 10 valid values (check the variable list).
    a. Inspect the frequency distributions of each independent variable in your hypotheses. If it appears that any have little valid data or were coded with more than 10 categories, substitute another independent variable.
    b. Generate cross tabulations that show the association between CAPPUN and each of the independent variables. Make sure that CAPPUN is the row variable and that you select "Column Percents."
    c. Does support for capital punishment vary across the categories of any of the independent variables? If so, by how much? Would you conclude that there is an association, as hypothesized, for any pairs of variables?
2. Now use the "HOMICIDE.por" data set, which contains a sample of homicide defendants in 30 of the largest counties in the United States. Do prior convictions influence the number of days to which homicide defendants are sentenced?
    a. Obtain a frequency distribution for the variable PRCONV (prior convictions). According to the data, do homicide defendants frequently have prior convictions? What do you hypothesize is the relationship between prior convictions and sentence length? Why?
    b. Compare the mean sentence length in days received by defendants against their number of prior convictions. For example, do defendants who had no prior convictions receive a shorter sentence length compared to those with at least one prior conviction? Do the data support your hypothesis? Do any of the categories deviate from what you hypothesized? Explain.

c. Recode the PRCONV variable into a new dichotomous variable, measuring whether the homicide defendant had prior convictions or no prior convictions. If necessary, reword your hypothesis to reflect the dichotomous nature of the new variable.

d. Test your hypothesis by comparing the mean sentence length in days received by defendants with prior convictions and those with no prior convictions. What conclusions do you make about the relationship between prior convictions and sentence length of homicide defendants?

Student Study Site

The companion Student Study Site for *Fundamentals of Research in Criminology and Criminal Justice* can be found at www.sagepub.com/bachmanfrccj2e.

Visit the Student Study Site to enhance your understanding of the chapter content and to discover additional resources that will take your learning one step further. You can enhance your understanding of the chapters by using the comprehensive study material, which includes interactive exercises, e-flashcards, web exercises, practice self-tests, and more. You will also find special features, such as Learning From Journal Articles, which incorporates Sage's online journal collection.

Survey Research

In this chapter, we will introduce you to survey research. You will learn about the challenges of designing a survey along with some basic rules of question construction. We will also discuss the ways in which surveys can be administered. Important ethical issues surrounding surveys are discussed in the final section. By the chapter's end, you should be well on your way to becoming an informed consumer of survey reports and a knowledgeable developer of survey designs. We hope you will have an increased appreciation for the fact that designing a survey involves a great deal of thought and planning and is much more difficult than putting a few questions together. In addition, you will become a more informed student of the methodological issues surrounding the measurement of violent victimization in the United States.

SURVEY RESEARCH IN ACTION: MEASURING VICTIMIZATION

Despite a research effort spanning more than three decades, the magnitude of rape, stalking, and intimate-perpetrated violence (IPV) against men and women is still frequently disputed. For many reasons, including the historical stigma attached to these crimes, victim fear of retaliation from their perpetrators, and other safety concerns, estimating incidence rates of this violence has always been a difficult task. You have already learned that one source of statistical information about violent crime in the United States is the Uniform Crime Reporting Program, which is compiled by the FBI from reports of victimization to police. In order to fill the gaps that we know exist in police reports, random sample surveys of the population are now being used as the social science tool of choice for measuring incidents of violent victimization, particularly violence within families. However, not unlike other research designs already discussed, surveys employ a diverse number of methodologies, and different definitions of violence result in widely varied estimates.

To increase our understanding of violent victimization, the National Institute of Justice and the Centers for Disease Control and Prevention cosponsored a national telephone survey called the National Violence Against Men and Women (NVAMW) Survey (Tjaden & Thoennes 2000). Respondents to the NVAMW Survey were asked about a number of health and safety concerns, including physical assault they experienced as children by adult caretakers, physical assault they experienced as adults by any type of perpetrator, and forcible rape or stalking they experienced at any time in their life by any type of perpetrator. In this chapter, we will use this project along with the U.S. Justice Department's National Crime Victimization Survey (NCVS) to illustrate some key features of survey research. After an initial review of the reasons for using survey methods, we will explain the major steps in questionnaire design, consider the features of four types of surveys, highlight the unique challenges associated with each, and then suggest possible solutions. Important ethical issues are discussed in the final section.

WHAT IS A SURVEY?

Survey research involves the collection of information from a sample of individuals through their responses to questions. In addition to social scientists, many newspaper editors, political pundits, and marketing gurus have turned to survey research because it is an efficient method for systematically collecting data from a broad spectrum of individuals and social settings. The results of surveys are broadcast daily on most network news programs.

The U.S. Bureau of the Census also began to supplement its decennial (every 10 years) census with more frequent surveys of population samples to monitor respondents' income and other economic variables. And in 1973, the U.S. Department of Justice implemented the National Crime Surveys to capture incidents of crime victimization not reported to police.

Since the early days of survey research, professional survey organizations have provided a base of support for social science researchers affiliated with universities. The development of computers also aided the growth of survey research and allowed for great increases in the speed and accuracy of data processing and reporting. Surveys soon became the most popular research method in the social sciences.

Attractive Features of Survey Research

Regardless of its scope, survey research owes its continuing popularity to three features: versatility, efficiency, and generalizability.

Versatility

The first and foremost reason for the popularity of survey methods is their versatility. Researchers can ask respondents questions about almost any topic you can imagine. Although a survey is not the ideal method for testing all hypotheses or learning about every social process, a well-designed survey can enhance our understanding of just about any social issue. In fact, there is hardly any topic of interest to social scientists that has not been studied at some time with survey methods.

Efficiency

Surveys also are popular because data can be collected from many people at relatively low cost and, depending on the survey design, relatively quickly. Surveys are efficient research methods because many variables can be measured without substantially increasing the time or cost of data collection. Mailed questionnaires can include up to 10 pages of questions before most respondents lose interest (and before more postage must be added). The maximum time limit for phone surveys seems to be about 45 minutes. In-person interviews can last much longer, more than an hour.

Generalizability

Survey methods lend themselves to probability sampling from large populations. Thus, survey research is very appealing when sample generalizability is a central research goal. In fact, survey research is often the only means available for developing a representative picture of the attitudes and characteristics of a large population.

Surveys also are the research method of choice when cross-population generalizability is a primary concern (see Chapter 5). They allow a range of social contexts and subgroups to be sampled, and the consistency of relationships can be examined across the various subgroups.

The Omnibus Survey

Most surveys are directed at a specific research question. In contrast, an omnibus survey covers a range of topics of interest to different social scientists. It has multiple sponsors or is designed to generate data useful to a broad segment of the social science community rather than answer one particular research question.

One of the most successful omnibus surveys is the General Social Survey (GSS) of the National Opinion Research Center at the University of Chicago. Starting in 1972, the National Science Foundation agreed to fund the GSS as an annual, publicly available national survey on topics of general interest to sociologists. In 1992, the GSS changed to a biennial schedule. Today, the GSS is administered every 2 years as a 90-minute interview to a probability sample of almost 3,000 Americans. It includes more than 500 questions about background characteristics and opinions, with an emphasis on social stratification, race relations, family issues, law and social control, and morale. Although the NVAMW Survey is not an omnibus survey, it was developed to obtain detailed information on a number of phenomena related to victimization. For example, because the Centers for Disease Control and Prevention were cosponsors of the survey, many questions were added to obtain detailed information on a respondent's history of health and injuries in addition to injuries specifically resulting from victimization.

The deficiency of the omnibus approach is the limited depth that can be achieved in any one substantive area. In some years, the GSS avoids this problem by going into greater depth in one particular area. But the best way to get survey data about one particular topic is still the survey developed around the topic alone. The surveys we will highlight in this chapter were all developed to measure one topic: victimization.

QUESTIONNAIRE DEVELOPMENT AND ASSESSMENT

The questionnaire (or interview schedule, as it is often called in interview-based studies) is the central feature of the survey process. Without a well-designed questionnaire tailored to the study's purposes, survey researchers have little hope of achieving their research goals.

Questionnaire The survey instrument containing the questions for a self-administered survey

Interview schedule The survey instrument containing the questions asked by the interviewer for an in-person interview or phone survey

---

The most effective design of a questionnaire varies with the specific survey method used and the other particulars of a survey project. There is no precise formula for a well-designed questionnaire. Nonetheless, some key principles should guide the design of any questionnaire, and some systematic procedures should be considered for refining it.

Maintain Focus

A survey (with the exception of an omnibus survey) should be guided by a well-defined inquiry and a definitively targeted population. Does the study seek to describe some phenomenon in detail, explain some behavior, or explore some type of social relationship? Is your aim to explain that behavior for everyone or only as it pertains to a select group? Until the research objective is clearly formulated, survey design cannot begin. Throughout the process of questionnaire design, this objective should be the primary basis for making decisions about what to include and exclude, and what to emphasize or treat with less importance. Moreover, the questionnaire should be viewed as an integrated whole, in which each section and every question serve a clear purpose related to the study's objective as well as complement other sections and questions.

Build on Existing Instruments

If evidence from previous surveys indicates that these already formulated questions provide a good measure of the concept or behaviors in which you are interested, then why reinvent the wheel? To measure incidents of physical assault, Tjaden and Thoennes (2000) modified a survey instrument that had already been widely used in the literature: the Conflict Tactics Scale (CTS) (Straus 1979). To measure incidents of rape and sexual victimization, Tjaden and Thoennes utilized questions that had already been used by Kilpatrick et al. at the University of South Carolina in the National Women's Study (National Victim Center and the Crime Victims Research and Treatment Center 1992). As you can see from Exhibit 7.1, these questions were very specific in nature and covered all behaviors that are legally defined as rape or sexual assault in most states. In contrast, you will also see that the screening questions still used by the NCVS to uncover incidents of rape and sexual assault do not make use of these behavior-specific questions, which have been proven to uncover more reports of victimization.

In the end, both surveys purport to measure incidents of rape in the United States, but which methodology is most appropriate? In the next section, we will provide you with some specific guidelines for writing questions, and you will see that the answer to this question is not so clear-cut.

> **Exhibit 7.1** Rape-Screening Questions Used by the NVAMW Survey and by the NCVS
>
> *National Violence Against Men and Women (NVAMW) Survey*
>
> [For females only] Regardless of how long ago it happened, has a man ever made you have sex by using force or threatening to harm you or someone close to you? Just so there is no mistake, by sex we mean putting a penis in your vagina.
>
> [For males and females] Has anyone, male or female, ever made you have oral sex by using force or threat of harm? Just so there is no mistake, by oral sex we mean that a man or boy put his penis in your mouth or someone, male or female, penetrated your vagina or anus with their mouth or tongue.
>
> [For males and females] Has anyone ever made you have anal sex by using force or threat of harm? Just so there is no mistake, by anal sex we mean that a man or boy put his penis in your anus.
>
> [For males and females] Has anyone, male or female, ever put fingers or objects in your vagina or anus against your will by using force or threats?
>
> [For males and females] Has anyone, male or female, ever attempted to make you have vaginal, oral, or anal sex against your will, but intercourse or penetration did not occur?
>
> *National Crime Victimization Survey (NCVS)*
>
> Incidents involving forced or unwanted sexual acts are often difficult to talk about. Have you been forced or coerced to engage in unwanted sexual activity by
>
> a. someone you didn't know before,
>
> b. a casual acquaintance, or
>
> c. someone you know well?

WRITING QUESTIONS

Asking people questions is the most common operation for measuring social variables, and probably the most versatile. In principle, survey questions can be a straightforward and efficient means of measuring individual characteristics, facts about events, levels of knowledge, and opinions of any sort. In practice, however, survey questions, if misleading or unclear, can result in inappropriate and unintended answers. All questions proposed for a survey must adhere to basic guidelines and then be tested and revised until the researcher feels confident they will be clear to the intended respondents (Fowler 1995).

Structurally, questions on surveys generally fall into two categories: those with explicit response choices and those without. Recall from Chapter 4 that **open-ended questions** are those without explicit response choices. This type of question is usually used only for explorative purposes when there is little known about a particular topic and the researcher wants to uncover as much about it as possible without restricting responses. For example, if you are investigating the perceptions of residents regarding a new community policing program instituted in the neighborhood, open-ended questions such as the following one could be very informative:

> In your opinion, what have been the benefits of the community policing program in your neighborhood?

Open-ended questions are also excellent tools for obtaining respondents' interpretations in greater detail and can often illuminate flaws in other questions. A survey researcher can also try to understand what respondents mean by their responses after the fact by including additional open-ended questions in the survey. Adding such **interpretive questions** after key survey questions is always a good idea, but it is of utmost importance when the questions in a survey have not been pretested. An example from a study of people with motor vehicle driving violations illustrates the importance of interpretive questions:

> When asked whether their emotional state affected their driving at all, respondents would reply that their emotions had very little effect on their driving habits. Then, when asked to describe the circumstances surrounding their last traffic violation, respondents typically replied, "I was mad at my girlfriend," or "I had a quarrel with my wife," or "We had a family quarrel," or "I was angry with my boss." (Labaw 1980: 71)

Were these respondents lying in response to the first question? Probably not. More likely, they simply did not interpret their own behavior in terms of a general concept such as "emotional state." But their responses to the first question would have likely told a different story without the further detail provided by answers to the second.

In summary, one strength of open-ended questions is the wealth of information they provide. This wealth of information, however, is exactly why many researchers do not use them. The verbatim text narratives obtained from open-ended questions take a great deal of time and energy to organize and summarize. In addition, many respondents may feel overwhelmed about writing a lengthy essay. If you want to ask a large number of open-ended questions, it is perhaps best to consider an in-person interview or phone interview instead of a questionnaire (both of which are discussed later in this chapter).

When respondents are offered explicit responses to choose from, this type of question is referred to as a **closed-ended question** or a **fixed-choice question**. For example, in the NVAMW Survey, respondents were asked the following:

> Overall, would you say that personal safety in this country has improved since you were a child, gotten worse since you were a child, or stayed about the same?
>
> ___ Improved
>
> ___ Gotten worse
>
> ___ Stayed about the same

Most surveys of a large number of people primarily contain fixed-choice questions, which are particularly easy to process and analyze with the use of computers and statistical software. With fixed-choice questions, respondents are also more likely to answer the question that researchers want them to answer. By including the response choices, the survey reduces ambiguity. However, fixed-choice questions can also obscure what people really think unless the choices are carefully designed to match the range of all possible responses to the question.

Regardless of the format used for questions, there are several rules to follow and pitfalls to avoid that will maximize the validity of your survey instrument. We will highlight these in the next section.

Constructing Clear and Meaningful Questions

All hope for achieving measurement validity is lost unless survey questions are clear and convey the intended meaning to respondents. You may verbally pose questions every day and have no trouble understanding the responses you receive, but writing clear and meaningful survey questions is a bit more difficult. Consider just a few of the differences between everyday conversations and standardized surveys:

- Survey questions must be asked of many people, not just one person.
- The same survey questions must be used with each person, not tailored to the specifics of a given conversation.
- Survey questions must be understood in the same way by people who differ in many ways.
- You will not be able to rephrase a survey question if someone does not understand it because that would result in asking the person a different question from the one you asked the others in your sample.
- Survey respondents do not know you and so cannot be expected to share the nuances of expression that you and those close to you use to communicate.

These features make a survey very different from natural conversation and make question writing a challenging and important task for survey researchers.

Questions must be very clear and specific. Note the differences in specificity between the rape-screening questions used by the NVAMW Survey and those of the NCVS displayed in Exhibit 7.1. When given multiple, behaviorally specific questions, survey respondents will be more likely to disclose victimizations compared to when answering the one question about sexual intercourse posed by the NCVS. In fact, results of the two surveys indicate that the NVAMW Survey uncovers about 4 times as many rapes as does the NCVS (Bachman 2000).

In addition to writing clear and meaningful questions, there are several other rules to follow and pitfalls to avoid that we will highlight next.

Avoid Confusing Phrasing and Vagueness

Good grammar is a basic requirement for clear questions. Clearly and simply phrased questions are most likely to have the same meaning for different respondents. The wordier and longer the question, the more likely you are to lose a respondent's attention and focus. Be brief and stick to the point. Virtually all questions about behavior and feelings will be more reliable if they refer to specific times or events (Turner & Martin 1984). Without identifying a reference period, or time frame around which a question is being asked, a researcher will not know how to interpret an answer. For example, the question "How often do you carry a method of self-protection such as pepper spray?" will produce answers that have no common reference period and therefore cannot reliably be compared with answers from other respondents. A more specific way to ask the question is, "In the last month, how many days did you carry a method of self-protection such as pepper spray?"

In general, research shows that the longer the reference period, the greater the underreporting of a given behavior (Cantor 1984, 1985; Kobelarcik et al. 1983). As a general rule, when respondents are being asked about mundane or day-to-day activities, reference periods should be no longer than "in the past month." However, when rare events are being measured, such as experiences with victimizations, "in the last 6 months," as utilized by the NCVS, or "in the past 12 months," as used by the NVAMW, are both more appropriate. By using longer reference periods like this, we will more likely capture these rarer events.

Avoid Negatives and Double Negatives

Picture yourself answering the following question: "Do you disagree that juveniles should not be tried as adults if they commit murder?" It probably took a long time for you to figure out whether you would actually agree or disagree with this statement because it is written as a double-negative question. For example, if you think juveniles who commit murder should be tried as adults, you would actually agree with this statement. Even questions that are written with a single negative are usually difficult to answer. For example, suppose you were asked to respond to "I can't stop thinking about the terrorist attacks on 9/11" using a 5-point response set of "very rarely" to "very often." A person who marks "very rarely" is actually saying, "I very rarely can't stop thinking about the terrorist attacks on 9/11." Confusing, isn't it? Even the most experienced survey researchers can unintentionally make this mistake.

Avoid Double-Barreled Questions

When a question is really asking more than one thing, it is called a double-barreled question. For example, asking people to respond to the statement, "I believe we should stop spending so much money building prisons and put it into building more schools," is really asking them two different questions. Some respondents may believe we should stop building so many prisons but may not want the revenue to go into building more schools. Double-barreled questions can also show up in the response categories. For example, the item below is really asking two questions:

Do you know anyone who has ever used cocaine?
____ Yes ____ No ____ I have used cocaine

Avoid Making Either Disagreement or Agreement Disagreeable

People often tend to "agree" with a statement just to avoid seeming disagreeable. You can see the impact of this human tendency in a Michigan Survey Research Center survey that asked who was to blame for crime and lawlessness in the United States (Schuman & Presser

1981: 208). When one item stated that individuals were more to blame than social conditions, 60% of the respondents agreed. But when the question was rephrased so respondents were asked, in a balanced fashion, whether individuals or social conditions were more to blame, only 46% chose individuals.

You can take several steps to reduce the likelihood of agreement bias. As a general rule, you should impartially present both sides of attitude scales in the question itself: "In general, do you believe that *individuals* or *social conditions* are more to blame for crime and lawlessness in the United States?" (Dillman 2000: 61–62, italics original). The response choices themselves should be phrased to make each one seem as socially approved, or as "agreeable," as the others. You should also consider replacing the word *agree* with a range of response alternatives. For example, "To what extent do you support or oppose the new health care plan?" (with response choices ranging from "strongly support" to "strongly oppose") is probably a better approach than the question, "To what extent do you agree or disagree with the statement, 'The new health care plan is worthy of support'?" (with response choices ranging from "strongly agree" to "strongly disagree").

When an illegal or socially disapproved behavior or attitude is the focus, we have to be concerned that some respondents will be reluctant to agree that they have ever done or thought such a thing. In this situation, the goal is to write a question and response choices that make agreement seem more acceptable or at the very least, not stigmatizing. For example, Dillman (2000) suggests that we ask, "Have you ever taken anything from a store without paying for it?" rather than "Have you ever shoplifted something from a store?" (p. 75). Asking about a variety of behaviors or attitudes that range from socially acceptable to socially unacceptable will also soften the impact of agreeing with those that are socially unacceptable.

Additional Guidelines for Fixed-Response Questions

Creating questions that are clear and meaningful is only half of the formula involved in creating a good survey instrument. The choices you provide respondents in fixed-choice questions are also important. In this section, we provide you with several rules that will help to ensure that the response choices you provide to your questions will also be clear and concise, as well as exhaustive.

Make Response Choices Mutually Exclusive

When you want respondents to make only one choice, the fixed-response categories must not overlap. For example, if you were interested in the ways foot patrol officers spent their time while working, you might ask the following question:

On average, how much time do you spend on the job each week taking care of traffic violations?
- Less than 1 hour
- 1–3 hours
- 3–6 hours
- 6–10 hours
- 10 hours or more

The choices provided for respondents in this question are not mutually exclusive responses because they overlap. Which choice would an officer select if he or she spent 3 hours a week on traffic violations? Choices that are mutually exclusive would look like this:

- 1 hour or less
- 2–3 hours
- 4–6 hours
- 7–10 hours
- 11 hours or more

Make the Response Categories Exhaustive

In addition to mutual exclusivity, fixed-response categories must also allow all respondents to select an option. Consider the same research question about foot patrol officers. Suppose we asked a question such as this:

In what activity do you spend the most time in an average week on the job?
- traffic violations
- disturbance-related issucs
- felony arrests
- misdemeanor arrests

Regardless of how exhaustive we think the response categories are, there must always be an option for respondents who require another choice. Exhaustive response categories can easily be created if respondents are provided with a choice labeled

- Other, please specify: _____

Note, however, that "Other" should be used only after you have included all options that you believe to be relevant. Otherwise, a large percentage of respondents will select the "Other" category and you will have to spend time coding their responses.

Utilize Likert-Type Response Categories

Likert-type responses generally ask respondents to indicate the extent to which they agree or disagree with statements. This format is generally believed to have been developed by Rensis Likert in the 1930s. Likert-type response categories list choices for respondents to select their level of agreement with a statement and may look something like this:

I think "three strikes" laws that increase penalties for individuals convicted of three or more felonies will help to decrease the crime rate.

Strongly Agree	Agree	Disagree	Strongly Disagree
1	2	3	4

Minimize Fence-Sitting and Floating

Two related problems in question writing stem from the respondent's desire to choose an acceptable or socially desirable answer and the desire to get through the survey as fast as possible. There is no uniformly correct solution to these problems, so you must carefully select an alternative.

Fence-sitters are people who see themselves as neutral in their attitudes toward a particular issue. If you are truly interested in those who do not have strong feelings on an issue, one alternative is to provide a neutral or undecided response option. The disadvantage of these options is that they may encourage some respondents to take the easy way out rather than really thinking about their feelings. They may also provide an out for respondents who do not want to reveal how they truly feel about an issue. On the other hand, not providing respondents who really have no opinion on an issue with an option such as "undecided" can be very frustrating for them and may encourage them to leave the item blank. Whatever you decide, it is generally a good idea to provide respondents with instructions that ask them to "select the choice in each item that most closely reflects your opinion." This should help make all respondents feel more comfortable about their answers, particularly those who only slightly feel one way or the other.

Floaters are respondents who choose a substantive answer even when they do not know anything about a particular question. For example, research has shown that one-third of the public will provide an opinion on a proposed law they know nothing about if they are not provided with a "don't know" response option (Schuman & Presser 1981). Of course, providing a "don't know" option has the same disadvantage as providing a neutral response option: Its inclusion leads some people who have an opinion to take the easy way out.

If you are really interested in informed opinions about an issue, it is best to provide detailed information about that issue when asking a question. For example, let us say we were interested in attitudes about the treatment of juvenile offenders by the criminal justice system and we asked respondents their opinion on the following statement: "The Juvenile Justice Bill before Congress will help reduce crime committed by juveniles." To avoid respondents replying "don't know" because they know nothing about the bill, it would be better to tell respondents exactly what the Juvenile Justice Bill entailed so they would be informed when they answered the question.

Utilize Filter Questions

The use of filter questions is important to ensure that questions are asked only of relevant respondents. For example, if you are interested in the utilization of police services by robbery victims, you would first need to establish victimization with a **filter question**. These filter questions create **skip patterns**. For example, respondents who answer "no" to one question are directed to skip ahead to another question, but respondents who answer "yes"

Exhibit 7.2 Filter Questions and Skip Patterns

14. In the past 6 months, has anyone taken something from you by force or the threat of force?

_____ Yes (If yes, please answer questions 15 through 16)

_____ No (If no, please skip to question 17)

15. What was the approximate monetary value of the items taken?

_____ Under $50

_____ $51 to $99

_____ $100 to $299

_____ $300 to $500

_____ Over $500

16. Was the incident reported to the police?

_____ Yes

_____ No

17. How fearful are you of walking alone at night in your neighborhood?

_____ Extremely afraid

_____ Afraid

_____ Unafraid

_____ Extremely unafraid

---

are to go on to the contingent question or questions. (Filter questions are sometimes called contingency questions.) Skip patterns should be indicated clearly with arrows or other direction in the questionnaire, as demonstrated in Exhibit 7.2.

Combining Questions Into an Index

Measuring variables with single questions is very popular. Public opinion polls based on answers to single questions are reported frequently in newspaper articles and TV news-casts: "Do you favor or oppose U.S. policy in . . . ?" "If you had to vote today, for which candidate would you vote?" The primary problem with using a single question is that if respondents misunderstand the question or have some other problem with the phrasing, there is no way to tell. Single questions are prone to this idiosyncratic variation, which occurs when individuals' responses vary because of their reactions to particular words or ideas in the question. Differences in respondents' background, knowledge, and beliefs almost guarantee that they will understand the same question differently. If a number of respondents do not know some of the words in a question, we may misinterpret their answers—if they answer at all. If a question is too complex, respondents may focus on different parts of the question. If prior experiences or culturally biased orientations lead different groups in the sample to interpret questions differently, answers will not have a consistent meaning because the question meant something different to each respondent.

As noted above, if just one question is used to measure a variable, the researcher may not realize respondents had trouble with a particular word or phrase in the question. Although writing carefully worded questions will help reduce idiosyncratic variation, when measuring concepts, the best option is to devise an index of multiple rather than single questions.

When several questions are used to measure one concept, the responses may be combined by taking the sum or average of the responses. A composite measure based on this type of sum or average is called an **index** or **scale.** The idea is that idiosyncratic variation in response to single questions will average out, so the main influence on the combined measure will be the concept focused on by the questions. In addition, the index can be considered a more complete measure of the concept than can any one of the component questions.

Creating an index, however, is not just a matter of writing a few questions that seem to focus on one concept. Questions that seem to you to measure a common concept might seem to respondents to concern several different issues. The only way to know that a given set of questions does effectively form an index is to administer the questions in a pretest to people similar to the sample you plan to study. If a common concept is being measured, people's responses to the different questions should display some consistency. Special statistics called **reliability measures** help researchers decide whether responses are consistent. Most respondent attitudes are complex and consist of many elements.

Be aware of *response sets* when constructing an index measuring attitudes. For example, some people tend to agree with almost everything asked of them, whereas others tend to disagree. Still others are prone to answer neutrally to everything if given the option. To decrease the likelihood of this happening, it is a good idea to make some statements both favorable and unfavorable to a particular attitude to vary the response choices and still reach an understanding of an individual's opinion. In this way, respondents are forced to be more careful in their responses to individual items. Exhibit 7.3 displays a hypothetical set of questions designed to solicit respondents' attitudes toward police in their community.

When scoring an index or scale made up of both favorable and unfavorable statements, you must remember to **reverse code** the unfavorable items. For example, marking "strongly agree" on the first item in Exhibit 7.3 should not be scored the same as a "strongly agree" response to the second item.

Demographic Questions

Almost all questionnaires include a section on demographic information such as sex, age, race or ethnicity, income, and religion. For many research studies, these questions are important independent variables. For example, research has shown that all five of these factors are related to the probability of victimization. Many researchers, however, include demographic questions that are not necessary for purposes of their research. In particular, try to avoid this for questions on income, because it makes the questionnaire more intrusive than necessary. In fact, many respondents feel that questions about their income invade their privacy. If you believe income is an essential variable for your study, providing fixed responses that include a range of values to select from is less intrusive than

Exhibit 7.3   Items in an "Attitude Toward Police" Index

1.   I think police officers are generally fair to all people regardless of their race or ethnicity.
_____ Strongly Agree _____ Agree _____ Disagree _____ Strongly Disagree

2.   Police officers are given too much freedom to stop and frisk community residents.
_____ Strongly Agree _____ Agree _____ Disagree _____ Strongly Disagree

3.   I think if someone resisted arrest, even a little, most police officers would become assaultive if they thought they could get away with it.
_____ Strongly Agree _____ Agree _____ Disagree _____ Strongly Disagree

4.   Police officers put their lives on the line every day trying to make it safe for residents of this community.
_____ Strongly Agree _____ Agree _____ Disagree _____ Strongly Disagree

5.   I think the majority of police officers have lied under oath at least once.
_____ Strongly Agree _____ Agree _____ Disagree _____ Strongly Disagree

6.   The majority of police officers are honest and fair.
_____ Strongly Agree _____ Agree _____ Disagree _____ Strongly Disagree

asking respondents for specific annual incomes. This format was utilized by the NVAMW Survey, as shown in Exhibit 7.4.

Care should also be taken when writing questions about race and ethnicity. Many people are justifiably sensitive to these questions. Even the U.S. Bureau of the Census has been struggling with appropriate categories to offer respondents. In fact, the Bureau still utilizes two questions, one on race and one for respondent ethnicity (Hispanic or non-Hispanic), which is obviously problematic. Most survey researchers now include questions such as the following:

Which of the following best describes your racial or ethnic background? Please check one.

___ Asian
___ Black or African American
___ White or Caucasian
___ Hispanic (may be of any race)
___ Native American
___ Of Mixed Race or Ethnicity
___ Other (Please specify: _____)

Exhibit 7.4   Question on Income From the NVAMW Survey

Including income from all sources, such as work, child support, and AFDC, how much income did you personally receive in 1995 before taxes? Stop me when I get to the category that applies. Was it . . .

01	Less than $5,000
02	$5,001 to $10,000
03	$10,001 to $15,000
04	$15,001 to $20,000
05	$20,001 to $25,000
06	$25,001 to $35,000
07	$35,001 to $50,000
08	$50,001 to $80,000
09	$80,001 to $100,000
10	Over $100,001
11	(Volunteer) None
12	(Volunteer) Don't Know
13	(Volunteer) Refused

Source: Tjaden & Thoennes (2000).

Deciding which categories to include remains difficult. Some researchers still prefer to exclude the Mixed category, because they believe most respondents will identify primarily with one race.

Questions on marital status can also be tricky to compose. The traditional categories of married, single, divorced, and widowed can be interpreted very differently by respondents. Why? Well, isn't someone who is currently divorced also single? And what about someone not officially divorced but separated? And what about someone who is in a civil union or domestic partnership? To avoid confusing respondents, the following response categories could be used: Married, Domestic Partnership, Separated, Widowed, Divorced, and Never Married.

Because demographic questions are usually perceived as private by respondents, some researchers place them in a section at the end of the questionnaire with an introduction reassuring respondents that the information will remain confidential. However, when the information being gathered in the rest of the questionnaire is even more sensitive, such as details of violence respondents may have experienced at the hands of a family member or intimate partner, some researchers opt to keep demographic questions near the beginning of the questionnaire. Asking less sensitive questions in the beginning of the survey allows interviews to gain more rapport with respondents before asking them to divulge more private information about themselves. For example, the NVAMW Survey included demographic questions after the first section, which asked respondents about their general perceptions of fear and safety before they were asked about personal victimizations.

Don't Forget to Pretest!

Adhering to the preceding question-writing guidelines will go a long way toward producing a useful questionnaire. However, simply asking what appear to be clear questions does not ensure that people will have a consistent understanding of what you are asking. You need some external feedback, and the more of it the better.

No questionnaire should be considered ready for use until it has been pretested. Try answering the questionnaire yourself, and then revise it. Try it out on some colleagues or other friends, and then revise it. Then select a small sample of individuals from the population you are studying or one very similar to it, and try out the questionnaire on them. Audiotape the test interviews for later review, or, for a written questionnaire, include in the pretest version some space for individuals to add comments on each key question.

It takes several drafts to create a good questionnaire. By the time you have gone through just a couple of drafts, you may not be scanning the instrument as clearly as you think. A very honest illustration of this is provided by Don Dillman, the director of the Social and Economic Sciences Research Center at Washington State University (cited in Seltzer 1996). His research team almost mailed a questionnaire with the following response categories:

What is your opinion?

Strongly oppose   Oppose   Neither   Favor   Strongly oppose

ORGANIZATION MATTERS

Once the basic topics and specific variables for a questionnaire have been identified, they can be sorted into categories (which may become separate sections), listed in tentative order, and later adjusted to develop the questionnaire's polish and coherence.

The first thing needed is a descriptive title for the questionnaire that indicates the overall topic. The title is essential because it sets the context for the entire survey. For example, the NCVS and the NVAMW Surveys are both interested in measuring the magnitude of crime victimization in the United States. The NVAMW Survey, however, is presented as a survey interested in a number of personal safety–related issues, including tactics used in conflict resolution. The NCVS is titled as a crime survey and is interested in obtaining information only about crimes respondents have experienced. Unfortunately, some survey participants still may not view assaults they have experienced by intimates and other family members as criminal acts.

In addition to the title, question order is important because this also can influence responses. For example, when a sample of the general public was asked, "Do you think it should be possible for a pregnant woman to obtain a legal abortion if she is married and does not want any more children?" 58% said yes. However, when this question was preceded by a less permissive question that asked whether the respondent would allow abortion of a defective fetus, only 40% said yes to the question, placing abortion in the context of "not wanting more children." Asking the question about the defective fetus altered respondents' frame of reference, perhaps making abortion simply to avoid having more children seem frivolous by comparison (Turner & Martin, 1984). The point to take away from this case is that question order is extremely important.

There is no real cure for this potential problem. However, a **split-ballot design** may help identify problems. In a split-ballot survey, some respondents can be given a survey with a particular question order while the other respondents can be given another. This design allows researchers to determine the effect of question order on responses. What is most important is to be aware of the potential for problems due to question order and to carefully evaluate the likelihood of their occurrence in any particular questionnaire. Survey results should mention, at least in a footnote, the order in which key questions were asked when more than one such question was used (Labaw 1980). Questionnaires should conform to several other organizational guidelines as well:

- Major topic divisions within the questionnaire should be organized in separate sections, and each section should be introduced with a brief statement.
- Instructions should be used liberally to minimize respondent confusion. Instructions should explain how each type of question is to be answered (such as circling a number or writing a response) in a neutral way that is not likely to influence responses. Instructions also should guide respondents through skip patterns.
- The questionnaire should look attractive, be easy to complete, and have substantial white space. Resist the temptation to cram as many questions as possible onto one page. Response choices should be printed in a different font or format from the questions and should be set off from them.
- Response choices should be designated by numbers to facilitate coding and data entry after the questionnaire is completed.

The **cover letter** for a mailed questionnaire and the introductory statement read by interviewers in telephone or in-person interviews are also critical to the survey's success. Similar to the context set by the title of the survey, the initial statement of the cover letter sets the tone for the entire questionnaire. For example, the first thing interviewers said to respondents of the NVAMW Survey was, "Hello, I'm _____ from SRBI, the national research organization. We are conducting a national survey on personal safety for the Center for Policy Research, under a grant from the federal government." Notice that, even though the survey's primary purpose was to uncover incidents of victimization, it was presented to respondents as a survey interested in issues of personal safety. This was done to increase the probability of respondents disclosing incidents of victimization even if they did not perceive them to be crimes. Also note that the introductory statement disclosed the researcher's affiliation and the project sponsor. In addition, the purpose of the survey should be briefly described and a contact number should be included for those who wish to ask questions or register complaints. In sum, the cover letter for a mailed questionnaire and the introductory statement for an interview should be credible, personalized, interesting, and responsible.

SURVEY DESIGNS

The five basic survey designs are the mailed survey, group-administered survey, phone survey, in-person survey, and electronic survey. Exhibit 7.5 summarizes the typical features of the five designs.

The five survey designs vary in their arrangement and application:

Manner of administration. Mailed, group, and electronic surveys are completed by the respondents themselves. During phone and in-person interviews, however, the researcher or a staff person asks the questions and records the respondent's answers.

Questionnaire structure. Survey designs also differ in the extent to which the content and order of questions are structured in advance by the researcher. Most mailed, group, phone, and electronic surveys are highly structured, fixing in advance the content and order of questions and response choices. Some of these types of surveys, particularly mailed surveys, may include some open-ended questions. In-person interviews are often highly structured, but they may include many questions without fixed-response choices. Moreover, some interviews may proceed from an interview guide rather than a fixed set of questions. In these relatively unstructured interviews, the interviewer covers the same topics with respondents but varies questions according to the respondent's answers to previous questions. Extra questions are added as needed to clarify or explore answers to the most important questions.

Exhibit 7.5 Typical Features of the Five Survey Designs

Design	Manner of Administration	Setting	Questionnaire Structure	Cost
Mailed survey	Self	Individual	Mostly structured	Low
Group survey	Self	Group	Mostly structured	Very low
Phone survey	Professional	Individual	Structured	Moderate
In-person interview	Professional	Individual	Structured or unstructured	High
Electronic survey	Self	Individual	Mostly structured	Very low

Setting. Most mail and electronic questionnaires and phone interviews are intended for completion by only one respondent. The same is usually true of in-person interviews, although sometimes researchers interview several family members at once. On the other hand, a variant of the standard survey is a questionnaire distributed simultaneously to a group of respondents, who complete the survey while the researcher (or assistant) waits. Students in classrooms are typically the group involved, although this type of group distribution also occurs in surveys administered to employees and members of voluntary groups.

Cost. As mentioned earlier, in-person interviews are the most expensive type of survey. Phone interviews are much less expensive, but surveying by mail is cheaper still. Electronic surveys are now the least expensive method because there are no interviewer costs; no mailing costs; and, for many designs, almost no costs for data entry. Of course, extra staff time and expertise is required to prepare an electronic questionnaire.

Because of their different features, the five designs vary in the types of errors to which they are most prone and the situations in which they are most appropriate. The rest of this section focuses on the unique advantages and disadvantages of each design.

Mailed Self-Administered Surveys

A **mailed (self-administered) survey** is conducted by mailing a questionnaire to respondents, who then administer the survey themselves. The principal drawback in using this method of survey administration is the difficulty maximizing the response rate—we have to rely on people to voluntarily return the surveys! The final response rate is unlikely to be much above 80%, and almost surely will be below 70% unless procedures to maximize the response rate are precisely followed. A response rate below 60% is a disaster, and even a 70% response rate is not much more than minimally acceptable. It is hard to justify the representativeness of the sample if more than a third of those surveyed fail to respond.

Related to the threat of nonresponse in mailed surveys is the hazard of incomplete response. Some respondents may skip some questions or just stop answering questions at some point in the questionnaire. Fortunately, this problem does not often occur with well-designed questionnaires. Potential respondents who decide to participate in the survey will usually complete it. Many researchers still rely on mailed surveys because they are relatively inexpensive and respondents are free to answer questions at their leisure, without the scrutiny of a survey administrator.

Group-Administered Surveys

A **group-administered survey** is completed by individual respondents assembled in a group. The response rate is not usually a concern in surveys that are distributed and collected in a group setting because most group members will participate. The difficulty with this method is that assembling a group is seldom feasible because it requires a captive audience. With the exception of students, employees, members of the armed forces, and some institutionalized populations, most populations cannot be sampled in such a setting.

One issue of special concern with group-administered surveys is the possibility that respondents will feel coerced to participate and as a result will be less likely to answer questions honestly. Also, because administering a survey to a group probably requires the approval of the group's supervisor, and the survey is likely conducted on the organization's premises, respondents may infer that the researcher is not at all independent of the sponsor. Even those who volunteer may still feel uncomfortable answering all questions, which may bias their responses. No complete solution to this problem exists, but it helps to make an introductory statement that emphasizes the researcher's independence, assures respondents that their survey answers will be completely anonymous, and gives participants a chance to ask questions about the survey.

Surveys by Telephone

In a phone survey, interviewers question respondents over the phone and then record their answers. Phone interviewing has become a very popular method of conducting surveys in the United States because almost all families have phones. But two matters may undermine the validity of a phone survey: not reaching the proper sampling units and not getting enough complete responses to make the results generalizable.

Reaching Sampling Units

Today, drawing a random sample is easier than ever due to random digit dialing (RDD) (Lavrakas 1987). A machine calls random phone numbers within designated exchanges, regardless of whether the numbers are published. When the machine reaches an inappropriate household (such as a business in a survey directed to the general population), the phone number is simply replaced with another.

The NVAMW Survey collected a national probability sample of 8,000 English- and Spanish-speaking women and 8,000 English- and Spanish-speaking men 18 years of age and older residing in households throughout the United States through RDD.

Maximizing Response to Phone Surveys

Three issues require special attention in phone surveys. First, because people often are not home, multiple callbacks will be necessary for many sample members. In addition, interviewers must be prepared for distractions if the respondent is interrupted by other household members. Sprinkling interesting or provocative questions throughout the questionnaire may help to maintain respondent interest. Lastly, respondents may feel a general lack of trust toward telephone interviewers who are strangers (Miller 1991).

Procedures can be standardized more effectively, quality control maintained, and processing speed maximized when phone interviewers are assisted by computers. This computer-assisted telephone interview has become known as CATI, and most large surveys are now performed in this way. There are several advantages to using CATI, but perhaps the primary one is that data collection and data entry can occur concurrently. Second, the CATI system has several machine edit features that help to minimize data entry error.

One method that dispenses with the interviewer altogether is computerized interactive voice response (IVR) survey technology. In an IVR survey, respondents receive automated calls and answer questions by pressing numbers on their touch-tone phones or speaking numbers that are interpreted by computerized voice-recognition software. These surveys can also record verbal responses to open-ended questions for later transcription. Although they present some difficulties when many answer choices must be used or skip patterns must be followed, IVR surveys have been used successfully with short questionnaires and when respondents are highly motivated to participate (Dillman 2000). When these conditions are not met, potential respondents may be put off by the impersonality of this computer-driven approach.

In summary, phone surveying is the best method to use for relatively short surveys of the general population. Response rates in phone surveys tend to be very high, often above 80%, because few individuals will hang up on a polite caller or refuse to stop answering questions (at least within the first 30 minutes or so). The NVAMW Survey obtained a response rate of 72% in the female survey and 69% in the male survey by conducting interviews via telephone.

In-Person Interviews

What is unique to the **in-person interview**, compared to the other survey designs, is the face-to-face social interaction between interviewer and respondent. If financial resources are available for hiring interviewers to go out and personally conduct the surveys with respondents, in-person interviewing is often the best survey design.

Although time-consuming and costly, in-person interviewing has several advantages. Response rates are higher for this survey design than for any other when potential respondents are approached by a courteous interviewer. In addition, in-person interviews can be much longer than mailed or phone surveys; the questionnaire can be complex, with both open-ended and closed-ended questions. The order in which questions are read and answered can be controlled by the interviewer, and the physical and social circumstances of the interview can be monitored. Lastly, respondents' interpretations of questions can be probed and clarified, if it is done consistently with all respondents.

As with phone interviewing, computers can be used to increase control of the in-person interview. In a computer-assisted personal interviewing (CAPI) project, interviewers carry a laptop computer programmed to display the interview questions and process the responses that the interviewer types in, as well as to check that these responses fall within the allowed ranges. Interviewers seem to like CAPI, and the quality of the data obtained is at least as good as for a noncomputerized interview (Shepherd et al. 1996). **Computer-assisted self interviewing (CASI)** is also an alternative. With audio-CASI, respondents interact with a computer-administered questionnaire by using a mouse and following audio instructions delivered via headphones. Audio-CASI is considered the most reliable way to administer questionnaires that probe sensitive or potentially stigmatizing information such as offending or victimization information (Miller et al. 1998; Tourangeau & Smith 1996; Turner et al. 1998). Wolf et al. (2006) used this technology to obtain information about the physical and sexual victimization experiences of male and female state prison inmates. They explain,

> The survey was administered using audio-CASI (computed-assisted self interviewing) and was available in English and Spanish. There were 30 computer stations set up at each facility and members of the research team were available to answer any questions and assist with the technology as needed. (p. 838)

Maximizing Response to Interviews

Even if the right balance is struck between maintaining control over interviews and achieving good rapport with respondents, in-person interviews can still have a problem. Due to the difficulty of catching all the members of a sample, response rates may suffer.

Several factors affect the response rate in interview studies. Contact rates tend to be lower in city centers, in part because of difficulties in finding people at home and gaining access to high-rise apartments and in part because of interviewer reluctance to visit some areas at night, when people are more likely to be home (Fowler 1988). Households with young children or elderly adults tend to be easier to contact, whereas single-person households are more difficult to reach (Groves & Couper 1998).

Electronic Surveys

The widespread use of personal computers and the growth of the Internet have created new possibilities for survey research. New data from the U.S. Census Bureau (2009) show that 62% of households reported using Internet access in 2007. These percentages are growing rapidly; it is not unreasonable to think that use of the Internet will soon become comparable to the use of telephones. As the proportion of the population that is connected increases, the Internet will become the preferred medium for survey research on many topics.

Electronic surveys can be prepared in two ways (Dillman 2000). E-mail surveys can be sent as messages to respondents' e-mail addresses. Respondents then mark their answers in the message and send them back to the researcher. This approach is easy for researchers to develop and for respondents to use. However, this approach is cumbersome for surveys that are more than four or five pages in length. By contrast, web surveys are designed on a server controlled by the researcher; respondents are then asked to visit the website and respond to the web questionnaire by checking answers. This approach requires more programming by the researcher and in many cases requires more skill on the part of the respondent. However, web surveys can be quite long, with questions that are inapplicable to a given respondent hidden from them so that the survey may actually seem much shorter than it is.

There are many free online services to aid you in developing a web survey, such as SurveyMonkey. However, many universities have also subscribed to more sophisticated survey engines such as Qualtrics. Using a random sample of University of Delaware students, the Center for Drug and Alcohol Studies conducted a College Risk Behavior Survey using Qualtrics. Exhibit 7.6 displays one screen of the survey, which was devoted to ascertaining the extent to which students engaged in all types of behavior including drinking and driving, using drugs, cheating on exams, victimizations, stealing, fighting, gambling, and illegally downloading material. Notice that the top of the screen told respondents how much of the survey they had left before they were finished. To enhance their response rate, the researchers offered students who completed the survey a $5 voucher that could be used at any university eating establishment.

Exhibit 7.6 A Page From the College Risk Behavior Survey

UNIVERSITY OF DELAWARE
2009 College Survey

Your responses to the previous section have been recorded.
You are 95% finished with this survey.
This is the final set of questions!

How often have you done the following:

	Never	Before, but not in the past year	A few times in the past year	1-3 times in the past month	4-8 times in the past month	9 or more times in the past month
Cheated on a test	○	○	○	○	○	○
Plagiarized/copied a paper	○	○	○	○	○	○
Threatened someone	○	○	○	○	○	○
Hit someone	○	○	○	○	○	○
Entered a building/vehicle I should not have been in	○	○	○	○	○	○
Stolen money	○	○	○	○	○	○
Stolen something other than money	○	○	○	○	○	○
Vandalized property other than your own	○	○	○	○	○	○
Committed fraud/forgery (includes using fake ID)	○	○	○	○	○	○
Carried a weapon	○	○	○	○	○	○
Drove under the influence of alcohol	○	○	○	○	○	○
Drove under the influence of marijuana or other drugs	○	○	○	○	○	○

Next Section

Survey Powered By Qualtrics

Web surveys are becoming the more popular form of Internet survey because they are so flexible. The design of the questionnaire can include many types of graphic and typographic features. Respondents can view definitions of words or instructions for answering questions by clicking on linked terms. Lengthy sets of response choices can be presented with pull-down menus. Pictures and audio segments can be added when they are useful. Because answers are recorded directly in the researcher's database, data entry errors are almost eliminated and results can be reported quickly.

The most important drawback to either Internet survey approach is the large portion of households that are not yet connected to the Internet. For special populations with high rates of Internet use, though, the technology makes possible fast and effective surveys. Also, access to a web survey must be limited to the sample members, perhaps by requiring use of a personal identification number (PIN) (Dillman 2000).

Mixed-Mode Surveys

Survey researchers increasingly are combining different survey designs. Mixed-mode surveys allow the strengths of one survey design to compensate for the weaknesses of another and can maximize the likelihood of securing data from different types of respondents. For example, a survey may be sent electronically to sample members who have e-mail addresses and mailed to those who do not. Alternatively, nonrespondents in a mailed survey may be interviewed in person or over the phone. As noted previously, an interviewer may use a self-administered questionnaire to present sensitive questions to a respondent.

A Comparison of Survey Designs

Which survey design should be used when? Group-administered surveys are similar in most respects to mailed surveys, except they require the unusual circumstance of having access to the sample in a group setting. We therefore do not need to consider this survey design by itself. Thus, we can focus our comparison on the four survey designs that involve the use of a questionnaire with individuals sampled from a larger population: mailed surveys, phone surveys, in-person surveys, and electronic surveys. Exhibit 7.7 summarizes their strong and weak points.

The most important consideration in comparing the advantages and disadvantages of the four survey designs is the likely response rate they will generate. Because of the great weakness of mailed surveys in this respect, they must be considered the least preferred survey design from a sampling standpoint. However, researchers may still prefer a mailed survey when they have to reach a widely dispersed population and do not have enough financial resources to hire and train an interview staff or to contract with a survey organization that already has an interview staff available in many locations.

Contracting with an established survey research organization for a phone survey is often the best alternative to a mailed survey. The persistent follow-up attempts necessary to secure an adequate response rate are much easier over the phone than in person or via mail.

In-person surveys are clearly preferable in terms of the possible length and complexity of the questionnaire itself, as well as the researcher's ability to monitor conditions while the questionnaire is being completed. Mailed surveys often are preferable for asking sensitive questions, although this problem can be lessened in an interview by giving respondents a separate sheet to fill out on their own. Although interviewers may themselves distort results, either by changing the wording of questions or failing to record answers properly, this problem can be lessened by careful training, monitoring, and tape-recording the answers.

The advantages and disadvantages of electronic surveys must be weighed in light of the potential respondents' capabilities at the time the survey is to be conducted. At this time, over 30% of households still lack Internet connections, and too many people who have computers lack adequate computer capacity for displaying complex web pages.

Exhibit 7.7	Advantages and Disadvantages of Four Survey Designs			
Characteristics of Design	*In-Person Survey*	*Mail Survey*	*Phone Survey*	*Electronic Survey*
Representative Sample				
Opportunity for inclusion is known				
For completely listed populations	High	High	High	Medium
For incompletely listed populations	High	Medium	Medium	Low
Selection within sampling units is controlled (e.g., specific family members must respond)	High	Medium	High	Low
Respondents are likely to be located	Medium	High	High	Low
If samples are heterogeneous	High	Medium	High	Low
If samples are homogeneous and specialized	High	High	High	High
Questionnaire Construction and Question Design				
Allowable length of questionnaire	High	Medium	Medium	Medium
Ability to include				
Complex questions	Medium	Low	High	High
Open questions	Low	High	High	Medium
Screening questions	Low	Low	High	
Tedious, boring questions	High	High	High	High
Ability to control question sequence	Low	High	High	High
Ability to ensure questionnaire completion	Medium	High	High	High
Distortion of Answers				
Odds of avoiding social desirability bias	High	Medium	Low	High
Odds of avoiding interviewer distortion	Low	High	Medium	
Odds of avoiding contamination by others	High	Medium	Medium	Medium
Administrative Goals				
Odds of meeting personnel requirements	High	High	Low	High
Odds of implementing quickly	Low	High	Low	High
Odds of keeping costs low	High	Medium	Low	High

Source: Adapted from Don A. Dillman, *Mail and Telephone Surveys: The Total Design Method.* Copyright © 1978 Don A. Dillman. Reprinted by permission of John Wiley & Sons, Inc.

These various points about the different survey designs lead to two general conclusions. First, in-person interviews are the strongest design and generally preferable when sufficient resources and a trained interview staff are available, but telephone surveys still offer many of the advantages of in-person interviews at a much lower cost. Second, we must take into account the unique features and goals of a study before deciding the best survey design to use.

ETHICAL ISSUES IN SURVEY RESEARCH

Survey research usually poses fewer ethical dilemmas than do experimental or field research designs. Potential respondents to a survey can easily decline to participate, and a cover letter or introductory statement that identifies the sponsors of and motivations for the survey gives them the information required to make this decision. The methods of data collection are quite obvious in a survey, so little is concealed from the respondents. The primary ethical issue in survey research involves protecting respondents.

Protection of Respondents

If the survey could possibly have any harmful effects for the respondents, these should be disclosed fully in the cover letter or introductory statement (recall the discussion of informed consent in Chapter 3). The procedures used to reduce such effects should also be delineated, including how the researcher will keep interviews confidential and anonymous. In addition, surveys such as the NVAMW Survey and NCVS that attempt to measure sensitive subject matter such as rape and intimate-perpetrated assault should also have other protections in place. By asking respondents to recall incidents of abuse and violence, there is always the possibility of causing victims serious emotional trauma. How can researchers ameliorate the negative consequences that responding to these surveys may have? What responsibility do researchers have in providing respondents with safety should they need it? We believe these important questions have received far too little attention. Respondents in the NVAMW Survey were given a toll-free number they could call if they needed to suddenly hang up during the course of the interview (e.g., if they felt they were in danger). In addition, interviewers for the NVAMW Survey were instructed to contact an attending supervisor at the first sign a respondent was becoming upset or emotionally distraught. These supervisors were provided with a sourcebook from the National Domestic Violence Coalition that listed rape crisis and domestic violence hotline numbers from around the country. The College Risk Behavior Survey discussed earlier in this chapter also gave respondents information about a number of avenues for help including the phone numbers to the University of Delaware Center for Counseling and Student Development, the Delaware Council on Gambling Problems, and the Delaware 24-hour Rape Crisis Hotline.

Confidentiality

Do any of the questions have the potential to embarrass respondents or otherwise subject them to adverse consequences such as legal sanctions? If the answer to this question is no—and it often is in surveys about general social issues—other ethical problems are unlikely. But if the questionnaire includes questions about attitudes or behaviors that are socially stigmatized or generally considered to be private, or questions about actions that are illegal, the researcher must proceed carefully and ensure that respondents' rights are protected.

The first step to take with potentially troublesome questions is to consider modifying them or omitting them entirely. If sensitive questions fall into this category, they probably should be omitted. There is no point in asking, "Have you ever been convicted of a felony?" if the answers are unlikely to be used in the analysis of survey results.

Many surveys—particularly surveys interested in delinquent or criminal offending behavior—do include some essential questions that might prove damaging to the subjects if their answers were disclosed. To prevent any possibility of harm to subjects due to disclosure of such information, it is critical to preserve subject confidentiality. No one other than research personnel should have access to information that could be used to link respondents to their responses, and even that access should be limited to what is necessary for specific research purposes. Only numbers should be used to identify respondents on their questionnaires, and the researcher should keep the names that correspond to these numbers in a separate, safe, and private location, unavailable to others who might otherwise come across them. Follow-up mailings or contact attempts that require linking the ID numbers with names and addresses should be carried out by trustworthy assistants under close supervision.

Only if no identifying information about respondents is obtained can surveys provide true anonymity to respondents. In this way, no identifying information is ever recorded to link respondents with their responses. However, the main problem with anonymous surveys is that they preclude follow-up attempts to encourage participation by initial nonrespondents, and they prevent panel designs, which measure change through repeated surveys of the same individuals. In-person surveys rarely can be anonymous because an interviewer must in almost all cases know the name and address of the interviewee. However, phone surveys that are meant only to sample opinion at one point in time, as in political polls, can safely be completely anonymous. When no follow-up is desired, group-administered surveys also can be anonymous. To provide anonymity in a mail survey, the researcher should omit identifying codes from the questionnaire but could include a self-addressed, stamped postcard so the respondent can notify the researcher that the questionnaire has been returned, without being linked to the questionnaire itself (Mangione 1995: 69).

CONCLUSION

Survey research is an exceptionally efficient and productive method for investigating a wide array of social research questions. In addition to the potential benefits for social science, considerations of time and expense frequently make a survey the preferred data collection method. One or more of the four survey designs reviewed in this chapter can be applied to almost any research question. It is no wonder that surveys have become the most popular research method in sociology and that they frequently influence discussion and planning about important social and political questions.

The relative ease of conducting at least some types of survey research leads many people to imagine that no particular training or systematic procedures are required. Nothing could be further from the truth. As a result of this widespread misconception, you will encounter a great deal of worthless survey results. You must be prepared to carefully examine the procedures used in any survey before accepting its finding as credible. Moreover, if you decide to conduct a survey, you must be prepared to invest the time and effort required to follow proper procedures.

KEY TERMS

Anonymity

Computer-assisted personal interviewing (CAPI)

Computer-assisted self-interviewing (CASI)

Computerized interactive voice response (IVR)

Contingent question

Cover letter

Double-barreled question

Double-negative question

Electronic survey

E-mail survey

Exhaustive responses

Fence-sitter

Filter question

Fixed-choice question

Floater

Group-administered survey

Idiosyncratic variation

Index

In-person interview

Interactive voice response (IVR)

Interpretive question

Interview schedule

Likert-type responses

Mailed (self-administered) survey

Mixed-mode survey

Mutually exclusive responses

Omnibus survey

Open-ended question

Phone survey

Pretest

Questionnaire

Reference period

Reliability measures

Reverse code

Scale

Skip pattern

Survey research

Web survey

HIGHLIGHTS

- Surveys are the most popular form of social research because of their versatility, efficiency, and generalizability. Many survey data sets, such as the General Social Survey (GSS), are available for social scientists to use in teaching and research.

- Surveys can fail to produce useful results due to problems in sampling, measurement, and overall survey design.

- A survey questionnaire or interview schedule should be designed as an integrated whole, with each question and section serving some clear purpose and complementing the others.

- Questions must be worded carefully to avoid confusing the respondents or encouraging a less-than-honest response. Inclusion of "don't know" choices and neutral responses may help, but the presence of such options also affects the distribution of answers. Open-ended questions can be used to determine the meaning that respondents attach to their answers. The answers to any survey questions may be affected by the questions that precede them in a questionnaire or interview schedule.

- Every questionnaire and interview schedule should be pretested on a small sample that is like the sample to be surveyed.

- The cover letter for a mailed questionnaire and the introductory statement for an interview should be credible, personalized, interesting, and responsible.

- Phone interviews using random digit dialing allow fast turnaround and efficient sampling.

- In-person interviews have several advantages over other types of surveys: They allow longer and more complex interview schedules, monitoring of the conditions when the questions are answered, probing for respondents' understanding of the questions, and high response rates.

- Electronic surveys may be e-mailed or posted on the web. At this time, use of the Internet is not sufficiently widespread to allow e-mail or web surveys of the general population, but these approaches can be fast and efficient for populations with high rates of computer use.

- Mixed-mode surveys allow the strengths of one survey design to compensate for the weaknesses of another.

- Most survey research poses few ethical problems because respondents are able to decline to participate. This option should be stated clearly in the cover letter or introductory statement. When anonymity cannot be guaranteed, confidentiality must be assured.

EXERCISES

Discussing Research

1. Who does survey research and how do they do it? These questions can be answered through careful inspection of ongoing surveys and the organizations that administer them at the website for the Cornell Institute for Social and Economic Research, www.ciser.cornell.edu/info/polls.shtml. Spend some time reading about the different survey research organizations, and write a brief summary of the types of research they conduct, the projects in which they are involved, and the resources they offer on their websites. What are the distinctive features of different survey research organizations?

2. Write 8 to 10 questions for a one-page questionnaire on fear of crime among students. Include some questions to measure characteristics (such as income or year in school) that might help to explain the attitudes. Make all but one of your questions closed-ended. What are some of the problems in trying to measure difficult concepts like "fear"? How about attitudes like "prejudice" and "intolerance"?

Finding Research on the Web

1. Go to the Social Information Gateway (SOSIG) at http://sosig.esrc.bris.ac.uk. Search SOSIG for electronic journal articles that use surveys to collect information on crime, criminal behavior, or criminal victimization. Find at least five articles and briefly describe each.

2. Go to the Research Triangle Institute website at www.rti.org. Click on "Tools and Methods," then "Surveys," and then "Survey Design and Development." Read about their methods for computer-assisted interviewing (under "Survey Methods") and their cognitive laboratory methods for refining questions (under "Usability Testing"). What does this add to your treatment of these topics in this chapter?

3. Go to The Question Bank at http://qb.soc.surrey.ac.uk/docs/home.htm. Go to the "Surveys" link and then click on one of the listed surveys or survey sections that interest you. Review 10 questions used in the survey, and critique them in terms of the principles for question writing that you have learned. Do you find any question features that might be attributed to the use of British English?

Critiquing Research

1. Read the original article reporting one of the surveys described in this book (Check the text of the chapters for ideas.). Critique the article using the questions presented in Appendix B as your guide. Focus particular attention on sampling, measurement, and survey design.

2. By interviewing two students, conduct a preliminary pretest of the questionnaire you wrote for Exercise 2 under "Discussing Research" (above). Follow up the closed-ended questions with open-ended questions that ask the students what they meant by each response or what came to mind when they were asked each question. Take account of the answers when you revise your questions. How do you draw the line between too much and too little data?

3. Make any necessary revisions to the questionnaire you wrote in Exercise 2 under "Discussing Research" (above). Write a cover letter that presumes the survey will be administered to students in a class at your school. Submit the questionnaire and cover letter to your instructor for comment and evaluation.

Making Research Ethical

1. In this chapter, we posed the questions, "How can researchers ameliorate the negative consequences that responding to these surveys may have? What responsibility do researchers have in providing respondents with safety should they need it?" Are there any conditions in which a researcher could justify emotional harm to respondents? Write a short statement in response to each question.

2. Tjaden and Thoennes (2000) sampled adults with random digit dialing in order to study violent victimization from a nationally representative sample of adults. We already asked you about the ethical dilemmas of reporting victimizations in Chapter 4. But what about respondents who are minors and are under the age of 18? What about children under the age of 12? Teachers and medical personnel are required by law to report cases they believe to represent incidents of child abuse. Should researchers have the same obligation? How would this affect large-scale surveys using random digit dialing in which you want to preserve the anonymity of respondents?

Developing a Research Proposal

1. Write 10 questions for a one-page questionnaire that concerns your proposed research question. Your questions should operationalize at least three of the variables on which you have

focused, including at least one independent and one dependent variable (You may have multiple questions to measure some variables.). Make all but one of your questions closed-ended. If you completed the "research proposal" exercises in Chapter 3, you can select your questions from the ones you developed for those exercises.

2. Conduct a preliminary pretest of the questionnaire by carrying out cognitive interviews with two students or other persons who are like those to whom the survey is directed. Follow up the closed-ended questions with open-ended probes that ask the students what they meant by each response or what came to mind when they were asked each question. Take account of the feedback you received when you revise your questions.

3. Polish up the organization and layout of the questionnaire, following the guidelines in this chapter. Prepare a rationale for the order of questions in your questionnaire. Write a cover letter directed to the target population that contains appropriate statements about research ethics (human subjects issues).

Performing Data Analysis in SPSS or Excel

Injuries are often sustained by victims of violent crime. Using NCVS9205.ASSAULT, a sample of assault incidents from the National Crime Victimization Survey, you can explore what factors most often lead to injury for victims of assault.

1. Browse the variables in the data set. What factors do you think are related to whether or not a victim of rape, robbery, or assault is injured?

2. Choose at least three of these variables, and state your hypotheses about the relationship between each of these variables and injury.

3. Generate cross-tabulations of your chosen variables and INJURY. (If you have had a statistics course, you may want to request the CHI-SQUARE statistic for each of the cross-tabulations.)

4. Describe the relationship you have found, noting the difference in the distribution of the dependent (row) variables between the categories of each independent (column) variable.

5. Do these relationships vary for the type of violent crime committed? Add the variable measuring the type of violent crime committed (TOC) as a CONTROL variable in your cross-tabulation request. Describe your results.

Student Study Site

The companion Student Study Site for *Fundamentals of Research in Criminology and Criminal Justice* can be found at www.sagepub.com/bachmanfrccj2e.

Visit the Student Study Site to enhance your understanding of the chapter content and to discover additional resources that will take your learning one step further. You can enhance your understanding of the chapters by using the comprehensive study material, which includes interactive exercises, e-flashcards, web exercises, practice self-tests, and more. You will also find special features, such as Learning From Journal Articles, which incorporates Sage's online journal collection.

Qualitative Methods and Data Analysis

In this chapter, you will learn from a variety of examples that some of our greatest insights into social processes can result from what appear to be very ordinary activities: observing, participating, and listening.

But you will also learn that qualitative research is much more than just doing what comes naturally in social situations. Qualitative researchers must keenly observe respondents, sensitively plan their participation, systematically take notes, and strategically question respondents. They must also prepare to spend more time and invest more of their whole selves than often occurs with experiments or surveys. Moreover, if we are to have any confidence in the validity of a qualitative study's conclusions, each element of its design must be reviewed as carefully as the elements of an experiment or survey.

WHAT DO WE MEAN BY QUALITATIVE METHODS?

> I mean, you try to touch on me, I'm gonna check you. If you try to touch on me, you being disrespectful. I'm saying, you engaged in sexual harassment. Some girls just play that. Laughing at it. That's how you know if a girl is a freak or not. That she wants to be touched for real. (quoted in Miller 2008: 146)

This was one young woman's description of her reaction to sexual harassment. The young woman was part of a study examining gendered violence that Jody Miller conducted using intensive interviewing techniques with 75 inner-city high school–aged men and women.

Qualitative methods (touched upon in Chapter 1) refers to three distinctive research designs: participant observation, intensive interviewing, and focus groups. Participant observation and intensive interviewing are often used in the same project; focus groups combine some elements of these two approaches into a unique data-collection strategy.

Participant observation A qualitative method for gathering data that involves developing a sustained relationship with people while they go about their normal activities

Intensive interviewing A qualitative method that involves open-ended, relatively unstructured questioning in which the interviewer seeks in-depth information on the interviewee's feelings, experiences, and perceptions (Lofland & Lofland 1984)

Focus groups A qualitative method that involves unstructured group interviews in which the focus group leader actively encourages discussion among participants on the topics of interest

Although these three qualitative designs differ in many respects, they share several features that distinguish them from experimental and survey research designs (Denzin & Lincoln 1994; Maxwell 1996; Wolcott 1995):

Collection primarily of qualitative rather than quantitative data. Any research design may collect both qualitative and quantitative data, but qualitative methods emphasize observations about natural behavior and artifacts that capture social life as it is experienced by the participants rather than in categories predetermined by the researcher.

Exploratory research questions, with a commitment to inductive reasoning. Qualitative researchers typically begin their projects seeking not to test preformulated hypotheses but to discover what people think and how and why they act in certain social settings. Only after many observations do qualitative researchers try to develop general principles to account for their observations (recall the research circle in Chapter 2).

A focus on previously unstudied processes and unanticipated phenomena. Previously unstudied attitudes and actions cannot adequately be understood with a structured set of questions or within a highly controlled experiment. Therefore, qualitative methods have their greatest appeal when we need to explore new issues, investigate hard-to-study groups, or determine the meaning people give to their lives and actions.

An orientation to social context, to the interconnections between social phenomena rather than to their discrete features. The context of concern may be a program, an organization, a neighborhood, or a broader social context.

A focus on human subjectivity, on the meanings that participants attach to events and that people give to their lives. "Through life stories, people account for their lives. . . . The themes people create are the means by which they interpret and evaluate their life experiences and attempt to integrate these experiences to form a self-concept" (Kaufman 1986: 24–25).

A focus on the events leading up to a particular event or outcome instead of general causal explanations. With its focus on particular actors and situations and the processes that connect them, qualitative research tends to identify causes of particular events embedded within an unfolding, interconnected action sequence (Maxwell 1996). The language of variables and hypotheses appears only rarely in the qualitative literature.

Reflexive research design. The design develops as the research progresses:

> Each component of the design may need to be reconsidered or modified in response to new developments or to changes in some other component. . . . The activities of collecting and analyzing data, developing and modifying theory, elaborating or refocusing the research questions, and identifying and eliminating validity threats are usually all going on more or less simultaneously, each influencing all of the others. (Maxwell 1996: 2–3)

Sensitivity to the subjective role of the researcher. Little pretense is made of achieving an objective perspective on social phenomena.

Origins of Qualitative Research

Anthropologists and sociologists laid the foundation for modern qualitative methods while doing field research in the early decades of the 20th century. Dissatisfied with studies of native peoples that relied on second-hand accounts and inspection of artifacts, anthropologists Franz Boas and Bronislaw Malinowski went to live in or near the communities they studied. Boas visited Native American villages in the Pacific Northwest; Malinowski lived among New Guinea natives. Neither truly participated in the ongoing social life of those they studied—Boas collected artifacts and original texts, and Malinowski reputedly lived as something of a nobleman among the natives he studied—but both helped to establish the value of intimate familiarity with the community of interest and thus laid the basis for modern anthropology (Emerson 1983).

Many of sociology's field research pioneers were former social workers and reformers. Some brought their missionary concern with the welfare of new immigrants to the Department of Sociology and Anthropology at the University of Chicago. Their successors continued to focus on sources of community cohesion and urban strain but came to view the city as a social science laboratory. They adopted the fieldwork methods of anthropology for studying the "natural areas" of the city and the social life of small towns (Vidich & Lyman 1994). By the 1930s, 1940s, and 1950s, qualitative researchers were emphasizing the value of direct participation in community life and sharing in subjects' perceptions and interpretations of events (Emerson 1983).

Case Study: Life in the Gang

The use of fieldwork techniques to study gangs has a long tradition in a variety of cities, including Thrasher's (1927) classic study of gangs in Chicago, and the work of others such as Hagedorn (1988), Padilla (1992), Sanchez-Jankowski (1991), Vigil (1988), and Whyte (1943). Joan Moore's research (1978, 1991) reflects over two decades studying the "homeboys" of Hispanic barrios all over the United States. All these researchers employed a fieldwork approach to the study of gangs rather than the more structured approaches offered by quantitative methods.

You can get a better feel for qualitative methods by reading the following excerpts from Decker and Van Winkle's (1996) book about gangs, *Life in the Gang: Family, Friends, and Violence*, and by reasoning inductively from their observations. See whether you can determine from these particulars some of the general features of field research. Ask yourself, "What were the research questions?" "How were the issues of generalizability, measurement, and causation approached?" "How did social factors influence the research?"

One of the first issues with which Decker and Van Winkle (1996) were challenged was precisely defining a gang (recall Chapter 4). The term *gang* could refer to many groups of youth, including a high school debate society or the Young Republicans. After reviewing the literature, Decker and Van Winkle developed a working definition of a gang as an "age-graded peer group that exhibits some permanence, engages in criminal activity, and has some symbolic representation of membership" (p. 31). To operationalize who was a gang member, they relied on self-identification. "Are you claiming . . .?" was a key screening question that was also verified, as often as possible, with other gang members.

There were several questions in which Decker and Van Winkle (1996) were interested:

First, we were interested in motivations to join gangs, the process of joining the gang, the symbols of gang membership, the strength of associational ties, the structure or hierarchy within the gang, motivations to stay (or leave) the gang. . . .
The second set of issues concerned the activities gang members engaged in. These included such things as turf protection, drug sales and use, and violence, as well as conventional activities. (pp. 54–55)[1]

With these research questions in mind, Decker and Van Winkle (1996) explain why they chose a fieldwork approach: "A single premise guided our study; the best information about gangs and gang activity would come from gang members contacted directly in the field" (p. 27). As stated earlier, Decker and Van Winkle combined two methods of qualitative data collection. With the help of a field ethnographer who spent the majority of each day "on the streets," direct observation was conducted along with the intensive interviewing conducted by Decker and Van Winkle.

You may wonder what the difference is between the interviews conducted by qualitative researchers and those discussed in the last chapter. The difference is structure. For example, Decker and Van Winkle (1996) did not rely on structured questionnaires with numerically coded, fixed responses; their data are primarily qualitative rather than quantitative.

As for their method, it was inductive. First, they gathered data. Then, as data collection continued, they figured out how to interpret the data and how to make sense of the social situations they were studying. Their analytic categories ultimately came not from social theory but from the categories by which the gang members themselves described one another and their activities and how they made sense of their social world. Instead of quantitatively measuring variables, Decker and Van Winkle (1996) uncovered themes as they emerged. They provided the field of criminology with in-depth descriptions and context-specific connections of sequences of events that could not have been obtained through other methodologies. The goal of much qualitative research is to create a thick description of the setting being studied, that is, a description that provides a sense of what it is like to experience that setting or group from the standpoint of the natural actors in that setting (Geertz 1973).

PARTICIPANT OBSERVATION

Other researchers have utilized a more direct observational strategy for studying gangs. For example, to illuminate the nuances and complexities of the role of a street gang in community social life, Venkatesh (1997) conducted intensive participant observation in Blackstone, a midsize public housing development located in a poor ghetto of a large Midwestern city. As Venkatesh describes, "Having befriended these gang members, I moved into their world, accompanying them into Blackstone and other spaces where they were actively involved in illicit economic activities, member recruitment, and the general expansion of their street-based organization" (p. 4). Participant observation, called fieldwork in anthropology, is a method of studying natural social processes as they happen (in the field rather than in the laboratory), leaving them relatively undisturbed and minimizing your presence as a researcher. It is the seminal field research method, a means for seeing the social world as the research subjects see it, in its totality, and for understanding subjects' interpretations of that world (Wolcott 1995: 66). By observing people and interacting with them in the course of their normal activities, participant observers seek to avoid the artificiality of experimental designs and the unnatural structured questioning of survey research (Koegel 1987: 8).

The term *participant observer* actually represents a continuum of roles (see Exhibit 8.1), ranging from being a complete observer who does not participate in group activities and is publicly defined as a researcher, to being a covert participant who acts just like other group members and does not disclose his or her research role. Many field researchers develop a role between these extremes, publicly acknowledging being a researcher but nonetheless participating in group activities. In some settings, it is possible to observe covertly without acknowledging being a researcher or participating.

Choosing a Role

The first concern of all participant observers is to decide what balance to strike between observing and participating and whether to reveal their role as researchers. These decisions must take into account the specifics of the social situation being studied, the researcher's own background and personality, the larger sociopolitical context, and ethical concerns. The balance of participating and observing that is most appropriate also changes many times during the majority of projects. Ultimately, the researcher's ability to maintain either a covert or an overt role can be challenged many times throughout the research effort.

Complete Observation

In her study of community policing, Susan Miller (1999) adopted the role of a complete observer. Community policing is an approach to policing that emphasizes building closer ties between police and members of the community. Miller was particularly interested in

Exhibit 8.1 The Observational Continuum

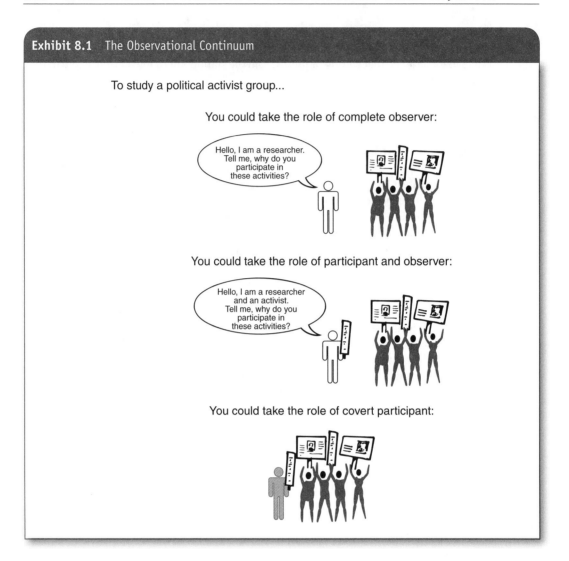

how gender affected the attitudes and behavior of community–police liaisons or neighborhood police officers (NPOs).

In complete observation, researchers try to see things as they happen, without disrupting the participants. Along with intensive interviews with police officers, Susan Miller (1999) also observed police officers on their daily shifts:

> Both neighborhood and patrol officers' shifts were observed, either on foot with neighborhood officers, or in squad cars with patrol officers. This component of the project also permitted gathering some observational information about citizens' reactions to police delivery of services. (pp. 232–233)

Of course, the researcher's presence as an observer alters the social situation being observed. It is not natural in most social situations to have an observer present, who at some point will record his or her observations for research and publication purposes. The observer thus sees what individuals do when they are being observed, which is not necessarily what they would do without an observer. This is called a reactive effect, and the extent to which it can be a problem varies with the situation. In Susan Miller's (1999) study, the extended measure of time she spent as an observer made her presence commonplace, thereby serving to decrease the problem of reactive effects. She states,

> Since I had spent so many hours over eighteen months with the Jackson City Police Department [fictional name], I had grown to be a familiar face; this, I believe, decreased respondents' tendencies toward social desirability. Officers took my presence for granted in the briefing room, the hallways, the interview rooms, and in the field, including me in jokes and informal conversation in the coffee shop. (p. 235)

Generally, in social settings involving many people, an observer may not attract attention. On the other hand, when the social setting involves few people and observing is apparent rather than camouflaged, or when the observer differs in obvious respects from the participants, the complete observer is more likely to have an impact.

Participation and Observation

Most field researchers adopt a role that involves some active participation in the setting. Usually they inform at least some group members of their research interests, but then they participate in enough group activities to develop trust and rapport with members and to gain a direct sense of what group members experience. This is not an easy balancing act.

In his classic study of corner gangs and other social organizations in the poor Boston community he called Cornerville, Whyte (1943) spent a large part of nearly 4 years trying to be accepted by the community and seen as a good fellow. He describes his efforts:

> My aim was to gain an intimate view of Cornerville life. My first problem, therefore, was to establish myself as a participant in the society so that I would have a position from which to observe. I began by going to live in Cornerville, finding a room with an Italian family. . . . It was not enough simply to make the acquaintance of various groups of people. The sort of information that I sought required that I establish intimate social relations, and that presented special problems. Since illegal activities are prevalent in Cornerville, every newcomer is under suspicion. . . . I put in a great deal of time simply hanging around with them [the men] and participating in their various activities. (pp. v–vii)[2]

Because of the great deal of time he spent with each gang and social organization he was studying, Whyte (1943) became accepted into each group and the community. Sudhir Alladi Venkatesh's (2000) book about gangs in Chicago, *American Project*, will almost certainly become a classic as well. In it, he describes the evolution of his research methodology from structured interviews to participant observation:

They read my survey instrument, informed me that I was "not going to learn shit by asking these questions," and said I would need to "hang out with them" if I really wanted to understand the experiences of African-American youth in the city. Over the next few months, I met with many of them informally to play racquetball, drink beer on the shores of Lake Michigan, attend their parties, and eat dinner with their families. . . . Over an eighteen-month period, I logged notes on the activities of their gang, called the Black Kings. (p. xiv)

Disclosing your research to participants has two clear ethical advantages. Because group members know the researcher's real role in the group, they can choose to keep some information or attitudes hidden. By the same token, the researcher can decline to participate in unethical or dangerous activities without fear of exposing his or her identity.

Even when researchers maintain a public identity as researchers, the ethical dilemmas arising from participation in group activities do not go away. In fact, researchers may have to prove themselves to group members by joining in some of their questionable activities. For example, police officers gave Van Maanen (1982) a nonstandard and technically prohibited pistol to carry on police patrols. Pepinsky (1980) witnessed police harassment of a citizen but did not intervene when the citizen was arrested.

Covert Participation

To lessen the potential for reactive effects and to gain entry to otherwise inaccessible settings, some field researchers have adopted the role of covert participant. By doing so, they keep their research secret and do their best to act like other participants in a social setting or group. Covert participation is also known as *complete participation.* Laud Humphreys (1970) served as a "watch queen" so that he could learn about men engaging in homosexual acts in a public restroom. Randall Alfred (1976) joined a group of Satanists to investigate group members and their interaction. Goffman (1961) worked as a state hospital assistant while studying the treatment of psychiatric patients.

Although the role of covert participant lessens some of the reactive effects encountered by the complete observer, covert participants confront other problems. The following are a few examples:

- *Covert participants cannot openly take notes or use any obvious recording devices.* They must write up notes based solely on memory and must do so at times when it is natural for them to be away from group members.
- *Covert participants cannot ask questions that will arouse suspicion.* Thus they often have trouble clarifying the meaning of other participants' attitudes or actions.
- *The role of covert participation is difficult to play successfully.* Covert participants will not know how regular participants act in every situation in which the researchers find themselves. Suspicion that researchers are not "one of us" may then have reactive effects, obviating the value of complete participation (Erikson 1967).
- *Covert participants must keep up the act at all times while in the setting under study.* Researchers may experience enormous psychological strain, particularly in situations where they are expected to choose sides in intragroup conflict or to

participate in criminal or other acts. Of course, some covert observers may become so wrapped up in their role that they adopt not just the mannerisms but also the perspectives and goals of the regular participants—they "go native." At this point, they abandon research goals and cease to critically evaluate their observations.

Ethical issues have been at the forefront of debate over the strategy of covert participation. Erikson (1967) argues that covert participation is by its very nature unethical and should not be allowed except in public settings. Covert researchers cannot anticipate the unintended consequences (e.g., gang violence) of their actions for research subjects, Erikson points out. In addition, other social research is harmed when covert research is disclosed, either during the research or upon its publication, because distrust of social scientists increases and future access to research opportunities may decrease.

But a total ban on covert participation would "kill many a project stone dead" (Punch 1994: 90). Studies of unusual religious or sexual practices and institutional malpractice would rarely be possible. According to Punch, "The crux of the matter is that some deception, passive or active, enables you to get at data not obtainable by other means" (p. 91). Therefore, some field researchers argue that covert participation is legitimate in certain circumstances. If the researcher maintains the confidentiality of others, keeps his or her commitments to them, and does not directly lie to the participants, some degree of deception may be justified in exchange for the knowledge gained (p. 90).

Entering the Field

Entering the field or the setting under investigation is a critical stage in a participant observation project, as the introduction can shape many subsequent experiences. Some background work is necessary before entering the field, at least enough to develop a clear understanding of what the research questions are likely to be and to review one's personal stance toward the people and problems likely to be encountered. With participant observation, researchers must also learn in advance about the participants' dress and their typical activities to avoid being caught completely unprepared.

Developing trust with at least one member of the group being studied is a necessity in qualitative research. Such a person can become a valuable informant throughout the project, and most participant observers make a point of developing trust with at least one informant in a group under study. For example, Susan Miller (1999) gained access to the police department she studied through a chief of police who was extremely open to research. She also had two friends on the police force at the time of her study.

In short, field researchers must be very sensitive to the impression they make and the ties they establish when entering the field. This stage of research lays the groundwork for collecting data from people who have different perspectives and for developing relationships that the researcher can use to overcome the problems that inevitably arise in the field.

Developing and Maintaining Relationships

Researchers must be careful to manage their relationships in the research setting so they can continue to observe and interview diverse members of the social setting throughout the long period typical of participant observation (Maxwell 1996: 66). Every action the researcher takes can develop or undermine this relationship. As Decker and Van Winkle (1996) describe, maintaining trust is the cornerstone to successful research engagement. They elaborate further:

> We were able to maintain good field relations with our subjects by strictly observing our own commitment to the confidentiality of their statements. Since we interviewed many individuals from the same gang, it was often the case that one member would want to know what an earlier participant had told us. We refused to honor such inquiries, reminding them that the same confidentiality that applied to their own answers also covered those of their fellow gang members. The strict confidentiality we were committed to was respected by our subjects, and appeared to enhance our own credibility as "solid" in their eyes. (p. 46)

Experienced participant observers (Whyte 1943: 300–306; Wolcott 1995: 91–95) have developed some sound advice for others seeking to maintain relationships in the field:

- Develop a plausible (and honest) explanation for yourself and your study.
- Maintain the support of key individuals in groups or organizations under study.
- Don't be too aggressive in questioning others (e.g., don't violate implicit norms that preclude discussion of illegal activity with outsiders). Being a researcher requires that you do not simultaneously try to be the guardian of law and order.
- Don't fake social similarity with your subjects. Taking a friendly interest in them should be an adequate basis for developing trust.
- Avoid giving and receiving monetary or other tangible gifts, but do not violate norms of reciprocity. Living with other people, taking others' time for conversations, and going out for a social evening all create expectations and incur social obligations. You cannot be an active participant without occasionally helping others. But you will lose your ability to function as a researcher if you are seen as someone who gives away money or other favors. Such small forms of assistance as an occasional ride to the store or advice on applying to college may strike the right balance.
- Be prepared for special difficulties and tensions if multiple groups are involved. It is hard to avoid taking sides or being used in situations of intergroup conflict.

Sampling People and Events

Decisions to study one setting or several settings and to pay attention to specific people and events will shape field researchers' ability to generalize about what they have found as well as the confidence that others can place in the results of their study. Limiting a particular study to a single setting allows a more intensive portrait of actors and activities in that setting, but also makes generalization of the findings questionable.

It is easy to be reassured by information indicating that a typical case was selected for study or that the case selected was appropriate in some way for the research question. We also must keep in mind that many of the most insightful participant observation studies were conducted in only one setting and draw their credibility precisely from the researcher's thorough understanding of that setting. Nonetheless, studying more than one case or setting almost always strengthens the causal conclusions and makes the findings more generalizable (King et al. 1994).

Most qualitative researchers utilize a purposive sampling technique (see Chapter 5), often adding a snowball aspect by asking respondents to recommend others. For example, Decker and Van Winkle (1996) utilized the technique of snowball sampling. Theoretical sampling is a systematic approach to sampling in participant observational research (Glaser & Strauss 1967). Decker and Van Winkle used this technique to ensure that various subgroups based on race, sex, or type of gang were represented within their sample. When field researchers discover in an investigation that particular processes seem to be important, implying that certain comparisons should be made or that similar instances should be checked, the researchers then modify their settings and choose new individuals to study, as shown in Exhibit 8.2 (Ragin 1994).

Exhibit 8.2 Theoretical Sampling

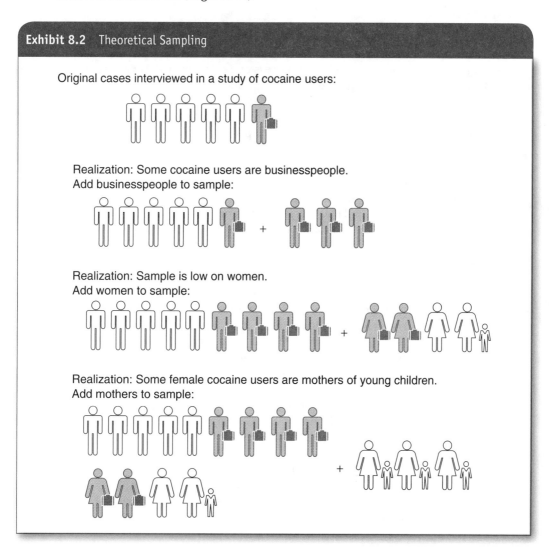

Original cases interviewed in a study of cocaine users:

Realization: Some cocaine users are businesspeople.
Add businesspeople to sample:

Realization: Sample is low on women.
Add women to sample:

Realization: Some female cocaine users are mothers of young children.
Add mothers to sample:

The resulting sample of gang members in Decker and Van Winkle's (1996) study represents 29 different gangs. Thus, Decker and Van Winkle's ability to draw from different gangs in developing conclusions gives us greater confidence in their study's generalizability.

Quota sampling also may be employed to ensure the representation of particular categories of participants. Using some type of intentional sampling strategy within a particular setting can allow tests of some hypotheses that would otherwise have to wait until comparative data could be collected from several settings (King et al. 1994). When field studies do not require ongoing, intensive involvement by researchers in the setting, the experience sampling method (ESM) can be used. The experiences, thoughts, and feelings of a number of people are randomly sampled as they go about their daily activities. Participants in an ESM study carry an electronic pager and fill out reports when they are beeped.

Taking Notes

Written field notes are the primary means of recording participant observation data (Emerson, Fretz, & Shaw 1995). It is almost always a mistake to try to take comprehensive notes while engaged in the field; the process of writing extensively is just too disruptive. The usual procedure is to jot down brief notes about the highlights of the observation period. These brief notes, called jottings, then serve as memory joggers when writing the actual field notes at a later time. With the aid of the brief notes and some practice, researchers usually remember a great deal of what happened, as long as the comprehensive field notes are written within the next 24 hours, that night or upon arising the next day. Many field researchers jot down partial notes while observing and then retreat to their computers to write up more complete notes on a daily basis. The computerized text can then be inspected and organized after it is printed out, or it can be marked up and organized for analysis using one of several computer programs designed especially for the task.

Usually, writing up notes takes as long as making the observations. Field notes must be as complete, detailed, and true to what was observed and heard as possible. Quotes should clearly be distinguished from the researcher's observations and phrased in the local vernacular; pauses and interruptions should be indicated. The surrounding context should receive as much attention as possible, and a map of the setting should always be included, with indications of where individuals were at different times.

Complete field notes must provide more than just a record of what was observed or heard. Notes also should include descriptions of the methodology: where researchers were standing while observing, how they chose people for conversation or observation, and what numerical counts of people or events they made and why. Sprinkled throughout the notes should be a record of the researchers' feelings and thoughts while observing, such as when they were disgusted by some statement or act, when they felt threatened or intimidated, or why their attention shifted from one group to another. Notes like these provide a foundation for later review of the likelihood of bias or inattention to some salient features of the situation.

Managing the Personal Dimensions

Our overview of participant observation is not complete without considering its personal dimensions. Because field researchers become a part of the social situation they are studying, they cannot help but be affected on a personal, emotional level. At the same time, those being studied react to researchers not just as researchers but as personal acquaintances—often as friends, sometimes as personal rivals. Managing and learning from this personal side of field research is an important part of any qualitative project.

The impact of personal issues varies with the depth of researchers' involvement in the setting. The more involved researchers are in multiple aspects of the ongoing social situation, the more important personal issues become and the greater the risk of "going native." Even when researchers acknowledge their role, "increased contact brings sympathy, and sympathy in its turn dulls the edge of criticism" (Fenno 1978: 277).

There is no formula for successfully managing the personal dimension of field research. It is much more art than science and flows more from the researcher's own personality and natural approach to other people than from formal training. Novice field researchers often neglect to consider how they will manage personal relationships when they plan and carry out their projects. Then, suddenly, they find themselves doing something they do not believe they should, just to stay in the good graces of research subjects, or juggling the emotions resulting from conflict within the group. These issues are even more salient when researchers place themselves in potentially dangerous situations. As Decker and Van Winkle (1996) explain,

> In part, gang members were of interest to us because of their involvement in violence. Because of this, we took steps to insure our own safety. One of the guiding principles was to limit the number of people being separately interviewed at the same time and location. In addition, we steadfastly avoided interviewing members of rival gangs at the same time. Despite our best efforts, there were occasions when these precautions did not work. The field ethnographer witnessed several drive-by shootings while on the way to pick up interview subjects, and on one occasion, he saw three of our subjects shot while waiting to be picked up for an interview. . . . Not all exposure to risk of physical danger comes through such obvious means, however; during one interview, when asked whether he owned any guns, a gang member reached into his coat pocket and pulled out a .32 caliber pistol. We assured him that we would have taken his word for it. (p. 46)

SYSTEMATIC OBSERVATION

Observations can be made in a more systematic, standardized design that allows systematic comparisons and more confident generalizations. A researcher using systematic observation develops a standard form on which to record variation within the observed setting in terms of his or her variables of interest. Such variables might include the frequency of some behavior(s), the particular people observed, the weather or other environmental conditions, and the number and state of repair of physical structures. In some systematic observation studies, records are obtained from a random sample of places or times.

Case Study: Systematic Observation in Chicago Neighborhoods

We discussed Robert Sampson and Stephen Raudenbush's (1999) study of disorder and crime in urban neighborhoods in Chapter 4. In this section, we will elaborate on their use of the method of systematic social observation of public spaces to learn more about Chicago neighborhoods. A systematic observational strategy increases the reliability of observational data by using explicit rules that standardize coding practices across observers (Reiss 1971). Sampson and Raudenbush's study was a multiple-methods investigation that combined observational research, survey research, and archival research. The observational component involved a stratified probability (random) sample of 196 Chicago census tracts. A specially equipped sport utility vehicle was driven down each street in these tracts at the rate of 5 miles per hour. Two video recorders taped the blocks on both sides of the street, while two observers peered out the vehicle's windows and recorded their observations in logs. The result was an observational record of 23,816 *face blocks* (the block on one side of the street is a face block). The observers recorded codes that indicated land use, traffic, physical conditions, and evidence of physical disorder (see Exhibit 8.3). Physical disorder was measured by counting such features as cigarettes or cigars in the street, garbage, empty beer bottles, graffiti, condoms, and syringes. Indicators of social disorder included adults loitering, drinking alcohol in public, fighting, and selling drugs.

Peter St. Jean (2007) advanced the research of Sampson and Raudenbush by examining the variation in collective efficacy, community disorder, and crime within specific blocks in one high-crime police district in Chicago. After examining official data and combining them with interviews asking residents where crime typically took place in the neighborhood, St. Jean found that "pockets of crime" emerged in which most crimes occurred on particular blocks within a neighborhood, while other blocks remained relatively untouched. The goal of St. Jean's work was to determine why. He used multiple methods for this project including resident surveys, participant observation, in-depth interviews with residents and offenders, and systematic social observation. For this last method, video cameras were mounted on each side of a vehicle while it was slowly driven through neighborhood streets so that physical and social appearances could be captured. An example of the video St. Jean captured is available on the Student Study Site for this text. Using the tapes, neighborhood characteristics were then coded for social disorder by using the conditions of the buildings, properties, and vacant lots and the prevalence of behaviors like loitering, public drinking, and panhandling. A snapshot from one of St. Jean's videos is displayed in Exhibit 8.4.

Innovatively, St. Jean (2007) not only coded the videos; he also used the footage as a visual cue when interviewing offenders about their reasons for selecting particular locations and victims. He explains,

> For instance, drug dealers and robbers were able to use the [Systematic Social Observation] movie to explain in detail how and why certain locations are more attractive than others. It also allowed offenders to identify the specific features of neighbourhoods that they considered distasteful, and to explain associated meanings, especially as such meanings pertain to the crimes they commit . . . it refreshed the subjects' memories of relevant events that they often claimed they would have forgotten to mention [without the video]. (p. 27)

Exhibit 8.3   Neighborhood Disorder Indicators Used in Systematic Observation Log

Variable	Category	Frequency
Physical Disorder		
Cigarettes, cigars on street or gutter	no yes	6,815 16,758
Garbage, litter on street or sidewalk	no yes	11,680 11,925
Empty beer bottles visible in street	no yes	17,653 5,870
Tagging graffiti	no yes	12,859 2,252
Graffiti painted over	no yes	13,390 1,721
Gang graffiti	no yes	14,138 973
Abandoned cars	no yes	22,782 806
Condoms on sidewalk	no yes	23,331 231
Needles or syringes on sidewalk	no yes	23,392 173
Political message graffiti	no yes	15,097 14
Social Disorder		
Adults loitering or congregating	no yes	14,250 861
People drinking alcohol	no yes	15,075 36
Peer group, gang indicators present	no yes	15,091 20
People intoxicated	no yes	15,093 18
Adults fighting or hostilely arguing	no yes	15,099 12
Prostitutes on street	no yes	15,100 11
People selling drugs	no yes	15,099 12

Source: Raudenbush, Stephen W. and Robert J. Sampson. 1999. "Ecometrics: Toward a Science of Assessing Ecological Settings With Application to the Systematic Social Observation of Neighborhoods." *Sociological Methodology, 29*: 1–41. Reprinted with permission.

Exhibit 8.4 One Building in St. Jean's (2007) Study

Source: © 2007 Peter K. B. St. Jean. Reprinted with permission.

Among other things, St. Jean discovered that even when offenders faced opposition from neighborhood reformers, they were not deterred from engaging in crime in an area when it offered "ecological advantages" such as retail establishments and bus stops.

These studies illustrate both the value of multiple methods and the technique of recording observations in a systematic form. The systematic observations, when combined with residents' own perceptions, provide us with much greater confidence in the measurement of relative neighborhood disorder. When these are combined with rich narrative accounts from neighborhood residents and active offenders, both the measurement validity of the constructs and the overall validity of the findings are significantly enhanced.

INTENSIVE INTERVIEWING

Asking questions is part of almost all qualitative research designs (Wolcott 1995). Many qualitative researchers employ intensive interviewing exclusively, without systematic observation of respondents in their natural setting. Unlike the more structured interviewing that may be used in survey research (discussed in Chapter 7), intensive interviewing relies on open-ended questions. Qualitative researchers do not presume to know the range of answers that respondents might give, and they seek to hear these answers in the respondents' own words. Rather than asking standard questions in a fixed order, intensive interviewers allow the specific content and order of questions to vary from one interviewee to another.

What distinguishes intensive interviewing from more structured forms of questioning is consistency and thoroughness. The goal is to develop a comprehensive picture of the interviewees' background, attitudes, and actions, in their own terms—to "listen to people as they describe how they understand the worlds in which they live and work" (Rubin & Rubin 1995: 3). For example, even though Decker and Van Winkle (1996) had an interview guide, they encouraged elaboration on the part of their respondents and "went to great lengths to insure that each person we interviewed felt they had received the opportunity to tell their story in their own words" (p. 45).

Random selection is rarely used to select respondents for intensive interviews, but the selection method still must be considered carefully. Researchers should try to select interviewees who are knowledgeable about the subject of the interview, who are open to talking, and who represent the range of perspectives (Rubin & Rubin 1995). Selection of new interviewees should continue, if possible, at least until the **saturation point** is reached, the point when new interviews seem to yield little additional information (see Exhibit 8.5). As new issues are uncovered, additional interviewees may be selected to represent different opinions about these issues.

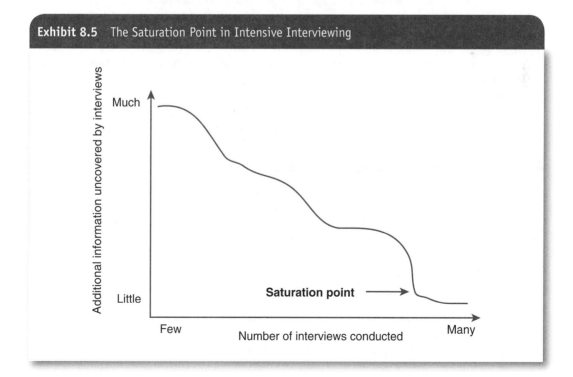

Exhibit 8.5   The Saturation Point in Intensive Interviewing

Research by Fleury-Steiner (2003) that examines the thoughts and emotions of jurors in death penalty cases is an excellent illustration of the tremendous insights that can be uncovered through intensive interviewing. In *Jurors' Stories of Death,* Fleury-Steiner reports on his work with the Capital Jury Project (CJP), which was a national study of the experiences of citizens who served as jurors on death penalty cases. To encourage respondents to tell stories about their experiences, the CJP survey explicitly asked jurors to tell interviewers about important moments during the trial and deliberations, and their impressions of the defendant. Fleury-Steiner states, "The goal of these questions was to facilitate jurors to construct their responses in their own ways. . . . Given the leeway to answer as they saw fit, in many instances jurors' stories emerged when I least expected them to" (p. 44).

Establishing and Maintaining a Partnership

Because intensive interviewing does not engage researchers as participants in subjects' daily affairs, the problems associated with entering the field are greatly reduced. However, the logistics of arranging long periods for personal interviews can still be fairly complicated. It is important to establish rapport with subjects by considering in advance how they will react to the interview arrangement and by developing an approach that does not violate their standards for social behavior. Interviewees should be treated with respect, as knowledgeable partners whose time is valued. (In other words, avoid being late for appointments.) Once again, a commitment to confidentiality should be stated and honored (Rubin & Rubin 1995).

It is important to highlight, however, that the intensive interviewer's relationship with the interviewee is not an equal partnership, for the researcher seeks to gain certain types of information and strategizes throughout to maintain an appropriate relationship. In the first few minutes of the interview, the goal is to show interest in the interviewee and to clearly explain the purpose of the interview (Kvale 1996). During the interview, the interviewer should maintain an appropriate distance from the interviewee, one that does not violate cultural norms; the interviewer should maintain eye contact and not engage in distracting behavior. An appropriate pace is also important; pause to allow the interviewee to reflect, elaborate, and generally not feel rushed (Gordon 1992). When an interview covers emotional or otherwise stressful topics, at the end the interviewer should give the interviewee an opportunity to unwind (Rubin & Rubin 1995).

Asking Questions and Recording Answers

Intensive interviewers must plan their main questions around an outline of the interview topic. The questions should generally be short and to the point. More details can then be elicited through nondirective probes (such as "Can you tell me more about that?"), and follow-up questions can be tailored to answers to the main questions. Interviewers should strategize throughout an interview about how best to achieve their objectives while taking into account interviewees' answers.

Decker and Van Winkle's (1996) interview narrative illustrates this well:

Nearly half of the gang members identified leaders as persons who could provide material advantage, thus ascribing a functional character to leadership within the gang. Since half of our sample were in their early teens, someone with the ability to procure cars, drugs, guns, or alcohol could play a valuable role in the gang.

Consequently, it was no surprise to find that over half of gang members identified leaders as persons who could "deliver." Because of the situational nature of leadership, persons moved in and out of this role. This was especially true in the case of being able to provide drugs in large quantities for street sales:

Q: Does someone have more juice in the gang?
A: Yeah, you always got someone that got more juice.

Q: What is the type of person who usually has more juice?
A: The one who got the connection with the drugs.

Q: Who has the most juice?
A: Dude named T-Loc.

Q: Why does he have more juice than everybody else?
A: 'Cause he travels a lot. Gets the good stuff.

Q: What's the good stuff?
A: Like guns, cocaine, weed.

Q: What gives him the juice? (pp. 97–98)

Do you see how the interviewer actively encouraged the subject to elaborate on answers? More important, intensive interviews can also uncover true meanings that questions utilizing fixed formats would surely miss.

Tape or digital voice recorders commonly are used to record intensive interviews. Most researchers who have recorded interviews feel that they do not inhibit most interviewees and, in fact, are routinely ignored. The occasional respondent who is very concerned with his or her public image may speak "for the recorder," but such individuals are unlikely to speak frankly in any research interview. In any case, constant note taking during an interview prevents adequate displays of interest and appreciation by the interviewer and hinders the degree of concentration that results in the best interviews.

FOCUS GROUPS

Focus groups are groups of individuals that are formed by a researcher and then led in group discussion of a topic. The researcher asks specific questions and guides the discussion to ensure that group members address these questions, but the resulting information is qualitative and relatively unstructured. Unlike most other survey designs, focus groups do not involve representative samples; instead, a few individuals are recruited for the group who have the time to participate and who share key characteristics with the target population.

Most focus groups involve 7 to 10 people, a size that facilitates discussion by all in attendance. Although participants usually do not know one another, they are chosen so that they are relatively homogeneous, which tends to reduce their inhibitions in discussion. Of course, the characteristics of individuals that determine their inclusion are based on the researcher's conception of the target population for the study. Focus group leaders must begin the discussion by creating the expectation that all will participate and that the researcher will not favor any particular perspective or participant.

Focus groups are interviewed to collect qualitative data using open-ended questions posed by the researcher (or group leader). Thus, a focused discussion mimics the natural process of forming and expressing opinions and may give some sense of validity. The researcher may also want to conduct a more traditional survey, asking a representative sample of the target population to answer closed-ended questions, to weigh the validity of data obtained from the focus group. No formal procedure exists for determining the generalizability of focus group answers, but the careful researcher should conduct at least several focus groups on the same topic and check for consistency in the findings as a partial test of generalizability.

As with other field research techniques, focus group methods emphasize discovering unanticipated findings and exploring hidden meanings. Although they do not provide a means for developing reliable, generalizable results (the traditional strong suits of survey research), focus groups can be an indispensable aid for developing hypotheses and survey questions, for investigating the meaning of survey results, and for quickly identifying the range of opinion about an issue.

Case Study: Combining Focus Groups With Official Records When Examining Police Searches

Racial profiling has generally been defined as the use of race by police as a key factor in deciding whether to make a traffic stop—that is, to pull over a driver for an infraction (Williams & Stahl 2008). As a response to lawsuits alleging racial profiling, many state and local law enforcement agencies have been mandated or have volunteered to collect traffic stop data to monitor the behavior of officers to determine the extent of such profiling. However, to actually determine if racial minorities like African Americans are stopped for an infraction like speeding more than whites, researchers would first have to determine the percentage of African American drivers relative to whites who were actually driving along a given highway, and then the percentage of these motorists who were actually speeding, to get a true base rate of speeding per population group. This would entail many hours of monitoring a given highway during various times of day. While some researchers have actually collected these data, Williams and Stahl decided to examine whether race was a determining factor in whether a driver was searched, not in the original police stop. The questions they asked were, "Who is being searched, and what are the results of these searches?" Using data collected in 24 local Kentucky law enforcement agencies along with two state agencies, they concluded that of the motorists pulled over on the interstate for compliance and courtesy stops, African American and Hispanic motorists were significantly more likely to be searched compared to white motorists. To test the second question, they examined whether there were differences in positive search results (e.g., finding contraband) across race or ethnic groups. Consistent with other research, there was no statistical difference in the likelihood that white, African American, or Hispanic motorists who were searched actually had illegal material.

To better contextualize these quantitative findings, Williams and Stahl (2008) also conducted focus groups with police officers to determine their perceptions about a number of issues including whether traffic stops and searches were effective in preventing some of the problems in their communities. A purposive sample (discussed in Chapter 5) of 24 officers participated in five focus groups. After comparing the perceptions, attitudes, and experiences across groups and individual officers, several themes emerged. The first was that drug use and sales as well as drunk driving were major community problems. The second was that the police perception was that if you wanted to target a particular problem, you had to target a particular group: African Americans were perceived to be associated with crack cocaine, driving under the influence was perceived to be associated with Hispanic motorists, and methamphetamine was perceived to be associated with whites. Moreover, officers were confident that traffic stops helped deter the drug trade and improve the quality of life of their local communities. Williams and Stahl concluded that the officers shared a perception that they were community problem solvers who profile the problems and not a particular group. However, these qualitative data, combined with the quantitative analysis of search data, led the researchers to conclude, "If police want to be efficient and effective in their efforts to stop drugs, it seems that they need to disregard the 'profile' as our analysis has found that it is an ineffective tool for turning up illegal substances" (p. 238). This triangulation of methods was extremely helpful in placing the quantitative data within the perceptions shared by police officers.

ANALYZING QUALITATIVE DATA

The distinctive features of qualitative data collection methods are also reflected in the methods used to analyze the data collected. The focus on text, on qualitative data rather than on numbers, is the most important feature of qualitative data analysis. The "text" that qualitative researchers analyze is most often transcripts of interviews or notes from participant observation sessions, but text can also refer to pictures or other images that the researcher examines.

Good qualitative data analyses are distinguished by their focus on the interrelated aspects of the setting, group, or person under investigation—the entire case—rather than breaking the whole into separate parts. The whole is always understood to be greater than the sum of its parts, and so the social context of events, thoughts, and actions becomes essential for interpretation. Within this framework, it would not make sense to focus on two variables out of an interacting set of influences and test the relationship between just those two.

Qualitative data analysis is a reflexive process that begins as data are being collected rather than after data collection has ceased (Stake 1995). Next to his or her field notes or interview transcripts, the qualitative analyst jots down ideas about the meaning of the text and how it might relate to other issues. This process of reading through the data and interpreting them continues throughout the project. The analyst adjusts the data collection process itself when it begins to appear that additional concepts need to be investigated or new relationships explored. This process is termed **progressive focusing** (Parlett & Hamilton 1976).

Progressive focusing The process by which a qualitative analyst interacts with the data and gradually refines his or her focus

---

Qualitative Data Analysis as an Art

The process of qualitative data analysis is described by some as involving as much "art" as science, or as a "dance," in the words of Miller and Crabtree (1999). In this artful way, analyzing text involves both inductive and deductive processes. The researcher generates concepts and linkages between them based on reading the text and also checks the text to see whether those concepts and interpretations are reflected.

Qualitative Compared With Quantitative Data Analysis

With these points in mind, let us review the ways in which qualitative data analysis differs from quantitative analysis (Denzin & Lincoln 2000; Patton 2002). Qualitative analysis features the following:

- A focus on meanings rather than on quantifiable phenomena;
- Collection of many data on a few cases rather than few data on many cases;
- In-depth study and attention to detail, without predetermined categories or directions, rather than emphasis on analyses and categories determined in advance;
- A conception of the researcher as an "instrument," rather than as the designer of objective instruments to measure particular variables;
- Sensitivity to context rather than a seeking of universal generalizations;
- Attention to the impact of the researcher's and others' values on the course of the analysis rather than presuming the possibility of value-free inquiry;
- A goal of rich descriptions of the world rather than measurement of specific variables.

You will also want to keep in mind features of qualitative data analysis that are shared with those of quantitative data analysis. Both qualitative and quantitative data analysis can involve making distinctions about textual data. You also know that textual data can be transposed to quantitative data through a process of categorization and counting. Some qualitative analysts also share with quantitative researchers a positivist goal of describing the world as it "really" is, but others have adopted a postmodern goal of trying to understand how different people see and make sense of the world, without believing that there is any "correct" description.

TECHNIQUES OF QUALITATIVE DATA ANALYSIS

The most typical steps that are shared by most approaches to qualitative data analysis include

- Documentation of the data and the process of data collection;
- Organization or categorization of the data into concepts;
- Connection of the data to show how one concept may influence another;

- Corroboration or legitimization, by evaluating alternative explanations, challenging validity, and searching for negative cases; and
- Representing the account (reporting the findings).

The analysis of qualitative research notes begins while interviewing or as early as the researcher enters the field; researchers identify problems and concepts that appear likely to help in understanding the situation. Simply reading the notes or transcripts is an important step in the analytic process. Researchers should make frequent notes in the margins to identify important statements and to propose ways of coding the data.

An interim stage may consist of listing the concepts reflected in the notes and diagramming the relationships among concepts (Maxwell 1996). In a large project, weekly team meetings are an important part of this process. Susan Miller (1999) described this process in her study of neighborhood police officers. Miller's research team members met both to go over their field notes and to resolve points of confusion, as well as to dialogue with other skilled researchers who helped to identify emerging concepts.

This process continues throughout the project and should assist in refining concepts during the report-writing phase, long after data collection has ceased. Let us examine each of the stages of qualitative research in more detail.

Documentation

The first formal analytical step is **documentation**. The various contacts, interviews, written documents, and whatever it is that preserves a record of what happened must all be saved and listed. Documentation is critical to qualitative research for several reasons: It is essential for keeping track of what will become a rapidly growing volume of notes, tapes, and documents; it provides a way of developing an outline for the analytic process; and it encourages ongoing conceptualizing and strategizing about the text.

What to do with all this material? Many field research projects have slowed to a halt because a novice researcher becomes overwhelmed by the quantity of information that has been collected. A 1-hour interview can generate 20 to 25 pages of single-spaced text (Kvale 1996: 169). Analysis is less daunting, however, if the researcher maintains a disciplined transcription schedule.

Making Sense of It: Conceptualization, Coding, and Categorizing

Identifying and refining important concepts is a key part of the iterative process of qualitative research. Sometimes conceptualizing begins with a simple observation that is interpreted directly, "pulled apart," and then put back together more meaningfully. Stake (1995) provides an example: "More often, analytic insights are tested against new observations, the initial statement of problems and concepts is refined, the researcher then collects more data, interacts with the data again, and the process continues" (p. 75).

Jody Miller (2000) provides an excellent illustration of the developmental process of conceptualization in her study of girls in gangs:

> I paid close attention to and took seriously respondents' reactions to themes raised in interviews, particularly instances in which they "talked back" by labeling a topic irrelevant, pointing out what they saw as misinterpretations on my part, or offering corrections. In my research, the women talked back the most in response to my efforts to get them to articulate how gender inequality shaped their experiences in the gang. Despite stories they told to the contrary, many maintained a strong belief in their equality within the gang. . . . As the research progressed, I also took emerging themes back to respondents in subsequent interviews to see if they felt I had gotten it right. In addition to conveying that I was interested in their perspectives and experiences, this process also proved useful for further refining my analyses. (p. 30)

The process described in this quote illustrates the reflexive nature of qualitative data collection and analysis. In qualitative research, the collection of data and their analysis are not typically separate activities. This excerpt shows how the researcher first was alerted to a concept by observations in the field, then refined her understanding of this concept by investigating its meaning. By observing the concept's frequency of use, she came to realize its importance.

Examining Relationships and Displaying Data

Examining relationships is the centerpiece of the analytic process, because it allows the researcher to move from simple description of the people and settings to explanations of why things happened as they did with those people in that setting. The process of examining relationships can be captured in a **matrix** that shows how different concepts are connected, or perhaps what causes are linked with what effects.

Exhibit 8.6 provides an excellent example of a causal model developed by Baskin and Sommers (1998) to explain the desistance process for the sample of violent female offenders they interviewed in the state of New York. They described the process for the women who made it out of their lives of crime as follows:

> Desistance is a process as complex and lengthy as the process of initial involvement. It was interesting to find that some of the key concepts in initiation of deviance—social bonding, differential association, deterrence, age—were equally important in the process of desistance. We see the aging offender take the threat of punishment seriously, reestablish links with conventional society and sever associations with subcultural street elements. We found, too, that the decision to give up crime was triggered by a shock of some sort that was followed by a period of crisis. They arrived at a point at which the deviant way of life seemed senseless. (p. 139)

Authenticating Conclusions

No set standards exist for evaluating the validity or "authenticity" of conclusions in a qualitative study, but the need to consider carefully the evidence and methods on which

Exhibit 8.6   The Desistance Process for Violent Female Offenders

Stage 1: Problems Associated With Criminal Participation

Socially Disjunctive Experiences	*Delayed Deterrence*
Hitting rock bottom	Increased probability of punishment
Fear of death	Increased difficulty in "doing time"
Tiredness	Increased severity of sanctions
Illness	Increasing fear

Assessment
Reappraisal of life and goals
Psychic change

Decision
Decision to quit or initial attempts at desistance
Continuing possibility of criminal participation

Stage 2: Restructuring of Self

Public pronouncement of decision to end criminal participation
Claim to a new identity

Stage 3: Maintenance of the Decision to Stop

Ability to successfully renegotiate identity
Support of significant others
Integration into new social networks
Ties to conventional roles
Stabilization of new social identity

Source: Baskin, Deborah R. and Ira B. Sommers. 1998. *Casualties of Community Disorder: Women's Careers in Violent Crime.* Boulder, CO: Westview. Reprinted by permission of Westview Press, a member of the Perseus Books Group.

conclusions are based is just as great as with other types of research. Data can be assessed in terms of at least three criteria (Becker 1958):

- *How credible was the informant?* Were statements made by someone with whom the researcher had a relationship of trust or by someone the researcher had just met? Did the informant have reason to lie? If the statements do not seem to be trustworthy as indicators of actual events, can they at least be used to help understand the informant's perspective?
- *Were statements made in response to the researcher's questions, or were they spontaneous?* Spontaneous statements are more likely to indicate what would have been said had the researcher not been present.
- *How does the presence or absence of the researcher or the researcher's informant influence the actions and statements of other group members?* Reactivity to being

observed can never be ruled out as a possible explanation for some directly observed social phenomena. However, if the researcher carefully compares what the informant says goes on when the researcher is not present, what the researcher observes directly, and what other group members say about their normal practices, the extent of reactivity can be assessed to some extent.

A qualitative researcher's conclusions should be assessed by their ability to provide a credible explanation for some aspect of social life. That explanation should capture group members' tacit knowledge of the social processes that were observed, not just their verbal statements about these processes. Tacit knowledge, "the largely unarticulated, contextual understanding that is often manifested in nods, silences, humor, and naughty nuances," is reflected in participants' actions as well as their words and in what they fail to state but nonetheless feel deeply and even take for granted (Altheide & Johnson 1994: 492–493). These features are evident in Whyte's (1955) analysis of Cornerville social patterns.

Comparing conclusions from a qualitative research project to those obtained by other researchers conducting similar projects can also increase confidence in their authenticity.

Reflexivity

Confidence in the conclusions from a field research study is also strengthened by an honest and informative account about how the researcher interacted with subjects in the field, what problems he or she encountered, and how these problems were or were not resolved. Such a "natural history" of the development of the evidence, sometimes termed reflexivity, enables others to evaluate the findings. Such an account is important primarily because of the evolving nature of field research.

Qualitative data analysts, more often than quantitative researchers, display real sensitivity to how a social situation or process is interpreted from a particular background and set of values and not simply based on the situation itself (Altheide & Johnson 1994). Researchers are only human, after all, and must rely on their own senses to process information through their own minds. By reporting how and why they think they did what they did, they can help others determine whether, or how, the researchers' perspectives influenced their conclusions. "There should be clear 'tracks' indicating the attempt [to show the hand of the ethnographer] has been made" (Altheide & Johnson 1994: 493).

ALTERNATIVES IN QUALITATIVE DATA ANALYSIS

The qualitative data analyst can choose from many interesting alternative approaches. Of course, the research question under investigation should shape the selection of an analytic approach, but the researcher's preferences and experiences will inevitably steer the research method selection. The alternative approaches we present here—ethnography and grounded theory—are two of the most frequently used (Patton 2002).

Ethnography

Ethnography is the study of a culture or cultures that a group of people share (Van Maanen 1995). As a method, it usually is meant to refer to the process of participant observation by a single investigator who immerses himself or herself in the group for a long period of time (often one or more years). Ethnographic research can also be called "naturalistic," because it seeks to describe and understand the natural social world as it really is, in all its richness and detail. There are no particular methodological techniques associated with ethnography, other than just "being there." The analytic process relies on the thoroughness and insight of the researcher to "tell it like it is" in the setting, as he or she experienced it.

Code of the Street, Elijah Anderson's (1999) award-winning study of Philadelphia's inner city, captures the flavor of this approach:

> My primary aim in this work is to render ethnographically the social and cultural dynamics of the interpersonal violence that is currently undermining the quality of life of too many urban neighborhoods. . . . How do the people of the setting perceive their situation? What assumptions do they bring to their decision making? (10–11)[3]

Like most traditional ethnographers, Anderson (1999) describes his concern with being "as objective as possible" and using his training as other ethnographers do, "to look for and to recognize underlying assumptions, their own and those of their subjects, and to try to override the former and uncover the latter" (p. 11).

From analysis of the data obtained in these ways, a rich description emerges of life in the inner city. Although we often do not "hear" the residents speak, we feel the community's pain in Anderson's (1999) description of "the aftermath of death":

> When a young life is cut down, almost everyone goes into mourning. The first thing that happens is that a crowd gathers about the site of the shooting or the incident. The police then arrive, drawing more of a crowd. Since such a death often occurs close to the victim's house, his mother or his close relatives and friends may be on the scene of the killing. When they arrive, the women and girls often wail and moan, crying out their grief for all to hear, while the young men simply look on, in studied silence. . . . Soon the ambulance arrives. (p. 138)

Anderson (1999) uses these descriptions as a foundation on which he develops the key concepts in his analysis, such as "code of the street":

> The "code of the street" is not the goal or product of any individual's action but is the fabric of everyday life, a vivid and pressing milieu within which all local residents must shape their personal routines, income strategies, and orientations to schooling, as well as their mating, parenting, and neighbor relations. (p. 326)

This rich ethnographic tradition is being abandoned by some qualitative data analysts, however. Many have become skeptical of the ability of social scientists to perceive the social world in a way that is not distorted by their own subjective biases or to receive impressions from the actors in that social world that are not altered by the fact of being studied (Van Maanen 2002). As a result, both specific techniques and alternative approaches to qualitative data analysis have proliferated. The next sections introduce several of these alternative approaches.

Grounded Theory

Theory development occurs continually in qualitative data analysis (Coffey & Atkinson 1996). The goal of many qualitative researchers is to create **grounded theory**—that is, to inductively build up a systematic theory that is "grounded" in, or based on, the observations. The observations are summarized into conceptual categories, which are tested directly in the research setting with more observations. Over time, as the conceptual categories are refined and linked, a theory evolves (Glaser & Strauss 1967; Huberman & Miles 1994). Exhibit 8.7 illustrates this process.

Exhibit 8.7 The Development of Grounded Theory

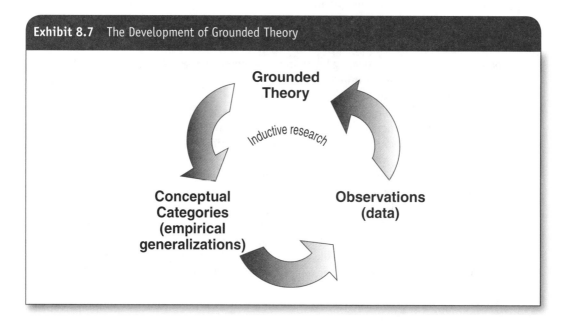

As observation, interviewing, and reflection continue, researchers refine their definitions of problems and concepts, and select indicators. They can then check the frequency and distribution of phenomena: How many people made a particular type of comment? Which people assigned similar meaning to the same patterns, behavior, or comparable social events? How often did social interaction lead to arguments? Social system models may then be developed, which specify the relationships among different phenomena. These models are modified as researchers gain experience in the setting. For the final analysis, the researchers check their models carefully against their notes and make a concerted attempt to discover negative evidence that might suggest the model is incorrect.

Computer-Assisted Qualitative Data Analysis

The analysis process can be enhanced in various ways by using a computer. Programs designed for qualitative data can speed up the analysis process, make it easier for researchers to experiment with different codes, test different hypotheses about relationships, and facilitate diagrams of emerging theories and preparation of research reports (Coffey & Atkinson 1996; Richards & Richards 1994). The steps involved in **computer-assisted qualitative data analysis** (preparation, coding, analysis, and reporting) parallel those used traditionally to analyze text such as notes, documents, or interview transcripts. We use two of the most popular programs to illustrate these steps: HyperRESEARCH and QSR NVivo. (See the Student Study Site, www.sagepub.com/bachmanfrccj2e, for an extended introduction to HyperRESEARCH. The software itself and the HyperRESEARCH tutorials are found on the study site as well.) However, there are many other programs from which to choose.

Computer-assisted analysis focuses on reviewing cases or text segments with similar codes and examining relationships among different codes. You may decide to combine codes into larger concepts, or you may specify additional codes to capture more fully the variation among cases. You can also test hypotheses about relationships among codes.

It is important to know that even with the many types of analyses and reports that can be developed with qualitative analysis software, the results still demand a careful evaluation of the quality of the data on which conclusions are based. In reality, using a qualitative data analysis computer program is not always as straightforward as it appears. Scott Decker and Barrik Van Winkle (1996) describe the difficulty they faced in using a computer program to identify instances of the concept of "drug sales":

> The software we used is essentially a text retrieval package. . . . One of the dilemmas faced in the use of such software is whether to employ a coding scheme within the interviews or simply to leave them as unmarked text. We chose the first alternative, embedding conceptual tags at the appropriate points in the text. An example illustrates this process. One of the activities we were concerned with was drug sales. Our first chore (after a thorough reading of all the transcripts) was to use the software to "isolate" all of the transcript sections dealing with drug sales.
>
> One way to do this would be to search the transcripts for every instance in which the word "drugs" was used. However, such a strategy would have the disadvantages of providing information of too general a character while often missing important statements about drugs. Searching on the word "drugs" would have produced a file including every time the word was used, whether it was in reference to drug sales, drug use, or drug availability—clearly more information than we were interested in. However, such a search would have failed to find all of the slang used to refer to drugs ("boy" for heroin, "Casper" for crack cocaine) as well as the more common descriptions of drugs, especially rock or crack cocaine. (pp. 53–54)

As you can see, coding interview transcripts is not so easy. Decker and Van Winkle solved this problem by parenthetically inserting conceptual tags in the text whenever talk of drug sales was found.

ETHICAL ISSUES IN QUALITATIVE RESEARCH

Qualitative research can raise some complex ethical issues. No matter how hard the field researcher strives to study the social world naturally, leaving no traces, the very act of research itself imposes something unnatural on the situation. It is up to the researchers to identify and take responsibility for the consequences of their involvement. Several ethical issues arise: voluntary participation, subject well-being, identity disclosure, confidentiality, establishing boundaries, and maintaining the safety of researchers in the field.

Voluntary Participation

Ensuring that subjects are participating in a study voluntarily is not often a problem with intensive interviewing and focus group research, but it is often a point of contention in participant observation studies. Few researchers or institutional review boards are willing to condone covert participation because it does not offer a way to ensure that participation by the subjects is voluntary. Even when the researcher's role is more open, interpreting the standard of voluntary participation still can be difficult. Most field research would be impossible if the participant observer were required to request permission of everyone having some contact, no matter how minimal, with a group or setting being observed. For instance, should the requirement of voluntary participation apply equally to every member of an organization being observed? What if the manager consents, the workers are ambivalent, and the union says no? Requiring everyone's consent would limit participant observation research only to settings without serious conflicts of interest.

The issue of voluntary participation is particularly important when interviewing or observing minors. At what age can individuals validly give their voluntary consent to participate in a project? It is customary for human subjects committees to want the consent of parents when their children are participating in research. This requirement poses a problem for research that may be investigating issues that parents or guardians may not want uncovered, such as abuse or neglect. In other instances, alerting parents or guardians about the nature of the study may compromise the confidentiality of the participants. For example, if Decker and Van Winkle (1996) had been forced to obtain parental approval for their gang member interviews, it would have violated the confidentiality they tried to provide to their respondents. To assure the human subjects committee that their participants understood their rights, Decker and Van Winkle obtained an advocate for each juvenile member of their sample. This advocate was responsible for making sure that the juveniles each understood his or her right to refuse or quit the interview at any time without penalty and the confidential nature of the project. Only after these issues were carefully explained did the participant sign a consent form. As noted in Chapter 3, issues of true voluntary participation also arise with other populations such as patients or inmates in a correctional facility.

Subject Well-Being

Before beginning a project, every field researcher should carefully consider how to avoid harm to subjects. It is not possible to avoid every theoretical possibility of harm or to be sure that any project will not cause adverse consequences to any individual. For example, some of the Cornerville men read Whyte's (1955) book and felt embarrassed or unnerved by it (while others found it enlightening). Direct harm to the reputations or feelings of particular individuals is what researchers must carefully avoid. They can do so in part by maintaining the confidentiality of research subjects. They must also avoid adversely affecting the course of events while engaged in a setting.

Jody Miller (2000) encountered a unique ethical dilemma while she was recruiting young women from a residential facility by paying them to refer other girls who were gang members to her research. These referral gratuities are common in snowball samples like this. Unfortunately, in this case one young woman decided to cash in on the deal by initiating new young women into her gang. Here, the ethical dilemma regarding "subject well-being" was that the initiation ceremony for this particular gang involved recruits to the gang being "beaten into the gang." Miller decided to stop conducting research at this location and ultimately lost several interviews. She states,

> It was a difficult decision to make because I had struggled for so long to locate gang girls in Columbus [Missouri]. Ultimately, I believe it was the right thing to do. My presence had stirred up trouble for the agency, and I had an ethical obligation to back away, regardless of the cost to me. (p. 26)

Identity Disclosure

How much disclosure about the study is necessary, and how hard should researchers try to make sure that their research purposes are understood? Less-educated subjects may not readily comprehend what a researcher does or be able to weigh the possible consequences of the research for themselves. Should researchers inform subjects if the study's interests and foci change while it is in progress? Current ethical standards require informed consent of research subjects. Can this standard be met in any meaningful way if researchers do not fully disclose their identity in the first place? But isn't some degree of deception a natural part of social life (Punch 1994)? Can a balance be struck between the disclosure of critical facts and a coherent research strategy?

Confidentiality

Field researchers normally use fictitious names for the people in their reports, but doing so does not always guarantee confidentiality for their research subjects. Individuals in the setting studied may be able to identify those whose actions are described and may thus become privy to some knowledge about their colleagues or neighbors that would otherwise have been kept from them. Researchers should therefore make every effort to expunge possible identifying material from published information and to alter unimportant aspects of a description when necessary to prevent identity disclosure. In any case, no field research project should begin if it is clear that some participants will suffer serious harm by being identified in project publications.

Confidentiality is particularly important if the research is uncovering deviant or illegal behavior. In research such as Decker and Van Winkle's (1996), it was almost inevitable that their information about illegal activity would be revealed during the course of observing or interviewing. Because they had promised confidentiality to their interviewees, Decker and Van Winkle would only refer to illegal activity in an aggregate form to describe the activities of gang members in general. They state, "had we violated this promise [of confidentiality], we would have placed the lives of several individuals (including the field worker) in jeopardy." In addition, Decker and Van Winkle told their subjects that they did not want to know about information concerning future crimes, as this information would not be protected by their pledge of confidentiality.

Appropriate Boundaries

This is an ethical issue that cuts across several of the others, including identity disclosure, subject well-being, and voluntary participation. You probably are familiar with this issue in the context of guidelines for professional practice: Therapists are cautioned to maintain appropriate boundaries with patients; teachers must maintain appropriate boundaries with students. This is a special issue in qualitative research because it often involves loosening the boundary between the "researcher" and the research "subject." Qualitative researchers may seek to build rapport with those they plan to interview by expressing an interest in their concerns and conveying empathy for their situation. Is this just "faking friendship" for the purpose of the research? Jean Duncombe and Julie Jessop (2002) posed the dilemma clearly in a book chapter titled "'Doing Rapport' and the Ethics of 'Faking Friendship.'"

> With deeper rapport, interviewees become more likely to explore their more intimate experiences and emotions. Yet they also become more likely to discover and disclose experiences and feelings which, upon reflection, they would have preferred to keep private from others . . . or not to acknowledge even to themselves. (p. 112)

Researcher Safety

Research "in the field," whether researchers are studying gang life or anything else, should not begin until any potential risks to researcher safety have been evaluated. Qualitative methods may provide the only opportunity to learn about organized crime in Russian ports (Belousov et al. 2007), street crime in the Dominican Republic (Gill 2004), or the other topics examined by studies in this chapter, but they should not be used if the risks to the researchers are unacceptably high. Safety needs to be considered at the time of designing the research, not as an afterthought on arriving at the research site. As Hannah Gill learned in the Dominican Republic, such advance planning can require more investigation than just reading the local newspapers: "Due to the community's marginality, most crimes, including murders, were never reported in newspapers, making it impossible to have known the insecurity of the field site ahead of time" (p. 2).

Being realistic about evaluating risk does not mean simply accepting misleading assumptions about unfamiliar situations or communities. For example, reports of a widespread breakdown in law and order in New Orleans were broadcast repeatedly after Hurricane Katrina, but researchers found that most nontraditional behavior in that period was actually "prosocial" rather than antisocial (Rodríguez, Trainor, & Quarantelli 2006):

One group named itself the "Robin Hood Looters." The core of this group consisted of eleven friends who, after getting their own families out of the area, decided to remain at some high ground and, after the floodwaters rose, commandeered boats and started to rescue their neighbors. . . . For about two weeks they kept searching in the area. . . . They foraged for food and water from abandoned homes, and hence [acquired] their group name. Among the important norms that developed were that they were going to retrieve only survivors and not bodies and that group members would not carry weapons. The group also developed informal understandings with the police and the National Guard. (p. 91)

These ethical issues cannot be evaluated independently. The final decision to proceed must be made after weighing the relative benefits and risks to participants. Few qualitative research projects will be barred by consideration of these ethical issues, except for those involving covert participation. The more important concern for researchers is to identify the ethically troublesome aspects of their proposed research, resolve them before the project begins, and act on new ethical issues as they come up during the project.

CONCLUSION

Qualitative research allows the careful investigator to obtain a richer and more intimate view of the social world than can be achieved with more quantitative methods. It is not hard to understand why so many qualitative studies have become classics in the literature. The emphases in qualitative research on inductive reasoning and incremental understanding help to stimulate and inform other research approaches. Research charting the dimensions of previously unstudied social settings and intensive investigations of the subjective meanings that motivate individual action are particularly well served by the techniques of participant observation, intensive interviewing, and focus groups.

The very characteristics that make qualitative research techniques so appealing restrict their use to a limited set of research problems. It is not possible to draw representative samples for study using participant observation, and for this reason the generalizability of any particular field study's results cannot really be known. Only the accumulation of findings from numerous qualitative studies permits confident generalization, but here again, the time and effort required to collect and analyze the data make it unlikely that many particular field research studies will be replicated.

Even if qualitative researchers made an effort to replicate key studies, attempting to compare findings would be hampered by their notion of developing and grounding explanations inductively in the observations made in a particular setting. Measurement reliability is thereby hindered, as are systematic tests for the validity of key indicators and formal tests for causal connections. Qualitative researchers do not necessarily seek to achieve the same generalizability standards as quantitative researchers; the agenda here is usually to tell *one* truth in the words of study participants.

In the final analysis, qualitative research involves a mode of thinking and investigating that is different from that used in experimental and survey research. Qualitative research is inductive; experiments and surveys tend to be conducted in a deductive, quantitative framework. Both approaches can help social scientists learn about the social world; the proficient researcher must be ready to use either. Qualitative data are often supplemented with many quantitative characteristics or activities, and quantitative data are often enriched with written comments and observations. The distinction between qualitative and quantitative research techniques is not always clear-cut, and increasingly, researchers are combining methods to advance knowledge.

NOTES

1. From *Life in the Gang: Family, Friends, and Violence,* by S. H. Decker, B. van Winkle, pp. 97–98. Copyright © 1996. Reprinted with permission of Cambridge University Press.

2. From *Street Corner Society: The Social Structure of an Italian Slum,* pp. v–vii, by W. F. Whyte, copyright © 1943. Reprinted with permission of The University of Chicago Press.

3. From *Code of the Street: Decency, Violence, and the Moral Life of the Inner City,* by Elijah Anderson. Copyright © 1999 by Elijah Anderson. Used by permission of W. W. Norton & Company, Inc.

KEY TERMS

Complete observation	Field research	Qualitative methods
Computer-assisted qualitative data analysis	Focus group	Reactive effect
	Grounded theory	Reflexivity
Covert (complete) participation	Intensive interviewing	Saturation point
Documentation	Jottings	Systematic observation
Ethnography	Matrix	Tacit knowledge
Experience sampling method (ESM)	Participant observation	Theoretical sampling
Field notes	Progressive focusing	Thick description

HIGHLIGHTS

- Qualitative researchers tend to develop ideas inductively, try to understand the social context and sequential nature of attitudes and actions, and explore the subjective meanings that participants attach to events. They rely primarily on participant observation; intensive interviewing; and, in recent years, focus groups.

- Participant observers may adopt one of several roles for a particular research project. Each role represents a different balance between observing and participating, which may or may not include public acknowledgment of the researcher's real identity. Many field researchers prefer a moderate role, participating as well as observing in a group but publicly acknowledging the researcher role.

- Field researchers must develop strategies for entering the field, developing and maintaining relations in the field, sampling, and recording and analyzing data.

- Recording and analyzing notes is a crucial step in field research. Detailed notes should be recorded and analyzed daily to refine methods and to develop concepts, indicators, and models of the social system observed.

- Intensive interviews involve open-ended questions and follow-up probes, with the content and order of specific questions varying from one interview to the next.

- Focus groups combine elements of participant observation and intensive interviewing. They can increase the validity of attitude measurement by revealing what people say when presenting their opinions in a group context.

- Case studies use thick description and other qualitative techniques to provide a holistic picture of a setting or group.

- Grounded theory connotes a general explanation that develops in interaction with the data and is continually tested and refined as data collection continues.

- The main ethical issues in field research concern voluntary participation, subject well-being, identity disclosure, confidentiality, appropriate boundaries, and researcher safety.

EXERCISES

Discussing Research

1. Review the experiments and surveys described in previous chapters. Choose one, and propose a field research design that would focus on the same research question but with participant observation techniques in a local setting. Propose the role that you would play in the setting, along the participant observation continuum, and explain why you would favor this role. Describe the stages of your field research study, including your plans for entering the field, developing and maintaining relationships, sampling, and recording and analyzing data. Then discuss what you would expect your study to add to the findings resulting from the study described in the book.

2. Develop an interview guide that focuses on a research question addressed in one of the studies in this book. Using this guide, conduct an intensive interview with one person who is involved with the topic in some way. Take only brief notes during the interview, and then write as complete a record of the interviews as you can immediately afterward. Turn in an evaluation of your performance as an interviewer and note taker, together with your notes.

3. Find the Qualitative Research lesson in the interactive exercises on the Student Study Site, www.sagepub.com/bachmanfrccj2e. Answer the questions in this lesson in order to review the types of ethical issues that can arise in the course of participant observation research.

4. Read about focus groups in one of the references cited in this chapter and then devise a plan for using a focus group to explore and explain student perspectives about crime on campus. How would you recruit students for the group? What types of students would you try to include? How would you introduce the topic and the method to the group? What questions would you ask? What problems would you anticipate (e.g., discord between focus group members or digressions from the chosen topic)? How would you respond to these problems?

Finding Research on the Web

1. Go to the *Annual Review of Sociology*'s website by following the publication link at http://soc. AnnualReviews.org. Search for articles that use field research as the primary method of gathering data on gangs or delinquency. Find at least three articles, and report on the specific method of field research used in each.

2. Search the web for information on focus groups (previous, upcoming, or ongoing) involving victims, offenders, fear of crime, crime prevention, or another criminological topic. List the websites you find, and write a paragraph about the purpose of each focus group and the sample involved. How might these focus groups be used to influence public policy?

3. Go to the Social Science Information Gateway (SOSIG) at www.intute.ac.uk/socialsciences/. Conduct a search for "qualitative methods" and then choose three or four interesting sites to find out more about field research—either professional organizations of field researchers or journals that publish their work. Explore the sites to find out what information they provide regarding field research, what kinds of projects are being done that involve field research, and the purposes that specific field research methods are being used for.

4. *The Qualitative Report* is an online journal about qualitative research. Inspect the table of contents for a recent issue at www.nova.edu/ssss/QR/index.html. Read one of the articles and write a brief article review.

Critiquing Research

1. Read and summarize one of the qualitative studies discussed in this chapter or another classic study recommended by your instructor. Review and critique the study using the article review questions presented in Appendix B. What questions are answered by the study? What questions are raised for further investigation?

2. Read the complete text of one of the qualitative studies presented in this chapter and evaluate its conclusions for authenticity, using the criteria in this chapter. If validity and authenticity are in any way debatable, what suggestions would you offer to improve the researcher's methodology?

3. Review one of the articles on the book's Student Study Site, www.sagepub.com/bachmanfrccj2e, that used qualitative methods. Describe the data that were collected, and identify the steps used in the analysis. What type of qualitative data analysis was this? If it is not one of the methods presented in this chapter, describe its similarities to and differences from one of these methods. How confident are you in the conclusions, given the methods of analysis used?

Making Research Ethical

1. The April 1992 issue of the *Journal of Contemporary Ethnography* is devoted to a series of essays reevaluating Whyte's (1943) classic field study, *Street Corner Society.* A social scientist interviewed some of the people described in Whyte's book and concluded that the researcher had made methodological and ethical errors. Whyte and others offer able rejoinders and further commentary. Reading the entire issue of this journal will improve your appreciation of the issues that field researchers confront. Do you agree or disagree with the claims? Why or why not?

2. Covert participation may be the only way for researchers to observe the inner workings of some criminal or other deviant groups, but this strategy is likely to result in the researcher witnessing, and perhaps being asked to participate in, illegal acts. Do you think that covert participation is ever ethical? If so, under what conditions? Can the standards of "no harm to subjects," "identity disclosure," and "voluntary participation" be maintained in covert research? In what circumstances would researcher safety advance to a priority status?

3. A *New York Times* reporter (Wines 2006) talked about the dilemma many reporters have: whether or not to provide monetary or other compensation, like food or medical supplies, to people they interview for a story. In journalism, paying for information is a "cardinal sin" because journalists are indoctrinated with the notion that they are observers. They are trained to report on situations, but not to influence a situation. This is what many scholars believe a researcher's role should be. Nevertheless, as we learned in this chapter, it is common in research to offer small gratuities for information and interviews. However, does paying for information unduly influence the truthfulness of the information being sought? What are your thoughts on paying for information? What if you were investigating the problems faced by families living below the poverty level, and during an interview you noticed that the family refrigerator and cupboards were empty and the baby was crying from hunger? What is the ethical reaction? If you believe the most ethical response would be to provide food or money for food, is it fair that there is another family next door in the same condition who did not happen to be on your interview list? How should gratuities be handled?

4. Recall our discussion of social norms and interpersonal comfort levels. Should any requirements be imposed on researchers who seek to study other cultures, to ensure that procedures are appropriate and interpretations are culturally sensitive? What practices would you suggest for cross-cultural researchers to ensure that ethical guidelines are followed? (Consider the wording of consent forms and the procedures for gaining voluntary cooperation.)

Developing a Research Proposal

Add a qualitative component to your proposed study. You can choose to do this with a participant observation project or intensive interviewing. Choose the method that seems most likely to help answer the research question for the overall survey project.

1. For a participant observation component, propose an observational plan that would complement the overall survey project. Present in your proposal the following information about your plan:

    a. Choose a site and justify its selection in terms of its likely value for the research.

    b. Choose a role along the participation–observation continuum and justify your choice.

    c. Describe access procedures and note any likely problems.

    d. Discuss how you will develop and maintain relations in the site.

    e. Review any sampling issues.

    f. Present an overview of the way in which you will analyze the data you collect.

2. For an intensive interview component, propose a focus for the intensive interviews that you believe will add the most to findings from the survey project. Present in your proposal the following information about your plan:

    a. Present and justify a method for selecting individuals to interview.

    b. Write out three introductory biographical questions and five "grand tour" questions for your interview schedule.

    c. List at least six different probes you may use.

    d. Present and justify at least two follow-up questions for one of your grand tour questions.

    e. Explain what you expect this intensive interview component to add to your overall survey project.

3. Which qualitative data analysis alternative is most appropriate for the qualitative data you proposed to collect for your project? Using the approach, develop a strategy for using the techniques of qualitative data analysis to analyze your textual data.

Performing Data Analysis in SPSS or Excel

The YOUTH.POR data set includes some questions on opinions regarding friends' attitudes toward delinquent acts and the extent to which getting caught for committing a crime would negatively affect the respondent's life.

1. Describe the opinions about friends' attitudes and personal misfortune based on the frequencies for these variables (V77, V79, V109, V119).

2. What explanation can you develop (inductively) for these attitudes? Do you believe that either friends' attitudes toward delinquent acts or getting caught for committing a crime would influence behavior? Explain.

3. Propose a participant observation, a focus group, or an intensive interview study to explore these attitudes further. Identify the sample for the study, and describe how you would carry out your observations, focus groups, or interviews.

Student Study Site

The companion Student Study Site for *Fundamentals of Research in Criminology and Criminal Justice* can be found at www.sagepub.com/bachmanfrccj2e.

    Visit the Student Study Site to enhance your understanding of the chapter content and to discover additional resources that will take your learning one step further. You can enhance your understanding of the chapters by using the comprehensive study material, which includes interactive exercises, e-flashcards, web exercises, practice self-tests, and more. You will also find special features, such as Learning From Journal Articles, which incorporates Sage's online journal collection.

Analyzing Content

Crime Mapping and Historical, Secondary, and Content Analysis

The research methods we have examined so far have relied on researchers collecting the data or information themselves. Increasingly, however, those interested in criminological research questions are relying on data previously collected by other investigators (Riedel 2000). As we noted in chapter 1, this is referred to as secondary data analysis. Secondary data analysis is simply the act of collecting or analyzing data that were originally collected by someone else at another time (Riedel 2000). Thus, if a researcher goes to a police department and personally compiles information from police reports to examine a research question, that researcher is still engaging in secondary data analysis because the police records were originally collected prior to his or her own research.

In this chapter, we will tell you about a number of data sets, including surveys and official records, which are publicly available for research purposes. Then we will examine several research methods that rely on secondary data, including historical events research, cross-cultural research, content analysis, and crime mapping. Next, we highlight the strengths and weaknesses of all types of methods and illustrate the importance of triangulating two or more methods when possible. Because using data originally gathered for other purposes poses unique concerns for a researcher, we spend the latter part of the chapter highlighting these methodological issues.

WHAT IS SECONDARY DATA?

In general, there are four major types of secondary data: surveys, official statistics, official records, and other historical documents. Although a data set can be obtained by an agreement between two or more researchers, many researchers obtain data through the Inter-University Consortium for Political and Social Research (ICPSR) (www.icpsr.umich.edu). Data stored at ICPSR primarily include surveys, official records, and official statistics. ICPSR stores data and information for nearly 5,000 sources and studies, including those conducted independently and those conducted by the U.S. government. The research introduced in Chapter 1 by MacDonald and his colleagues (2005) relied on the secondary analysis of the Youth Risk Behavior Survey (YRBS) to examine the factors related to violent offending. The YRBS data can be easily downloaded from ICPSR.

Case Study: Gender and Offending

The research possibilities are almost limitless with the wealth of data already made available to researchers interested in issues of criminology and criminal justice. For example, Heimer and De Coster (1999) used the National Youth Survey (NYS) to examine the mechanisms explaining variation in violent delinquency between male and female youth. Generally, studies of self-reported violent delinquency find gender ratios (self-reports of delinquency of males compared to females) ranging from approximately 1.1 to 5.3, depending on the specific aggressive offense being measured. These ratios show that, although males generally commit more violent acts than females, young females do engage in violence. One of the primary mechanisms related to violent offending that Heimer and De Coster examined was "cultural definitions of violence." That is, they believed that one factor affecting the different offending patterns between males and females was that, on average, boys tend to acquire attitudes more favorable to violence than females. To operationalize the concepts of violent definitions and gender definitions, Heimer and De Coster used several questions in the National Youth Survey, which are displayed in Exhibit 9.1 along with the questions used to uncover incidents of violent offending. After statistically controlling for other important factors proven to be related to violent offending, such as socioeconomic status, age, prior violent delinquency, association with aggressive friends, and attachments to family, the results of the analyses of the NYS data provided support for both hypotheses. Heimer and De Coster concluded that girls are less violent than boys mainly because they are influenced more strongly by bonds to family, where they learn fewer violent definitions and are taught that violence is inconsistent with the meaning of being female.

HISTORICAL EVENTS RESEARCH

The central insight behind considering the causes and impacts of historical events is that we can improve our understanding of social processes when we make comparisons with other times and places. Although there are no rules for determining how far in the past the focus of research must be in order for it to be considered historical, in practice, research tends to be considered historical when it focuses on a period prior to the experience of most of those conducting the research (Abbott 1994).

Historical events research in the social sciences differs from traditional historical research because researchers seek to develop general theoretical explanations of historical events and processes instead of just detailed, "fact-centered" descriptions of them (Monk-konen 1994: 8). Social scientists do not ignore the details of historical events; rather, they "unravel" unique events to identify general patterns (Abrams 1982: 200). However, as in traditional history, the focus on the past presents special methodological challenges. Documents and other evidence may have been lost or damaged, and what evidence there

Exhibit 9.1   Questions From the National Youth Survey Used to Measure Violent Definitions, Gender Definitions, and Violent Delinquent Offending

Violent Delinquency

The below items were coded 1 = never; 2 = once or twice a year; 3 = once or twice every 2–3 months; 4 = once a month; 5 = once every 2–3 weeks; 6 = once a week; 7 = 2–3 times a week; 8 = once a day; 9 = 2–3 times a day.

How may times in the past year have you

a) carried a hidden weapon other than a plain pocket knife?

b) attacked someone with the idea of seriously hurting or killing them?

c) been involved in gang fights?

d) hit or threatened to hit a teacher or other adult at school?

e) hit or threatened to hit your parents?

f) hit or threatened to hit other students?

g) had or tried to have sexual relations with someone against their will?

h) used force (strong-arm methods) to get money or things from other students?

i) used force (strong-arm methods) to get money or things from a teacher or adult at school?

j) used force (strong-arm methods) to get money or things from other people (not teachers or students)?

Violent Definitions

The following questions were coded 1 = strongly disagree; 2 = disagree; 3 = neither agree nor disagree; 4 = agree; 5 = strongly agree.

a) In order to gain respect from your friends, it is sometimes necessary to beat up on other kids.

b) It is alright to beat up another person if he or she called you a dirty name.

c) It is alright to beat up another person if he or she started the fight.

d) Hitting another person is an acceptable way to get him or her to do what you want.

Gender Definitions

a) In general, the father should have greater authority than the mother in the bringing up of children.

b) Women with children should not work outside the home unless there is no one else to support the family.

c) In a marriage, it is the woman's responsibility to care for any children and take care of the home.

d) Women are too emotional to solve problems well.

e) Women are physically and emotionally weaker than men and therefore need male protection and support.

Source: K. Heimer and S. De Coster (1999), "The Gendering of Violent Delinquency." *Criminology, 37*(2): 277–318. Reprinted with permission.

is may represent a sample that is biased toward those who were more newsworthy figures or who were more prone to writing. The feelings of individuals involved in past events may be hard, if not impossible, to reconstruct. Nonetheless, in many situations the historical record may support very systematic research on what occurred in the past. When research on past events does not follow processes for a long period of time, when it is basically cross-sectional, it is usually referred to as historical events research.

Case Study: Race, Rape, and Capital Punishment

In his book *The Martinsville Seven: Race, Rape, and Capital Punishment,* Eric Rise (1995) offers an in-depth example of historical events research. On January 8, 1949, a 32-year-old white woman in Martinsville, Virginia, accused seven young black men of violently raping her. These men became known as the "Martinsville Seven." Within 2 days of the allegation, state and local police had arrested and obtained confessions from each of the suspects. In a rapid succession of brief trials held over the course of 11 days, six separate juries convicted the defendants of rape and sentenced each to death. During the first week of February 1951, each of the Martinsville Seven died in the electric chair at the Virginia State Penitentiary. At a time when African Americans were beginning to assert their civil rights vigorously, the executions provided a stark reminder of the harsh treatment reserved for African Americans who violated Southern racial codes.

In his analysis of the case, Rise (1995) examined a wealth of historical documents, including legal papers that the lawyers involved in the cases made available, official transcripts of the cases, briefs and petitions to the Virginia State Supreme Court, related case law from the Supreme Court, annual reports from the Virginia Department of Corrections for 1946–1951, and newspaper accounts.

The large number of defendants, the rapid pace of the trials, and the specter of multiple executions attracted national media attention and brought sentencing disparity arguments to the foreground of contemporary race relations. Rise's (1995) analysis revealed the critical effect that this historical event had on subsequent developments. The revelation that capital sentencing disparities existed between white and African American defendants during the appeals process of the Martinsville Seven was significant for modern jurisprudence. Specifically, the Martinsville case was the first time courtroom attorneys presented equal protection arguments that challenged the racial disparity of death sentences for rape.

COMPARATIVE METHODS

The limitations of examining data from a single location have encouraged many social scientists to turn to comparisons among many geographical entities. As noted in the 2001 American Academy of Criminal Justice Sciences' Presidential Address by Richard Bennett (2004), **comparative research** in criminal justice and criminology took on a new importance after the attacks of September 11. Bennett described two types of comparative research:

1. Research that seeks to understand the structure, nature, or scope of a nation's or nations' criminal justice systems or rates of crime is descriptive comparative research.

2. Research that seeks to understand how national systems work and the factors related to their operations is analytic comparative research.

There is also variability in the *scope* of comparative research. Studies can examine crime patterns in single nations, make a comparison across several nations, or conduct transnational research, which generally explores how cultures and nations deal with crime that transcends their borders. Investigating terrorism is one emerging form of transnational research. Bennett (2004) notes,

> One of the outcomes of the terrorist attacks in 2001 was a shocking awareness that terrorism is international and inextricably tied to transnational criminal activity. . . . We need to understand how criminal and terrorist organizations fund themselves and exploit our inability to link and analyze criminal activity that transcends national borders. (p. 8)

Although comparative methods are often associated with cross-national comparisons, research examining smaller aggregates such as states and cities can also be subsumed under the comparative research umbrella. Comparative research methods allow for a broader vision about social relations than is possible with cross-sectional research limited to one location.

Case Study: Homicide Across Nations

One of the first large comparative research projects undertaken in criminology was the development of the Comparative Crime Data File (CCDF), which was created by Archer and Gartner (1984). The authors articulated the need for comparative research in the field succinctly:

> The need for cross-national comparisons seems particularly acute for research on crime and violence since national differences on these phenomena are of a remarkable magnitude. In some societies, homicide is an hourly, highly visible, and therefore somewhat unexceptional cause of death. In other nations, homicides are so infrequent that, when they do occur, they receive national attention and lasting notoriety. (p. 4)

The CCDF was launched in 1984, with extensive crime data from 110 nations and 44 major international cities covering the period from approximately 1900 to 1970, and has been regularly updated ever since. In their work, Archer and Gartner (1984) examined many research questions using the CCDF. One of these questions is related to the idea that war might increase the level of homicide within the nations once the war ends. There are several theoretical models that speculate about the possible effects of wars on later (postwar) violence within a nation. For example, the social solidarity model posits a wartime *decrease* in violence because of the increase in social solidarity among a nation's citizenry. At a more individual level, the violent veteran model predicts that postwar levels of violence within a nation will *increase* as a result of the violent acts of returning war veterans. At a societal level, the legitimization of violence model postulates that during a war, a society reverses its prohibitions against killing and instead honors acts of violence that would be regarded as murderous in peacetime. This social approval or legitimation of violence, this model suggests, may produce a lasting reduction of inhibitions against taking human life, even after the war, thereby increasing levels of violence within nations. To examine the effects of war on postwar violence, Archer and Gartner compared national rates of homicide before and after many wars, both small and large, including the two world wars. They found that most combatant nations experienced substantial increases in their rates of homicide following both small and large wars.

A recent transnational study by Savage, Bennett, and Danner (2008) examined the relationship between social welfare spending and homicide for 52 nations. They wanted to know if welfare spending encouraged dependency and weakened personal initiative, thereby increasing crime, or, alternatively, if it equalized inequality, thereby decreasing crime. When looking at variation in welfare spending across localities in the United States, evidence tended to support the latter. Savage et al. used a data set called the Correlates of Crime (COC), which contains data for a sample of 52 diverse nations from every region of the globe for the years 1960 through 1984.

Social welfare spending was operationalized as the amount of governmental spending in U.S. dollar equivalents for social welfare programs per person. Over the time period studied, Savage et al. (2008) found that social welfare spending was negatively related to both theft and homicide; that is, as social welfare spending increased, rates of these crimes generally decreased. This was true even after controlling for other important factors like the gross domestic product and unemployment.

CONTENT ANALYSIS

Do media accounts of crime, such as newspaper and television news coverage, accurately portray the true nature of crime? The methodologies discussed thus far may not be helpful for answering this question. **Content analysis,** or the "the systematic, objective, quantitative analysis of message characteristics" (Neuendorf 2002: 1), would be an appropriate tool. Using this method, we can learn a great deal about popular culture and many other areas by studying the characteristics of messages delivered through the mass media and other sources.

The goal of a content analysis is to develop inferences from text (Weber 1985). You could think of a content analysis as a "survey" of some documents or other records of prior communication. In fact, a content analysis is a survey designed with fixed-choice responses so that it produces quantitative data that can be analyzed statistically.

Content analysis bears some similarities to qualitative data analysis because it involves coding and categorizing text, discovering relationships among constructs identified in the text, and a statistical analysis of those findings. Content analysis is also similar to secondary data analysis because it involves taking data or text that already exists and subjecting it to a new form of "analysis"; however, unlike secondary analysis of previously collected quantitative data, content analysis also involves sampling and measurement of primary data. Content analysis techniques can be used with all forms of messages, including visual images, sounds, and interaction patterns, as well as written text (Neuendorf 2002: 24–25).

Identifying a Population of Documents or Other Textual Sources

The population of documents that is selected for analysis should be appropriate to the research question of interest. Words or other features of these units are then coded in order to measure the variables involved in the research question. The content analysis involves the following steps or stages (Weber 1985).

1. *Identify a population of documents or other textual sources for study.* This population should be selected for its appropriateness to the research question of interest. Perhaps the population will be all newspapers published in the United States, college student newspapers, nomination speeches at political party conventions, or "state of the nation" speeches by national leaders.

2. *Determine the units of analysis.* These could be newspaper articles, whole newspapers, television episodes, or political conventions.

3. *Select a sample of units from the population.* The most basic strategy might be a simple random sample of documents. However, a stratified sample might be needed to ensure adequate representation of community newspapers in large and small cities, or of weekday and Sunday papers, or of political speeches during election years and in off years (see Chapter 4).

4. *Design coding procedures for the variables to be measured.* This requires deciding what unit of text to code, such as words, sentences, paragraphs, or newspaper pages. Then, the categories into which the units are to be coded must be defined. These categories may be broad, such as "supports democracy," or narrow, such as "supports universal suffrage."

5. *Test and refine the coding procedures.* Clear instructions and careful training of coders are essential.

6. *Base statistical analyses on counting occurrences of particular items.* These could be words, themes, or phrases. You will also need to test relations between different variables.

Developing reliable and valid coding procedures is not an easy task. The meaning of words and phrases is often ambiguous. As a result, coding procedures cannot simply categorize and count words; text segments in which the words are embedded must also be inspected before codes are finalized. Because different coders may perceive different meanings in the same text segments, explicit coding rules are required to ensure coding consistency. Special dictionaries can be developed to keep track of how the categories of interest are defined in the study (Weber 1985).

After coding procedures are developed, their reliability should be assessed by comparing different coders' codes for the same variables. The criteria for judging quantitative content analyses of text reflect the same standards of validity applied to data collected with other quantitative methods. We must review the sampling approach, the reliability and validity of the measures, and the controls used to strengthen any causal conclusions.

Case Study: Crime and TV

Researchers interested in the media and crime have used content analysis in a number of ways. For example, scholars analyzing crime depictions presented in the media often conclude that newspaper and television coverage of crime is frequently inaccurate and misleading; stories disproportionately report violent crimes, and reporters tend to focus attention on sensational matters such as the capture of a criminal or high-status offenders.

One type of television program presents vignettes depicting actual crimes in which theories of crime are dramatized. These dramatizations feature actors, actual photographs or film footage, and interviews conducted with participants and the police. Viewers are urged to call the police or program representatives with information related to the crime, and police officers are on standby in the television studio to take these calls and facilitate action. Two examples of these sorts of programs are *America's Most Wanted* (AMW) and *Unsolved Mysteries* (UM).

To analyze the images these programs revealed to viewers, Cavender and Bond-Maupin (2000) conducted a content analysis of AMW and UM programs that aired between January 25 and May 31, 1989. All programs that aired during this time period were videotaped, and a subsample of 77 crime vignettes was randomly selected as the study's units of analysis. The coding protocol used for data collection was focused on three aspects of the programs:

1. *Demographics.* Types of crime and general information on the crime, criminals, and victims

2. *Characterizations.* Specific depictions of crime, criminals, and victims, such as brutality, dangerousness, or a victim's vulnerability

3. *Worldview.* The relative safety of people and places, the terror and randomness of crime, and what the audience should do about crime

Exhibit 9.2 presents the percentage of program vignettes that depicted offense types for both AMW and UM.

Cavender and Bond-Maupin (2000) concluded that the overwhelming majority of criminals on these shows were depicted as dangerous people who were beyond the help of social control or rehabilitation. In addition, both shows regularly featured criminals who were characterized with deviant psychological labels such as a "crazed killer, a psycho, a maniac," schizophrenic, emotionally disturbed, or showing no emotion. Other criminals were portrayed as Satanists, gang members, and drug dealers. On the other hand, victims were usually

Exhibit 9.2 Number and Percentage of Vignettes Depicted by the Programs *Unsolved Mysteries* and *America's Most Wanted*

	%	n
Murder	52	40
Theft or fraud extortion	13	10
Escape	12	9
Bank robbery or armed robbery	10	8
Illegal arms or terrorism	3	2
Unexplained death or missing	7	5
Rape	5	4
Kidnapping	5	4
Child molestation	5	4
Attempted murder	3	2
Drug dealing	3	2
Other	7	5

Source: Adapted from Cavender and Bond-Maupin (2000).

presented as upstanding citizens that you would like to have as a neighbor. The camera most often took the victims' perspective as well, achieving what Cavender and Bond-Maupin called the "good/evil dichotomy," with the victim and the audience aligned against the criminal. In sum, they concluded that the message sent to viewers by both programs was that danger lurks everywhere, awaiting the victim and, by implication, the viewer at home.

CRIME MAPPING

Many of us have adopted the image of crime mapping that involves a police precinct wall with pushpins stuck all over it identifying the location of crime incidents. Crime mapping for general research purposes has a long history in criminological research. It is generally used to identify the spatial distribution of crime along with the social indicators such as poverty and social disorganization that are similarly distributed across areas (e.g., neighborhood, census tracts). Rachel Boba (2009) defines crime mapping as "the process of using a geographic information system to conduct special analysis of crime problems and other police-related issues" (p. 7). She also describes the three main functions of crime mapping:

1. It provides visual and statistical analyses of the spatial nature of crime and other events.

2. It allows the linkage of crime data to other data sources, such as census information on poverty or school information, which allows relationships between variables to be established.

3. It provides maps to visually communicate analysis results.

Although applied crime mapping has been used for over 100 years to assist the police in criminal apprehension and crime prevention, the type of crime mapping we will discuss here is related to mapping techniques used for traditional research purposes (e.g., testing theory about the causes of crime), not for investigative purposes. With the advent of computing technology, crime mapping has become an advanced form of statistical data analysis. The **geographic information system (GIS)** is the software tool that has made crime mapping increasingly available to researchers since the 1990s.

Case Study: Mapping Crime in Cities

Although they were not the first researchers to use crime mapping, Shaw and McKay (1942) conducted a landmark analysis in criminology on juvenile delinquency in Chicago neighborhoods back in the 1930s. These researchers mapped thousands of incidents of juvenile delinquency and analyzed relationships between delinquency and various social conditions such as social disorganization. After analyzing rates of police arrests for delinquency, using police records to determine the names and addresses of those arrested in Chicago between 1927 and 1935, Shaw and McKay observed a striking pattern that persisted over the years. They found there was a decrease in rates of delinquency as the distance from the Loop (city center) increased. When rates of other community characteristics were similarly mapped (e.g., infant mortality, tuberculosis cases, percentage of families who own their own homes, percentage of foreign-born residents, percentage of families receiving federal aid), the conclusions were stark. Shaw and McKay concluded,

> The communities with the highest rates of delinquents are occupied by these segments of the population whose position is most disadvantageous in relation to the distribution of economic, social, and cultural values. Of all the communities in the city, these have the fewest facilities for acquiring the economic goods indicative of status and success in our conventional culture. (pp. 318–319)

Case Study: Gang Homicides in St. Louis, Missouri

Contemporary researchers interested in issues related to crime and criminology have access to more sophisticated computer technology that allows the creation of more enhanced crime maps. The purpose of crime maps, however, remains the same: to illuminate the relationship between some category of crime and corresponding character-istics such as poverty and disorganization across given locations. Using GIS software, Rosenfeld, Bray, and Egley (1999) examined the mechanisms through which gangs facili-tate violent offending in St. Louis, Missouri. The primary purpose of this research was to study whether gang membership pushes members to engage in violence or merely exposes them to violent persons and situations. Rosenfeld and colleagues compared gang-affiliated, gang-motivated, and nongang youth homicides occurring in St. Louis between 1985 and 1995. In one part of their analysis, they examined the spatial distribution of gang and non-gang youth homicide in relation to attributes of the neighborhood context (e.g., economic deprivation or the inability to obtain resources to establish a lifestyle comparable to those around you) in which the incidents occurred.

To examine the spatial relationship between these three types of homicides and the relationship they had to neighborhood disadvantage (such as economic deprivation or social disorganization) and instability (such as residents moving in and out of the neighbor-hood), the researchers used the census block group as their unit of analysis. Exhibit 9.3 displays the map of block groups where gang-affiliated and gang-motivated homicides occurred, along with the extent of neighborhood disadvantage in each block for 1990–1995 (Rosenfeld et al. 1999).

From this map, you can see that gang homicides were concentrated in disadvantaged areas. Other maps revealed a similar finding with regard to neighborhood instability: Homi-cides were concentrated in neighborhoods with moderate levels of instability regardless of whether they were gang-affiliated, gang-motivated, or nongang-related. Rosenfeld and colleagues (1999) concluded,

> Our results offer powerful evidence of the clustering of both gang and nongang youth homicides in areas characterized by high levels of social-economic disadvantage and racial isolation. Although the accumulated evidence for gang facilitation of violence is quite compelling, our results serve as a reminder that concentrated disadvantage and racial isolation remain the fundamental sources of lethal violence in urban areas. (p. 514)

These conclusions echo those made over half a century earlier by Shaw and McKay (1942). As such, we are compelled to note Ernest W. Burgess's words in the introduction of Shaw and McKay's original work:

> We must realize that the brightest hope in reformation is in changing the neighborhood and in control of the gang in which the boy moves, lives, and has his being and to which he returns after this institutional treatment. . . . We must reaffirm our faith in prevention, which is so much easier, cheaper, and more effective than cure and which begins with the home, the play group, the local school, the church, and the neighborhood. (p. xiii)

Exhibit 9.3   Neighborhoods in St. Louis Where Gang-Affiliated and Gang-Motivated Homicides Occurred

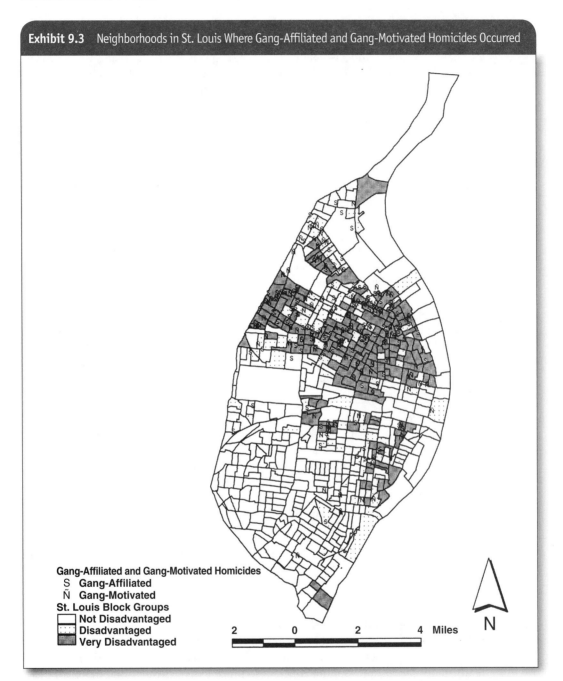

Gang-Affiliated and Gang-Motivated Homicides
S Gang-Affiliated
Ñ Gang-Motivated
St. Louis Block Groups
Not Disadvantaged
Disadvantaged
Very Disadvantaged

2   0   2   4 Miles

N

Source: R. Rosenfeld, T. M. Bray, and Arlen Egley (1999), "Facilitating Violence: A Comparison of Gang-Motivated, Gang-Affiliated, and Nongang Youth Homicides." *Journal of Quantitative Criminology*, *15*(4): 496–516. Reprinted with permission.

Case Study: Using Google Earth to Track Sexual Offending Recidivism

While the GIS software that was utilized by Rosenfeld et al. (1999) has many research advantages for displaying the spatial distributions of crime, researchers have begun to take advantage of other research mapping tools including Google Earth. One such endeavor was conducted by Duwe, Donnay, and Tewksbury (2008), who sought to determine the effects of Minnesota's residency restriction statute on the recidivism behavior of registered sex offenders. Many states have passed legislation that restricts where sex offenders are allowed to live. These policies are primarily intended to protect children from child molesters by deterring the offenders' direct contact with schools, day care centers, parks, and so on. Most of these statutes are applied to all sex offenders, regardless of their offending history or perceived risk of reoffense. The impact of such laws on sexual recidivism, however, remains unclear. Duwe et al. attempted to fill this gap in our knowledge. They examined 224 sex offenders who had been reincarcerated for a new sex offense between 1990 and 2005 and asked several research questions, including "Where did offenders initially establish contact with their victims, and where did they commit the offense?" and "What were the physical distances between an offender's residence and both the offense and first contact locations?" (p. 488). The researchers used *Google Earth* to calculate the distance from an offender's place of residence to the place where first contact with the victim occurred, and from these locations to the place of the offense.

Duwe and his colleagues (2008) investigated four criteria to classify a reoffense as preventable: (a) the means by which offenders established contact with their victims, (b) the distance between an offender's residence and where first contact was established (i.e., 1,000 feet, 2,500 feet, or 1 mile), (c) the type of location where contact was established (e.g., was it a place where children congregated?), and (d) whether the victim was under the age of 18. To be classified as preventable through housing restrictions, an offense had to meet certain criteria. For example, the offender would have had to establish direct contact with a juvenile victim within 1 mile of his residence at a place where children congregate (e.g., park, school). Results indicated that the majority of offenders, as in all cases of sexual violence, victimized someone they already knew. Only 35% of the sex offender recidivists established new direct contact with a victim, but these victims were more likely to be adults than children, and the contact usually occurred more than a mile away from the offender's residence. Of the few offenders who directly established new contact with a juvenile victim within close proximity of their residence, none did so near a school, a park, a playground, or other locations included in residential restriction laws.

The authors concluded that residency restriction laws were not that effective in preventing sexual recidivism among child molesters. Duwe et al. (2008) state, "Why does residential proximity appear to matter so little with regard to sexual reoffending? Much of it has to do with the patterns of sexual offending in general. . . . Sex offenders are much more likely to victimize someone they know" (p. 500).

Clearly, the power of mapping technologies has changed not only the way law enforcement officials are preventing crime, but also the way in which researchers are examining the factors related to crime and crime control.

COMBINING RESEARCH DESIGNS

Designing research means deciding how to measure empirical phenomena, how to identify causal connections, and how to generalize findings not as separate decisions but in tandem, with each decision having implications for the others. The carefully controlled laboratory conditions that increased the causal validity of Bushman's (1995) experiments on media violence decreased the generalizability of his conclusions (Chapter 7). The representative sampling plan that increased the generalizability of Tjaden and Thoennes's (2000) national study of violent victimization limited their options for estimating causal effects (Chapter 8). The observations that underlay Decker and Van Winkle's (1996) descriptions of gang members would not be feasible in a national sample of gang members (Chapter 8).

Comparing Research Designs

It is not enough to ask of a study you critique, or one that you plan, such questions as, "Were the measures valid?" and "Were the causal conclusions justified?" You must also consider how the measurement approach might have affected the causal validity of the researcher's conclusions and how the sampling strategy might have altered the quality of measures. In fact, you must be concerned with how each component of the research design influenced (or might influence) the other components.

In the real world of social and criminological research, the boundaries separating different methods of data collection often overlap: Experiments may be conducted in the field, surveys may involve some intensive open-ended questioning, and field research may utilize quantitative counts of phenomena or random samples of events. The central features of experiments, surveys, and qualitative methods provide distinct perspectives even when used to study the same social processes. Comparing subjects randomly assigned to a treatment and a comparison group, asking standard questions of the members of a random sample, and observing while participating in a natural social setting involve markedly different decisions about measurements, causality, and generalizability. No method can reasonably be graded as superior to the others, and each varies in its suitability to different research questions and goals.

In general, experimental designs are strongest for testing causal hypotheses and most appropriate for studies of treatment (see Chapter 6). Despite this clear advantage, experimental designs require a degree of control that cannot always be achieved outside of the laboratory, and what appears to be a treatment effect or noneffect may be something else altogether.

Laboratory experiments permit much more control over conditions, but at the cost of less generalizable findings. People must volunteer for most laboratory experiments, so there is a good possibility that experimental subjects differ from those who do not volunteer. The problem of generalizability in an experiment using volunteers lessens only when the object of investigation is an orientation, a behavior, or a social process that is relatively invariable among people.

Most social science surveys facilitate the collection of vast descriptive data and rely on random sampling for their selection of cases from a larger population, and it is this feature that makes them preferable for maximizing generalizability (Chapter 4). However, meticulous survey design is integral to research findings, and subject response rates and confidentiality protections are ongoing concerns. Qualitative methods presume an intensive measurement approach in which indicators of concepts are drawn from direct observation or in-depth commentary (Chapter 8). This approach is most appropriate when it is not clear what meaning people attach to a concept or when researchers seek to explore a new or poorly understood social setting. Intensive measurement also limits many field research efforts to small numbers of people or unique social settings. Furthermore, for hypothesis testing, the impossibility of taking into account many possible extraneous influences in such limited comparisons makes qualitative methods a weak approach. As discussed in this chapter, historical event research, crime mapping, and content analysis range from cross-national quantitative surveys to qualitative comparisons of social features and political events. Their suitability for exploration, description, explanation, and evaluation varies in relation to the particular method used. If the same methods are used to study multiple eras or nations rather than just one nation at one time, the results are likely to be enhanced generalizability and causal validity.

In reality, none of these methods of data collection provides a foolproof means for achieving measurement validity, causal validity, or generalizability. Each will have some liabilities in a specific research application, and all can benefit from combination with one or more other methods (Sechrest & Sidani 1995). To benefit from this multiple-method approach, researchers have been using a triangulated methodology—that is, combining different methods in the same project to reveal different dimensions of the same phenomenon. It is to this subject that we now turn.

Triangulating Research Designs

As mentioned earlier in the book, the use of multiple methods to study one research question is called **triangulation.** The term suggests that a researcher can get a clearer picture of the social reality being studied by viewing it from several different perspectives. The term is actually derived from land surveying, where knowing a single landmark allows you to locate yourself only somewhere along a line in a single direction from the landmark. However, with two landmarks you can take bearings on both and locate yourself at their intersection.

Case Study: Triangulation in Action—School Security and Discipline

Aaron Kupchik provides an excellent example of triangulation in practice in his recent book *Homeroom Security* (2010). In his research, he was primarily interested in how school security measures, particularly the presence of police officers, affect students. Logging over 100 hours of observation at each of four high schools, two in a southwestern state and two in a mid-Atlantic state, Kupchik shadowed administrators and security guards, and he surveyed classrooms and common areas. He also conducted over 100 semi-structured interviews with administrators, security personnel, students, and parents. These interviews "sought to acquire an understanding of the respondents' views of the school rules and punishments, his or her experiences with school discipline, and his or her perceptions of school violence and appropriate responses to it." (p. 225). In addition to these two methods, student survey data was also collected at each school that, among other things, asked students about their experiences with punishment at school and their perceptions of the fairness of these incidents. Thus, to more fully understand the reality of school discipline, Kupchik used three very different research methods, each providing him with a somewhat different angle from which to examine the issue, and each method complemented the other's weaknesses.

The school observations allowed Kupchik (2010) to observe the interactions in the school in real time. He observed on numerous occasions how relatively minor problems escalated into larger problems as a result of police involvement, causing students to unnecessarily be sent through the criminal justice system rather than having their issues dealt with at the school level only. With the in-depth interviews, Kupchik was able to identify how some of the school administrators perceived the behavior of the police officers in their schools. For example, one school administrator stated,

> The biggest problem that I see is that . . . police officers are trained to deal with adults. . . . [T]hey are not trained to deal with children. . . . They deal with them terribly. In their day-to-day interactions . . . they deal with them like criminals, they do not trust anything they say, they assume they are lying before they even open their mouths. And it's not their fault. They've been trained to do that. (p. 108)

Finally, the survey data allowed Kupchik to make generalizations regarding perceptions and experiences of discipline to the larger student population. For example, the survey data indicated that boys were more likely to report that they had gotten in trouble for rule violations than girls, as were African American and Latino/a students compared to whites.

Of course, these are only a sampling of the many findings from this research. The central point we want to illustrate is how the use of all three methodologies provided a more complete picture of school discipline compared to the use of a single method. The research provided in-depth, detailed descriptions of the reality of school discipline from both administrator and student perspectives. It also provided a quantitative assessment of students' experiences that could be generalized to a larger student population.

ETHICAL ISSUES WHEN ANALYZING AVAILABLE DATA AND CONTENT

When analyzing historical documents or quantitative data collected by others, the potential for harm to human subjects that can be a concern when collecting primary data is greatly reduced. It is, however, still important to be honest and responsible in working out arrangements for data access and protection. Researchers who conclude that they are being denied access to public records of the federal government may be able to obtain the data by filing a Freedom of Information Act (FOIA) request. The FOIA stipulates that all persons have a right to access all federal agency records unless the records are specifically exempted (Riedel 2000: 130–131). Researchers who review historical or government documents must also try to avoid embarrassing or otherwise harming named individuals or their descendants by disclosing sensitive information.

Subject confidentiality is a key concern when original records are analyzed. Whenever possible, all information that could identify individuals should be removed from the records to be analyzed so that no link is possible to the identities of living subjects or the living descendants of subjects (Huston & Naylor 1996: 1698). When you used data that have already been archived, you need to find out what procedures were used to preserve subject confidentiality. The work required to ensure subject confidentiality probably will have been done for you by the data archivist. For example, the ICPSR examines carefully all data deposited in the archive for the possibility of disclosure risk. All data that might be used to identify respondents is altered to ensure confidentiality, including removal of information such as birth dates or service dates, specific incomes, or place of residence that could be used to identify subjects indirectly (see www.icpsr.umich.edu/icpsrweb/ICPSR/access/deposit/confidentiality.jsp). If all information that could be used in any way to identify respondents cannot be removed from a data set without diminishing its quality (such as by preventing links to other essential data records), ICPSR restricts access to the data and requires that investigators agree to conditions of use that preserve subject confidentiality.

It is not up to you to decide whether there are any issues of concern regarding human subjects when you acquire a data set for secondary analysis from a responsible source. The institutional review board (IRB) for the protection of human subjects at your college, university, or other institution has the responsibility to decide whether they need to review and approve proposals for secondary data analysis. The federal regulations are not entirely clear on this point, so the acceptable procedures will vary among institutions based on what their IRBs have decided.

Ethical concerns are multiplied when surveys are conducted or other data are collected in other countries. If the outside researcher lacks much knowledge of local norms, values, and routine activities, the potential for inadvertently harming subjects is substantial. For this reason, cross-cultural researchers should spend time learning about each of the countries in which they plan to collect primary data and establish collaborations with researchers in those countries (Hantrais & Mangen 1996). Local advisory groups may also be formed in each country so that a broader range of opinion is solicited when key decisions must be made. Such collaboration can also be invaluable when designing instruments, collecting data, and interpreting results.

CONCLUSION

Each of the research methods highlighted in this chapter can help researchers gain new insights into processes like factors related to homicide offending and other criminological topics. This chapter has also highlighted the strengths and weaknesses of each research method examined in this text, and the important benefit using a mixed-method approach, called triangulation, has when investigating any research question.

KEY TERMS

Analytic comparative research

Comparative research

Content analysis

Crime mapping

Descriptive comparative research

Geographic information system (GIS)

Historical events research

Transnational research

Triangulation

HIGHLIGHTS

- Secondary data analysis is the act of collecting or analyzing data that was originally collected for another purpose.

- In general, there are four major types of secondary data: surveys, official statistics, official records, and other historical documents including written text or media representations (e.g., trial transcripts, newspaper articles, television shows).

- The central insight behind historical and comparative methods is that we can improve our understanding of social processes when we make comparisons to other times and places.

- Content analysis is a tool for systematic analysis of documents and other textual data. It requires careful testing and control of coding procedures to achieve reliable measures.

- Crime mapping for research purposes is generally used to identify the spatial distribution of crime along with the social indicators such as poverty and social disorganization that are similarly distributed across areas (e.g., neighborhoods, census tracts).

- Using multiple research designs to answer the same research question, called triangulation, enhances generalizability, measurement validity, and causal validity.

EXERCISES

Discussing Research

1. Recall some of the other studies mentioned in this text. Think of how historical events may change our conceptualization of social behavior (e.g., Virginia Tech, O. J. Simpson, Abu Ghraib). Pick one phenomenon and assess how you would perform a media content analysis concerning this particular theme. Focus particular attention on procedures for measurement, sampling, and establishing causal relations.

2. What historical events have had a major influence on social patterns in the nation? The possible answers are too numerous to list, ranging from any of the wars to major internal political conflicts, economic booms and busts, scientific discoveries, and legal changes. Choose one such event in your own nation for this exercise. Find one historical book on this

event and list the sources of evidence used by the author(s). What additional evidence would you suggest for a social science investigation of the event?

3. Select a current crime or political topic that has been the focus of news articles. Propose a content analysis strategy for this topic, using newspaper articles or editorials as your units of analysis. Your strategy should include a definition of the population, selection of the units of analysis, a sampling plan, and coding procedures for key variables. Now find an article on this topic and use it to develop your coding procedures. Test and refine your coding procedures with another article on the same topic.

Finding Research on the Web

1. Using your library's government documents collection or the U.S. Census Bureau website (www.census.gov), select one report by the U.S. Census Bureau about the population of the United States or some segment of it. Outline the report and list all the tables included in it. Summarize the report in two paragraphs. Suggest a historical or comparative study for which this report would be useful.

2. The Bureau of Justice Statistics (BJS) home page can be found at www.ojp.usdoj.gov/bjs. The site contains an extensive list of reports published by the BJS along with links to the data used in the reports. You can access tables of data that display phenomena over time and across various geographical locations.
   a. Using data or reports available from the National Crime Victimization Survey, conduct an analysis of the rates of violent victimization from 1993 until the most recent date the data report is available. What do you conclude about the trends of violent victimization?
   b. Find a report available on the site that makes cross-national comparisons. Summarize the methods by which the data were collected. Now summarize the findings of the report.

3. The National Institute of Justice has a wealth of information on crime mapping located at www.ncjrs.org. Search the site for information on "crime mapping," and you will find that it contains a multitude of information, including the latest technological advances in crime-mapping strategies for police departments as well as full-text articles discussing recent research that uses crime-mapping techniques. Select a report available online and summarize its findings.

Critiquing Research

1. Review the survey data sets available through the Inter-University Consortium for Political and Social Research (ICPSR), using either its published directory or its Internet site (www.icpsr.umich.edu). Select two data sets that might be used to study a research question in which you are interested. Use the information ICPSR reports about them to determine whether the data set contains the relevant variables you will need to answer your research question? Are the issues of confidentiality and anonymity appropriately addressed? Is the information provided enough to ensure that all ethical guidelines were followed? What are the advantages and disadvantages of using one of these data sets to answer your research question compared to designing a new study?

2. Read the original article reporting one of the studies described in this chapter. Critique the article, using the article review questions presented in Appendix B as your guide. Focus particular attention on procedures for measurement, sampling, and establishing causal relations.

Making Research Ethical

1. In your opinion, does a researcher have an ethical obligation to urge government officials or others to take action in response to social problems that they have identified? Why or why not?

2. Should any requirements be imposed on researchers who seek to study other cultures, in order to ensure that procedures are appropriate and interpretations are culturally sensitive? What practices would you suggest for cross-cultural researchers in order to ensure that ethical guidelines are followed? (Consider the wording of consent forms and the procedures for gaining voluntary cooperation.)

3. Oral historians can uncover disturbing facts about the past. What if a researcher were conducting an oral history project such as the Depression Writer's Project and learned from an interviewee about his previously undisclosed involvement in a predatory sex crime many years ago? Should the researcher report what she learned to a government attorney who might decide to bring criminal charges? What about informing the victim or her surviving relatives? Would you change your answers to these questions if the statute of limitations had expired and as a result, the offender could not be prosecuted any longer? Do you think researchers should be protected from being subpoenaed to testify before a grand jury?

4. When using methodological triangulation techniques, do you think that researchers must take extra care to protect respondents' identities? Theoretically, the more sources data are pulled from, the more chances there are to link interview data with official records. Where should the line be drawn between the pursuit of rich data collection that surpasses single-method findings and subject confidentiality? If official records are publicly available anyway, should this be a concern?

Developing a Research Proposal

Add a historical or comparative dimension to your proposed study.

1. Consider which of the four types of comparative-historical methods would best be suited to an investigation of your research question. Think of possibilities for qualitative and quantitative research on your topic with the method you prefer. Will you conduct a variable-oriented or case-oriented study? Write a brief statement justifying the approach you choose.

2. Review the possible sources of data for your comparative-historical project. Search the web and relevant government, historical, and international organization sites or publications. Search the social science literature for similar studies and read about the data sources they used.

3. Specify the hypotheses you will test or the causal sequences you will investigate. Describe what your cases will be (nations, regions, years, etc.). Explain how you will select cases. List the sources of your measures and describe the specific type of data you expect to obtain for each measure.

4. Review the list of potential problems in comparative-historical research and discuss those that you believe will be most troublesome in your proposed investigation. Explain your reasoning.

Performing Data Analysis in SPSS or Excel

1. Using the data set STATE2000, examine the rates of violence and murder across the four regions of the United States (REGION). The best procedure to use for this is called MEANS. You can access this under ANALYZE, then COMPARE MEANS, then click on MEANS. In the Mean dialog box, place the rate of violence you wish to compare first (VIOLENT or MURDER) in the dependent variables box and REGION in the independent variable box. Summarize your findings. Now, using this same procedure, examine whether there are similar differences across regions for rates of poverty, which are often found to be associated with rates of violence. That is, geographical locations that have higher rates of poverty and over-deprivation also tend to have higher rates of violence. What do you conclude?

2. Now use the General Social Survey (GSS) file that is located on the student study site. Because the GSS file is cross-sectional, we cannot use it to conduct historical research. However, we can develop some interesting historical questions by examining differences in the attitudes of Americans in different birth cohorts.

   a. Inspect the distributions of a set of variables in which you are interested (e.g., attitudes toward the death penalty, attitudes toward women). Would you expect any of these attitudes and behaviors to have changed during the 20th century? State your expectations in the form of hypotheses.

   b. Request a cross tabulation of these variables by birth COHORT.

   c. What appear to be the differences among the cohorts? Which differences do you think are due to historical change, and which do you think are due to the aging process? Which attitudes and behaviors would you expect to still differentiate the baby boom generation and the post-Vietnam generation in 20 years?

Student Study Site

The companion Student Study Site for *Fundamentals of Research in Criminology and Criminal Justice* can be found at www.sagepub.com/bachmanfrccj2e.

Visit the Student Study Site to enhance your understanding of the chapter content and to discover additional resources that will take your learning one step further. You can enhance your understanding of the chapters by using the comprehensive study material, which includes interactive exercises, e-flashcards, web exercises, practice self-tests, and more. You will also find special features, such as Learning From Journal Articles, which incorporates Sage's online journal collection.

CHAPTER 10

Evaluation and Policy Analysis

In this chapter, we will provide you with an overview of evaluation research in the field of criminology and criminal justice. Although all the research we have discussed in this text is ultimately useful, evaluation research is inherently so because the results generally have an impact on policy choices in the immediate future. As such, evaluation research is often referred to as *applied research* because the findings can immediately be utilized and applied. We will first provide you with a brief history of evaluation research. Then, after describing the different types of evaluation research, we will offer case studies that illustrate the various methodologies used to assess the impacts of programs and policies in criminology and criminal justice. We will conclude with a discussion of the differences between basic science and applied research and highlight the emerging demand for evidence-based policy.

WHY DO WE NEED EVALUATION?

Every year, the U.S. Department of Justice (DOJ) spends an average of $3 billion in grants to help state and local law enforcement and communities prevent and ameliorate the consequences of crime. But similar to virtually every government agency, very little money has been allocated by the DOJ to determine whether these prevention programs actually work. In 1996, Congress required the Attorney General to provide a "comprehensive evaluation of the effectiveness" of the programs that had been implemented with this money. Not only does the money go for such traditional prevention programs as after-school recreation programs, but it also supports such efforts as community-oriented policing, drug raids, prisoner rehabilitation, boot camps, home confinement and electronic monitoring, job corps and vocational training for prison inmates, preschool education programs, and other programs too numerous to mention. Most of the Department of Justice money set aside for prevention, however, is allocated most heavily in police and prisons, with very little support for prevention programs in other institutions (Sherman et al. 1997). As the mandate from Congress suggests, evaluation plays an increasingly important role in the fields of criminology and criminal justice.

Many of the studies we have already highlighted in this text were conducted to evaluate the effectiveness of some program or policy (e.g., violent prevention programs in schools, mandatory arrest policies, the effects of drug courts). In this chapter, we will illustrate other research focused on different types of evaluation. However, we will first provide you with an overview of evaluation research in the field of criminology and criminal justice. Because evaluation research is frequently used to inform policies or to implement changes in a programs, it is often referred to as applied research because the findings can immediately be utilized and applied.

A BRIEF HISTORY OF EVALUATION RESEARCH

Evaluation research is not a method of data collection, like survey research or experiments, nor is it a unique component of research designs, like sampling or measurement. Instead, evaluation research is social research that is conducted for a distinctive purpose: to investigate social programs (such as substance abuse treatment programs, welfare programs, criminal justice programs, or employment and training programs). Rossi and Freeman (1989) define evaluation research as "the systematic application of social research procedures for assessing the conceptualization, design, implementation, and utility of social intervention programs" (p. 18). What exactly does *systematic* mean? Well, regardless of the treatment or program being examined, evaluations are systematic because they employ social research approaches to gathering valid and reliable data. Note the plural *approaches* instead of the singular *approach*. Evaluation research covers the spectrum of research methods that we have discussed in this text.

For each project, an evaluation researcher must select a research design and a method of data collection that are useful for answering the particular research questions posed and appropriate for the particular program investigated.

You can see why we placed this chapter after most of the others in the text: When you review or plan evaluation research, you have to think about the research process as a whole and how different parts of that process can best be combined.

Although scientific research methods had been used prior to the 1950s (in fact, as early as the 1700s) to evaluate outcomes of particular social experiments and programs, it was not until the end of the 1950s that social research became immersed in the workings of government with the common goal of improving society. During the 1960s, the practice of evaluation research increased dramatically, not only in the United States but also around the world. One of the main initiatives that spawned this growth of evaluation research in the United States was the so-called War on Poverty that was part of the Great Society legislation of the 1960s. When the federal government began to take a major role in alleviating poverty and the social problems associated with it, such as delinquency and crime, the public wanted accountability for the tax dollars spent on such programs. Were these programs actually having their intended effects? Did the benefits outweigh the costs? During this time, the methods of social science were utilized like never before to evaluate this proliferation of new programs.

By the mid-1970s, evaluators were called on not only to assess the overall effectiveness of programs, but also to determine whether programs were being implemented as intended and to provide feedback to help solve programming problems as well. As an indication of the growth of evaluation research during this time, several professional organizations emerged to assist in the dissemination of ideas from the burgeoning number of social scientists engaged in this type of research in the United States, along with similar organizations in other countries (Patton 1997).

By the 1990s, the public wanted even more accountability. Unfortunately, clear answers were not readily available. Few social programs could provide hard data on results achieved and outcomes obtained. Of course, government bureaucrats had produced a wealth of data on other things, including exactly how funds in particular programs were spent, for whom this money was spent, and for how many. However, these data primarily measured whether government staff were following the rules and regulations, not whether the desired results were being achieved. Instead of being rewarded for making their programs produce the intended outcomes (e.g., more jobs, fewer delinquents), the bureaucracy of government had made it enough simply to do the required paperwork of program monitoring.

The results of evaluations that were conducted rarely saw the light of day. This, in turn, was interpreted by many politicians and individual citizens alike as "nothing works." Professional evaluation researchers soon realized that it was not enough simply to perform rigorous experiments to determine program efficacy; they must also be responsible for making sure their results could be understood and utilized by the practitioners (e.g., government officials, corporations, and nonprofit agencies) to make decisions about scrapping or modifying existing programs. In addition, there was increased concern in the field regarding fiscal accountability, documenting the worth of social program expenditures in relation to their costs.

It was in this context that professional evaluators began discussing standards for the field of evaluation research. In 1981, a Joint Committee on Standards published the list of features all evaluations should have. These standards still exist today (Joint Committee 1994, as cited in Patton 1997: 17):

Utility: The utility standards are intended to ensure that an evaluation will serve the practical information needs of intended users.

Feasibility: The feasibility standards are intended to ensure that an evaluation will be realistic, prudent, diplomatic, and frugal.

Propriety: The propriety standards are intended to ensure that an evaluation will be conducted legally, ethically, and with due regard for the welfare of those involved in the evaluation, as well as those affected by its results.

Accuracy: The accuracy standards are intended to ensure that an evaluation will reveal and convey technically adequate information about the features that determine worth or merit of the program being evaluated.

To the surprise of many in the field, utility was at the top of the list. This conveyed the idea that an evaluation only met the standards if, in fact, it served the needs of intended users. Professionals in the field responded accordingly. For example, Patton (1997) developed the practice of and coined the term "utilization-focused evaluation" as a way to fulfill the utility standard. Utilization-focused evaluation offered both a philosophy of evaluation and a practical framework for designing and conducting evaluations. The primary premise of this method was that evaluations should be judged by their utility and actual use. Use concerned how real people in the real world applied evaluation findings and experienced the evaluation process.

EVALUATION BASICS

Exhibit 10.1 illustrates the process of evaluation research as a simple systems model. First, clients, customers, students, or some other persons or units—cases—enter the program as inputs. Students may begin a new D.A.R.E. program, sex offenders may enter a new intense probation program, or crime victims may be sent to a victim advocate. Resources and staff required by a program are also program inputs.

Inputs Resources, raw materials, clients, and staff that go into a program

---

Next, some service or treatment is provided to the cases. This may be attendance in a class, assistance with a health problem, residence in new housing, or receipt of special cash benefits. The process of service delivery (program process) may be simple or complicated, short or long, but it is designed to have some impact on the cases, as inputs are consumed and outputs are produced.

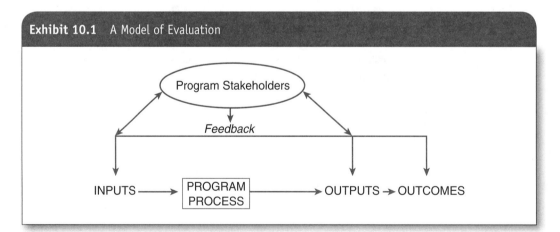

Exhibit 10.1   A Model of Evaluation

Source: Adapted from Martin, Lawrence L. & Peter M. Kettner. 1996. *Measuring the Performance of Human Service Programs.* Thousand Oaks, CA: Sage. Used with permission.

Program process The complete treatment or service delivered by the program

---

The direct products of the program's service delivery process are its **outputs**. Program outputs may include clients served, case managers trained, food parcels delivered, or arrests made. The program outputs may be desirable in themselves, but they primarily serve to indicate that the program is operating.

Outputs The services delivered or new products produced by the program process

---

Program **outcomes** indicate the impact of the program on the cases that have been processed. Outcomes can range from improved test scores or higher rates of job retention to fewer criminal offenses and lower rates of poverty. There are likely to be multiple outcomes of any social program, some intended and some unintended, some positive and others that are viewed as negative.

Outcomes The impact of the program process on the cases processed

---

Variation in both outputs and outcomes in turn influences the inputs to the program through a **feedback** process. If not enough clients are being served, recruitment of new clients may increase. If too many negative side effects result from a trial medication, the trials may be limited or terminated. If a program does not appear to lead to improved outcomes, clients may go elsewhere.

Feedback Information about service delivery system outputs, outcomes, or operations that is available to any program inputs

---

Evaluation research enters into this picture as a more systematic approach to feedback that strengthens the feedback loop through credible analyses of program operations and outcomes. Evaluation research also broadens this loop to include connections to parties outside of the program itself. A funding agency or political authority may mandate the research; outside experts may be brought in to conduct the research; and the evaluation research findings may be released to the public, or at least funders, in a formal report.

The evaluation process as a whole, and the feedback process in particular, can only be understood in relation to the interests and perspectives of program stakeholders. **Stakeholders** are those individuals and groups who have some basis of concern with the program. They might be clients, staff, managers, funders, or the public. The board of a program or agency, the parents or spouses of clients, the foundations that award program grants, the auditors who monitor program spending, and the members of Congress are all potential program stakeholders, and each has an interest in the outcome of any program evaluation. Some may fund the evaluation; some may provide research data; and some may review, and even approve, the research report (Martin & Kettner 1996). Who the program stakeholders are and what role they play in the program evaluation will have tremendous consequences for the research.

Stakeholders Individuals and groups who have some basis of concern with the program

---

Can you see the difference between evaluation research and traditional social science research? Unlike explanatory social science research, evaluation research is not designed to test the implications of a social theory; the basic issue is often just, "What is the program's impact?" Process evaluation often uses qualitative methods, but unlike traditional exploratory research, the goal is not to create a broad theoretical explanation for what is discovered; instead, the question is, "How does the program do what it does?" Unlike social science research, the researchers cannot design evaluation studies simply in accord with the highest scientific standards and the most important research questions; instead, it is program stakeholders who set the agenda, but there is no sharp boundary between the two: In their attempt to explain how and why the program has an impact, and whether the program is needed, evaluation researchers often bring social theories into their projects.

EVALUATION ALTERNATIVES

Today, the field of evaluation research remains somewhat of a dichotomy. There are those who conduct evaluation research for the sake of knowledge alone, whereas others strive to make their products useful for some action (the more specific program evaluation research, such as that performed by Sherman and Berk, 1984, discussed in Chapter 2). Regardless of the emphasis, however, all evaluation is empirical and data-driven. Both program evaluation and evaluation research in general offer empirical answers to questions of policy and policy effectiveness. Objective and empirical assessments of policies and programs are the cornerstone of the evaluation field.

Evaluation research may be undertaken for a variety of reasons: for management and administrative purposes; to test hypotheses derived from theory; to identify ways to improve the delivery of services; or to decide whether to continue, cut, or modify a particular program. The goal of evaluation research, however, is primarily the same as the goal for all social science research: to design and implement a study that is objective and grounded in the rules of scientific methodology. These methods run the gamut of the methods we have discussed in this text. They can range from the strictly quantitative experimental and quasi-experimental designs to the qualitative methodologies of observation and intensive interviewing.

Evaluation projects can focus on several questions related to the operation of social programs and the impact they have:

- Is the program needed? (evaluation of need)
- Can the program be evaluated? (evaluability assessment)
- How does the program operate? (process evaluation)

- What is the program's impact? (impact evaluation)
- How efficient is the program? (efficiency analysis)

The specific methods used in an evaluation research project depend, in part, on which of these questions is being addressed.

Do We Need the Program?

Is a new program needed or is an old one still required? Is there a need at all? A **needs assessment** attempts to answer these questions with systematic, credible evidence. The initial impetus for implementing programs to alleviate social problems and other societal ailments typically comes from a variety of sources, including advocacy groups, moral leaders, community advocates, and political figures. Before a program is designed and implemented, however, it is essential to obtain reliable information on the nature and the scope of the problem, and the target population in need of the intervention. Evaluation researchers often contribute to these efforts by applying research tools to answer such questions as "What is the magnitude of this problem in this community?" "How many people in this community are in need of this program?" "What are the demographic characteristics of these people (e.g., age, gender, and race or ethnicity)?" and "Is the proposed program or intervention appropriate for this population?"

Can the Program Be Evaluated?

Evaluation research will be pointless if the program itself cannot be evaluated. Yes, some type of study is always possible, but a study conducted specifically to identify the effects of a particular program may not be possible within the available time and resources. So researchers may carry out an **evaluability assessment** to learn this in advance, rather than expend time and effort on a fruitless project.

Knowledge about the program gleaned through the evaluability assessment can be used to refine evaluation plans. Because they are preliminary studies to "check things out," evaluability assessments often rely on qualitative methods. Program managers and key staff may be interviewed in depth, or program sponsors may be asked about the importance they attach to different goals. These assessments also may have an "action research" aspect, because the researcher presents the findings to program managers and encourages changes in program operations.

Is the Program Working as Planned?

What actually happens in a program? Once a program has been started, evaluators are often called on to document the extent to which implementation has taken place, whether the program is reaching the target individuals or groups, whether the program is actually operating as expected, and what resources are being expended in the conduct of the program. This is often called **process evaluation** or **program monitoring**. Rossi and Freeman (1989) define program monitoring as the systematic attempt by evaluation researchers to examine program coverage and delivery. Assessing program coverage consists of estimating the extent to which a program is reaching its intended target population; evaluating program delivery consists of measuring the degree of congruence between the plan for providing services and treatments and the ways they are actually provided.

Process evaluations are extremely important, primarily because there is no way to reliably determine whether the intended outcomes have occurred without being certain the program is working according to plan. For example, imagine you are responsible for determining whether an anti-bullying curriculum implemented in a school has been successful in decreasing the amount of bullying behavior by the students. You conduct a survey of the students both before and after the curriculum began and determine that rates of bullying have not significantly changed in the school since the curriculum started. After you write your report, however, you find out that, instead of being given in a 5-day series of 1-hour sessions as intended, the curriculum was actually crammed into a 2-hour format delivered on a Friday afternoon. A process evaluation would have revealed this implementation problem. If a program has not been implemented as intended, there is obviously no need to ask whether it had the intended outcomes.

A process evaluation can take many forms. Because most government and private organizations inherently monitor their activities through such things as application forms, receipts, and stock inventories, it should be relatively easy to obtain quantitative data for monitoring the delivery of services. This information can be summarized to describe things such as the clients served and the services provided. In addition to this quantitative information, a process evaluation will also likely benefit from qualitative methodologies such as unstructured interviews with people using the service or program. Interviews can also be conducted with staff to illuminate what they perceive to be obstacles to their delivery of services.

Process evaluation can employ a wide range of indicators. Program coverage can be monitored through program records, participant surveys, community surveys, or number of utilizers versus dropouts and ineligibles. Service delivery can be monitored through service records completed by program staff, a management information system maintained by program administrators, or reports by program recipients (Rossi & Freeman 1989).

Qualitative methods are often a key component of process evaluation studies because they can be used to understand internal program dynamics, even those that were not anticipated (Patton 2002; Posavac & Carey 1997). Qualitative researchers may develop detailed descriptions of how program participants engage with each other, how the program experience varies for different people, and how the program changes and evolves over time.

Case Study: Evaluating the D.A.R.E. Program

The evaluation of D.A.R.E. by Research Triangle Institute researchers Ringwalt et al. (1994: 7) included a process evaluation with three objectives:

1. Assess the organizational structure and operation of representative D.A.R.E. programs nationwide.

2. Review and assess factors that contribute to the effective implementation of D.A.R.E. programs nationwide.

3. Assess how D.A.R.E. and other school-based drug prevention programs are tailored to meet the needs of specific populations.

The process evaluation (called an "implementation assessment" by the researchers) was an ambitious research project in itself, with site visits, informal interviews, discussions, and surveys of D.A.R.E. program coordinators and advisors. These data indicated that D.A.R.E. was operating as designed and was running relatively smoothly. As shown in Exhibit 10.2, drug prevention coordinators in D.A.R.E. school districts rated the program components as much more satisfactory than did coordinators in school districts with other types of alcohol and drug prevention programs.

Exhibit 10.2   Components of D.A.R.E. and Other Alcohol and Drug Prevention Programs Rated as Very Satisfactory (in percentages)

Component	D.A.R.E. Program (N = 222)	Other AOD Programs (N = 406)
Curriculum	67.5	34.2
Teaching	69.7	29.8
Administrative requirements	55.7	23.1
Receptivity of students	76.5	34.6
Effects on students	63.2	22.8

Source: Ringwalt et al. (1994: 58).

Process evaluation also can be used to identify the specific aspects of the service delivery process that have an impact. This, in turn, will help explain why the program has an effect and which conditions are required for these effects. For example, implementation problems identified in site visits included insufficient numbers of officers to carry out the program as planned and a lack of Spanish-language D.A.R.E. books in a largely Hispanic school (Ringwalt et al. 1994).

Did the Program Work?

If a process study shows that the implementation of the program has been delivered to the target population as planned, the next role for an evaluator is to assess the extent to which the program achieved its goals. "Did the program work?" "Did the program have the intended consequences?" This question should by now be familiar to you; stated more like a research question we are used to, "Did the treatment or program (independent variable) effect change in the dependent variable?" It all comes back to the issue of causality. This part of the research is variously called **impact evaluation** or **impact analysis.**

Impact evaluation (or analysis) Analysis of the extent to which a treatment or other service has an effect

The bulk of the published evaluation studies in our field are devoted to some type of impact assessment. The D.A.R.E. program (independent variable), for instance, tries to reduce drug use (dependent variable). When the program is present, we expect less drug use. In a more elaborate study, we might have multiple values of the independent variable; for instance, we might look at "no program," "D.A.R.E. program," and "other drug or alcohol education" conditions and compare the results of each.

As in other areas of research, an experimental design is the preferred method for maximizing internal validity—that is, for making sure your causal claims about program impact are justified. Cases are assigned randomly to one or more experimental treatment groups and to a control group so that there is no systematic difference between the groups at the outset (see Chapter 6). The goal is to achieve a fair, unbiased test of the program itself, so that the judgment about the program's impact is not influenced by differences between the types of people who are in the different groups. It can be a difficult goal to achieve, because the usual practice in social programs is to let people decide for themselves whether they want to enter a program or not and also to establish eligibility criteria that ensure people who enter the program are different from those who do not (Boruch 1997). In either case, a selection bias is introduced.

Of course, program impact may also be evaluated with quasi-experimental designs or survey or field research methods, without a randomized experimental design. But if current participants who are already in a program are compared with nonparticipants, it is unlikely that the treatment group will be comparable to the control group. Participants will probably be a selected group, different at the outset from nonparticipants. As a result, causal conclusions about program impact will be on much shakier ground. For instance, when a study at New York's maximum-security prison for women found that "Inmate Education [i.e., classes] Is Found to Lower Risk of New Arrest," the conclusions were immediately suspect: The research design did not ensure that the women who enrolled in the prison classes were similar to (e.g., in offense type) those who had not enrolled in the classes, "leaving open the possibility that the results were due, at least in part, to self-selection, with the women most motivated to avoid reincarceration being the ones who took the college classes" (Lewin 2001).

Impact analysis is an important undertaking that fully deserves the attention it has been given in government program funding requirements. However, you should realize that more rigorous evaluation designs are less likely to conclude that a program has the desired effect; as the standard of proof goes up, success is harder to demonstrate.

Case Study: The Risk Skills Training Program (RSTP) Compared to D.A.R.E.

D'Amico and Fromme's (2002) study of a new Risk Skills Training Program (RSTP) compared the impact of RSTP on children 14 to 19 years of age to that of an abbreviated version of D.A.R.E. and to a control group. The impacts they examined included positive and negative "alcohol expectancies" (the anticipated effects of drinking) as well as perception of peer risk taking and actual alcohol consumption. D'Amico and Fromme found that negative alcohol expectancies increased for the RSTP group in the posttest but not for the D.A.R.E. group or the control group, while weekly drinking and "positive expectancies" for drinking outcomes actually *increased* for the D.A.R.E. group and the control group by the 6-month follow-up but not for the RSTP group (see Exhibit 10.3).

Is the Program Worth It?

Whatever the program's benefits, are they sufficient to offset the program's costs? Are taxpayers getting their money's worth? What resources are required by the program? These efficiency questions can be the primary reason that funders require evaluation of the programs they fund. As a result, efficiency analysis, which compares program effects with costs, is often a necessary component of an evaluation research project.

A cost–benefit analysis must identify the specific program costs and the procedures for estimating the economic value of specific program benefits. This type of analysis also requires that the analyst identify whose perspective will be used in order to determine what can be considered a benefit rather than a cost.

A cost-effectiveness analysis focuses attention directly on the program's outcomes rather than on the economic value of those outcomes. In a cost-effectiveness analysis, the specific costs of the program are compared with the program's outcomes, such as the number of jobs obtained, the extent of improvement in reading scores, or the degree of decline in crimes committed. For example, one result might be an estimate of how much it cost the program for each job obtained by a program participant.

Efficiency analysis A type of evaluation research that compares program costs with program effects. It can be either a cost–benefit analysis or a cost-effectiveness analysis.

Cost–benefit analysis A type of evaluation research that compares program costs with the economic value of program benefits

Cost-effectiveness analysis A type of evaluation research that compares program costs with actual program outcomes

---

Social science training often does not give much attention to cost–benefit analysis, so it can be helpful to review possible costs and benefits with an economist or business school professor or student. Once potential costs and benefits have been identified, they must be measured. It is a need highlighted in recent government programs.

In addition to measuring services and their associated costs, a cost–benefit analysis must be able to make some type of estimation of how clients benefited from the program. Normally, this will involve a comparison of some indicators of client status before and after clients received program services, or between clients who received program services and a comparable group who did not.

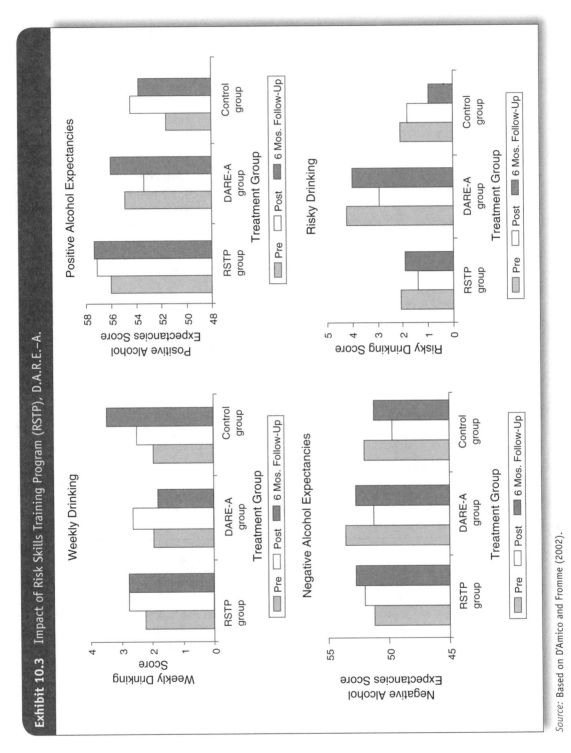

Exhibit 10.3 Impact of Risk Skills Training Program (RSTP), D.A.R.E.–A.

Source: Based on D'Amico and Fromme (2002).

266

Case Study: Cost–Benefit Analysis of Therapeutic Communities

A recent study of therapeutic communities provides a clear illustration. A therapeutic community is an alternative to the traditional correctional response to drug addiction, which is typically incarceration for those convicted of either the possession or trafficking of illegal substances. In therapeutic communities, abusers participate in an intensive, structured living experience with other addicts who are attempting to stay sober. Because the treatment involves residential support as well as other types of services, it can be quite costly. Are those costs worth it?

Sacks et al. (2002) conducted a cost–benefit analysis of a modified therapeutic community (TC). A total of 342 homeless, mentally ill chemical abusers were randomly assigned to either a TC or a "treatment-as-usual" comparison group. Employment status, criminal activity, and utilization of health care services were each measured for the 3 months prior to entering treatment and the 3 months after treatment. Earnings from employment in each period were adjusted for costs incurred by criminal activity and utilization of health care services.

Was it worth it? The average cost of TC treatment for a client was $20,361. In comparison, the economic benefit (based on earnings) to the average TC client was $305,273, which declined to $273,698 after comparing post- to pre-program earnings, but was still $253,337 even after adjustment for costs. The resulting benefit–cost ratio was 13:1, although this ratio declined to only 5.2:1 after further adjustments (for cases with extreme values). Nonetheless, the TC program studied seems to have had a substantial benefit relative to its costs.

DESIGN DECISIONS

Once we have decided on, or identified, the goal or focus for a program evaluation, there are still important decisions to be made about how to design the specific evaluation project. The most important decisions are the following:

- Black box or program theory: Do we care how the program gets results?
- Researcher or stakeholder orientation: Whose goals matter most?
- Quantitative or qualitative methods: Which methods provide the best answers?

Black Box Evaluation or Program Theory

The "meat and potatoes" of most evaluation research involves determining whether a program has the intended effect. If the effect occurred, the program "worked"; if the effect didn't occur, then some would say the program should be abandoned or redesigned. In this approach, the process by which a program has an effect on outcomes is often treated as a black box—that is, the focus of the evaluation researcher is on whether cases seem to have changed as a result of their exposure to the program, between the time they entered the program as inputs and when they exited the program as outputs (Chen 1990). The assumption is that program evaluation requires only the test of a simple input–output model. There may be no attempt to open the black box of the program process.

If an investigation of program process is conducted, a program theory may be developed. A **program theory** describes what has been learned about how the program has its effect. When a researcher has sufficient knowledge before the investigation begins, outlining a program theory can help to guide the investigation of program process in the most productive directions. This is termed a **theory-driven evaluation.**

A program theory specifies how the program is expected to operate and identifies which program elements are operational (Chen 1990). In addition, a program theory specifies how a program is to produce its effects and so improves understanding of the relationship between the independent variable (the program) and the dependent variable (the outcome or outcomes).

Researcher or Stakeholder Orientation

Whose prescriptions specify how the program should operate, what outcomes it should try to achieve, or who it should serve? Most social science research assumes that the researcher specifies the research questions, the applicable theory or theories, and the outcomes to be investigated. Social science research results are most often reported in a professional journal or at professional conferences where scientific standards determine how the research is received. In program evaluation, however, the research question is often set by the program sponsors or the government agency that is responsible for reviewing the program. It is to these authorities that research findings are reported. Most often this authority also specifies the outcomes to be investigated. The first evaluator of the evaluation research is therefore the funding agency, not the professional social science community. Evaluation research is research for a client, and its results may directly affect the services, treatments, or even punishments (e.g., in the case of prison studies) that program users receive. In this case, the person who pays the piper gets to call the tune.

Should an evaluation researcher insist on designing the evaluation project and specifying its goals, or should he or she accept the suggestions and adopt the goals of the funding agency? What role should the preferences of program staff or clients play? What responsibility does the evaluation researcher have to politicians and taxpayers when evaluating government-funded programs? The different answers that various evaluation researchers have given to these questions are reflected in different approaches to evaluation (Chen 1990: 66–68).

Stakeholder approaches encourage researchers to be responsive to program stakeholders. Issues for study are to be based on the views of people involved with the program, and reports are to be made to program participants. The program theory is developed by the researcher to clarify and develop the key stakeholders' theory of the program (Shadish, Cook, & Leviton 1991). In one stakeholder approach, termed *utilization-focused evaluation,* the evaluator forms a task force of program stakeholders who help to shape the evaluation project so that they are most likely to use its results (Patton 2002). In evaluation research termed *action research* or *participatory research,* program participants are engaged with the researchers as coresearchers and help to design, conduct, and report the research. One research approach that has been termed *appreciative inquiry* eliminates the professional researcher altogether in favor of a structured dialogue about needed changes among program participants themselves (Patton 2002).

Social science approaches emphasize the importance of researcher expertise and maintenance of some autonomy in order to develop the most trustworthy, unbiased program evaluation. It is assumed that "evaluators cannot passively accept the values and views of the other stakeholders" (Chen 1990: 78). Evaluators who adopt this approach derive a program theory from information they obtain on how the program operates and extant social science theory and knowledge, not from the views of stakeholders.

Integrative approaches attempt to cover issues of concern to both stakeholders and evaluators, and to include stakeholders in the group from which guidance is routinely sought (Chen & Rossi 1987). The emphasis given to either stakeholder or social concern is expected to vary with the specific project circumstances. Integrated approaches seek to balance the goal of carrying out a project that is responsive to stakeholder concerns with the goal of objective, scientifically trustworthy, and generalizable results. When the research is planned, evaluators are expected to communicate and negotiate regularly with key stakeholders and to take stakeholder concerns into account. Findings from preliminary inquiries are reported back to program decision makers so that they can make improvements in the program before it is formally evaluated. When the actual evaluation is conducted, the evaluation research team is expected to operate more autonomously, minimizing intrusions from program stakeholders.

Ultimately, evaluation research takes place in a political context, in which program stakeholders may be competing or collaborating to increase program funding or to emphasize particular program goals. It is a political process that creates social programs, and it is a political process that determines whether these programs are evaluated and what is done with evaluation findings (Weiss 1993). Developing supportive relations with stakeholder groups will increase the odds that political processes will not undermine evaluation practice.

EVALUATION IN ACTION

Case Study: Problem-Oriented Policing in Violent Crime Areas

Several studies have found that over half of all crimes in a city are committed at a few criminogenic places within communities. These places have been called "hot spots" by some criminologists (Sherman, Gartin, & Buerger 1989; Weisburd, Maher, & Sherman 1992). Even within the most crime-ridden neighborhoods, it has been found that crime clusters at a few discrete locations while other areas remain relatively crime-free. The clustering of violent crime at particular locations suggests that there are important features or dynamics at these locations that give rise to violent situations. As such, focused crime prevention efforts should be able to modify these criminogenic conditions and reduce violence.

Problem-oriented policing strategies are increasingly utilized by urban jurisdictions to reduce crime in these high-activity crime places. Problem-oriented policing challenges officers to identify and analyze the causes of problems behind a string of criminal incidents. Once the underlying conditions that give rise to crime problems are known, police officers can then develop and implement appropriate responses. Braga et al. (1999) created a novel experiment designed to determine the effectiveness of problem-oriented policing in decreasing the incidence of violent street crime in Jersey City, New Jersey. The methodology they employed for their study was a true randomized experimental design. Recall from Chapter 5 that this design allows researchers to assume that the only systematic difference between a control and an experimental group is the presence of the intervention—in this case, the presence or absence of problem-oriented policing strategies.

To determine which places would receive the problem-oriented strategies and which places would not, 56 neighborhoods were matched into 28 pairs with equal levels of crime, which were then randomly assigned to receive the problem-oriented policing treatment (experimental places). Remember that a key feature of true experimental designs is this **random assignment.** The places that were not selected from the flip in each pair did not receive the new policing strategies (control places). The design of this experimental evaluation is illustrated in Exhibit 10.4.

In each of the experimental places, police officers from the Violent Crime Unit (VCU) of the Jersey City Police Department established networks consistent with problem-oriented policing. For example, community members were used as information sources to discuss the nature of the problems the community faced, the possible effectiveness of proposed responses, and the assessment of implemented responses. In most places, the VCU officers believed that the violence that distinguished these places from other areas of the city was closely related to the disorder of the place. Although specific tactics varied from place to place, most attempts to control violence in these places were actually targeted at the social disorder problems. For example, some tactics included cleaning up the environment of the place through aggressive order maintenance and making physical improvements such as

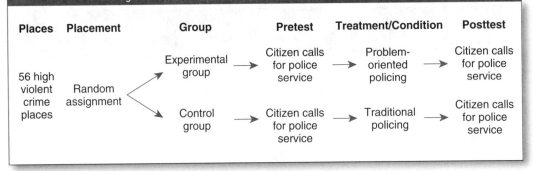

Exhibit 10.4   Randomized Experimental Design Used to Evaluate Problem-Oriented Policing Strategies

Places	Placement	Group	Pretest	Treatment/Condition	Posttest
56 high violent crime places	Random assignment	Experimental group	Citizen calls for police service	Problem-oriented policing	Citizen calls for police service
		Control group	Citizen calls for police service	Traditional policing	Citizen calls for police service

Source: Braga, Anthony A. et al. (1999), "Problem-Oriented Policing in Violent Crime Places: A Randomized Controlled Experiment." *Criminology, 37*(4): 541–580. Reprinted with permission.

securing vacant lots or removing trash from the street. The independent variable or treatment, then, was the use of problem-oriented policing, which comprised a number of specific tactics implemented by police officers to control the physical and social disorder at experimental violent places. In contrast, control places did not receive these problem-solving efforts; they received traditional policing strategies such as arbitrary patrol interventions and routine follow-up investigations by detectives. No problem-oriented strategies were employed.

Braga et al. (1999) examined the efficacy of these problem-oriented policing strategies by using three separate dependent variables: incident report data, citizen emergency calls for service within each place, and physical observation of each place during the pretest and posttest periods. This variable was used to indicate changes in both physical incivilities at places such as vacant lots, trash, graffiti, or broken windows, and social incivilities such as drinking in public and loitering. These variables were measured for 6-month preintervention and postintervention periods. If the problem-oriented policing approach was effective, then Braga and colleagues should have seen a decrease in incidents and emergency calls for service in the experimental areas in the posttest compared to the control areas. They should also have seen decreased signs of physical and social incivilities in the experimental areas compared to the control areas. Results indicated that the problem-oriented policing strategies examined in this evaluation research appear to have had a great deal of success in controlling and preventing crime.

STRENGTHS OF RANDOMIZED EXPERIMENTAL DESIGNS IN IMPACT EVALUATIONS

The research design used by Braga et al. (1999) meets all three criteria for a true experimental design. First, they used at least two comparison groups. In the Braga et al. research, some communities received the problem-oriented patrol strategies (experimental groups), while the other comparison communities received traditional police patrol (control groups). Finally, the assessment of change in the dependent variables used in their study was performed after the experimental condition (problem-oriented strategies) had been delivered.

Because the communities in Braga et al.'s (1999) study were randomly assigned to receive either problem-oriented or traditional patrol strategies, the relationship found between these strategies (independent variable) and the dependent variables (incidents of crime, etc.) are unambiguous. Braga and colleagues monitored their dependent variables both before and after the different policing strategies were implemented, so there is also no question that the strategies came before the change in the dependent variable. Finally, the random assignment of the communities to either the problem-oriented or traditional police conditions controlled for a host of possible extraneous influences that may have created spurious relationships.

The extent to which the findings of these studies can be generalized to the larger population, however, is another issue. Can Braga et al.'s (1999) findings be generalized to the larger population in New Jersey (sample generalizability) or to other states and communities (external validity)? Issues of sample generalizability, you will recall, are related to selecting a random sample from the population in the first place (random selection), not random assignment. However, because Braga and colleagues' study utilized several experimental and control communities, this increases the likelihood that their findings are generalizable to their respective populations. In addition, because the study was performed in the field (i.e., the real world) and not in a laboratory, their findings are more likely to be generalizable to the larger population.

WHEN EXPERIMENTS ARE NOT FEASIBLE

We have already learned that many research questions or situations are not amenable to a true experimental design. The same is true in evaluation research. There are many reasons why it may be impossible to use randomized experiments to evaluate the impacts of programs and policies. The primary reason why randomization is likely not possible in evaluation research is that the program is usually outside the control of the evaluator. As Rossi and Freeman (1989) state, "for political, human subject or other considerations, program staff, sponsors, or other powerful stakeholders resist randomization" (p. 313). Obtaining the cooperation of the program staff and sponsors is often an obstacle in evaluation research. In fact, when there are several locations implementing similar programs, the sites included in an evaluation study may be selected based primarily on the cooperation of the staff and sponsors.

In general, quasi-experimental designs are the most powerful alternatives to true randomized experimental designs. The more similar the experimental and control groups are to each other, particularly on characteristics thought to be related to the intervention or treatment, the more confident we can be in a study's findings.

Case Study: Boot Camps

Since their beginning in 1983 in Georgia, the use of correctional boot camps, sometimes called shock incarceration programs, has skyrocketed in both state and federal prison systems. For politicians and citizens alike, the notion of a strict, military-style punishment as an alternative to extended incarceration is attractive. Many questions remain, however, about the value of boot camps. Do they work? Because there are so many different types of boot camps (e.g., some have a military-style atmosphere whereas others do not), there is no easy answer to this question.

In 1990, Doris MacKenzie evaluated boot camp program efficacy in eight states: Florida, Georgia, Illinois, Louisiana, New York, Oklahoma, South Carolina, and Texas. These sites were selected because they incorporated the core elements of a boot camp program, including (1) strict rules, discipline, and a military boot camp–like atmosphere; (2) mandatory participation in military drills and physical training; and (3) separation of program participants from other prison inmates.

The evaluation was extensive and resulted in many publications (Brame & MacKenzie 1996; MacKenzie 1994; MacKenzie et al. 1995; MacKenzie & Souryal 1995). We will

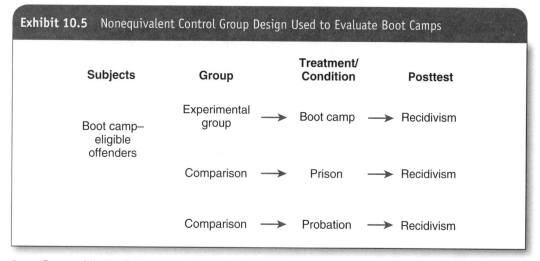

Exhibit 10.5   Nonequivalent Control Group Design Used to Evaluate Boot Camps

Source: Brame and MacKenzie (1996).

highlight the results of the impact assessments for recidivism here. To determine whether boot camps were more likely than traditional prison time to reduce recidivism after release, MacKenzie and colleagues utilized a quasi-experimental design. In each state, a sample of male boot camp program graduates was used as the experimental condition. Two other offender samples were used as comparison groups and usually included regular prison parolees, probationers, and boot camp dropouts. The individuals from all samples, however, met the eligibility requirements for the boot camp programs. This nonequivalent control group design is illustrated in Exhibit 10.5.

After being sentenced to probation or released from boot camps and prison, subjects were tracked for a follow-up period of up to 2 years of community supervision. Recidivism was measured by arrests and revocations for new crimes or for technical violations.

Were boot camps successful in meeting their goals? Results were mixed: Programs with more intensive long-term follow-up supervision had a decrease in recidivism, while traditional boot camps without such long-term supervision did not.

The weakness of this quasi-experimental design lay in the fact that MacKenzie and colleagues were not able to randomly assign offenders to the boot camps or the comparison treatments. Therefore, there is less confidence in the findings, primarily because there is no assurance that the offenders were equivalent before they received the treatments.

QUALITATIVE AND QUANTITATIVE METHODS

Evaluation research that attempts to identify the effects of a treatment, law, or program typically is quantitative. It is fair to say that when there is an interest in comparing outcomes between an experimental and a control group, or tracking change over time in a systematic manner, quantitative methods are favored.

But qualitative methods can add much to quantitative evaluation research studies, including more depth, detail, nuance, and exemplary case studies (Patton 1997). Perhaps the greatest contribution qualitative methods can make in many evaluation studies is in investigating the program process—finding out what is "inside the black box." Although it is possible—even recommended—to track the process of service delivery with quantitative measures like staff contact hours, frequency of complaints, and the like, the goal of finding out what is happening to program clients and how clients experience the program can often best be achieved by observing program activities and interviewing staff and clients intensively.

Another good reason for using qualitative methods in evaluation research is the importance of learning how different individuals react to the treatment. Qualitative methods can also help in understanding how social programs actually operate. Complex social programs have many different features, and it is not always clear whether it is the combination of those features or some particular features that are responsible for the program's effect, or for the absence of an effect.

The more complex the social program, the more value qualitative methods can add to the evaluation process. For the most part, the strengths and weaknesses of methodologies used in evaluation research are those of the methods we have already discussed throughout this text. As Patton (1997) contends, "There are no perfect [evaluation] studies. And there cannot be, for there is no agreement on what constitutes perfection" (p. 23). There are, however, methods that are better able to infer cause and effect. Because the basic question of most impact evaluations is, "Does program (cause) have its intended consequences (effect)?" there are basic methodological criteria we can use to judge the methods discussed in this chapter.

In their review of the crime prevention evaluation literature, Sherman et al. (1997) adopted a way to judge the "methodological rigor" of evaluation studies using a 5-point scale. The researchers gave each study examined in their review a "scientific methods score" of 1 to 5, with 5 being the strongest scientific evidence. Only studies that used random assignment to a program (experimental group) and comparison group (control group) were assigned a score of 5. Studies that used a comparison between multiple groups or units within and outside the program, controlling for other factors, or a nonequivalent comparison group that has only minor differences evident between the groups, received a score of 4.

Despite the fact that a randomized experiment is the best way to determine the impact of a program, it is also important to remember that the methodology selected for an evaluation project should be relevant to the policy makers and planners who intend to use the results. Although some researchers vehemently contend that only a randomized experimental design can provide reliable information on the impacts of a program, others just as vehemently disagree.

Increasing Demand for Evidence-Based Policy

As you have seen in this chapter, evaluation studies come in many forms. A single study, such as the Minneapolis Domestic Violence Experiment (recall Chapter 2), can be very influential and have an enormous effect on police policies. But we have seen that replications of studies answering the same question often result in very different conclusions. Obviously, learning what works should rely on more than one study. Evaluation specialists are increasingly encouraging policy makers to enact **evidence-based policies,** which are based on a **systematic review** of all available evidence that assesses what works and what doesn't. Petrosino and Lavenberg (2007) define systematic reviews as follows:

> In systematic reviews, researchers attempt to gather relevant evaluative studies, critically appraise them, and come to judgments about what works using explicit, transparent, state-of-the-art methods. In contrast to traditional syntheses, a systematic review will include detail about each stage of the decision process, including the question that guided the review, the criteria for studies to be included, and the methods used to search for and screen evaluation reports. It will also detail how analyses were done and how conclusions were reached. (p. 1)

The reviews often try to quantify the successfulness of particular programs and interventions, sometimes using a technique called meta-analysis, which we describe later. Although these reviews are designed to be objective, there are still controversies surrounding any particular review, including conflict about the inclusion or exclusion of studies and what qualifies as a rigorous study design (e.g., is a true experimental design the only way to determine causality?).

Systematic reviews are increasingly sponsored by both private and government entities. One private organization that has become a leader in publicizing reviews related to criminal justice policy research is the Campbell Collaboration. The **Campbell Collaboration** is an international research network that prepares and disseminates systematic reviews of social science evidence in three fields including crime and justice, education, and social welfare. The collaboration's mission "is to promote positive social change, by contributing to better-informed decisions and better-quality public and private services around the world" (www.campbellcollaboration.org). All reports are peer reviewed and are available on the collaboration's website. One example from the online Campbell Library (www .campbellcollaboration.org/library.php) is a systematic review by Tolan et al. (2008) that examined the impact of mentoring interventions in decreasing delinquency and other problems. If you read the report, you will see that all decisions made by the authors are explicitly stated. For example, they were very specific in their criteria for mentoring, which had to meet four criteria: (a) an interaction between two individuals over an extended period of time; (b) inequality of experience, knowledge, or power between the mentor and mentee, with the mentor possessing the greater share; (c) the mentee is in a position to imitate and benefit from the knowledge, skill, ability, or experience of the mentor; and (d) the absence of inequality that typifies other helping relationships and is marked by professional training, certification, or predetermined status differences such as parent–child or teacher–student relationships.

When selecting studies for their review, Tolan et al. (2008) also clearly stated four criteria: (a) studies that focused on youth who were at risk for juvenile delinquency or who were currently involved in delinquent behavior; (b) studies that focused on prevention or treatment for those at-risk youth; (c) studies that measured at least one quantitative effect on at least one outcome including delinquency, substance abuse, academic achievement, or aggression; and (d) studies that were conducted in predominately English-speaking countries reported between 1980 and 2005. As you can see, systematic reviews are, well, extremely systematic! For the record, the review found that there was a modest impact of mentoring in reducing delinquency and aggression, but less of relationship was found between mentoring and drug use and academic achievement.

Meta-Analyses

Meta-analyses are often used in systematic reviews. A **meta-analysis** is a quantitative method for identifying patterns in findings across multiple studies of the same research question (Cooper & Hedges 1994). Unlike a traditional literature review, which describes previous research studies verbally, meta-analyses treat previous studies as cases, whose features are measured as variables and then analyzed statistically. It is like conducting a survey in which the "respondents" are previous studies. Meta-analysis shows how evidence about social processes varies across research studies. If the methods used in these studies varied, then meta-analysis can describe how this variation affected the study findings. If social contexts varied across the studies, then meta-analysis will indicate how social context affected the study findings.

Meta-analysis can be used when a number of studies have attempted to answer the same research question using similar quantitative methods. Meta-analysis is not appropriate for evaluating results from qualitative studies or from multiple studies that used different methods or measured different dependent variables. It is also not very sensible to use meta-analysis to combine study results when the original case data from these studies are available and can actually be combined and analyzed together (Lipsey & Wilson 2001). Meta-analysis is a technique for combination and statistical analysis of published research reports.

After a research problem is formulated based on the findings of prior research, the literature must be searched systematically to identify the entire population of relevant studies. Typically, multiple bibliographic databases are used; some researchers also search for relevant dissertations and conference papers. Once the studies are identified, their findings, methods, and other features are coded (e.g., sample size, location of sample, and strength of the association between the independent and dependent variables). Like all systematic reviews, eligibility criteria must be specified carefully to determine which studies to include and which to omit as too different.

Statistics are then calculated to identify the average effect of the independent variable on the dependent variable, as well as the effect of methodological and other features of the studies (Cooper & Hedges 1994). The **effect size** statistic is the key to capturing the association between the independent and dependent variables across multiple studies. It is a standardized measure of association—often the difference between the mean of the experimental group and the mean of the control group on the dependent variable, adjusted for the average variability in the two groups (Lipsey & Wilson 2001).

The meta-analytic approach to synthesizing research findings can result in much more generalizable findings than those obtained with just one study. Methodological weaknesses in the studies included in the meta-analysis are still a problem, however; it is only when other studies without particular methodological weaknesses are included that we can estimate effects with some confidence. In addition, before we can place any confidence in the results of a meta-analysis, we must be confident that all (or almost all) relevant studies were included and that the information we need to analyze was included in all (or most) of the studies (Matt & Cook 1994).

Case Study: The Effectiveness of Anti-Bullying Programs

The 2005 School Crime Supplement to the National Crime Victimization Survey reported that about 14% of teens between the ages of 12 and 18 had been bullied in the past 6 months. The effects of bullying are numerous and include perceived fear, behavior problems, negative consequences for school performance, depression, and other physical ailments. There have been many different programs designed to decrease bullying in schools, but the effectiveness of these programs remains largely unknown. To examine the effects of anti-bullying programs across studies, Ferguson et al. (2007) performed a meta-analysis of randomized experimental studies examining the efficacy of such programs.

Studies included in the Ferguson et al. (2007) meta-analysis had several selection criteria: (a) They had to be published between 1995 and 2006, (b) the outcome variables had to clearly measure some element of bullying behavior toward peers, (c) they had to involve some form of control group to test program effectiveness, (d) the intervention programs had to be school-based, and (e) only manuscripts published in peer-reviewed journals were included. Results of the meta-analysis indicated that the positive impact of anti-bullying programs ranged from less than 1% for low-risk children to 3.6% for high-risk children. Ferguson and his colleagues (2007) stated, "Thus, it can be said that although anti-bullying programs produce a small amount of positive change, it is likely that this change is too small to be practically significant or noticeable" (p. 408).

Meta-analyses such as this make us aware of how hazardous it is to base understanding of social processes on single studies that are limited in time, location, and measurement. Of course, we need to have our wits about us when we read reports of meta-analytic studies. It is not a good idea to assume that a meta-analysis is the definitive word on a research question just because it cumulates the results of multiple studies.

ETHICS IN EVALUATION

Evaluation research can make a difference in people's lives while it is in progress, as well as after the results are reported. Educational and vocational training opportunities in prison, the availability of legal counsel, and treatment for substance abuse are all potentially important benefits, and an evaluation research project can change both their type and their availability. This direct impact on research participants, and potentially their families, heightens the attention that evaluation researchers have to give to human subjects concerns. Although the particular criteria that are at issue and the decisions that are most ethical vary with the type of evaluation research conducted and the specifics of a particular project, there are always serious ethical as well as political concerns for the evaluation researcher (Boruch 1997; Dentler 2002).

Assessing needs, determining evaluability, and examining the process of treatment delivery have few special ethical dimensions. Cost–benefit analyses in themselves also raise few ethical concerns. It is when the focus is program impact that human subjects considerations multiply. What about assigning persons randomly to receive some social program or benefit? One justification given by evaluation researchers has to do with the scarcity of these resources. If not everyone in the population who is eligible for a program can receive it, due to resource limitations, what could be a fairer way to distribute the program benefits than through a lottery? Random assignment also seems like a reasonable way to allocate potential program benefits when a new program is being tested with only some members of the target recipient population. However, when an ongoing entitlement program is being evaluated and experimental subjects would normally be eligible for program participation, it may not be ethical simply to bar some potential participants from the programs. Instead, evaluation researchers may test alternative treatments or provide some alternative benefit while the treatment is being denied.

It is important to realize that it is costly to society and potentially harmful to participants to maintain ineffective programs. In the long run, at least, it may be more ethical to conduct an evaluation study than to let the status quo remain in place.

CONCLUSION

In recent years, the field of evaluation research has become an increasingly popular and active research specialty within the fields of criminology and criminal justice. Many social scientists find special appeal in evaluation research because of its utility.

The research methods applied to evaluation research are no different from those covered elsewhere in this text; they can range from qualitative intensive interviews to rigorous randomized experimental designs. In process evaluations, qualitative methodologies can be particularly advantageous. However, the best method for determining cause and effect, or for determining whether a program had its intended consequences (impacts), is the randomized experimental design. Although this may not always be possible in the field, it is the "gold standard" with which to compare methodologies used to assess the impacts of all programs or policies.

KEY TERMS

Accuracy	Cost-effectiveness analysis	Evaluation of process
Black box evaluation	Effect size	Evidence-based policies
Campbell Collaboration	Efficiency analysis	Experimental designs
Comparison group	Evaluation of efficiency	Feasibility
Control group	Evaluation of impact	Feedback
Cost–benefit analysis	Evaluation of need	Formative evaluation

Impact evaluation	Meta-analysis	Program theory
Improvement-oriented evaluation	Needs assessment	Propriety
	Nonequivalent control group design	Quasi-experimental design
Inputs		Random assignment
Judgment-oriented evaluation	Outcomes	Stakeholders
Knowledge-oriented evaluation	Outputs	Systematic review
Mechanisms	Program process	Utility

HIGHLIGHTS

- The evaluation process as a whole, and the feedback process in particular, can be understood only in relation to the interests and perspectives of program stakeholders.
- The process by which a program has an effect on outcomes is often treated as a "black box," but there is good reason to open the black box and investigate the process by which the program operates and produces, or fails to produce, an effect.
- A program theory may be developed before or after an investigation of program process is completed. It may be either descriptive or prescriptive.
- There are five primary types of program evaluation: needs assessment, evaluability assessment, process evaluation (including formative evaluation), impact evaluation, and efficiency (cost–benefit) analysis.
- True randomized experiments are the most appropriate method for determining cause and effect, and as such, for determining the impact of programs and policies.
- Evidence-based policy is increasingly demanded by government agencies, which require systematic reviews that synthesize the results of the best available research on a given topic using transparent procedures.
- Meta-analysis is a quantitative analysis of findings from multiple studies.
- Evaluation research raises complex ethical issues because it may involve withholding desired social benefits.

EXERCISES

Discussing Research

1. Read one of the articles reviewed in this chapter. Fill in the answers to the article review questions (Appendix B) not covered in the chapter. Do you agree with the answers to the other questions discussed in the chapter? Could you add some points to the critique provided by the author of the text or to the lessons on research design drawn from these critiques?

2. Propose a randomized experimental evaluation of a social program with which you are familiar. Include in your proposal a description of the program and its intended outcomes. Discuss the strengths and weaknesses of your proposed design.

Finding Research on the Web

1. Go to the American Evaluation Association website at www.eval.org. Choose "Publications" and then "Guiding Principles for Evaluator." What are the five guiding principles discussed in this document? Provide a summary of each principle.

2. Go to the National Criminal Justice Reference Organization (NCJRS) at www.ncjrs.org and search for a publication that has conducted an evaluation of a program of your choice. Read the report and write a brief summary, making sure to include a summary of the methodology used in the report.

3. Describe the resources available for evaluation researchers at one of the following three websites:

   www.wmich.edu/evalctr

   www.worldbank.org/oed

Critiquing Research

1. Evaluate the ethics of one of the studies reviewed in which human subjects were used. Sherman and Berk's (1984) study of domestic violence raises some interesting ethical issues, but there are also points to consider in most of the other studies. Which ethical guidelines (see Chapter 2) seem most difficult to adhere to? Where do you think the line should be drawn between not taking any risks at all with research participants and developing valid scientific knowledge? Be sure to consider various costs and benefits of the research.

2. Find a recent article that evaluates a policy or program from a criminal justice policy journal such as *Crime and Public Policy*. Describe its strengths and weaknesses. Do the author(s) make claims about causality that are supported by their methodology?

Making Research Ethical

1. The Manhattan Bail Project randomly assigned some defendants with strong community ties to be recommended for release without bail and some not to be recommended. The project found a very high (99%) rate of appearance at trial for those released without bail, but of course the researchers did not know that this would be the case before they conducted the study. Would you consider this study design ethical? What if one of the persons in the 1% who did not come to trial murdered someone when they should have been at court? Are there any conditions when randomization should not be permitted when evaluating criminal justice programs?

2. A large body of evaluation research suggested that the D.A.R.E. program was not effective in reducing drug use in schools, but many school and police officials, parents, and students insisted on maintaining the program without change for many years. Do you think that government agencies should be allowed to de-fund programs that numerous evaluation research studies have shown to be ineffective? Should government agencies be *required* to justify funding for social programs on the basis of evaluation research results?

Developing a Research Proposal

Imagine that you are submitting a proposal to the U.S. Justice Department to evaluate the efficacy of a new treatment program for substance abusers within federal correctional institutions.

1. What would your research question be if you proposed a process evaluation component to your research?

2. For the outcome evaluation, what is your independent variable and what would your dependent variable be? How would you operationalize both?

3. What type of research design would you propose to answer both the process evaluation and outcome evaluation components in your proposal?

Performing Data Analysis in SPSS or Excel

Do hospitals provide equal treatment across race and social class? Although the data available do not provide enough information for an in-depth evaluation of hospital procedures or quality of care, NCVS9205.ASSAULT enables you to explore the relationship between the total amount of medical expenses incurred as a result of injuries sustained from an assault (MEDEXP) and the victim's family income (INCOME), race or ethnicity (PPRACE), and coverage by any medical insurance or other type of health benefits program (INSURANC).

1. Write at least three hypotheses about the relationship between medical expenses incurred from rape, robbery, or assault across race and social class based on the variables discussed above.

2. Obtain a frequency distribution for INCOME. Recode INCOME to measure victim's family income into three or four categories.

3. Select all cases in which the victim sustained injuries (YES = 1). Compare the mean amount of expenses incurred as a result of the victim's injuries across categories of each independent variable. Describe the results; be sure to note the number of victims for each category when interpreting your results.

4. Were your hypotheses supported? What conclusions do you make about these relationships? Can you determine whether hospitals provide equal treatment across race and social class based on these data? Explain.

Student Study Site

The companion Student Study Site for *Fundamentals of Research in Criminology and Criminal Justice* can be found at www.sagepub.com/bachmanfrccj2e.

Visit the Student Study Site to enhance your understanding of the chapter content and to discover additional resources that will take your learning one step further. You can enhance your understanding of the chapters by using the comprehensive study material, which includes interactive exercises, e-flashcards, web exercises, practice self-tests, and more. You will also find special features, such as Learning from Journal Articles, which incorporates Sage's online journal collection.

CHAPTER 11

Quantitative Data Analysis

"*Oh no, not data analysis and statistics!*" We now hit the chapter you may have been fearing all along: the one on data analysis and the use of statistics. This chapter describes what you need to do after your data have been collected. You now need to analyze what you have found, interpret it, and decide how to present your data so that you can most clearly make the points you wish to make.

We would like to state at the beginning, however, that you have relatively little to fear. If you can add, subtract, multiply, and divide, and are willing to put some effort into carefully reading this chapter, you will do well in the statistical analysis of your data. One helpful way to think of statistics is that it consists of a set of tools that you will use to examine your data to help you answer the questions that motivated your research in the first place. In the course of this chapter, we will add some fundamental tools to that toolbox.

This chapter will introduce several common types of statistics and highlight the factors that must be considered in using and interpreting statistics. Two preliminary sections lay the foundation for studying statistics. In the first, we discuss the role of statistics in the research process, returning to themes and techniques you already know. In the second preliminary section, we outline the process of acquiring data for statistical analysis. In the rest of the chapter, we explain how to describe the distribution of single variables and the relationship between variables. Along the way, we address ethical issues related to data analysis. This chapter will be successful if it encourages you to see statistics responsibly and evaluate them critically, and gives you the confidence necessary to seek opportunities for extending your statistical knowledge.

WHY WE NEED STATISTICS

Statistics play a key role in achieving valid research results, in terms of measurement, causal validity, and generalizability. Some statistics are useful primarily to describe the results of measuring single variables and to construct and evaluate multi-item scales. These statistics include frequency distributions, graphs, measures of central tendency and variation, and reliability tests. Other statistics are useful primarily in achieving causal validity, by helping us describe the association among variables and to control for, or otherwise take into account, other variables.

Crosstabulation is one technique for measuring association and controlling other variables and is introduced in this chapter. All these statistics are called descriptive statistics because they are used to describe the distribution of and relationship among variables.

It is also important for an analyst to choose statistics that are appropriate to the level of measurement of the variables to be analyzed. As you learned in Chapter 4, numbers used to represent the values of variables may not actually signify different quantities, meaning that many statistical techniques will be inapplicable. Some statistics, for example, will only be appropriate when the variable you are examining is measured at the nominal level. Other kinds of statistics will require interval-level measurement. To use the right statistic, then, you must be very familiar with the measurement properties of your variables (and you thought that stuff would go away!).

Case Study: The Causes of Delinquency

Throughout this chapter, we will use research on the causes of delinquency for our examples. More specifically, our data will be a subset of a much larger study of a sample of approximately 1,200 high school students selected from the metropolitan and suburban high schools of a city in South Carolina (Paternoster et al. 1983). These students, all of whom were in the tenth grade, completed a questionnaire that asked about such things as how they spent their spare time; how they got along with their parents, teachers, and friends; their attitudes about delinquency; whether their friends committed delinquent acts; and their own involvement in delinquency. One specific hypothesis, derived from deterrence theory, predicts that youths who believe they are likely to get caught by the police for committing delinquent acts are less likely to commit delinquency than others. This hypothesis is shown in Exhibit 11.1. The variables from this study that we will use in our chapter examples are displayed in Exhibit 11.2.

PREPARING DATA FOR ANALYSIS

We used the Windows version of the Statistical Package for the Social Sciences (SPSS) for the analysis in this chapter; you will find examples of SPSS commands required to define and analyze data on the Student Study Site for this text, http://www.sagepub.com/bachmanfrccj2e.

Exhibit 11.1   Perceived Fear of Punishment and Delinquency

Fear of getting caught by police → Delinquency

Exhibit 11.2   List of Variables for Class Examples of Causes of Delinquency

Variable	SPSS Variable Name	Description
Gender	V1	Sex of respondent.
Age	V2	Age of respondent.
TV	V21	Number of hours per week the respondent watches TV.
Study	V22	Number of hours per week the respondent spends studying.
Supervision	V63	Do parents know where respondent is when he or she is away from home?
Friends think theft wrong	V77	How wrong respondent's best friends think is it to commit petty theft.
Friends think drinking wrong	V79	How wrong respondent's best friends think is it to drink liquor under age.
Punishment for drinking	V109	If respondent was caught drinking liquor under age and taken to court, how much of a problem it would be.
Cost of vandalism	V119	How much would respondent's chances of having good friends be hurt if he or she was arrested for petty theft.
Parental supervision	PARSUPER	Added scale from items that ask respondent if parents know where he or she is and who he or she is with when away from home. A high score means more supervision.
Friend's opinion	FROPINON	Added scale that asks respondent if his or her best friend thought that committing various delinquent acts was all right. A high score means more support for delinquency from friends.
Friend's behavior	FRBEHAVE	Added scale that asks respondent how many of his or her best friends commit delinquent acts.
Certainty of punishment	CERTAIN	Added scale that measures how likely respondent thinks it is that he or she will be caught by police if he or she were to commit delinquent acts. A high score means more fear of getting caught.
Morality	MORAL	Added scale that measures how morally wrong respondent thinks it is to commit diverse delinquent acts. A high score means strong moral inhibitions against committing delinquency.
Delinquency	DELINQ1	An additive scale that counts the number of times respondent admits to committing a number of different delinquent acts in the past year. The higher the score, the more delinquent acts committed.

DISPLAYING UNIVARIATE DISTRIBUTIONS

The first step in data analysis is usually to display the variation in each variable of interest in what are called *univariate frequency distributions*. For many descriptive purposes, the analysis may go no further. Frequency distributions and graphs of frequency distributions are the two most popular approaches for displaying variation; both allow the analyst to display the distribution of cases across the value categories of a variable. Graphs have the advantage over numerically displayed frequency distributions because they provide a picture that is easier to comprehend. Frequency distributions are preferable when exact numbers of cases with particular values must be reported, and when many distributions must be displayed in a compact form.

No matter which type of display is used, the primary concern of the data analyst is to accurately display the distribution's shape—that is, to show how cases are distributed across the values of the variable. Three features of the shape of a distribution are important: central tendency, variability, and skewness (lack of symmetry). All three of these features can be represented in a graph or in a frequency distribution.

Central tendency The most common value (for variables measured at the nominal level) or the value around which cases tend to cluster (for a quantitative variable)

Variability The extent to which cases are spread out through the distribution or clustered in just one location

Skewness The extent to which cases are clustered more at one or the other end of the distribution of a quantitative variable rather than in a symmetric pattern around the center. Skew can be positive (a "right skew"), with the number of cases tapering off in the positive direction, or negative (a "left skew"), with the number of cases tapering off in the negative direction.

A variable's level of measurement is the most important determinant of the appropriateness of particular statistics. For example, we cannot talk about the skewness (lack of symmetry) of a qualitative variable (measured at the nominal level, e.g., of gender). If the values of a variable cannot be ordered from lowest to highest, that is, if the ordering of the values is arbitrary, we cannot say whether the distribution is symmetric because we could just reorder the values to make the distribution more (or less) symmetric. Some measures of central tendency and variability are also inappropriate for qualitative variables.

The distinction between variables measured at the ordinal level and those measured at the interval or ratio level should also be considered when selecting statistics to use, but social researchers differ on just how much importance they attach to this distinction. Many social researchers think of ordinal variables as imperfectly measured interval-level variables, and believe that in most circumstances statistics developed for interval-level variables also provide useful summaries for ordinal variables. Other social researchers believe that variation in ordinal variables will often be distorted by statistics that assume an interval level of measurement. We will touch on some of the details of these issues in the following sections on particular statistical techniques.

We will now examine graphs and frequency distributions that illustrate these three features of shape. Summary statistics used to measure specific aspects of central tendency and variability will be presented in a separate section. There is a summary statistic for the measurement of skewness, but it is used only rarely in published research reports and will not be presented here.

Graphs

It is true that a picture often is worth a thousand words. Graphs can be easy to read, and they very nicely highlight a distribution's shape. They are particularly useful for exploring data because they show the full range of variation and identify data anomalies that might be in need of further study. Moreover, good, professional-looking graphs can now be produced relatively easily with software available for personal computers. There are many types of graphs, but the most common and most useful are bar charts and histograms. Each has two axes, the vertical axis (y-axis) and the horizontal axis (x-axis), and labels to identify the variables and the values with tick marks showing where each indicated value falls along the axis. The vertical y-axis of a graph is usually in frequency or percent units, whereas the horizontal x-axis displays the values of the variable being graphed. There are different kinds of graphs you can use to descriptively display your data, depending upon the level of measurement of the variable.

A **bar chart** contains solid bars separated by spaces. It is a good tool for displaying the distribution of variables measured at the nominal level and other discrete categorical variables because there is, in effect, a gap between each of the categories. In our delinquency data, one of the questions asked of respondents was whether their parents knew where they were when they were away from home. We graphed the responses to this question in a bar chart, which is shown in Exhibit 11.3. In this bar chart, we report both the frequency count for each value and the percentage of the total that each value represents. The bar chart in Exhibit 11.3 indicates that very few of the respondents (only 16, or 1.3%) reported that their parents "never" knew where they were when they were not at home. Almost one half (562, or 44.3%) of the youths reported that their parents "usually" knew where they were. What you can also see by noticing the height of the bars above "usually" and "always" is that most youths report that their parents provide very adequate supervision. You can also see that the most frequent response was "usually" and the least frequent was "never." Because the response "usually" is the most frequent value, it is called the *mode* or *modal response*. With ordinal data like these, the mode is the most appropriate measure of central tendency. (We will cover more about this later.)

A **histogram** is like a bar chart, but it has bars that are adjacent, or right next to each other, with no gaps. This is done to indicate that data displayed in a histogram, unlike the data in a bar chart, are quantitative variables that vary along a continuum (see the discussion of levels of measurement for variables in Chapter 3). Exhibit 11.4 shows a histogram from the delinquency data set we are using. The variable being graphed is the number of hours per week the respondent reported to be studying. Notice that the cases cluster at the

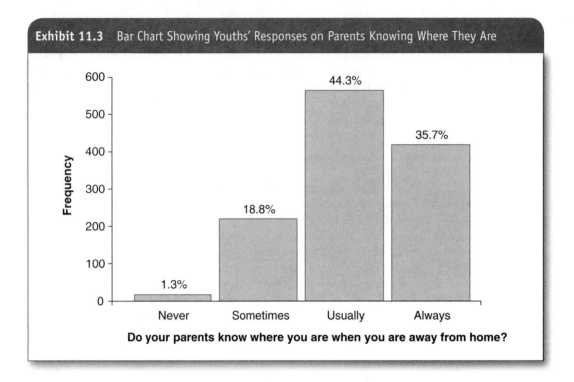

Exhibit 11.3   Bar Chart Showing Youths' Responses on Parents Knowing Where They Are

low end of the values. In other words, there are a lot of youths who spend between 0 and 15 hours per week studying. After that, there are only a few cases at each different value with a "spike" occurring at 25, 30, 38, and 40 hours studied. This distribution is clearly not symmetric. In a symmetric distribution, there is a lump of cases or a "spike" with an equal number of cases to the left and right of that spike. In the distribution shown in Exhibit 11.4, most of the cases are at the left end of the distribution (i.e., at low values), and the distribution trails off on the right side. The ends of a histogram like this are often called the *tail* of a distribution. In a symmetric distribution, the left and right tails are approximately the same length. As you can clearly see in Exhibit 11.4, however, the right tail is much longer than the left tail. When the tails of the distribution are uneven, the distribution is said to be asymmetrical or skewed. A skew is either positive or negative. When the cases cluster to the left and the right tail of the distribution is longer than the left, as in Exhibit 11.4, our variable distribution is positively skewed. When the cases cluster to the right side and the left tail of the distribution is long, our variable distribution is negatively skewed.

Frequency Distributions

A frequency distribution displays the number, the percentage (the relative frequencies), or both for cases corresponding to each of a variable's values or group of values. The components of the frequency distribution should be clearly labeled, with a title, a stub (labels for the values of the variable), a caption (identifying whether the distribution includes

Exhibit 11.4   Histogram

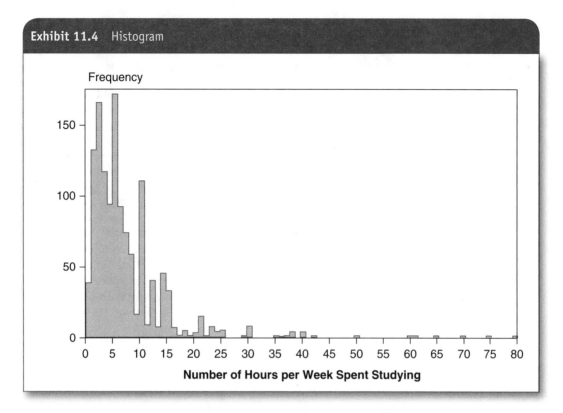

frequencies, percentages, or both), and perhaps the number of missing cases. If percentages are presented rather than frequencies (sometimes both are included), the total number of cases in the distribution (the base N) should be indicated (see Exhibit 11.5). Remember that a percentage is simply a relative frequency. A percentage shows the frequency of a given value relative to the total number of cases times 100.

Ungrouped Data

Constructing and reading frequency distributions for variables with few values are not difficult. In Exhibit 11.5, we created the frequency distribution from the variable "Punishment for Drinking" found in the delinquency data set (see Exhibit 11.2). This variable asked the youths to respond to the following question: "How much of a problem would it be if you went to court for drinking liquor under age?" The frequency distribution in Exhibit 11.5 shows the frequency for each value and its corresponding percentage.

As another example of calculating the frequencies and percentages, suppose we had a sample of 25 youths and asked them their gender. From this group of 25 youths, 13 were male and 12 were female. The frequency of males (symbolized here by f) would be 13 and the frequency of females would be 12. The percentage of males would be 52%, calculated by f / the total number of cases × 100 (13 / 25 × 100 = 52%). The percentage of females would be 12 / 25 × 100 = 48%.

Exhibit 11.5 Frequency Distribution

How much of a problem would it be if you went to court for drinking liquor under age?

Value	Frequency (f)	Percentage (%)
No problem at all	14	1.1
Hardly any problem	53	4.2
A little problem	196	15.4
A big problem	421	33.1
A very big problem	588	46.2
Total	1,272	100.0

In the frequency distribution shown in Exhibit 11.5, you can see that only a very small number of youths (14 out of 1,272) thought that they would experience "no problem" if they were caught and taken to court for drinking liquor under age. You can see that most, in fact 1,009, of these youths—or 79.3% of them—thought that they would have either "a big problem" or "a very big problem" with this.

Exhibit 11.5 is a frequency distribution of an ordinal-level variable; it has a very small number of discrete categories. In Exhibit 11.6, we provide an illustration of a frequency distribution with a continuous quantitative variable. This variable is one we have already looked at and graphed from the delinquency data, the number of hours per week the respondent spent studying. Notice that this variable, like many continuous variables in criminological research, has a large number of values. Although this is a reasonable frequency distribution to construct—you can, for example, still see that the cases tend to cluster in the low end of the distribution and are strung way out at the upper end—it is a little difficult to get a good sense of the distribution of the cases. The problem is that there are too many values to easily comprehend. It would be nice if we could simplify distributions like these that have a large number of different values. Well, we can. We can construct what is called a **grouped frequency distribution**.

Grouped Data

Many frequency distributions, such as that in Exhibit 11.6, and many graphs require grouping of some values after the data are collected. There are two reasons for grouping:

1. There are more than 15–20 values to begin with, a number too large to be displayed in an easily readable table.

2. The distribution of the variable will be clearer or more meaningful if some of the values are combined.

Inspection of Exhibit 11.6 should clarify these reasons. In this distribution, it is very difficult to discern any shape, much less the central tendency. What we would like to do

Exhibit 11.6 Frequency Distribution With Continuous Quantitative Data: Hours Studied per Week		
Value	**Frequency (f)**	**Percentage (%)**
0	38	3.0
1	132	10.4
2	165	13.0
3	116	9.1
4	94	7.4
5	171	13.4
6	92	7.2
7	73	5.7
8	58	4.6
9	16	1.3
10	110	8.6
11	9	0.7
12	40	3.1
13	7	0.6
14	45	3.5
15	32	2.5
16	7	0.6
17	5	0.4
18	4	0.3
19	1	0.1
20	15	1.2
21	8	0.6
22	1	0.1
23	1	0.1
24	4	0.3
25	5	0.4
29	1	0.1
30	8	0.6
35	1	0.1
37	1	0.1
40	4	0.3
42	1	0.1
50	1	0.1
60	1	0.1
61	1	0.1
65	1	0.1
70	1	0.1
75	1	0.1
80	1	0.1
Total	1,272	100.0

now to make the features of the data more visible is change the values into intervals of values, or a range of values. For example, rather than having five separate values of 0, 1, 2, 3, 4 hours studied per week, we can have a range of values or an interval for the first value, such as 0–4 hours studied. Then we can get a count or frequency of the number of cases (and percentage of the total) that fall within that interval.

Once we decide to group values or categories, we have to be sure that in doing so we do not distort the distribution. Adhering to the following guidelines for combining values in a frequency distribution will prevent many problems.

- Categories should be logically defensible and preserve the distribution's shape.
- Categories should be mutually exclusive and exhaustive, so every case is classifiable in one and only one category.
- The first interval must contain the lowest value and the last interval must contain the highest value in the distribution.
- Each interval width, the number of values that fall within each interval, should be the same size.
- There should be between 7 and 13 intervals. This is a tough rule to follow. The key is not to have so few intervals that your data are clumped or clustered into only a few intervals (or you will lose too much information about your distribution) and not to have so many intervals that the data are not much clearer than an ungrouped frequency distribution.

Let us use the data in Exhibit 11.6 on the number of hours studied by these youths to create a grouped frequency distribution. We will follow a number of explicit steps:

Step 1: Determine the number of intervals you think you want. This decision is arbitrary, but try to keep the number of intervals you have in the 7 to 13 range. For our example, let us say we initially decided we wanted to have 10 intervals. (Note: If you do your frequency distribution and it looks too clustered or there are too many intervals, redo your distribution with a different number of intervals.) Don't worry, there are no hard-and-fast rules for the correct number of intervals, and constructing a grouped frequency distribution is as much art as science. Just remember that the frequency distribution you make is supposed to convey information about the shape and central tendency of your data.

Step 2: Decide on the width of the interval (symbolized by w_i). The interval width is the number of different values that fall into your interval. For example, an interval width of 5 has five different values that fall into it, say, the values 0, 1, 2, 3, or 4 hours studied. There is a simple formula to approximate what your interval width should be, given the number of intervals you decided on in the first step: Determine the range of the data, where the range is simply the highest score in the distribution minus the lowest score. In our data, with the number of hours studied, the range is 80 because the high score is 80 and the low score is 0, so the range = 80 – 0 = 80. Then determine the width of the interval by dividing the range by the number of intervals you want from Step 1. We wanted 10 intervals, so our interval width would be

w_i = 80 / 10 = 8. We should therefore have an interval width of 8. If you use this simple formula for determining your interval width and you end up with a decimal, say 8.2 or 8.6, then simply round up or down to an integer.

Step 3: Make your first interval so that the lowest value falls into it. Our lowest value is 0 (for studied 0 hours per week), so our first interval begins with the value 0. Now, if the beginning of our first interval is 0 and we want an interval width of 8, is the last value of our interval 7 (with a first interval of 0–7 hours), or is the last value of our interval 8 (with a first interval of 0–8 hours)? One easy way to make a grouped frequency distribution is to do the following: Take the beginning value of your first interval (in our case, it is 0), and add the interval width to that value (8). This new value is the first value of your next interval. What we know, then, is that the first value of our first interval is 0, and the first value of our second interval is 8 (0–?, 8–?). This must mean that the last value to be included in our first interval is one less than 8, or 7. Our first interval, therefore, includes the ranges of values 0–7. If you count the number of different values in this interval, you will find that it includes eight different values (0, 1, 2, 3, 4, 5, 6, 7). This is our interval width of 8.

Step 4: After your first interval is determined, the next intervals are easy. They must be the same width and not overlap (mutually exclusive). You must make enough intervals to include the last value in your variable distribution. The highest value in our data is 80 hours per week, so we construct the grouped frequency distribution as follows:

0–7

8–15

16–23

24–31

32–39

40–47

48–55

56–63

64–71

72–79

80–87

Notice that in order to include the highest value in our data (80 hours), we had to make 11 intervals instead of the 10 we originally decided upon in Step 1. No problem. Remember, the number of intervals is arbitrary and this is as much art as science.

Step 5: Count the number or frequency of cases that appear in each interval and their percentage of the total.

The completed grouped frequency distribution is shown in Exhibit 11.7. Notice that this grouped frequency distribution conveys the important features of the distribution of this data. Most of the data cluster at the low end of the number of hours studied. In fact, more than two-thirds of these youths studied fewer than 8 hours per week. Notice also that the frequency of cases thins out at each successive interval. In other words, there is a long right tail to this distribution indicating a positive skew because fewer youths studied a high number of hours. Notice also that the distribution was created in such a way that the interval widths are all the same and each case falls into one and only one interval (i.e., the intervals are exhaustive and mutually exclusive). We would have run into trouble if we had two intervals like 0–7 and 7–14 because we would not know where to place those youths who spent 7 hours a week studying. Should we put them in the first or second interval? If the intervals are mutually exclusive, as they are here, you will not run into these problems.

SUMMARIZING UNIVARIATE DISTRIBUTIONS

Summary statistics, sometimes called descriptive statistics, focus attention on particular aspects of a distribution and facilitate comparison among distributions. For example,

Exhibit 11.7 Example of a Grouped Frequency Distribution From Hours Studied

Value	Frequency (f)	Percentage (%)
0–7	881	69.26
8–15	317	24.92
16–23	42	3.30
24–31	18	1.42
32–39	2	0.16
40–47	5	0.39
48–55	1	0.08
56–63	2	0.16
64–71	2	0.16
72–79	1	0.08
80–87	1	0.08
Total	1,272	100.00

Note: Total may not equal 100.0% due to rounding error.

suppose you wanted to report the rate of violent crimes for each city in the United States with over 100,000 in population. You could report each city's violent crime rate, but it is unlikely that two cities would have the same rate and you would have to report approximately 200 rates, one for each city. This would be a frequency distribution that many, if not most, people would find difficult to comprehend. One way to interpret your data for your audience would be to provide a summary measure that indicates what the average violent crime rate is in large U.S. cities. That is the purpose of the set of summary statistics called measures of *central tendency*. You would also want to provide another summary measure that shows the variability or heterogeneity in your data—in other words, a measure that shows how different the scores are from each other or from the central tendency. That is the purpose of the set of summary statistics called measures of *variation* or *dispersion*. We will discuss each type of measurement in turn.

Measures of Central Tendency

Central tendency is usually summarized with one of three statistics: the mode, the median, or the mean. For any particular application, one of these statistics may be preferable, but each has a role to play in data analysis. To choose an appropriate measure of central tendency, the analyst must consider a variable's level of measurement, the skewness of a quantitative variable's distribution, and the purpose for which the statistic is used. In addition, the analyst's personal experiences and preferences inevitably will play a role.

Mode

The mode is the most frequent value in a distribution. For example, refer to the data in Exhibit 11.7, which shows the grouped frequency distribution for the number of hours studied. The value with the greatest frequency in that data is the interval 0–7 hours; this is the mode of that distribution. Notice that the mode is the most frequently occurring value; it is not the frequency of that value. In other words, the mode in Exhibit 11.7 is 0–7 hours; the mode is not 881, which is the frequency of the modal category. When a variable distribution has one case or interval that occurs more often than the others, it is called a unimodal distribution.

Sometimes a distribution has more than one mode because there are two values that have the highest frequency. This distribution would be called bimodal. Some distributions are trimodal in that there are three distinctively high frequency values, and other distributions have no mode. In saying that there is no mode, though, you are communicating something very important about the data: that no case is more common than the others. Another potential problem with the mode is that it might happen to fall far from the main clustering of cases in a distribution. It would be misleading in this case, then, to say simply that the variable's central tendency was the same as the modal value.

Nevertheless, there are occasions when the mode is very appropriate. Most important, the mode is the only measure that can be used to characterize the central tendency of variables measured at the nominal level. In Exhibit 11.8, we have the frequency distribution of the conviction offense for 1,000 offenders convicted in a criminal court. The central tendency of the distribution is property offense, because more of the 1,000 offenders were

Exhibit 11.8 Frequency Distribution of Offense Convicted for 1,000 Offenders

Offense	Frequency (f)
Violent	125
Drug	210
Property	480
Public order	100
Other	85
Total	1,000

convicted of a property crime than any other crime. For the variable "type of offense convicted of," the most common value is property crime. The mode also is often referred to in descriptions of the shape of a distribution. The terms *unimodal* and *bimodal* appear frequently, as do descriptive statements such as "The typical [most probable] respondent was in her thirties."

Median

The median is the score in the middle of a rank-ordered distribution. It is, then, the score or point that divides the distribution in half (the 50th percentile). The median is inappropriate for variables measured at the nominal level because their values cannot be put in ranked order (remember, there is no "order" to nominal-level data), and so there is no meaningful middle position. To determine the median, we simply need to do the following: First, rank-order the values from lowest to highest. If there is an odd number of scores, then you can find the position of the median in the rank order of scores by using the following simple formula:

$$N + 1 \div 2$$

where N is equal to the total number of cases. If there is an even number of scores, then you can find the position of the median in the rank order of scores by finding the midpoint of the scores in the following two positions:

$$\text{Position } 1 = \frac{N}{2}$$
$$\text{Position } 2 = \frac{N+2}{2}$$

The midpoint of the two scores can be found by adding the scores in the two positions and dividing by 2. Please note that in both formulas, you use the formula to find the

Exhibit 11.9   Rate of Violent Crime for Selected U.S. Cities

City	Number of Violent Crimes per 100,000
Atlanta	3,571
Boston	1,916
Cleveland	1,530
Dallas	1,589
Los Angeles	2,059
New Orleans	1,887
New York	1,861
Philadelphia	1,322
San Francisco	1,461
Atlanta	3,571
Boston	1,916
Cleveland	1,530
Dallas	1,589
Los Angeles	2,059
New Orleans	1,887
New York	1,861
Philadelphia	1,322

position of the median; the formula does not give you the value of the median. Let us do an example.

In Exhibit 11.9, we first list a sample of nine U.S. cities and their hypothetical rate of violent crime. In the bottom panel of Exhibit 11.9, we drop one of the cities (San Francisco) and are left with eight cities.

Let us determine the median for both lists. First, we rank-order the violent crime rates for the first list.

Rank	Crime Rate
1	1,322
2	1,461
3	1,530
4	1,589
5	1,861
6	1,887
7	1,916
8	2,059
9	3,571

Because we have an odd number of scores (N = 9), the position of the median is determined by (9 + 1) / 2 = 10 / 2 = 5. The median violent crime rate, then, is in the fifth position in this rank order. Starting either at the top of the scores and counting down to the fifth position or the bottom and counting up, we find that in the fifth position is the score 1,861 violent crimes per 100,000, which is the median violent crime rate for these nine U.S. cities. Now, let us find the median in the second list. We first rank-order these eight scores.

Rank	Crime Rate
1	1,322
2	1,530
3	1,589
4	1,861
5	1,887
6	1,916
7	2,059
8	3,571

Because we now have an even number of scores (notice that the violent crime rate for San Francisco is missing from this list), we know that the median position is the midpoint in between the fourth (8 / 2 = 4) and fifth ([8 + 2] / 2) positions. The score at the fourth position is 1,861 and at the fifth it is 1,887. The value of the median can now be found by adding these two scores and dividing by two. The median rate of violent crime is equal to (1,861 + 1,887) / 2 = 1,874 violent crimes per 100,000 population. Of the cities, 50% had a violent crime rate below 1,874 and 50% had a violent crime rate above 1,874.

Mean

The **mean** is simply the arithmetic average of all scores in a distribution. It is computed by adding up the value of all the cases and dividing by the total number of cases, thereby taking into account the value of each case in the distribution:

Mean = Sum of value of all cases / number of cases

The symbol for the mean is $\bar{X}$ (pronounced "x-bar"). In algebraic notation, the equation is

$$\bar{X} = \frac{\sum_{1}^{n} x_i}{N}$$

where x_i is a symbol for each ith score and i's go from 1 to N; N is the total number of cases. What the algebraic equation says to do is to sum all scores, starting at the first score and continuing until the last, or *N*th, score; then divide this sum by the total number of cases (*N*).

We will calculate the mean rate of violent crime for the nine U.S. cities listed in Exhibit 10.9:

$$\bar{X} = \frac{(3{,}571 + 1{,}916 + 1{,}530 + 1{,}589 + 2{,}059 + 1{,}887 + 1{,}861 + 1{,}332 + 1{,}461)}{9}$$

$$= 1{,}910.7$$

The mean rate of violent crime for these nine U.S. cities, then, is 1,910.7 violent crimes per 100,000 population. Notice that in calculating the mean, we do not first have to rank-order the scores. The mean takes every score into account, so it does not matter whether we add 3,571 first, in the middle, or last.

Computing the mean requires adding up the values of the cases, so it makes sense to compute a mean only if the values of the cases can be treated as actual quantities—that is, if they reflect an interval or ratio level of measurement, or if they are ordinal and we assume that ordinal measures can be treated as interval. It would make no sense, however, to calculate the mean for a nominal-level variable like racial or ethnic status, or for the variable gender. Thus, both the median and the mean are inappropriate measures of central tendency for variables measured at the nominal level.

Median or Mean?

Both the median and the mean are used to summarize the central tendency of quantitative variables, but their suitability for a particular application must be assessed carefully.

The key issues to be considered in this assessment are the variable's level of measurement, the shape of its distribution, and the purpose of the statistical summary. Level of measurement is a key concern because, to calculate the mean, we must add up the values of all the cases, a procedure that assumes the variable is measured at the interval or ratio level. The shape of a variable's distribution should also be taken into account when deciding whether to use the median or the mean. When a distribution is perfectly symmetric (i.e., when the distribution is bell shaped), the distribution of values below the median is a mirror image of the distribution of values above the median, and the mean and median will be the same. But the values of the mean and median are affected differently by skewness, or the presence of cases with extreme values on one side of the distribution but not the other side. The median takes into account only the number of cases above and below the median point, not the value of these cases, so it is not affected in any way by extreme values. The mean is based on adding the value of all the cases, so it will be pulled in the direction of exceptionally high (or low) values. When the value of the mean is larger than the median, we know that the distribution is skewed in a positive direction, with proportionately more cases with lower than higher values. When the mean is smaller than the median, the distribution is skewed in a negative direction.

This differential impact of skewness on the median and mean is illustrated in Exhibit 11.10. The first list shows the crime rate per 1,000 residents for seven neighborhoods in a hypothetical city. The crime rates range from a low of 51.7 per 1,000 to 135.3 per 1,000.

Exhibit 11.10 Rates of Crime in Selected Neighborhoods

Community	Crime Rate per 1,000
Valley View	51.7
Glen Commons	63.1
Springdale	75.3
Green Acres	98.7
Oceanside	113.4
Meadowbrook	125.9
King's Crossing	135.3
Valley View	51.7
Glen Commons	63.1
Springdale	75.3
Green Acres	98.7
Oceanside	113.4
Meadowbrook	125.9
West Chester	697.5
Pleasantville	5.3
Glen Commons	63.1
Springdale	75.3
Green Acres	98.7
Oceanside	113.4
Meadowbrook	125.9
King's Crossing	135.3

When we calculate the mean crime rate for these seven neighborhoods, we find that it is 94.8 crimes per 1,000; the median is 98.7 crimes per 1,000. Notice that this is a relatively symmetrical distribution, with the values of the mean and the median very comparable to each other. With these data, both the mean and the median provide an accurate description of the central tendency.

In the second list of neighborhoods, we replace the neighborhood that had the highest crime rate (i.e., King's Crossing) with West Chester, which has a substantially higher crime rate: 697.5 per 1,000. It is then an unusually high score. When we calculate the mean for these data, we find that it is 175.1 per 1,000; it has increased from its previous value of 94.8. The median, however, remains the same; it is still 98.7 crimes per 1,000. When an unusually high score is added to a distribution, the mean thus gets inflated relative to the median.

In distributions that are positively skewed, the mean is of greater magnitude than the median. Notice also that, with this unusually high crime rate added, the median is still an accurate picture of the central tendency, whereas the mean of 175.1 is no longer accurate. In the third list of neighborhoods, we replace the neighborhood that has the lowest crime rate (i.e., Valley View) with Pleasantville, which has a substantially lower crime rate, 5.3 per 1,000. It is, then, an unusually low score. When we calculate the mean for these data, we find that it is 88.1 per 1,000; it has decreased from the value in the first list, which was 94.8. The median, however, remains the same; it is still 98.7 crimes per 1,000. When an unusually low score is added to a distribution, then, the mean gets deflated relative to the median. In distributions that are negatively skewed, the mean is less than the median. Notice also that, even with this unusually low crime rate added, the median is still an accurate picture of the central tendency, whereas the mean of 88.1 is no longer as accurate.

This example illustrates one of the problems with using the mean as a measure of central tendency. If the data are skewed (either positively or negatively), then the mean will be affected by the extreme scores in the distribution and will not give as accurate an estimate of the central tendency of the data as the median. The lesson is that one should probably report both the mean and the median. In general, the mean is the most commonly used measure of central tendency for quantitative variables, because it takes into account the value of all cases in the distribution and it is the foundation for many other more advanced statistics. However, the mean's very popularity results in its use in situations for which it is inappropriate. Keep an eye out for this problem.

Measures of Variation

You have learned that central tendency is only one aspect of the shape of a distribution. Although the measure of center is the most important aspect for many purposes, it is still just a piece of the total picture. A summary of distributions based only on their central tendency can be very incomplete, even misleading. For example, three towns might have the same mean and median crime rate but still be very different in their social character due to the shape of the crime distributions. We show three distributions of community crime rates for three different towns in Exhibit 11.11. If you calculate the mean and median crime rate for each town, you will find that they are the same for all three. In terms of its crime rate, then, each community has the same central tendency. As you can see, however, there is something very different about these towns. Town A is a very heterogeneous town; crime rates in its neighborhoods are neither very homogeneous nor clustered at either the low or high end. Rather, the crime rates in its communities are spread out from one another. Crime rates in these neighborhoods are, then, very diverse. Town B is characterized

Exhibit 11.11   Neighborhood Crime Rates in Three Different Towns

Town A	Town B	Town C
19.5	58.1	8.9
28.2	59.7	15.4
35.7	60.1	18.3
41.9	62.7	21.9
63.2	63.2	63.2
75.8	63.9	103.5
92.0	64.2	104.2
95.7	64.5	110.7
109.4	65.0	105.3

by neighborhoods with very homogeneous crime rates; there are no real high- or low-crime areas because each neighborhood is not far from the overall mean of 62.4 crimes per 1,000. Town C is characterized by neighborhoods with either very low crime rates or very high crime rates. Crime rates in the first four neighborhoods are much lower than the mean (62.4 crimes per 1,000), whereas the last four neighborhoods are much higher than the mean. Although they share identical measures of central tendency, these three towns have neighborhood crime rates that are very different.

The way to capture these differences is with statistical measures of variation. Three popular measures of variation are the range, the variance, and the standard deviation (which is the most popular measure of variability). To calculate each of these measures, the variable must be at the interval or ratio level. Statistical measures of variation are used infrequently with qualitative variables, so these measures will not be presented here.

Range

The **range** is a simple measure of variation, calculated as the highest value in a distribution minus the lowest value:

Range = Highest value – Lowest value

It often is important to report the range of a distribution, to identify the whole range of possible values that might be encountered. However, because the range can be drastically altered by just one exceptionally high or low value (called an **outlier**), it does not do an adequate job of summarizing the extent of variability in a distribution. For our three towns in Exhibit 11.11, the range in crimes rates for Town A is 89.9 (109.4 – 19.5), for Town B it is 6.9 (65.0 – 58.7), and for Town C it is 106.4 (115.3 – 8.9).

Variance

If the mean is a good measure of central tendency, then it would seem that a good measure of variability would be the distance each score is away from the mean. Unfortunately, we cannot simply take the average distance of each score from the mean. One property of the mean is that it exactly balances negative and positive distances from it, so if we were to sum the difference between each score in a distribution and the mean of that distribution, it would always sum to zero. What we can do, though, is to square the difference of each score from the mean so the distance retains its value. This is the notion behind the variance as a measure of variability.

The **variance** is the average square deviation of each case from the mean, so it takes into account the amount by which each case differs from the mean. The equation to calculate the variance is

$$\sigma^2 = \frac{\Sigma_1^N (x - \bar{X})^2}{N}$$

In words, this formula says to take each score and subtract the mean, then square this difference, then sum all these differences, then divide this sum by N or the total number of scores. We will calculate the variance for the crime rate data from Town A in Exhibit 11.11.

x	$(x - \bar{X})$	$(x - \bar{X})^2$
19.5	(19.5 – 62.4) = -42.9	1,840.41
28.2	(28.2 – 62.4) = -34.2	1,169.64
35.7	(35.7 – 62.4) = -26.7	712.89
41.9	(41.9 – 62.4) = -20.5	420.25
63.2	(63.2 – 62.4) = -0.8	0.64
75.8	(75.8 – 62.4) = 13.4	179.56
92.0	(92.0 – 62.4) = 29.6	876.16
95.7	(95.7 – 62.4) = 33.3	1,108.89
109.4	(109.4 – 62.4) = 47.0	2,209.00
		$\Sigma(x - \bar{X})^2 = 8{,}517.44$

We can now determine that the variance is

$$\sigma^2 = \frac{8{,}517.44}{9} = 946.38$$

The variance of these data, then, is 946.38. In "squared deviation units," the variance tells us the amount of variation the distribution has around its mean. We had to square the original deviation units before summing them because $\Sigma(x - \bar{X}) = 0$. For most people, however, it is difficult to grasp "squared deviation units." For this reason, we typically take the square root of this value, called the standard deviation, to bring the variable back to its original units of measurement.

Standard Deviation

The standard deviation is simply the square root of the variance. It is the square root of the average squared deviation of each case from the mean:

$$\sigma = \sqrt{\frac{\Sigma_1^N (x - \bar{X})^2}{N}}$$

To find the standard deviation, simply calculate the variance and take the square root. For our example, the standard deviation is

$$\sigma = \sqrt{946.38} = 30.76$$

When the standard deviation is calculated from sample data, the denominator is supposed to be $N - 1$, rather than N, an adjustment that has no discernible effect when the number of cases is reasonably large. This value tells us that, on average, the neighborhood crime rates in Town A vary 30.76 around their mean of 62.4.

CROSSTABULATING VARIABLES

Most data analyses focus on relationships among variables to test hypotheses or just to describe or explore relationships. For each of these purposes, we must examine the association among two or more variables. Crosstabulation (crosstab) is one of the simplest methods for doing so. A crosstabulation displays the distribution of one variable for each category of another variable; it can also be called a *bivariate distribution*. Crosstabs also provide a simple tool for statistically controlling one or more variables while examining the associations among others. In this section, you will learn how crosstabs used in this way can help to test for spurious relationships and evaluate causal models. Crosstabulations are usually used when both variables are measured at either the nominal or ordinal level—that is, when the values of both variables are categories.

We are going to provide a series of examples of crosstabulations from our delinquency data. In our first example, the independent variable we are interested in is the youth's gender (V1; see Exhibit 11.2), and the dependent variable is the youth's self-reported involvement in delinquent behavior (DELINQ1). To use the delinquency variable in a crosstabulation, however, we first need to recode it into a categorical variable. We will make three approximately equal categories of self-reported delinquency: low, medium, and high.

Anyone who reported from 0 to 2 delinquent acts is now coded as 1, or low delinquency; anyone reporting from 3 to 13 delinquent acts is now coded as 2, or medium delinquency; and anyone reporting more than 14 delinquent acts is now coded as 3, or high delinquency. If you were to do a frequency distribution of this new variable, DELINQ2, you would see that there are three approximately equal groups.

We are interested in the relationship between gender and delinquency because a great deal of delinquency theory would predict that males are more likely to be delinquent than females. The gender of the youth is the independent variable, and the level of self-reported delinquency is the dependent variable.

Exhibit 11.12 shows the crosstabulation of gender with DELINQ2. Some explanation of this table is in order. Notice that there are two values of gender (male and female) that comprise the two rows of the table, and three values of delinquency (low, medium, and high) that comprise the three columns of the table. Crosstabulations are usually referred to by the number of rows and columns the table has. Our crosstabulation in Exhibit 11.12 is a 2 × 3 (pronounced "two-by-three") table because there are two rows and three columns. Notice also that there are values at the end of each row and at the end of each column. These totals are referred to as the *marginals* of the table. These marginal distributions provide the sum of the frequencies for each column and each row of the table. For example, there are 680 females in the data and 592 males. These row marginals should sum to the total number of youths in the data set: 1,272. There are 450 youths who are low in delinquency, 348 youths who are medium in delinquency, and 251 youths who are high on the delinquency variable. These column marginals should also sum to the total number of youths in the data set: 1,272.

Now notice that there are 2 × 3 or 6 data entries in the table (ignoring the percentages for now). These data entries are called the *cells* of the crosstabulation and represent the joint distribution of the two variables: gender and delinquency. The table in Exhibit 11.12 has six cells for the joint distribution of two levels of gender with three levels of delinquency. Notice where the value for female converges with the value of low for delinquency. You see a frequency number of 275 in this cell. This frequency indicates how many times there is the joint occurrence of a female and low delinquency; it shows that 275 females were also low in delinquency. Moving to the cell to the right of this, we see that there are 182 females who were medium in delinquency, and moving to the right again we see that there are 223 females who are high in delinquency. The sum of these three numbers is equal to the total number of females, 680. Likewise, the row for the males shows the joint distribution of males with each level of delinquency.

What we would like to know is whether there is a relationship or association between gender and delinquency. In other words, are males more likely to be delinquent than females? Because raw frequencies can provide a deceptive picture, we determine whether there is any relationship between our independent and dependent variables by looking at the percentages. Keep in mind that the idea in looking at relationships is that we want to know if variation on the independent variable has any effect on the dependent variable. To determine this, what we always do in crosstabulation tables is calculate our percentages on each value of the independent variable. For example, notice that in Exhibit 11.12, gender is our independent variable. We calculated our percentages so that for each value of gender, the percentages would sum to 100% at the end of each row. The percentages for both females and males, therefore, sum to 100% at the end of the row. Now we take a given

Exhibit 11.12 Crosstabulation of Respondents' Gender by Delinquency

		SELF-REPORTED DELINQUENCY			
		Low	Medium	High	Total
GENDER	Female	275 40.4%	182 26.8%	223 32.8%	680 100%
	Male	175 29.6%	166 28.0%	251 42.4%	592 100%
	Total	450	348	474	1,272

category of the dependent variable and ask what percentage of each independent variable value falls into that category of the dependent variable. Another way to say this is that we calculate our percentages on the independent variable and compare them on the dependent variable. We compare the percentages for different levels of the independent variable on the same category or level of the dependent variable.

In Exhibit 11.12, for example, notice that 40.4% of the female youths were low in delinquency, but only 29.6% of the males were low. This tells us that females are more likely to be low in delinquency than males. Now let us look at the high category. We can see that 32.8% of the females were high in delinquency and 42.4% of the males were high. Together, this tells us that females are more likely to be low in delinquency and males are more likely to be high in delinquency. There is, then, a relationship between gender and delinquency. Also notice that the independent variable was the row variable, and the dependent variable was the column variable. It does not always have to be this way; the independent variable could just as easily have been the column variable. The important general rule to remember is to always calculate your percentages on the levels of the independent variable (e.g., use marginal totals for the independent variable as denominators), and compare percentages on a level of the dependent variable.

In Exhibit 11.12, an association exists, although we can only say that it is a modest association. The percentage difference at the low and high ends of the delinquency variables is approximately 10 percentage points.

We provide another example of a crosstabulation in Exhibit 11.13. This is a 3 × 3 table that shows the relationship between how morally wrong a youth thinks delinquency is (the independent variable) and his or her self-reported involvement in delinquency (the dependent variable). This table reveals a very strong relationship between moral beliefs and delinquency. We can see that 5.6% of youths with weak moral beliefs are low on delinquency; this increases to 33.8% for those with medium beliefs and to 62.8% for those with strong moral beliefs. At the high end, over two-thirds (72.1%) of those youths with weak moral beliefs are high in delinquency, 29.4% of those with medium moral beliefs are high

Exhibit 11.13 Crosstabulation of Respondents' Morals by Delinquency

SELF-REPORTED DELINQUENCY

		Low	Medium	High	Total
	Weak	20 5.6%	79 22.3%	256 72.1%	355 100%
MORALS	Medium	170 33.8%	185 36.8%	148 29.4%	503 100%
	Strong	260 62.8%	84 20.3%	70 16.9%	414 100%
	Total	450	348	474	1,272

in delinquency, and only 16.9% of those youths with strong moral beliefs are high in delinquency. Clearly, then, having strong moral beliefs serves to effectively inhibit involvement in delinquent behavior. This is exactly what control theory would have us believe.

You will find when you read research reports and journal articles that social scientists usually make decisions about the existence and strength of association on the basis of more statistics than just percentage differences in a crosstabulation table. A **measure of association** is a type of descriptive statistic used to summarize the strength of an association.

Inferential statistics are used in deciding whether it is likely that an association exists in the larger population from which the sample was drawn. Even when the association between two variables is consistent with the researcher's hypothesis, it is possible that the association was just due to chance or to the vagaries of sampling on a random basis (Of course, the problem is even worse if the sample is not random.). It also is conventional in statistics to avoid concluding that an association exists in the population from which the sample was drawn unless the probability that the association was due to chance is less than 5%. In other words, a statistician normally will not conclude that an association exists between two variables unless he or she can be at least 95% confident that the association was not due to chance. Estimation of the probability that an association is not due to chance will be based on one of several inferential statistics, **chi-square** being the one used in most crosstabular analyses.

When an association passes muster in this way, when the analyst feels reasonably confident (at least 95% confident) that it was not due to chance, it is said that the association is statistically significant. **Statistical significance** means that an association is not likely to be due to chance, according to some criterion set by the analyst. Convention (and the desire to avoid concluding that an association exists in the population when it does not) dictates that the criterion be a probability less than 5%.

ANALYZING DATA ETHICALLY: HOW NOT TO LIE ABOUT RELATIONSHIPS

It is when the data analyst begins to examine relationships among variables in some real data that social science research becomes most exciting. The moment of truth, it would seem, has arrived. Either the hypotheses are supported or not. But, in fact, this is also a time to proceed with caution, and to evaluate the analyses of others with even more caution. Once large data sets are entered into a computer, it becomes very easy to check out a great many relationships; when relationships are examined among three or more variables at a time, the possibilities become almost endless.

This range of possibilities presents a great hazard for data analysis. It becomes very tempting to search around in the data until something interesting emerges. Rejected hypotheses are forgotten in favor of highlighting what's going on in the data. It is not wrong to examine data for unanticipated relationships; the problem is that inevitably some relationships between variables will appear just on the basis of chance association alone. If you search hard and long enough, it will be possible to come up with something that really means nothing.

A reasonable balance must be struck between deductive data analysis to test hypotheses and inductive analysis to explore patterns in a data set. Hypotheses formulated in advance of data collection must be tested as they were originally stated; any further analyses of these hypotheses that involve a more exploratory strategy must be labeled as such in research reports. Serendipitous findings do not need to be ignored, but they must be reported. Subsequent researchers can try to deductively test the ideas generated by our explorations.

We also have to be honest about the limitations of using survey data to test causal hypotheses. The usual practice for those who seek to test a causal hypothesis with nonexperimental survey data is to test for the relationship between the independent and dependent variables, controlling for other variables that might possibly create spurious relationships. We must always think about the possibilities and be cautious in our causal conclusions.

CONCLUSION

This chapter has demonstrated how a researcher can describe phenomena in criminal justice and criminology, identify relationships among them, explore the reasons for these relationships, and test hypotheses about them. Statistics provide a remarkably useful tool for developing our understanding of the social world, a tool that we can use to test our ideas and generate new ones.

Unfortunately, to the uninitiated, the use of statistics can seem to end debate right there; you cannot argue with the numbers. But you now know better than that. The numbers will be worthless if the methods used to generate the data are not valid, and the numbers will be misleading if they are not used appropriately, taking into account the type of data to which they are applied. Even assuming valid methods and proper use of statistics, there is one more critical step, for the numbers do not speak for themselves. Ultimately, it is how we interpret and report the numbers that determines their usefulness. It is this topic we turn to in the next chapter.

KEY TERMS

Bar chart	Inferential statistics	Range
Base N	Marginal distributions	Secondary data analysis
Bimodal distribution	Mean	Skewness
Central tendency	Measure of association	Spurious
Chi-square	Median	Standard deviation
Crosstabulation (crosstab)	Mode	Statistical significance
Descriptive statistics	Negatively skewed	Unimodal distribution
Frequency distribution	Outlier	Variability
Grouped frequency distribution	Percentage	Variance
Histogram	Positively skewed	

HIGHLIGHTS

- Bar charts, histograms, and frequency polygons are useful for describing the shape of distributions. Care must be taken with graphic displays to avoid distorting a distribution's apparent shape.

- Frequency distributions display variation in a form that can easily be inspected and described. Values should be grouped in frequency distributions in a way that does not alter the shape of the distribution. Following several guidelines can reduce the risk of problems.

- Summary statistics are often used to describe the central tendency and variability of distributions. The appropriateness of the mode, mean, and median vary with a variable's level of measurement, the distribution's shape, and the purpose of the summary.

- The variance and standard deviation summarize variability around the mean. The degree of skewness of a distribution is usually described in words rather than with a summary statistic.

- Crosstabulations should normally be percentaged within the categories of the independent variable.

- Inferential statistics are used with sample-based data to estimate the confidence that can be placed in a statistical estimate of a population parameter. Estimates of the probability that an association between variables may have occurred on the basis of chance are also based on inferential statistics.

EXERCISES

Discussing Research

1. Create frequency distributions from lists in the FBI Uniform Crime Reports on characteristics of arrestees in at least 100 cases (cites). You will have to decide on a grouping scheme for the

distribution scheme of variables such as race, age, and crime committed, and how to deal with outliers in the frequency distribution.

   a. Decide what summary statistics to use for each variable of interest. How well were the features of each distribution represented by the summary statistics? Describe the shape of each distribution.

   b. Propose a hypothesis involving two of these variables, and develop a crosstabulation to evaluate the support for this hypothesis.

   c. Describe each relationship in terms of the four aspects of an association, after making percentages within each table within the categories of the independent variable. Which hypotheses appear to have been supported?

Finding Research on the Web

1   Search the web for a crime-related example of statistics. Using the key terms from this chapter, describe the set of statistics you have identified. What phenomena are described by this set of statistics? What relationships, if any, do the statistics identify?

2.   Search the web for a crime-related example of statistics. The Bureau of Justice Statistics is a good place to start: www.ojp.usdoj.gov/bjs/. Using the key terms from this chapter, describe the set of statistics you have identified. What phenomena does this set of statistics describe? What relationships, if any, do the statistics identify?

3.   Do a web search for information on a criminological subject that interests you. How much of the information you found relies on statistics as a tool for understanding the subject? How do statistics allow researchers to test their ideas about the subject and generate new ideas? Write your findings in a brief report, referring to the websites you found.

Critiquing Research

1.   Become a media critic. For the next week, scan a newspaper or some magazines for statistics related to crime or criminal victimization. How many can you find using frequency distributions, graphs, and the summary statistics introduced in this chapter? Are these statistics used appropriately and interpreted correctly? Would any other statistics have been preferable or useful in addition to those presented? If so, which ones?

Making Research Ethical

1.   Review the frequency distributions and graphs in this chapter. Change one of these data displays so that you are "lying with statistics." You might consider using the graphic technique discussed by Orcutt and Turner (1993).

2.   Consider the relationship between gender and delinquency that is presented in this chapter. What third variable do you think should be controlled in the analysis to better understand the basis for this relationship? How might criminal justice policies be affected by finding out that this relationship was due to differences in teacher expectations rather than to genetic differences in violence propensity?

Developing a Research Proposal

Use the General Social Survey data to add a pilot study to your proposal. A pilot study is a preliminary effort to test out the procedures and concepts that you have proposed to research.

1. Review the GSSCRJ2K variable list and identify some variables that have at least some connection to your research problem. If possible, identify one variable that might be treated as independent in your proposed research and one that might be treated as dependent.

2. Request frequencies for these variables.

3. Request a crosstabulation of the dependent variable by the independent variable (if you were able to identify any). If necessary, recode the independent variable to three or fewer categories.

4. Write a brief description of your findings and comment on their implications for your proposed research. Did you learn any lessons from this exercise for your proposal?

Performing Data Analysis in SPSS or Excel

1. Develop a description of homicide defendants and their sentence length from HOMICIDE. POR. Examine each characteristic with three statistical techniques: a graph, a frequency distribution, and a measure of central tendency.

2. Describe the distribution of each variable, noting any skewness or outliers.

3. Collapse the categories for defendant's age (DAGE) and sentence length (PRITIME). Examine the data distributions using a graph and frequency distribution. Does the general shape of the distributions change as a result of changing how the data are measured?

4. Look at the relationship between these two variables. Indicate which is the dependent variable and which is the independent variable.

5. Run a crosstabulation on these data (using your newly created categorical variables). Be sure to obtain percentiles for categories of the independent variable (either row or column).

6. Propose two variables that might create a spurious relationship between defendant's age and sentence length. Explain your thinking.

CHAPTER 12

Reporting Research Results

The goal of research is not just to discover something but to communicate that discovery to a larger audience—other social scientists, government officials, your teachers, the general public, perhaps several of these audiences. Whatever the study's particular outcome, if the research report enables the intended audience to comprehend the results and learn from them, the research can be judged a success. If the intended audience is *not* able to learn about the study's results, the research should be judged a failure no matter how expensive the research, how sophisticated its design, or how much of yourself you invested in it.

The time for congratulations is when credible results are released and they serve some useful function, not when the research project is first approved. Furthermore, if you have conducted a worthwhile research project, consider whether some of the results might be appropriate for more than one report to different audiences.

The primary goals of this chapter are to help you develop worthwhile reports for any research you conduct and to guide you in evaluating reports produced by others. We begin by teaching you how to write research proposals, because a formal proposal lays the groundwork for a final research report. The next section highlights problems that are unique to the main types of reports: student papers and theses, journal articles, and unpublished reports for specific clients. The chapter's final sections present suggestions for writing and organizing reports, techniques for displaying statistical results, and ethical issues to be considered.

RESEARCH REPORT GOALS

The research report will present research findings and interpretations in a way that reflects some combination of the researcher's goals, the research sponsor's goals, the concerns of the research subjects, and perhaps the concerns of a wider anticipated readership. Understanding the goals of these different groups will help the researcher begin to shape the final report even at the start of the research. In designing a proposal and in negotiating access to a setting for the research, commitments often must be made to produce a particular type of report, or at least to cover certain issues in the final report. As the research progresses, feedback about the research from its participants, sponsoring agencies, collaborators, or other interested parties may suggest the importance of focusing on particular issues in the final report. Social researchers traditionally have tried to distance themselves from the concerns of such interested parties, paying attention only to what is needed to advance scientific knowledge. But in recent years, some social scientists have recommended bringing these interested parties into the research and reporting process itself.

Advance Scientific Knowledge

Most social science research reports are directed to other social scientists working in the area of study, so they reflect orientations and concerns that are shared within this community of interest. The traditional scientific approach encourages a research goal to advance scientific knowledge by providing reports to other scientists. This approach also treats value considerations as beyond the scope of science: "An empirical science cannot tell anyone what he should do but rather what he can do and under certain circumstances what he wishes to do" (Weber 1949: 54).

The idea is that developing valid knowledge about how society is organized or how we live our lives does not tell us how society *should* be organized or how we *should* live our lives. There should, as a result, be a strict separation between the determination of empirical facts and the evaluation of these facts as satisfactory or unsatisfactory (Weber 1949). Social scientists must not ignore value considerations, which are viewed as a legitimate basis for selecting a research problem to study. After the research is over and a report has been written, many scientists also consider it acceptable to encourage government officials or private organizations to implement the findings. During a research project, however, value considerations are to be held in abeyance.

Shape Social Policy

As we highlighted in our discussion of applied research in Chapter 10, many social scientists seek to influence social policy through their writing. By now, you have been exposed to several such examples in this text, including all the evaluation research (Chapter 10). These particular studies, like much policy-oriented social science research, are similar to those that aim strictly to increase knowledge. In fact, these studies might even be considered contributions to knowledge first and to social policy debate second. What distinguishes the reports of these studies from strictly academic reports is their attention to policy implications.

Other social scientists who seek to influence social policy explicitly reject the traditional scientific, rigid distinction between facts and values (Sjoberg & Nett 1968). Bellah et al. (1985) have instead proposed a model of "social science as public philosophy," in which social scientists focus explicit attention on achieving a more just society:

> Social science makes assumptions about the nature of persons, the nature of society, and the relation between persons and society. It also, whether it admits it or not, makes assumptions about good persons and a good society and considers how far these conceptions are embodied in our actual society.

Social science as public philosophy, by breaking through the iron curtain between the social sciences and the humanities, becomes a form of social self-understanding or self-interpretation. . . . By probing the past as well as the present, by looking at "values" as much as at "facts," such a social science is able to make connections that are not obvious and to ask difficult questions. (p. 301)

This perspective suggests more explicit concern with public policy implications when reporting research results. But it is important to remember that we all are capable of distorting our research and our interpretations of research results to correspond to our own value preferences. The temptation to see what we want to see is enormous, and research reports cannot be deemed acceptable unless they avoid this temptation.

Organize Social Action—Participatory Action Research

For the same reasons that value questions are traditionally set apart from the research process, many social scientists consider the application of research a nonscientific concern. William Foote Whyte, whose *Street Corner Society* (1943) study you encountered in Chapter 9, has criticized this belief and proposed an alternative research and reporting strategy he calls participatory action research (PAR). Whyte (1991) argues that social scientists must get "out of the academic rut" and engage in applied research to develop better understanding of social phenomena (p. 285).

In PAR, the researcher involves as active participants some members of the setting studied. Both the organizational members and the researcher are assumed to want to develop valid conclusions, to bring unique insights, and to desire change, but Whyte (1991) believed that these objectives were more likely to be obtained if the researcher collaborated actively with the persons he studied. PAR can bring researchers into closer contact with participants in the research setting through groups that discuss and plan research steps and then take steps to implement research findings. Stephen Kemmis and Robin McTaggart (2005) summarize the key features of PAR research as "a spiral of self-reflecting cycles" involving

- Planning a change;
- Acting and observing the process and consequences of the change;
- Reflecting on these processes and consequences;
- Replanning;
- Acting and observing again.

In contrast with the formal reporting of results at the end of a research project, these "cycles" make research reporting an ongoing part of the research process.

Case Study: Seeking Higher Education for Inmates

While prison populations in the United States have been significantly increasing, access to college programs within prisons has been essentially eliminated. Primarily because of the "tough on crime" policies of the 1990s, by 1995, only eight of the existing 350 college programs in prisons remained open nationwide (Torre & Fine 2005). To remedy this situation, Torre and Fine became involved in participatory action research to facilitate a college and college-bound program at the Bedford Hills Correctional Facility (BHCF), a maximum-security women's prison in New York. To conduct a study of the effects of the program, Michelle Fine was the principal investigator along with four prisoner-researchers and four researchers from the Graduate Center of the City University of New York. This "participatory research team" asked several questions: (a) Who are the women in the college program? (b) What is the impact of the college experience on inmate students and their children? (c) What is the impact of the college experience on the prison environment? (d) What is the impact of the college experience beyond college on recidivism? and (e) What is the cost of such a program to taxpayers? The researchers used a triangulated methodology employing quantitative analysis of recidivism rates and costs of the program along with in-depth interviews with the participants; focus groups with inmates, faculty, children, and college presidents; and surveys of faculty who taught in the program. Although not using a randomized experimental design, Torre and Fine, along with their coinvestigators, tracked participants in the college program after release and found that women who had not participated in the program were four times more likely to be returned to custody than women who had participated.

The narratives from the interviews with college inmates also illuminated the positive benefits of the education. One inmate college student said, "Because when you take some-body that feels that they're not gonna amount to anything, and you put them in an environ-ment, like, when you're in college it takes you away from the prison . . . it's like you're opening your mind to a whole different experience" (Torre & Fine 2005: 582). The positive impact of college on the inmates was also transferred to their children. The cost–benefit analysis of the program indicated that the savings based on decreased recidivism rates for those who attended the college far outweighed the initial cost of the program itself. In sum, with just a small grant from a private foundation, the participatory action research team brought together universities, prisoners, churches, community organizations, and prison administrators to resurrect a college at BHCF. The authors concluded, "Key elements of this program include broad-based community involvement, strong prisoner participation in design and governance, and the support of the prison administration" (p. 591). A full report of this research can be found at http://web.gc.cuny.edu/che/changingminds.html. As you can see, participatory action research has the potential to be life changing for all involved.

TYPES OF RESEARCH REPORTS

Research projects designed to produce student papers and theses, applied research reports, and academic articles all have unique features that will influence the final research report. For example, student papers are written for a particular professor or for a thesis committee and often are undertaken with almost no financial resources and in the face of severe time constraints. Applied research reports are written for an organization or agency that usually also has funded the research and has expectations for a particular type of report. Journal articles are written for the larger academic community and will not be published until they are judged acceptable by some representatives of that community (e.g., after the article has gone through extensive peer review).

These unique features do not really match up so neatly with the specific types of research products. For example, a student paper that is based on a research project conducted in collaboration with a work organization may face some constraints for a project designed to produce an applied research report. An academic article may stem from an applied research project conducted for a government agency. An applied research report often can be followed by an academic article on the same topic. In fact, one research study may lead to all three types of research reports as students write course papers or theses for professors who write both academic articles and applied research reports.

Student Papers and Theses

What is most distinctive about a student research paper or thesis is the audience for the final product: a professor or, for a thesis, a committee of professors. In light of this, it is important for you to seek feedback early and often about the progress of your research and about your professor's expectations for the final paper. Securing approval of a research proposal is usually the first step, but it should not be the last occasion for seeking advice prior to writing the final paper. Do not become too anxious for guidance, however. Professors require research projects in part so that their students can work through, at least somewhat independently, the many issues they confront. A great deal of insight into the research process can be gained in this way. So balance your requests for advice with some independent decision making.

Most student research projects can draw on few resources beyond the student's own time and effort, so it is important that the research plan not be overly ambitious. Keep the paper deadline in mind when planning the project, and remember that almost every researcher tends to underestimate the time required to carry out a project.

The Thesis Committee

Students who are preparing a paper for a committee, usually at the MA or PhD level, must be prepared to integrate the multiple perspectives and comments of committee members into a plan for a coherent final report. (The thesis committee chair should be the primary guide in this process; careful selection of faculty to serve on the committee is also important.) As much as possible, committee members should have complementary areas of expertise that are each important for the research project: perhaps one methodologist, one specialist in the primary substantive area of the thesis, and one specialist in a secondary area.

It is very important that you work with your committee members in an ongoing manner, both individually and collectively. In fact, it is vitally important to have a group meeting with all committee members at the beginning of the project to ensure everyone on the committee supports the research plan. Doing this will avoid obstacles that arise due to miscommunication later in the research process.

Journal Articles

It is the peer review process that makes preparation of an academic journal article most unique. Similar to a grant review, the journal's editor sends submitted articles to two or three experts (peers), who are asked whether the paper should be accepted more or less as is, revised and then resubmitted, or rejected. Reviewers also provide comments—which are sometimes quite lengthy—to explain their decision and to guide any required revisions. The process is an anonymous one at most journals; reviewers are not told the author's name, and the author is not told the reviewers' names. Although the journal editor has the final say, editors' decisions are normally based on the reviewers' comments.

This peer review process must be anticipated in designing the final report. Peer reviewers are not pulled out of a hat. They are experts in the field or fields represented in the paper and usually have published articles themselves in that field. It is critical that the author be familiar with the research literature and be able to present the research findings as a unique contribution to that literature. In most cases, this hurdle is much harder to jump with journal articles than with student papers or applied research reports. In fact, most leading journals have a rejection rate of over 90%, so that hurdle is quite high indeed. Of course, there is also a certain luck of the draw involved in peer review. One set of two or three reviewers may be inclined to reject an article that another set of reviewers would accept. But in general, the anonymous peer review process results in higher-quality research reports because articles are revised prior to publication in response to the suggestions and criticisms of the experts.

Criminological and criminal justice research is published in myriad journals within several disciplines, including criminology, law, sociology, psychology, and economics. As a result, there is no one formatting style by which all criminological literature abides. If, for example, you are submitting your paper to a psychology-related journal, you must abide by the formatting style dictated by the *Publication Manual of the American Psychological Association*. The easiest way to determine how to format a paper for a particular journal is to examine recent volumes of the journal and format your paper accordingly. There are numerous articles available on the Student Study Site for this text, www.sagepub.com/bachmanfrccj2e.

Despite the slight variations in style across journals, there are typically seven standard sections within a journal article in addition to the title page:

1. *Abstract*. This should be a concise and nonevaluative summary of your research paper (no more than 120 words) that describes the research problem, the sample, the method, and the findings.

2. *Introduction*. The body of a paper should open with an introduction that presents the specific problem under study and describes the research strategy. Before writing this section, you should consider the following questions: What is the point of the study? How do the hypotheses and the research design relate to the problem? What are the theoretical implications of the study, and how does the study relate to previous work in the area? What are the theoretical propositions tested, and how were they derived? A good introduction answers these questions in a few paragraphs by summarizing the relevant argument and the data, giving the reader a sense of what was done and why.

3. *Literature Review*. Discuss the relevant literature in a way that relates each previous study cited to your research, not in an exhaustive historical review. Citation of and specific credit to relevant earlier works is part of the researcher's scientific and

scholarly responsibility. It is essential for the growth of cumulative science. This section should demonstrate the logical continuity between previous research and the research at hand. At the end of this section, you are ready to conceptually define your variables and formally state your hypotheses.

4. *Method.* Describe in detail how the study was conducted. Such a description enables the reader to evaluate the appropriateness of your methods and the reliability and the validity of your results. It also permits experienced investigators to replicate the study if they so desire. In this section, you can include subsections that describe the sample, the independent and dependent variables, and the analytical or statistical procedure you will use to analyze the data.

5. *Results.* Summarize the results of the statistical or qualitative analyses performed on the data. It can include tables and figures that summarize findings. If statistical analyses are performed, tests of significance should also be highlighted.

6. *Discussion.* Take the opportunity to evaluate and interpret your results, particularly with respect to your original hypotheses and previous research. Here, you are free to examine and interpret your results as well as draw inferences from them. In general, this section should answer the following questions: What have I contributed to the literature here? How has my study helped to resolve the original problem? What conclusions and theoretical implications can I draw from my study? What are the limitations of my study? What are the implications for future research?

7. *References.* All citations in the manuscript must appear in the reference list, and all references must be cited in the text.

Applied Reports

Unlike journal articles, applied reports are usually commissioned by a particular government agency, corporation, or nonprofit organization. As such, the most important problem that applied researchers confront is the need to produce a final report that meets the funding organization's expectations. This is called the "hired gun" problem. Of course, the extent to which being a hired gun is a problem varies greatly with the research orientation of the funding organization and with the nature of the research problem posed. The ideal situation is to have few constraints on the nature of the final report, but sometimes research reports are suppressed or distorted because the researcher comes to conclusions that the funding organization does not like.

Applied reports that are written in a less highly charged environment can face another problem—even when they are favorably received by the funding organization, their conclusions are often ignored. This problem can be more a matter of the organization not really knowing how to use research findings than it not wanting to use them. This is not just a problem of the funding organization; many researchers are prepared only to present their findings, without giving any thought to how research findings can be translated into organizational policies or programs.

CURBING THE FRUSTRATIONS OF WRITING

Perfectionism is the voice of the oppressor, the enemy of the people. It will keep you cramped and insane your whole life and it is the main obstacle between you and a shitty first draft. (Lamott 1994: 28)

We often hear lamentations from students such as, "It is impossible to know where to begin," or "I have a hard time getting started." To this we say only, "Begin wherever you are most comfortable but begin early!" You do not have to start with the introduction; start in the method section if you prefer. The main point is to begin somewhere and then keep typing, keep typing, and keep typing! It is always easier to rewrite a paper than it is to write the first draft. The fine art of writing is really in the rewriting!

Those of you who began with a research proposal have a head start; you will find that the final report is much easier to write. It is very disappointing to discover that something important was left out when it is too late to do anything about it. We do not need to point out that students (and professional researchers) often leave final papers (and reports) until the last possible minute (often for understandable reasons, including other course work and job or family responsibilities). But be forewarned: The last-minute approach does not work for research reports.

A successful report must be well organized and clearly written. Getting to such a product is a difficult but not impossible goal. Consider the following principles formulated by experienced writers (Booth, Colomb, & Williams 1995: 150–151):

- Start with an outline.
- Respect the complexity of the task, and do not expect to write a polished draft in a linear fashion. Your thinking will develop as you write, causing you to reorganize and rewrite.
- Leave enough time for dead ends, restarts, revisions, and so on, and accept the fact that you will discard much of what you write.
- Write as fast as you comfortably can. Do not worry about spelling, grammar, and so on until you are polishing things up.
- Ask all the people whom you trust for their reactions to what you have written.
- Write as you go along, so you have notes and report segments drafted even before you focus on writing the report.

It is important to remember that no version of a manuscript is ever final. As you write, you will get new ideas about how to organize the report. Try them out. As you review the first draft, you will see many ways to improve your writing. Focus particularly on how to shorten and clarify your statements. Make sure each paragraph concerns only one topic. Remember the golden rule of good writing: Writing is revising!

Another useful tip is to use a method called reverse outlining. After you have written a first complete draft, outline it on a paragraph-by-paragraph basis, ignoring the actual section headings you used. See if the paper you wrote actually fits the outline you planned. How could the organization be improved?

Perhaps most important, leave yourself enough time so that you can revise—several times if possible—before turning in the final draft.

A well-written research report requires (to be just a bit melodramatic) blood, sweat, and tears and more time than you will at first anticipate. But the process of writing one will help you to write the next, and the issues you consider, if you approach your writing critically, will be sure to improve your subsequent research projects and sharpen your evaluations of others.

Those of you interested in a more focused discussion of writing in general (e.g., grammar, elements of style, emotional aspects of writing) should see Becker (1986); Booth, et al. (1995); Mullins (1977), Strunk and White (1979); and Turabian (1967).

ETHICS AND REPORTING

It is at the time of reporting research results that the researcher's ethical duty to be honest becomes paramount. Here are some guidelines.

- *Provide an honest accounting of how the research was carried out and where the initial research design had to be changed.* Readers do not have to know about every change you made in your plans and each new idea you had, but they should be informed about major changes in hypotheses or research design.
- *Maintain a full record of the research project so that questions can be answered if they arise.* Many details will have to be omitted from all but the most comprehensive reports, but these omissions should not make it impossible to track down answers to specific questions about research procedures that may arise in the course of data analysis or presentation.
- *Avoid "lying with statistics" or using graphs to mislead.*
- *Acknowledge the sponsors of the research.* In part, this is so that others can consider whether this sponsorship may have tempted you to bias your results in some way. Make sure to also thank staff who made major contributions.
- *Be sure that the order of authorship for coauthored reports is discussed in advance and reflects agreed-upon principles. Be sensitive to coauthors' needs and concerns.*

Ethical research reporting should not mean ineffective reporting. You need to tell a coherent story in the report and to avoid losing track of the story in a thicket of miniscule details. You do not need to report every twist and turn in the conceptualization of the research problem or the conduct of the research, but be suspicious of reports that do not seem to admit to the possibility of any room for improvement. Social science is an ongoing enterprise in which one research report makes its most valuable contribution by laying the groundwork for another, more sophisticated research project. Highlight important findings in the research report, but use the report also to point out what are likely to be the most productive directions for future researchers.

Plagiarism

It may seem depressing to end a book on research methods with a section on plagiarism, but it would be irresponsible to avoid the topic. We realize that you may have a course syllabus detailing instructor or university policies about plagiarism and specifying the penalties for violating that policy, so we're not simply going to repeat that kind of warning. Unfortunately, the practice of selling term papers is revoltingly widespread. When you understand the dimensions of the problem and the way it affects research, you should be better able to detect plagiarism in other work and avoid it in your own.

You learned in Chapter 3 that maintaining professional integrity—honesty and openness in research procedures and results—is the foundation for ethical research practice. When it comes to research publications and reports, being honest and open means avoiding plagiarism—that is, presenting as one's own the ideas or words of another person or persons for academic evaluation without proper acknowledgment (Hard, Conway, & Moran 2006). In essence, plagiarism is a form of stealing.

An increasing body of research suggests that plagiarism is a growing problem on college campuses. For example, Hard et al. (2006) conducted an anonymous survey in one university and found very high plagiarism rates: 60.6% of students reported that they had copied "sentences, phrases, paragraphs, tables, figures or data directly or in slightly modified form from a book, article, or other academic source without using quotation marks or giving proper acknowledgment to the original author or source" (p. 1069), and 39.4% reported that they had "copied information from Internet Web sites and submitted it as [their] work" (p. 1069).

The plagiarism problem is not just about purchasing term papers—although that is really about as bad as it gets (Broskoske 2005); plagiarism is also about what you do with the information you obtain from a literature review or an inspection of research reports. However, rest assured that this is not only about student papers; it also is about the work of established scholars and social researchers who publish reports that you want to rely on for accurate information. Several noted historians have been accused of plagiarizing passages that they used in popular books; some have admitted to not checking the work of their research assistants, to not keeping track of their sources, or to being unable to retrieve the data they claimed they had analyzed. Whether the cause is cutting corners to meet deadlines or consciously fudging facts, the effect is to undermine the trustworthiness of social research.

A primary way to avoid plagiarism is to maintain careful procedures for documenting the sources that you rely on for your own research and papers, but you should also think about how best to reduce temptations among others. After all, what people believe about what others do is a strong influence on their own behavior (Hard et al. 2006).

Reviewing the definition of plagiarism and how it is enforced by your discipline's professional association is essential. These definitions and procedures reflect a collective effort to help social scientists maintain standards throughout the discipline. Awareness is the first step (American Sociological Association [ASA] 1999). In addition, your college or university also has rules that delineate its definition of and consequences for plagiarism.

The next step toward combating the problem and temptation of plagiarism is to keep focused on the goal of social research methods: investigating the social world. If researchers are motivated by a desire to learn about social relations, to study how people understand society, and to discover why conflicts arise and how they can be prevented, they will be as concerned with the integrity of their research methods as are those, like yourself, who read and use the results of their research. Throughout this text, you have been learning how to use research processes and practices that yield valid findings and trustworthy conclusions. Failing to report honestly and openly on the methods used or sources consulted derails progress toward that goal.

It works the same as with cheating in school. When students are motivated only by the desire to "ace" their tests and receive better grades than others, they are more likely to plagiarize and use other illicit means to achieve that goal. Students who seek first to improve their understanding of the subject matter and to engage in the process of learning are less likely to plagiarize sources or cheat on exams (Kohn 2008). They are also building the foundation for becoming successful social researchers who help others understand our world.

CONCLUSION

Much research lacks one or more of the three legs of validity—measurement validity, causal validity, or generalizability—and sometimes contributes more confusion than understanding about particular issues. Top journals generally maintain very high standards, partly because they have good critics in the review process and distinguished editors who make the final acceptance decisions. But some daily newspapers do a poor job of screening, and research reporting standards in many popular magazines, TV shows, and books are often abysmally poor. Keep your standards high and your view critical when reading research reports, but not so high or so critical that you turn away from studies that make tangible contributions to the literature, even if they do not provide definitive answers. However, don't be so intimidated by the need to maintain high standards that you shrink from taking advantage of opportunities to conduct research yourself.

Of course, social research methods are no more useful than the commitment of the researchers to their proper application. Research methods, like all knowledge, can be used poorly or well, for good purposes or bad, when appropriate or not. A claim that a belief is based on social science research in itself provides no extra credibility. As you have discovered throughout this book, we must first learn which methods were used, how they were applied, and whether interpretations square with the evidence. To investigate the social world, we must keep in mind the lessons of research methods.

KEY TERMS

Participatory action research

Peer review

Plagiarism

Reverse outlining

HIGHLIGHTS

- Proposal writing should be a time for clarifying the research problem, reviewing the literature, and thinking ahead about the report that will be required.

- Relations with research subjects and consumers should be developed in a manner that achieves key research goals and preparation of an effective research report. The traditional scientific approach of minimizing the involvement of research subjects and consumers in research decisions has been challenged by proponents of participatory action research and adherents of the constructivist paradigm.

- Research reports should include an introductory statement of the research problem, a literature review, a methodology section, a findings section with pertinent data displays, and a conclusions section that identifies any weaknesses in the research design and points out implications for future research and theorizing. This basic report format should be modified according to the needs of a particular audience.

- All reports should be revised several times and critiqued by others before they are presented in final form.

- The central ethical concern in research reporting is to be honest. This honesty should include providing a truthful accounting of how the research was carried out, maintaining a full record about the project, using appropriate statistics and graphs, acknowledging the research sponsors, and being sensitive to the perspectives of coauthors.

- Plagiarism is a grievous violation of scholarly ethics. All direct quotes or paraphrased material from another author's work must be appropriately cited.

EXERCISES

Discussing Research

1. Select a recent article published in a peer-reviewed criminological journal and answer the following questions: How effective is the article in conveying the design and findings of the research? Could the article's organization be improved at all? Are there bases for disagreement about the interpretation of the findings?

2. Call a local criminal justice official and arrange for an interview. Ask the official about his or her experience with applied research reports and his conclusions about the value of social research and the best techniques for reporting to practitioners.

3. Rate four criminological journal articles for overall quality of the research and for effectiveness of the writing and data displays. Discuss how each could have been improved.

Finding Research on the Web

1. Go to the National Science Foundation's Law and Social Science Program website at http://nsf .gov/dir/index.jsp?org = sbe. What are the components that this program looks for in a proposed piece of research in the social sciences? Write a detailed outline for a research proposal to study a subject of your choice to be submitted to the National Science Foundation for funding.

2. Using the Internet, find five different examples of criminological research projects that have been completed. Briefly describe each. How does each differ in its approach to reporting the

research results? To whom do you think the author(s) of each is "reporting" (i.e., who is the "audience")? How do you think the predicted audience has helped to shape the author's approach to reporting the results? Be sure to note the websites at which you located each of your five examples.

Critiquing Research

1. Rate four criminological journal articles for overall quality of the research and for effectiveness of the writing and data displays. Discuss how each could have been improved.

2. How firm a foundation do social research methods provide for understanding the social world? Stage an in-class debate, with the pro and con arguments focusing on the variability of social research findings across different social contexts and the difficulty of understanding human subjectivity.

Making Research Ethical

1. Some researchers do not make their data publicly available. As a result, other researchers are not able to replicate the original findings. Would you recommend legal regulations about the release of research data? What would those regulations be? Would they differ depending on the researcher's source of funding? Would you allow researchers exclusive access to their own data for some period of time after they have collected it?

2. Plagiarism is not a joke. What are the regulations on plagiarism of class papers at your school? What do you think the ideal policy would be? Should this policy take into account cultural differences in teaching practices and learning styles? Do you think this ideal policy is likely to be implemented? Why or why not? Based on your experiences, do you believe that most student plagiarism is the result of misunderstanding about proper citation practices, or is it the result of dishonesty? Do you think that students who plagiarize while in school are less likely to be honest as social researchers? Why or why not?

3. Full disclosure of sources of research as well as of other medically related funding has become a major concern for medical journals. Should researchers publishing in criminology and criminal justice journals also be required to fully disclose all sources of funding? Should full disclosure of all previous funds received by criminal justice agencies be required in each published article? What about disclosure of any previous jobs or paid consultations with criminal justice agencies? Write a short justification of the regulations you propose.

Developing a Research Proposal

Now it is time to bring all the elements of your proposal together.

1. Organize the proposal material you wrote for previous chapters in a logical order. Based on your research question, select the most appropriate research method as your primary method (see Chapters 6–9).

2. To add another component to your research design, select an additional research method that could contribute knowledge about your research question.

Performing Data Analysis in SPSS or Excel

1. How do friends' opinions and support for delinquent activities influence levels of delinquency among youth? A combined frequency display of the distributions of a series of YOUTH.POR variables will help you to answer this question.

   a. Obtain a frequency distribution and descriptive statistics for friends' attitudes toward delinquent acts index (FROPINION), index of friends' engagement in delinquent acts (FRBEHAVE), and the delinquency index at time 11 (DELINQ1).
   b. Using the mean as the measure of center, recode the three indexes to measure low and high levels of each variable (e.g., all values below the mean represent low levels of a given variable and all values above the mean represent high levels of the given variable).
   c. Use the percentages in these distributions to prepare a combined frequency display.
   d. Discuss what you have learned about the influence of friends' delinquent tendencies on delinquency levels among youth.

Student Study Site

The companion Student Study Site for *Fundamentals of Research in Criminology and Criminal Justice* can be found at www.sagepub.com/bachmanfrccj2e.

   Visit the Student Study Site to enhance your understanding of the chapter content and to discover additional resources that will take your learning one step further. You can enhance your understanding of the chapters by using the comprehensive study material, which includes interactive exercises, e-flashcards, web exercises, practice self-tests, and more. You will also find special features, such as Learning From Journal Articles, which incorporates Sage's online journal collection.

Glossary

Alternate-forms reliability: A procedure for testing the reliability of responses to survey questions in which subjects' answers are compared after the subjects have been asked slightly different versions of the questions or when randomly selected halves of the sample have been administered slightly different versions of the questions

Analytic comparative research: Research that seeks to understand how national systems work and the factors related to their operations

Anomalous findings: Unexpected findings in data analysis that are inconsistent with most other findings with that data

Anonymity: Provided by research in which no identifying information is recorded that could be used to link respondents to their responses

Applied research: Research that is designed to solve practical problems of the modern world, rather than to acquire knowledge for knowledge's sake

Authenticity: When the understanding of a social process or social setting is one that reflects fairly the various perspectives of participants in that setting

Availability sampling: Sampling in which elements are selected on the basis of convenience

Bar chart: A graphic for qualitative variables in which each variable's distribution is displayed with solid bars separated by spaces

Base N: The total number of cases in a distribution

Before-and-after designs: A quasi-experimental design consisting of before–after comparisons involving the same variables and sometimes the same groups, but sometimes these designs may even include different groups in the pretests and posttests

Belmont Report: A 1979 National Commission for the Protection of Human Subjects of Biomedical and Behavioral Research report that established three basic ethical principles for the protection of human subjects, including respect for persons, beneficence, and justice

Bimodal: A distribution that has two nonadjacent categories with about the same number of cases, and these categories have more cases than any other categories

Black box evaluation: A type of evaluation that occurs when an evaluation of program outcomes ignores, and does not identify, the process by which the program produced the effect

Campbell Collaboration: An international research network that prepares and disseminates systematic reviews of social science evidence in crime and justice, education, and social welfare

Causal effect: When variation in one phenomenon, an independent variable, leads to or results, on average, in variation in another phenomenon, the dependent variable

Causal validity: Exists when a conclusion that A leads to or results in B is correct

Census: Research in which information is obtained through the responses that all available members of an entire population give to questions

Central tendency: The most common value (for variables measured at the nominal level) or the value around which cases tend to cluster (for a quantitative variable)

Certificate of Confidentiality: Document that protects researchers from being legally required to disclose confidential information

Ceteris paribus: Latin phrase meaning "other things being equal"

Chi-square: An inferential statistic used to test hypotheses about relationships between two or more variables in a crosstabulation

Closed-ended (fixed-choice) question: A survey question that provides preformatted response choice for the respondent to circle or check

Cluster: A naturally occurring, mixed aggregate of elements of the population

Cluster sampling: Sampling in which elements are selected in two or more stages, with the first stage being the random selection of naturally occurring clusters and the last stage being the random selection of elements within clusters

Cohort: Individuals or groups with a common starting point. Examples include college class of 2010, General Motors employees who started work between 2005 and 2006, and so on.

Comparative research: Research comparing data from more than one time period or more than one culture or country

Compensatory rivalry (John Henry effect): A type of contamination in experimental designs that occurs when control group members perceive that they are being denied some advantage that the experimental group members are getting and increase their efforts by way of compensation

Complete observation: A role in participant observation in which the researcher does not participate in group activities and is publicly defined as a researcher

Computer-assisted qualitative data analysis: Uses special computer software to assist qualitative analyses through creation, application, and refinement of categories; tracing linkages between concepts; and making comparisons between cases and events

Computer-assisted self-interviewing (CASI): A system within which respondents interact with a computer-administered questionnaire by using a mouse and following audio instructions delivered via headphones

Computer-assisted telephone interviews (CATI): An interview in which data collection and data entry can occur concurrently and data entry error is minimized. Most large surveys are performed in this way.

Computer Interactive Voice Response (IVR): Software that uses a touch-tone telephone to interact with people in order to acquire information from or enter data into the database

Concept: A mental image that summarizes a set of similar observations, feelings, or ideas

Constant: A characteristic or property that does not vary but takes on only one value

Construct validity: The type of validity that is established by showing that a measure is related to other measures as specified in a theory

Constructivism: A perspective that emphasizes how different stakeholders in social settings construct their beliefs

Contamination: A source of causal invalidity that occurs when either the experimental or the comparison group is aware of the other group and is influenced in the posttest as a result

Content analysis: A research method for systematically analyzing and making inferences from text

Content validity: The type of validity that exists when the full range of a concept's meaning is covered by the measure.

Context: A focus on idiographic causal explanation. A particular outcome is understood as part of a larger set of interrelated circumstances.

Contextual effects: Relationships among variables that vary among geographic units or other social settings

Contingent questions: Questions that are asked of only a subset of survey respondents

Control group: In an experiment or study, a comparison group that receives no treatment

Cost–benefit analysis: A type of evaluation research that compares program costs with the economic value of program benefits

Cost-effectiveness analysis: A type of evaluation research that compares program costs with actual program outcomes

Cover letter: The letter sent with a mailed questionnaire. It explains the survey's purpose and auspices and encourages the respondent to participate

Covert participation: A role in field research in which the researcher does not reveal his or her identity as a researcher to those who are observed. The covert participant has adopted the role of a "complete participant"

Crime mapping: Geographical mapping strategies used to visualize a number of things including location, distance, and patterns of crime and their correlates

Criminological research question: A question that is answered through the collection and analysis of firsthand, verifiable, empirical data

Criterion validity: The type of validity that is established by comparing the scores obtained on the measure being validated to those obtained with a more direct or already validated measure of the same phenomenon

Cross-population generalizability: Exists when findings about one group, population, or setting hold true for other groups, populations, or settings. This is also called *external validity.*

Cross-sectional research design: A study in which data are collected at only one point in time

Crosstabulation (crosstab): A bivariate (two-variable) distribution showing the distribution of one variable for each category of another variable

Debriefing: A researcher's informing of subjects after an experiment about the experiment's purposes and methods and evaluating subjects' personal reactions to the experiment

Deductive research: The type of research in which a specific explanation is deduced from a general premise and is then tested; compare to *inductive research*

Dependent variable: A variable that is hypothesized to vary depending on or under the influence of the independent variable

Descriptive comparative research: Research that seeks to understand the structure, nature, or scope of a nation or nations' criminal justice systems or rates of crime

Descriptive research: Research in which social phenomena are defined and described

Descriptive statistics: Statistics used to describe the distribution of and relationship among variables

Differential attrition: A problem that occurs in experiments when comparison groups become different because subjects are more likely to drop out of one of the groups for various reasons

Disproportionate stratified sampling: Sampling in which elements are selected from strata in different proportions from those that appear in the population

Distribution of benefits: An ethical issue about how much researchers can influence the benefits subjects receive as part of the treatment being studied in field experiments

Double-barreled question: A single survey question that actually asks two questions but allows only one answer

Double-blind procedure: An experimental method in which neither the subjects nor the staff delivering experimental treatments know which subjects are getting the treatment and which are receiving the placebo

Double-negative question: A question or statement that contains two negatives, which can muddy the meaning

Ecological fallacy: An error in reasoning in which incorrect conclusions about individual-level processes are drawn from group-level data

Effect size: A standardized measure of association that is often the difference between the mean of the experimental group and the mean of the control group on the dependent variable

Efficiency analysis: A type of evaluation research that compares program costs with program effects. It can be either a cost–benefit analysis or a cost-effectiveness analysis.

Electronic survey: A survey that is sent and answered by computer, either through e-mail or on the web

Elements: The individual members of the population whose characteristics are to be measured

E-mail survey: A survey that is sent and answered through e-mail

Empirical generalization: A statement that describes patterns found in data

Endogenous change: A source of causal invalidity that occurs when natural developments or changes in the subjects, independent of the experimental treatment itself, account for some or all of the observed change from the pretest to the posttest

Ethnography: The study of a culture or cultures that some group of people share, using participant observation over an extended period of time

Evaluability assessment: A method to determine the possibility of a study being able to specifically identify the effects of a particular program within the available time and with the available resources

Evaluation research: Research about social programs or interventions

Event-based design (cohort study): A type of longitudinal study in which data are collected at two or more points in time from individuals in a cohort

Evidence-based policies: Programs and policies that are based on a systematic review of all available evidence that assesses what works and what doesn't

Exhaustive attributes: A variable's attributes or values are exhaustive when every case can be classified into one of the categories

Exhaustive response attributes: A variable's attributes or values in which every case can be classified as having one attribute

Expectancies of the experimental staff: A source of treatment misidentification in experiments that occurs when change among experimental subjects is due to the positive expectancies of the staff who are delivering the treatment rather than to the treatment itself; also called a self-fulfilling prophecy

Experience sampling method (ESM): A technique for drawing a representative sample of everyday activities, thoughts, and experiences. Participants carry a pager and are beeped at random times over several days or weeks; upon hearing the beep, participants complete a report designed by the researcher.

Experimental approach: An approach in which the researcher assigns individuals to two or more groups in a way that equates the characteristics of individuals in the groups, except for variation in the groups' exposure to the independent variable

Experimental group: In an experiment, the group of subjects that receives the treatment or experimental manipulation

Explanatory research: Research that seeks to identify causes or effects of social phenomena

Exploratory research: Research in which social phenomena are investigated without a priori expectations, in order to develop explanations of them

Ex post facto control group designs: A nonexperimental design in which comparison groups are selected after the treatment or program has occurred

External events: A source of causal invalidity that occurs when events external to the study influence posttest scores; also called *history effects*

External validity: The applicability of a treatment effect (or noneffect) across subgroups within an experiment or across different populations, times, or settings

Face validity: The type of validity that exists when an inspection of items used to measure a concept suggests that they are appropriate on their face

Falsifiable: A theoretical statement must be capable of being proven wrong; that is, it must have the capacity to be empirically tested and falsified

Federal Policy for the Protection of Human Subjects: Federal regulations established in 1991 that are based on the principles of the Belmont Report (see *Belmont Report*)

Feedback: Information about service delivery system outputs, outcomes, or operations that is available to any program inputs

Fence-sitters: Survey respondents who see themselves as being neutral on an issue and choose a middle (neutral) response that is offered

Field experiment: A study conducted in a real-world setting

Field notes: Notes that describe what has been observed, heard, or otherwise experienced in a participant observation study; these notes usually are written after the observational session

Field research: Research in which natural social processes are studied as they happen and left relatively undisturbed

Filter question: A survey question used to identify a subset of respondents who then are asked other questions

Fixed-choice (closed-ended) question: Survey question providing preformulated response choices for the respondent to circle or check

Fixed-sample panel design (panel study): A type of longitudinal study in which data are collected from the same individuals—the panel—at two or more points in time

Floaters: Survey respondents who provide an opinion on a topic in response to a closed-ended question that does not include a "don't know" option, but will choose "don't know" if it is available

Focus groups: A qualitative method that involves unstructured group interviews in which the focus group leader actively encourages discussion among participants on the topics of interest

Generalizability: Exists when a conclusion holds true for the population, group, setting, or event that the researcher says it does, given the conditions that he or she specifies

Geographic Information System (GIS): The software tool that has made crime mapping increasingly available to researchers since the 1990s

Grounded theory: Systematic theory developed inductively, based on observations that are summarized into conceptual categories, reevaluated in the research setting, and gradually refined and linked to other conceptual categories

Group-administered survey: A survey that is completed by individual respondents who are assembled in a group

Grouped frequency distribution: A frequency distribution in which the data are organized into categories, either because there are more values than can be easily displayed or because the distribution of the variable will be clearer or more meaningful

Hawthorne effect: A type of contamination in experimental designs that occurs when members of the treatment group change in terms of the dependent variable because their participation in the study makes them feel special

Histogram: A graphic for quantitative variables in which the variable's distribution is displayed with adjacent bars

Historical events research: Research in which social events of only one time period in the past are studied

History effects: A source of causal invalidity that occurs when something other than the treatment influences scores on the posttest. Also called *external events*

Hypotheses: A tentative statement about empirical reality, involving a relationship between two or more variables

Idiosyncratic variation: Variation in responses to a question that is caused by individuals' reactions to particular words or ideas in the question instead of by variation in the concept that the question is intended to measure

Illogical reasoning: When someone prematurely jumps to conclusions or argues on the basis of invalid assumptions

Impact evaluation or analysis: Analysis of the extent to which a treatment or other service has an effect

Independent variable: A variable that is hypothesized to cause, or lead to, variation in the dependent variable

Index: A composite measure based on summing, averaging, or otherwise combining the responses to multiple questions that are intended to measure the same variable

Inductive research: The type of research in which general conclusions are drawn from specific data; compare to *deductive research*

In-person interview: A survey in which an interviewer questions respondents and records their answers

Inputs: Resources, raw materials, clients, and staff that go into a program

Institutional Review Board: A group of organizational and community representatives required by federal law to review the ethical issues in all proposed research that is federally funded, involves human subjects, or has any potential for harm to subjects

Integrative approach: An orientation to evaluation research that expects researchers to respond to the concerns of people involved with the program as well as to the standards and goals of the social scientific community

Intensive interviewing: A qualitative method that involves open-ended, relatively unstructured questioning in which the interviewer seeks in-depth information on the interviewee's feelings, experiences, and perceptions (from Lofland & Lofland 1984: 12)

Inter-item reliability: An approach that calculates reliability based on the correlation among multiple items used to measure a single concept; also known as internal consistency

Internal validity (causal validity): The type of validity that is achieved when a conclusion that one phenomenon leads to or results in another phenomenon—or doesn't lead to or result in another—is correct

Inter-observer reliability: When similar measurements are obtained by different observers rating the same persons, events, or places

Interpretive questions: Questions included in a questionnaire or interview schedule to help explain answers to other important questions

Interpretivism: The belief that reality is socially constructed and that the goal of social scientists is to understand what meanings people give to that reality. Max Weber termed the goal of interpretivist research *verstehen*, or "understanding."

Intersubjective agreement: Agreement between scientists about the nature of reality; often upheld as a more reasonable goal for science than certainty about an objective reality

Interval level of measurement: A measurement of a variable in which the numbers indicating a variable's values represent fixed measurement units but have no absolute, or fixed, zero point

Interview schedule: The survey instrument containing the questions asked by the interviewer for an in-person interview or phone survey

Intra-observer or intra-rater reliability: Consistency of ratings by an observer of an unchanging phenomenon at two or more points in time

John Henry effect (compensatory rivalry): A type of contamination in experimental designs that occurs when control group members perceive that they are being denied some advantage that the experimental group members are getting and increase their efforts by way of compensation

Jottings: Brief notes that serve as memory joggers when writing actual field notes at a later time

Level of measurement: The mathematical precision with which the values of a variable can be expressed. The nominal level of measurement, which is qualitative, has no mathematical interpretation; the quantitative levels of measurement (ordinal, interval, and ratio) are progressively more precise mathematically.

Likert-type responses: Survey responses in which respondents indicate the extent to which they agree or disagree with statements

Longitudinal research design: A study in which data are collected that can be ordered in time; also defined as research in which data are collected at two or more points in time

Mailed (self-administered) survey: A survey involving a mailed questionnaire to be completed by the respondent

Marginal distributions: The summary distributions in the margins of a crosstabulation that correspond to the frequency distribution of the row variable and of the column variable

Matching: A procedure for equating the characteristics of individuals in different comparison groups in an experiment

Matrix: A form on which can be recorded systematically particular features of multiple cases or instances that a qualitative data analyst needs to examine

Mean: The arithmetic, or weighted average, computed by adding up the value of all the cases and dividing by the total number of cases

Measure of association: A type of descriptive statistic that summarizes the strength of an association

Measurement validity: Exists when a measure actually measures what we think it does

Mechanism: A discernible process that creates a causal connection between two variables

Median: The position average, or the point that divides a distribution in half (the 50th percentile)

Meta-analysis: The quantitative analysis of findings from multiple studies

Mixed-mode surveys: Surveys that are conducted by more than one method, allowing the strengths of one survey design to compensate for the weaknesses of another and maximizing the likelihood of securing data from different types of respondents; for example, nonrespondents in a mailed survey may be interviewed in person or over the phone

Mode: The most frequent value in a distribution; also termed the probability average

Multiple group before-and-after design: A type of quasi-experimental design in which several before-and-after comparison are made involving the same independent and dependent variables but different groups

Mutually exclusive attributes: A variable's attributes or values are mutually exclusive when every case can be classified as having only one attribute

Needs assessment: A type of evaluation research that attempts to determine the needs of some population that might be met with a social program

Negatively skewed: A distribution in which cases cluster to the right side, and the left tail of the distribution is longer than the right

Nominal level of measurement: Variables whose values have no mathematical interpretation; they vary in kind or quality, but not in amount

Nonequivalent control group design: A quasi-experimental design in which there are experimental and comparison groups that are designated before the treatment occurs but are not created by random assignment

Nonprobability sampling methods: Sampling methods in which the probability of selection of population elements is unknown

Nonresponse: Entities such as people who do not participate in a study even though they were selected for the sample

Nonspurious: A criterion for establishing a causal relationship between two variables; when a relationship between two variables is not due to variation in a third variable

Nuremberg War Crimes Trials: U.S.-conducted court trials that exposed horrific medical experiments conducted by Nazi doctors and others in the name of "science"

Omnibus survey: A survey that covers a range of topics of interest to different social scientists

Open-ended question: A survey question to which the respondent replies in his or her own words, either by writing or by talking

Operationalization: The process of specifying the operations that will indicate the value of a variable for each case

Operations: A procedure for identifying or indicating the value of cases on a variable

Ordinal level of measurement: A measurement of a variable in which the numbers indicating a variable's value specify only the order of the cases, permitting "greater than" and "less than" distinctions

Outcomes: The impact of the program process on the cases processed

Outlier: An exceptionally high or low value in a variable distribution

Outputs: The services delivered or new products produced by the program process

Overgeneralization: Occurs when we unjustifiably conclude that what is true for some cases is true for all cases

Participant observation: A qualitative method for gathering data that involves developing a sustained relationship with people while they go about their normal activities

Participatory action research: A type of research in which the researcher involves some organizational members as active participants throughout the process of studying an organization; the goal is making changes in the organization

Peer review: A process in which a journal editor sends a submitted article to two or three experts who judge whether the paper should be accepted, revised and resubmitted, or rejected; the experts also provide comments to explain their decision and guide any revisions

Percentages: Relative frequencies, computed by dividing the frequency of cases in a particular category by the total number of cases and multiplying by 100

Periodicity: A sequence of elements in a list to be sampled that varies in some regular, periodic pattern

Phone survey: A survey in which interviewers question respondents over the phone and then record their answers

Placebo effect: A source of treatment misidentification that can occur when subjects receive a treatment that they consider likely to be beneficial and improve because of the expectation rather than because of the treatment

Population: The entire set of elements (e.g., individuals, cities, states, countries, prisons, schools) in which we are interested

Positively skewed: Describes a distribution in which the cases cluster to the left, and the right tail of the distribution is longer than the left

Positivism: The belief, shared by most scientists, that there is a reality that exists quite apart from our own perception of it, although our knowledge of this reality may never be complete

Postpositivism: The belief that there is an empirical reality but that our understanding of it is limited by its complexity and by the biases and other limitations of researchers

Posttest: In experimental research, this is the measurement of an outcome (dependent) variable after an experimental intervention or treatment (independent variable)

Pretest: In experimental research, this is the measurement of an outcome (dependent) variable prior to an experimental intervention or treatment (independent variable)

Pretested questionnaire: A questionnaire that has been tested in advance of actual use in a study; in pretesting, the researchers may try answering the questions themselves, or they may try the questionnaire on a small sample of individuals

Privacy Certificate: A document that protects researchers from being legally required to disclose confidential information

Probability of selection: The likelihood that an element will be selected from the population for inclusion in the sample

Probability sampling methods: Sampling methods that allow us to know in advance how likely it is that any element will be selected from the population for inclusion in the sample. In a census, of all the elements of a population, the probability that any particular element will be selected is 1.0 because everyone will be selected. If half the elements in the population are sampled on the basis of chance (say, by tossing a coin), the probability of selection for each element is one half, or 0.5. When the size of the sample as a proportion of the population decreases, so does the probability of selection.

Process evaluation (program monitoring): Evaluation research that investigates the process of service delivery

Program process: The complete treatment or service delivered by the program

Program theory: A descriptive or prescriptive model of how a program operates and produced effects

Progressive focusing: The process by which a qualitative analyst interacts with the data and gradually refines his or her focus

Proportionate stratified sampling: Sampling method in which elements are selected from strata in exact proportion to their representation in the population

Purposive sampling: A nonprobability sampling method in which elements are selected for a purpose, usually because of their unique position

Qualitative methods: Methods such as participant observation, intensive interviewing, and focus groups that are designed to capture social life as participants experience it, rather than in categories predetermined by the researcher. Data that are treated as qualitative are mostly written or spoken words, or observations that do not have a direct numerical interpretation.

Quantitative methods: Methods such as surveys and experiments that record variation in social life in terms of categories that vary in amount. Data that are treated as quantitative are either numbers or attributes that can be ordered in terms of magnitude.

Quasi-experimental design: A research design in which there is a comparison group that is comparable with the experimental group in critical ways, but subjects are not randomly assigned to the comparison and experimental groups

Questionnaire: The survey instrument containing the questions for a self-administered survey

Quota sampling: A nonprobability sampling method in which elements are selected to ensure that the sample represents certain characteristics in proportion to their prevalence in the population

Random assignment: A procedure by which each experimental subject is placed in a group randomly

Random digit dialing: The random dialing by a machine of phone numbers within designated prefixes, which creates a random sample for phone surveys

Random number table: A table containing lists of numbers that are ordered solely on the basis of chance; it is used for drawing random samples

Random sampling error: Differences between the population and the sample that are due only to chance factors (random error), not to systematic sampling error. Random sampling error may or may not result in an unrepresentative sample. The magnitude of sampling error due to chance factors can be estimated statistically.

Random selection: The fundamental element of probability samples. The essential characteristic of random selection is that every element of the population has a known and independent chance of being selected into the sample.

Range: The true upper limit in a distribution minus the true lower limit (or the highest rounded value minus the lowest rounded value, plus one)

Ratio level of measurement: A measurement of a variable in which the numbers indicating a variable's values represent fixed measuring units and an absolute zero point

Reactive effects: The changes in individual or group behavior that are due to being observed or otherwise studied

Reductionism or reductionist fallacy: An error in reasoning that occurs when incorrect conclusions about group-level processes are based on individual-level data

Reference period: A time frame in which a survey question asks respondents to place a particular behavior (e.g., in the last 6 months)

Reflexivity: A narrative provided by the researcher that offers a reflection on the process of research, including any obstacles encountered

Reliability measures: A measure is reliable when it yields consistent scores or observations of a given phenomenon on different occasions. Reliability is a prerequisite for measurement validity.

Repeated cross-sectional design (trend study): A longitudinal study in which data are collected at two or more points in time from different samples of the same population

Repeated measures panel design: A quasi-experimental design consisting of several pretest and posttest observations of the same group

Replacement sampling: A method of sampling in which sample elements are returned to the sampling frame after being selected so they may be sampled again

Replications: Repetitions of a study using the same research methods to answer the same research question

Representative sample: A sample that looks like the population from which it was selected in all respects that are potentially relevant to the study. The distribution of characteristics among the elements of a representative sample is the same as the distribution of those characteristics among the total population. In an unrepresentative sample, some characteristics are overrepresented or underrepresented.

Research circle: A diagram of the elements of the research process, including theories, hypotheses, data collection, and data analysis

Resistance to change: The reluctance to change our ideas in light of new information

Reverse code: Recoding response choices that were originally coded to reflect both favorable and unfavorable attitudes toward a phenomenon as indicative of either all favorable or all unfavorable, so the index is measuring the same thing

Reverse outlining: Outlining the sections in an already written draft of a paper or report to improve its organization in the next draft

Sample: A subset of elements from the larger population

Sample generalizability: Exists when a conclusion based on a sample, or subset, of a larger population holds true for that population

Sampling error: Any difference between the characteristics of a sample and the characteristics of the population from which it was drawn. The larger the sampling error, the less representative the sample is of the population.

Sampling frame: A list of all elements or other units containing the elements in a population

Sampling interval: The number of cases from one sampled case to another in a systematic random sample

Sampling units: Units listed at each stage of a multistage sampling design

Saturation point: The point at which subject selection is ended in intensive interviewing, when new interviews seem to yield little additional information

Scale: A composite measure of one concept created from a series of two or more questions

Secondary data analysis: Analysis of data collected by someone other than the researcher or the researcher's assistant

Selection bias: A source of internal (causal) invalidity that occurs when the characteristics of experimental and comparison groups are not equivalent

Selective observation: Choosing to look only at things that are in line with our preferences or beliefs

Serendipitous findings: Unexpected patterns in data, which stimulate new ideas or theoretical approaches; also known as *anomalous findings*

Simple random sampling: A method of sampling in which every sample element is selected only on the basis of change, through a random process

Skewness: The extent to which cases are clustered more at one or the other end of the distribution of a quantitative variable rather than in a symmetric pattern around the center. Skew can be positive (a "right skew"), with the number of cases tapering off in the positive direction, or negative (a "left skew"), with the number of cases tapering off in the negative direction.

Skip pattern: The unique combination of questions created in a survey by *filter questions* and *contingent questions*

Social science: A set of logical, systematic, documented methods for investigating nature and natural processes; the knowledge produced by these investigations

Social science approach: An orientation to evaluation research that expects researchers to emphasize the importance of researcher expertise and maintenance of autonomy from program stakeholders

Solomon four-group design: A type of experimental design that combines a randomized pretest–posttest control group design with a randomized posttest-only design, resulting in two experimental groups and two comparison groups

Split-ballot design: Unique questions or other modifications in a survey administered to randomly selected subsets of the total survey sample, so that more questions can be included in the entire survey or so that responses to different question versions can be compared

Split-halves reliability: Reliability achieved when responses to the same questions by two randomly selected halves of a sample are about the same

Spurious relationship: A relationship between two variables that is due to variation in a third variable

Stakeholder approach: An orientation to evaluation research that expects researchers to be responsive primarily to the people involved with the program

Stakeholders: Individuals and groups who have some basis of concern with the program

Standard deviation: The square root of the average squared deviation from the mean of each case

Statistical significance: An association that is not likely to be due to chance, judged by the analyst using a criterion set

Stratified random sampling: A method of sampling in which sample elements are selected separately from population strata that are identified in advance by the researcher

Subject fatigue: Problems caused by panel members growing weary of repeated interviews and dropping out of a study or becoming so used to answering the standard questions in the survey that they start giving stock or thoughtless answers

Survey research: Research in which information is obtained from a sample of individuals through their responses to questions about themselves or others

Surveys: Popular and versatile research instruments using a question format. Surveys can either be self-administered or read by an interviewer.

Systematic observation: A strategy that increases the reliability of observational data by using explicit rules that standardize coding practices across observers

Systematic random sampling: A method of sampling in which sample elements are selected from a list or from sequential files, with every nth element being selected after the first element is selected randomly within the first interval

Systematic review: A paper that attempts to gather relevant evaluative studies, critically appraise them, and come to judgments about what works using explicit, transparent, state-of-the-art methods

Systematic sampling error: Overrepresentation or underrepresentation of some population characteristics in a sample due to the method used to select the sample. A sample shaped by systematic sampling error is a biased sample.

Tacit knowledge: In field research, a credible sense of understanding of social processes that reflects the researcher's awareness of participants' actions as well as their words, and of what they fail to state, feel deeply, and take for granted

Target population: A set of elements larger than or different from the population sampled, to which the researcher would like to generalize study findings

Test–retest reliability: A measurement showing that measures of a phenomenon at two points in time are highly correlated, if the phenomenon has not changed, or have changed only as much as the phenomenon itself

Theoretical constructs: Constructs that describe what is important to look at to understand, explain, or predict a phenomenon

Theoretical sampling: A sampling method recommended for field researchers by Glaser and Strauss (1967). A theoretical sample is drawn in a sequential fashion, with settings or individuals selected for study as earlier observations or interviews indicate that these settings or individuals are influential.

Theory: A logically interrelated set of propositions about empirical reality. Examples of criminological theories are social learning, routine activities, labeling, general strain, and social disorganization theory. *See also specific theories.*

Theory-driven evaluation: A program evaluation that is guided by a theory that specifies the process by which the program has an effect

Thick description: A method used in case reports that clarifies the context and makes it possible for the reader vicariously to experience it

Time order: A criterion for establishing a causal relationship between two variables. The variation in the independent variable must occur before the variation in the dependent variable.

Time series design: A quasi-experimental design consisting of many pretest and posttest observations of the same group

Transnational research: Explores how cultures and nations deal with crime that transcends their borders

Treatment misidentification: A problem that occurs in an experiment when the treatment itself is not what causes the outcome, but rather the outcome is caused by some intervening process that the research has not identified and is not aware of

Triangulation: The use of multiple methods to study one research question

True experiment: Experiment in which subjects are assigned randomly to an experimental group that receives the treatment or other manipulation of the independent variable and a comparison group that does not receive the treatment. Outcomes are measured in a posttest.

Unimodal: A distribution of a variable in which there is only one value that is most frequent

Unit of analysis: The level of social life on which a research question is focused, such as individuals, groups, towns, or nations

Units of observation: The cases about which measures actually are obtained in a sample

Unobtrusive measure: A measurement based on physical traces or other data that are collected without the knowledge or participation of the individuals or groups that generated the data

Variability: The extent to which cases are spread out through the distribution or clustered in just one location

Variable: A characteristic or property that can vary (take on different values or attributes)

Variance: A statistic that measures the variability of a distribution as the average squared deviation of each score from the mean of all scores

Verstehen: Understanding human behavior by identifying the meaning that social actors give to their actions (term coined by Max Weber)

Web survey: A survey designed on a server; respondents are asked to visit a website and respond to the web questionnaire by checking answers.

References

Abbott, Andrew. 1994. "History and Sociology: The Lost Synthesis." Pp. 77–112 in *Engaging the Past: The Uses of History Across the Social Sciences,* edited by Eric H. Monkkonen. Durham, NC: Duke University Press.

Abrams, Philip. 1982. *Historical Sociology.* Ithaca, NY: Cornell University Press.

Academy of Criminal Justice Sciences (ACJS). 2000. "Code of Ethics." Retrieved September 26, 2009, from http://www.acjs.org.pubs./167_171_2922.cfm

Adair, G., T. W. Dushenko, and R. C. L. Lindsay. 1985. "Ethical Regulations and Their Impact on Research Practice." *American Psychologist* 40: 59–72.

Agnew, R. 1986. "Work and Delinquency Among Juveniles Attending School." *Journal of Criminal Justice* 9: 19–41.

Agnew, R. 1992. "Foundations of General Strain Theory of Crime and Delinquency." *Criminology,* 30: 475–499.

Alarid, Leanne Fiftal, Velmer S. Burton, Jr., and Francis T. Cullen, 2000. "Gender and Crime Among Felony Offenders: Assessing the Generality of Social Control and Differential Association Theories." *Journal of Research in Crime and Delinquency* 37: 171–199.

Alfred, Randall. 1976. "The Church of Satan." Pp. 180–202 in *The New Religious Consciousness,* edited by Charles Glock and Robert Bellah. Berkeley: University of California Press.

Altheide, David L. and John M. Johnson. 1994. "Criteria for Assessing Interpretive Validity in Qualitative Research." Pp. 485–499 in *Handbook of Qualitative Research,* edited by Norman K. Denzin and Yvonna S. Lincoln. Thousand Oaks, CA: Sage.

Amenta, E. and J. D. Poulsen. 1994. "Where to Begin: A Survey of Five Approaches to Selecting Independent Variables for Qualitative Comparative Analysis." *Sociological Methods and Research* 23(1): 22–53.

American Sociological Association. 1997. *Code of Ethics.* Washington, DC: American Sociological Association.

American Sociological Association. 1999. *Code of Ethics and Policies and Procedures of the ASA Committee on Professional Ethics.* Washington, DC: Author.

Anderson, Elijah. 1999. *Code of the Street: Decency, Violence, and the Moral Life of the Inner City.* New York: Norton.

Anderson, Elijah. 2003. "Jelly's Place: An Ethnographic Memoir." *Symbolic Interaction* 26: 217–237.

Archer, Dane and Rosemary Gartner. 1984. *Violence and Crime in Cross-National Perspective.* New Haven, CT: Yale University Press.

Arwood, T. and S. Panicker. 2007. "Assessing Risk in Social and Behavioral Sciences." *Collaborative Institutional Training Initiative.* Retrieved June 5, 2008, from https://www.citiprogram.org/members/learners

Asmussen, Kelly J. and John W. Creswell. 1995. "Campus Response to a Student Gunman." *Journal of Higher Education,* 66(5): 575–591.

Babor, Thomas F., Robert S. Stephens, and G. Alan Marlatt. 1987. "Verbal Report Methods in Clinical Research on Alcoholism: Response Bias and Its Minimization." *Journal of Studies on Alcohol* 48(5): 410–424.

Bachman, Ronet. 2000. "A Comparison of Annual Incidence Rates and Contextual Characteristics of Intimate Perpetrated Violence Against Women From the National Crime Victimization Survey (NCVS) and the National Violence Against Women Survey (NVAWS)." *Violence Against Women* 6(8): 839–867.

Bachman, Ronet and Linda Saltzman. 1995. "Violence Against Women: Estimates From the Redesigned National Crime Victimization Survey." *Bureau of Justice Statistics Special Report.* Washington, DC: U.S. Department of Justice.

Ball, R. A. and G. D. Curry. 1995. "The Logic of Definition in Criminology: Purposes and Methods for Defining Gangs." *Criminology* 33(2): 225–245.

Bandura, Albert, Dorothea Ross, and Sheila A. Ross. 1963. "Imitation of Film-Mediated Aggressive Models." *Journal of Abnormal and Social Psychology* 66: 3–11.

Barringer, Felicity. 1993. "Majority in Poll Back Ban on Handguns." *New York Times,* June 4, p. A14.

Baskin, D. R. and I. B. Sommers. 1998. *Casualties of Community Disorder: Women's Careers in Violent Crime.* Boulder, CO: Westview Press.

Baumrind, D. 1964. "Some Thoughts on Ethics of Research: After Reading Milgram's 'Behavioral Study of Obedience.'" *American Psychologist* 19(6): 421–423.

Baumrind, D. 1985. "Research Using Intentional Deception: Ethical Issues Revisited." *American Psychologist* 40(2):165–174.

Becker, Howard S. 1958. "Problems of Inference and Proof in Participant Observation." *American Sociological Review* 23: 652–660.

Becker, Howard S. 1963. *The Outsiders: Studies in the Sociology of Deviance.* New York: Free Press.

Becker, Howard S. 1986. *Writing for Social Scientists.* Chicago: University of Chicago Press. (This can be ordered directly from the American Sociological Association, 1722 N Street NW, Washington, DC 20036, 202–833–3410.)

Bellah, Robert N., Richard Madsen, William M. Sullivan, Ann Swidler, and Steven M. Tipton. 1985. *Habits of the Heart: Individualism and Commitment in American Life.* New York: Harper & Row.

Belousov, Konstantin, Tom Horlick-Jones, Michael Bloor, Jakov Gilinsky, Valentin Golbert, Jakov Kostikovsky, et al. 2007. "Any Port in a Storm: Fieldwork Difficulties in Dangerous and Crisis-Ridden Settings." *Qualitative Research* 7: 155–175.

Bench, L. L. and T. D. Allen. 2003. "Investigating the Stigma of Prison Classification: An Experimental Design." *The Prison Journal* 83(4): 367–382.

Bennett, Lauren, Lisa Goodman, and Mary Ann Dutton. 1999. "Systematic Obstacles to the Criminal Prosecution of a Battering Partner: A Victim Perspective." *Journal of Interpersonal Violence,* 14: 761–772.

Bennett, R. R. 2004. "Comparative Criminology and Criminal Justice Research: The State of Our Knowledge." *Justice Quarterly* 21(1): 1–21.

Berk, Richard A., Alec Campbell, Ruth Klap, and Bruce Western. 1992. "The Deterrent Effect of Arrest: A Bayesian Analysis of Four Field Experiments." *American Sociological Review,* 57: 698–708.

Beyer, William H., Ed. 1968. *CRC Handbook for Tables for Probability and Statistics,* 2nd ed. Boca Raton, FL: CRC Press.

Binder, Arnold and James W. Meeker. 1993. "Implications of the Failure to Replicate the Minneapolis Experimental Findings." *American Sociological Review* 58 (December): 886–888.

Black, Donald J., Ed. 1984. *Toward a General Theory of Social Control.* Orlando, FL: Academic Press.

Boba, Rachel. 2009. *Crime Analysis With Crime Mapping.* Thousand Oaks, CA: Sage.

Booth, Wayne C., Gregory G. Colomb, and Joseph M. Williams. 1995. *The Craft of Research.* Chicago: University of Chicago Press.

Boruch, Robert F. 1997. *Randomized Experiments for Planning and Evaluation: A Practical Guide.* Thousand Oaks, CA: Sage.

Braga, A. A., D. L. Weisburd, E. J. Waring, L. G. Mazerolle, W. Spelman, and F. Gajewski. 1999. "Problem-Oriented Policing in Violent Crime Places: A Randomized Controlled Experiment." *Criminology* 37(4): 541–580.

Brame, R. and D. L. MacKenzie. 1996. "Shock Incarceration and Positive Adjustment During Community Supervision: A Multisite Evaluation." In *Correctional Boot Camps: A Tough Intermediate Sanction,* edited by D. L. MacKenzie and E. E. Herbert, Washington, DC: National Institute of Justice, U.S. Department of Justice.

Brener, Nancy D., Thomas R. Simon, Etienne G. Krug, and Richard Lowry. 1999. "Recent Trends in Violence-Related Behaviors Among High School Students in the United States." *Journal of the American Medical Association* 282(5): 133–147.

Brewer, J. and Hunter, A. 1989. *Multimethod Research: A Synthesis of Styles.* Newbury Park, CA: Sage.

Bridges, George S. and Joseph G. Weis. 1989. "Measuring Violent Behavior: Effects of Study Design on Reported Correlates of Violence." Pp. 14–24 in *Violent Crime, Violent Criminals,* edited by Neil Alan Weiner and Marvin E. Wolfgang. Newbury Park, CA: Sage.

Broder, David S. 2000. "Don't Toy With the Census." *The Washington Post,* April 4, p. A29.

Broskoske, Steve. 2005. "How to Prevent Paper Recycling." *The Teaching Professor* 19: 1–4.

Bureau of Justice Statistics. 1994. *Sourcebook of Criminal Justice Statistics: 1994.* Washington, DC: U.S. Department of Justice.

Bureau of Justice Statistics. 1995. *Sourcebook of Criminal Statistics: 1995.* Washington, DC: U.S. Department of Justice.

Bureau of Justice Statistics. 2002. "Nation's Violent Crime Victimization Rate Falls 10 Percent." Press Release, September 9. Retrieved November 15, 2009, from www.ojp.usdoj.gov/bjs/pub/press/cv01pr.htm

Bureau of Justice Statistics. 2006. "Prison Statistics." Retrieved November 15, 2009, from www.ojp.usdoj.gov/bjs/ prisons.htm

Burt, Martha R. 1996. "Homelessness: Definitions and Counts." Pp. 15–23 in *Homelessness in America,* edited by Jim Baumohl. Phoenix, AZ: Oryx.

Bushman, Brad J. 1995. "Moderating Role of Trait Aggressiveness in the Effects of Violent Media on Aggression." *Journal of Personality and Social Psychology* 69(5): 950–960.

Bushway, S. and P. Reuter. 1997. "Labor Markets and Crime Risk Factors." In *Preventing Crime: What Works, What Doesn't, What's Promising,* edited by L. W. Sherman, D. Gottfredson, D. MacKenzie, J. Eck, P. Reuter, and S. Bushway. Unpublished report by the Department of Criminology and Criminal Justice, University of Maryland.

Butterfield, Fox. 1996. "After 10 Years, Juvenile Crime Begins to Drop." *New York Times,* August 9, pp. A1, A25.

Buzawa, Eva S. and Carl G. Buzawa. 1996. *Domestic Violence: The Criminal Justice Response,* 2nd ed. Thousand Oaks, CA: Sage.

Campbell, Donald T. and Julian C. Stanley. 1996. *Experimental and Quasi-Experimental Designs for Research.* Chicago: Rand McNally.

Campbell, Donald T. and M. Jean Russo. 1999. *Social Experimentation.* Thousand Oaks, CA: Sage.

Campbell, Richard T. 1992. "Longitudinal Research." Pp. 1146–1158 in *Encyclopedia of Sociology,* edited by Edgar F. Borgatta and Marie L. Borgatta. New York: Macmillan.

Campbell, T. T. and D. W. Fiske. 1959. "Convergent and Discriminant Validity by the Multi-Trait, Multi-Method Matrix." *Psychological Bulletin* 56: 126–139.

Cantor, David. 1984. *Comparing Bounded and Unbounded Three- and Six-Month Reference Periods in Rate Estimation.* Washington, DC: Bureau of Social Science Research.

Cantor, David. 1985. "Operational and Substantive Differences in Changing the NCS Reference Period." Pp. 125–137 in *Proceedings of the American Statistical Association, Social Statistics Section.* Washington, DC: American Statistical Association.

Cao, L., A. Adams, and V. J. Jensen. 1997. "A Test of the Black Subculture of Violence Thesis: A Research Note." *Criminology* 35(2): 367–379.

Carrington, P. J., and J. L. Schulenberg. 2008. "Structuring Police Discretion: The Effect on Referrals to Youth Court." *Criminal Justice Policy Review* 19: 349–367.

Catalano, Shannan. 2006. *Criminal Victimization, 2005.* (NCJ 214644.) Washington, DC: U.S. Department of Justice, Bureau of Justice Statistics.

Cava, A., R. Cushman, and K. Goodman. 2007. "HIPPA and Human Subjects Research." *Collaborative Institutional Training Initiative.* Retrieved June 5, 2008, from https://www.citiprogram.org/members/learners

Cavender, Gray and Lisa Bond-Maupin. 2000. "Fear and Loathing on Reality Television: An Analysis of *America's Most Wanted* and *Unsolved Mysteries.*" Pp. 51–57 in *Criminology: Perspectives,* edited by Steven Cooper. Bellevue, WA: Coursewise.

Chalk, Rosemary and Joel H. Garner. 2001. "Evaluating Arrest for Intimate Partner Violence: Two Decades of Research and Reform." *New Directions for Evaluation* 90: 9–23.

Chen, H. 1990. *Theory-Driven Evaluations.* Newbury Park, CA: Sage.

Chen, Huey-Tsyh and Peter H. Rossi. 1987. "The Theory-Driven Approach to Validity." *Evaluation and Program Planning* 10: 95–103.

Coffey, Amanda and Paul Atkinson. 1996. *Making Sense of Qualitative Data: Complementary Research Strategies.* Thousand Oaks, CA: Sage.

Converse, J. M. 1984. Attitude measurement in psychology and sociology: The early years. Pp. 3–40, in *Surveying Subjective Phenomena, vol. 2,* edited by Charles F. Turner and Elizabeth Martin. New York: Russell Sage Foundation.

Cook, Philip J. and John H. Laub. 1998. "The Epidemic in Youth Violence." In *Youth Violence: Crime and Justice* (vol. 24), edited by Michael Tonry and Mark H. Moore. Chicago: University of Chicago Press.

Cook, Thomas D. and Donald T. Campbell. 1979. *Quasi-Experimentation: Design and Analysis Issues for Field Settings.* Chicago: Rand McNally.

Cooper, Harris and Larry V. Hedges. 1994. "Research Synthesis as a Scientific Enterprise." Pp. 3–14 in *The Handbook of Research Synthesis*, edited by Harris Cooper and Larry V. Hedges. New York: Russell Sage Foundation.

Costner, Herbert L. 1989. "The Validity of Conclusions in Evaluation Research: A Further Development of Chen and Rossi's Theory-Driven Approach." *Evaluation and Program Planning* 12: 345–353.

Cullen, Dave. 2009. *Columbine.* New York: Twelve.

D'Amico, Elizabeth J. and Kim Fromme. 2002. "Brief Prevention for Adolescent Risk-Taking Behavior." *Addiction* 97: 563–574.

Davis, Ryan. 1999. "Study: Search Engines Can't Keep Up With Expanding Net." *The Boston Globe,* July 8, pp. C1, C3.

Decker, Scott H. and Barrik Van Winkle. 1996. *Life in the Gang: Family, Friends, and Violence.* Cambridge, UK: Cambridge University Press.

Dentler, Robert A. 2002. *Practicing Sociology: Selected Fields.* Westport, CT: Praeger.

Denzin, Norman K. and Yvonna S. Lincoln. 1994. "Introduction: Entering the Field of Qualitative Research." Pp. 1–17 in *Handbook of Qualitative Research,* edited by Norman K. Denzin and Yvonna S. Lincoln. Thousand Oaks, CA: Sage.

Denzin, Norman K. and Yvonna S. Lincoln, Eds. 2000. *The Handbook of Qualitative Research,* 2nd ed. Thousand Oaks, CA: Sage.

Dewan, Shaila K. 2004a. "As Murders Fall, New Tactics Are Tried Against Remainder." *New York Times,* December 31, pp. A24–A25.

Dewan, Shaila K. 2004b. "New York's Gospel of Policing by Data Spreads Across U.S." *New York Times,* April 26, pp. A1, C16.

Dillman, Don A. 1978. *Mail and Telephone Surveys: The Total Design Method.* New York: Wiley.

Dillman, Don A. 2000. *Mail and Internet Surveys: The Tailored Design Method,* 2nd ed. New York: John Wiley & Sons.

Duggan, Paul, Michael D. Shear, and Marc Fisher. 1999. "Killers Fused Violent Fantasy, Reality." *The Washington Post,* April 22, p. A1.

Duncombe, Jean and Julie Jessop. 2002. "'Doing Rapport' and the Ethics of 'Faking Friendship.'" Pp. 107–122 in *Ethics in Qualitative Research,* edited by Melanie Mauthner, Maxine Birch, Julie Jessop, and Tina Miller. Thousand Oaks, CA: Sage.

Dunford, Franklyn W., David Huizinga, and Delbert Elliott. 1990. "The Role of Arrest in Domestic Assault: The Omaha Police Experiment." *Criminology* 28: 183–206.

Duwe, G., W. Donnay, and R. Tewksbury. 2008. "Does Residential Proximity Matter? A Geographic Analysis of Sex Offense Recidivism." *Criminal Justice and Behavior,* 35: 484–505.

Ehrlich, I. 1975. "The Deterrent Effect of Capital Punishment: A Question of Life and Death." *American Economic Review* 65: 397–417.

Emerson, Robert M., Ed. 1983. *Contemporary Field Research.* Prospect Heights, IL: Waveland Press.

Emerson, Robert M., Rachel I. Fretz, and Linda L. Shaw. 1995. *Writing Ethnographic Fieldnotes.* Chicago: University of Chicago Press.

Erikson, Kai T. 1966. *Wayward Puritans: A Study in the Sociology of Deviance.* New York: Wiley.

Erikson, Kai T. 1967. "A Comment on Disguised Observation in Sociology." *Social Problems* 12: 366–373.

Farrington, David P. 1977. "The Effects of Public Labeling." *British Journal of Criminology* 17(2): 112–125.

Fenno, Richard F. Jr. 1978. *Home Style: House Members in Their Districts.* Boston: Little, Brown.

Ferguson, C. J., C. San Miguel, J. C. Kilburn, J. R. Sanchez, and P. Sanchez. 2007. "The Effectiveness of School-Based Anti-bullying Programs: A Meta-analytic Review." *Criminal Justice Review* 32(4): 401–414.

Fink, Arlene. 1998. *Conducting Research Literature Reviews: From Paper to the Internet.* Thousand Oaks, CA: Sage.

Fleury-Steiner, Benjamin. 2003. *Jurors' Stories of Death: How America's Death Penalty Invests in Inequality.* Ann Arbor: University of Michigan Press.

Fowler, Floyd J. 1988. *Survey Research Methods,* rev. ed. Newbury Park, CA: Sage.

Fowler, Floyd J. 1995. *Improving Survey Questions: Design and Evaluation.* Thousand Oaks, CA: Sage.

Fox, James Alan and Marianne W. Zawitz. 2009. *Homicide Trends in the United States.* Washington, DC: Bureau of Justice Statistics. Retrieved July 1, 2009, from http://www.ojp.usdoj.gov/bjs/homicide/hom trnd.htm

Fraker, Thomas and Rebecca Maynard. 1987. "Evaluating Comparison Group Designs with Employment-Related Programs." *Journal of Human Resources* 22(2): 194–227.

Gallup, G. 1986. *Public Opinion, 1985.* Wilmington, DE: Scholarly Resources Press.

Gallup Poll. 2007. *Americans Skeptical About Preventing Virginia Tech-Like Incidents.* Retrieved July 15, 2010, from http://www.gallup.com/poll/27430/Americans-Skeptical-About-Preventing-Virginia-TechLike-Incidents.aspx

Garner, Joel, Jeffrey Fagan, and Christopher Maxwell. 1995. "Published Findings From the Spousal Assault Replication Program: A Critical Review." *Journal of Quantitative Criminology* 11: 3–28.

Geertz, Clifford. 1973. "Thick Description: Toward an Interpretive Theory of Culture." Pp. 3–30 in *The Interpretation of Cultures,* edited by Clifford Geertz. New York: Basic Books.

Gill, Hannah E. 2004. "Finding a Middle Ground Between Extremes: Notes on Researching Transnational Crime and Violence." *Anthropology Matters Journal* 6: 1–9.

Glaser, Barney G. and Anselm L. Strauss. 1967. *The Discovery of Grounded Theory: Strategies for Qualitative Research.* London: Weidenfeld and Nicholson.

Glover, Judith. 1996. "Epistemological and Methodological Considerations in Secondary Analysis." Pp. 28–38 in *Cross-National Research Methods in the Social Sciences,* edited by Linda Hantrais and Steen Mangen. New York: Pinter.

Goffman, Erving. 1961. *Asylums: Essays on the Social Situation of Mental Patients and Other Inmates.* Garden City, NY: Doubleday.

Goldfinger, Stephen M., Russell K. Schutt, Larry J. Seidman, Winston M. Turner, Walter E. Penk, and George S. Tolomiczenko. 1996. "Self-Report and Observer Measures of Substance Abuse Among Homeless Mentally Ill Persons in the Cross-Section and Over Time." *Journal of Nervous and Mental Disease* 184(11): 667–672.

Goleman, Daniel. 1993. "Pollsters Enlist Psychologists in Quest for Unbiased Results." *New York Times,* September 7, pp. C1, C11.

Gordon, Raymond. 1992. *Basic Interviewing Skills.* Itasca, IL: Peacock.

Gottfredson, D. C. and T. Hirschi. 1990. *A General Theory of Crime.* Palo Alto, CA: Stanford University Press.

Gregg v. Georgia, 428 U.S. 153 (1976).

Grinnell, Frederick. 1992. *The Scientific Attitude*, 2nd ed. New York: Guilford Press.

Grossman, David C., Jolly J. Neckerman, Thomas D. Koepsell, Ping-Yu Liu, Kenneth N. Asher, Kathy Beland, et al. 1997. "Effectiveness of a Violence Prevention Curriculum Among Children in Elementary School: A Randomized Controlled Trial." *Journal of the American Medical Association* 277(20), 1605–1612.

Groves, Robert M. and Mick P. Couper. 1998. *Nonresponse in Household Interview Surveys.* New York: Wiley.

Gruenewald, Paul J., Andrew J. Treno, Gail Taff, and Michael Klitzner. 1997. *Measuring Community Indicators: A Systems Approach to Drug and Alcohol Problems.* Thousand Oaks, CA: Sage.

Guba, Egon G. and Yvonna S. Lincoln. 1989. *Fourth Generation Evaluation.* Newbury Park, CA: Sage.

Guba, Egon G. and Yvonna S. Lincoln. 1994. "Competing Paradigms in Qualitative Research." Pp. 105–117 in *Handbook of Qualitative Research,* edited by Norman K. Denzin and Yvonna S. Lincoln. Thousand Oaks, CA: Sage.

Gubrium, Jaber F. and James A. Holstein. 1997. *The New Language of Qualitative Method.* New York: Oxford University Press.

Gubrium, Jaber F. and James A. Holstein. 2000. "Analyzing Interpretive Practice." Pp. 487–508 in *The Handbook of Qualitative Research*, 2nd ed., edited by Norman Denzin and Yvonna S. Lincoln. Thousand Oaks, CA: Sage.

Hafner, Katie. 2005. "In Challenge to Google, Yahoo Will Scan Books." *New York Times,* October 3, pp. C1, C4.

Hagan, John. 1994. *Crime and Disrepute.* Thousand Oaks, CA: Pine Forge Press.

Hage, Jerald and Barbara Foley Meeker. 1988. *Social Causality.* Boston: Unwin Hyman.

Hagedorn, John. 1988. *People and Folks.* Chicago: Lake View Press.

Haney, C., C. Banks, and Philip G. Zimbardo. 1973. "International Dynamics in a Simulated Prison." *International Journal of Criminology and Penology* 1: 69–97.

Hantrais, Linda and Steen Mangen. 1996. "Method of Management of Cross-National Social Research." Pp. 1–12 in *Cross-National Research Methods in the Social Sciences*, edited by Linda Hantrais and Steen Mangen. New York: Pinter.

Hard, Stephen F., James M. Conway, and Antonia C. Moran. 2006. "Faculty and College Student Beliefs About the Frequency of Student Academic Misconduct." *Journal of Higher Education* 77: 1058–1080.

Harding, Sandra. 1989. "Value-Free Research Is a Delusion." *New York Times,* October 22, p. E24.

Hart, Chris. 1998. *Doing a Literature Review: Releasing the Social Science Research Imagination.* London: Sage.

Heckathorn, Douglas D. 1997. "Respondent-Driven Sampling: A New Approach to the Study of Hidden Populations." *Social Problems* 44: 174–199.

Heimer, Karen and Stacy De Coster. 1999. "The Gendering of Violent Delinquency." *Criminology* 37(2): 277–318.

Hirschel, J. David, Ira W. Hutchison III, and Charles W. Dean. 1992. "The Failure of Arrest to Deter Spouse Abuse." *Journal of Research in Crime and Delinquency* 29(1): 7–33.

Hock, Randolph. 2004. *The Extreme Searcher's Internet Handbook: A Guide for the Serious Searcher.* Medford, NJ: CyberAge.

Hoover, Kenneth R. 1980. *The Elements of Social Scientific Thinking*, 2nd ed. New York: St. Martin's Press.

Howell, J. C. 2003. *Preventing and Reducing Juvenile Delinquency: A Comprehensive Framework.* Thousand Oaks, CA: Sage.

Hoyle, Carolyn and Andrew Sanders. 2000. "Police Response to Domestic Violence: From Victim Choice to Victim Empowerment." *British Journal of Criminology* 40: 14–26.

Huberman, A. Michael and Matthew B. Miles. 1994. "Data Management and Analysis Methods." Pp. 428–444 in *Handbook of Qualitative Research*, edited by Norman K. Denzin and Yvonna S. Lincoln. Thousand Oaks, CA: Sage.

Humphrey, Nicholas. 1992. *A History of the Mind: Evolution and the Birth of Consciousness.* New York: Simon & Schuster.

Humphreys, Laud. 1970. *Tearoom Trade: Impersonal Sex in Public Places.* Chicago: Aldine.

Hunt, Morton. 1985. *Profiles of Social Research: The Scientific Study of Human Interactions.* New York: Russell Sage Foundation.

Huston, P. and C. D. Naylor. 1996. "Health Services Research: Reporting on Studies Using Secondary Data Sources." *Canadian Medical Association Journal 155:* 1697–1702.

James. T. S. and J. M. Granville. 1984. "Practical Issues in Vocational Education for Serious Juvenile Offenders." Pp. 486–506 in *Violent Juvenile Offenders: An Anthology,* edited by R. Mathias, P. DeMuro, and R. Allison. San Francisco: National Council on Crime and Delinquency.

Jervis, Robert. 1996. "Counterfactuals, Causation, and Complexity." Pp. 309–316 in *Counterfactual Thought Experiments in World Politics: Logical, Methodological, and Psychological Perspectives*, edited by Philip E. Tetlock and Aaron Belkin. Princeton, NJ: Princeton University Press.

Johnson, Dirk. 1997. "Party Animals in Fraternities Face the Threat of Extinction." *New York Times*, May 15, pp. A1, A29.

Kandakai, Tina L., James H. Price, Susan K. Telljohann, and Carter A. Wilson. 1999. "Mothers' Perceptions of Factors Influencing Violence in Schools." *Journal of School Health* 69(5): 189–205.

Kaplan, Fred. 2002. "NY Continues to See Plunge in Number of Felonies." *The Boston Globe,* April 15, p. A3.

Kaufman, Sharon R. 1986. *The Ageless Self: Sources of Meaning in Late Life.* Madison: University of Wisconsin Press.

Kemmis, S. and R. McTaggart. 2005. "Participatory Action Research: Communicative Action and the Public Sphere." Pp. 559–603 in *The Sage Handbook of Qualitative Research,* 3rd ed., edited by Norman K. Denzin and Yvonna S. Lincoln. Thousand Oaks, CA: Sage.

Kennedy, David M., Anne M. Piehl, and Anthony A. Braga. 1996. "Youth Violence in Boston: Gun Markets, Serious Youth Offenders, and a Use-Reduction Strategy." *Law and Contemporary Problems* 59: 147–196.

Kincaid, Harold. 1996. *Philosophical Foundations of the Social Sciences: Analyzing Controversies in Social Research.* Cambridge, UK: Cambridge University Press.

King, Gary, Robert O. Keohane, and Sidney Verba. 1994. *Scientific Inference in Qualitative Research.* Princeton, NJ: Princeton University Press.

Klein, Malcolm W. 1971. *Street Gangs and Street Workers.* Englewood Cliffs, NJ: Prentice Hall.

Kobelarcik, E. L., C. A. Alexander, R. P. Singh, and G. M. Shapiro. 1983. "Alternative Reference Periods for the National Crime Survey." In *Proceedings of the American Statistical Association: Section on Survey Methods.* Washington, DC: American Statistical Association.

Koegel, Paul. 1987. *Ethnographic Perspectives on Homeless and Homeless Mentally Ill Women.* Washington, DC: Alcohol, Drug Abuse, and Mental Health Administration, Public Health Service, U.S. Department of Health and Human Services.

Kohn, Alfie. 2008. "Who's Cheating Whom?" *Education Digest* 73: 4–11.

Kohn, Melvin L. 1987. "Cross-National Research as an Analytic Strategy." *American Sociological Review* 52: 713–731.

Korn, J. H. 1997. *Illusions of Reality: A History of Deception in Social Psychology.* Albany: State University of New York Press.

Kupchik, A. 2010. *Homeroom Security: School Discipline in an Age of Fear.* New York: New York University Press.

Kvale, Steinar. 1996. *InterViews: An Introduction to Qualitative Research Interviewing.* Thousand Oaks, CA: Sage.

Kvale, Steinar. 2002. "The Social Construction of Validity." Pp. 299–325 in *The Qualitative Inquiry Reader,* edited by Norman K. Denzin and Yvonna S. Lincoln. Thousand Oaks, CA: Sage.

Labaw, Patricia. 1980. *Advanced Questionnaire Design.* Cambridge, MA: ABT Books.

Lamott, Anne. 1994. *Bird by Bird: Some Instructions on Writing and Life.* New York: Anchor Books.

Larson, Calvin J. 1993. *Pure and Applied Sociological Theory: Problems and Issues.* New York: Harcourt Brace Jovanovich.

Lavrakas, Paul J. 1987. *Telephone Survey Methods: Sampling, Selection, and Supervision.* Newbury Park, CA: Sage.

Lempert, Richard. 1989. "Humility Is a Virtue: On the Publicization of Policy-Relevant Research." *Law & Society Review* 23: 146–161.

Lempert, Richard and Joseph Sanders. 1986. *An Invitation to Law and Social Science: Desert, Disputes, and Distribution.* New York: Longman.

Levine, J. P. 1976. The Potential for Crime Overreporting in Criminal Victimization Surveys. *Criminology* 14: 307–330.

Lewin, Tamar. 2001. "Inmate Education Is Found to Lower Risk of New Arrest." *New York Times,* November 16, p. A18.

Lichtblau, Eric. 2000. "Crime Dip Levels Off; Assault, Rape Up." *New York Times,* December 19, p. A2.

Lipsey, Mark W. and David B. Wilson. 2001. *Practical Meta-Analysis.* Thousand Oaks, CA: Sage.

Liptak, Adam. 2004. "Long Term in Drug Case Fuels Debate on Sentencing." *New York Times,* September 12, p. 16.

Listwan, S. J., J. L. Sundt, A. M. Halsinger, and E. H. Katessam. 2003. "The Effect of Drug Court Programming on Recidivism: The Cincinnati Experience." *Crime and Delinquency* 49: 389–411.

Litwin, Mark S. 1995. *How to Measure Survey Reliability and Validity.* Thousand Oaks, CA: Sage.

Locke, Lawrence F., Stephen J. Silverman, and Waneen Wyrick Spirduso. 1998. *Reading and Understanding Research.* Thousand Oaks, CA: Sage.

Lofland, John and Lyn H. Lofland. 1984. *Analyzing Social Settings: A Guide to Qualitative Observation and Analysis,* 2nd ed. Belmont, CA: Wadsworth.

Lovibond, S. H., X. Mithiran, and W. G. Adams. 1979. "The Effects of Three Experimental Prison Environments on the Behaviour of Non-Convict Volunteer Subjects." *Australian Psychologist* 14: 273–287.

Lynch, Michael and David Bogen. 1997. "Sociology's Asociological 'Core': An Examination of Textbook Sociology in Light of the Sociology of Scientific Knowledge." *American Sociological Review* 62: 481–493.

MacDonald, J. M., A. R. Piquero, R. F. Valois, and K. J. Zullig. 2005. "The Relationship Between Life Satisfaction, Risk-Taking Behaviors, and Youth Violence." *Journal of Interpersonal Violence* 20(11): 1495–1518.

MacKenzie, D. L. 1994. "Results of a Multisite Study of Boot Camp Prisons." *Federal Probation* 58(2): 60–66.

MacKenzie, D. L., R. Brame, D. McDowall, and C. Souryal. 1995. "Boot Camp, Prisons and Recidivism in Eight States." *Criminology* 33(3): 401–430.

MacKenzie, D. L. and C. Souryal. 1995. "Inmate Attitude Change During Incarceration: A Comparison of Boot Camp with Traditional Prison." *Justice Quarterly* 12(2): 125–150.

Mangione, Thomas W. 1995. *Mail Surveys: Improving the Quality.* Thousand Oaks, CA: Sage.

Marini, Margaret Mooney and Burton Singer. 1988. "Causality in the Social Sciences." Pp. 347–409 in *Sociological Methodology*, vol. 18, edited by Clifford C. Clogg. Washington, DC: American Sociological Association.

Marshall, G. D. and P. G. Zimbardo. 1979. "Affective Consequences of Inadequately Explained Physiological Arousal." *Journal of Personality and Social Psychology* 37: 970–988.

Martin, Lawrence L. and Peter M. Kettner. 1996. *Measuring the Performance of Human Service Programs.* Thousand Oaks, CA: Sage.

Martin, Linda G. and Kevin Kinsella. 1995. "Research on the Demography of Aging in Developing Countries." Pp. 356–403 in *Demography of Aging,* edited by Linda G. Martin and Samuel H. Preston. Washington, DC: National Academy Press.

Matt, Georg E. and Thomas D. Cook. 1994. "Threats to the Validity of Research Syntheses." Pp. 503–520 in *The Handbook of Research Synthesis*, edited by Harris M. Cooper and Larry V. Hedges. New York: Russell Sage Foundation.

Maxwell, Joseph A. 1996. *Qualitative Research Design: An Interactive Approach.* Thousand Oaks, CA: Sage.

McLellan, A. Thomas, Lester Luborsky, John Cacciola, Jeffrey Griffith, Frederick Evans, Harriet L. Barr, et al. 1985. "New Data From the Addiction Severity Index: Reliability and Validity in Three Centers." *Journal of Nervous and Mental Disease* 173(7): 412–423.

Merton, Robert K. 1983. "Social Structure and Anomie." *American Sociological Review* 3: 672–682.

Messner, Steven F. and Richard Rosenfeld. 1994. *Crime and the American Dream.* Belmont, CA: Wadsworth.

Milgram, Stanley. 1963. "Behavioral Study of Obedience." *Journal of Abnormal and Social Psychology* 67(3): 371–378.

Milgram, Stanley. 1964. "Issues in the Study of Obedience: A Reply to Baumrind." *American Psychologist* 19: 848–852.

Milgram, Stanley. 1965. "Some Conditions of Obedience and Disobedience to Authority." *Human Relations* 18: 57–75.

Milgram, Stanley. 1974. *Obedience to Authority: An Experimental View.* New York: Harper & Row.

Milgram, Stanley. 1992. *The Individual in a Social World: Essays and Experiments,* 2nd ed. New York: McGraw-Hill.

Miller, Arthur G. 1986. *The Obedience Experiments: A Case Study of Controversy in Social Science.* New York: Praeger.

Miller, Delbert C. 1991. *Handbook of Research Design and Social Measurement*, 5th ed. Newbury Park, CA: Sage.

Miller, H. G., J. N. Gribble, L. C. Mazade, and C. F. Turner. 1998. "Abortion and Breast Cancer: Fact or Artifact?" In *Science of Self Report,* edited by A. Stone. Mahwah, NH: Lawrence Erlbaum.

Miller, JoAnn 2003. "An Arresting Experiment: Domestic Violence Victim Experiences and Perceptions." *Journal of Interpersonal Violence* 18: 695–716.

Miller, Jody. 2000. *One of the Guys: Girls, Gangs, and Gender.* New York: Oxford University Press.

Miller, Jody. 2008. *Getting Played: African American Girls, Urban Inequality and Gendered Violence.* New York University Press.

Miller, Susan. 1999. *Gender and Community Policing: Walking the Talk.* Boston: Northeastern University Press.

Miller, Walter. 1992. *Crime by Youth Gangs and Groups in the United States.* Washington, DC: Office of Juvenile Justice and Delinquency Prevention.

Miller, William L. and Benjamin F. Crabtree. 1999. "Clinical Research: A Multimethod Typology and Qualitative Roadmap." Pp. 3–30 in *Doing Qualitative Research,* 2nd ed., edited by Benjamin Crabtree and William L. Miller. Thousand Oaks, CA: Sage.

Mills, C. Wright. 1959. *The Sociological Imagination.* New York: Oxford University Press.

Mohr, Lawrence B. 1992. *Impact Analysis for Program Evaluation.* Newbury Park, CA: Sage.

Monkkonen, Eric H. 1994. "Introduction." Pp. 1–8 in *Engaging the Past: The Uses of History Across the Social Sciences.* Durham, NC: Duke University Press.

Moore, Joan W. 1978. *Homeboys: Gangs, Drugs, and Prison in the Barrios of Los Angeles.* Philadelphia: Temple University Press.

Moore, Joan W. 1991. *Going Down to the Barrio: Homeboys and Homegirls in Change.* Philadelphia: Temple University Press.

Mosher, Clayton J., Terance D. Miethe, and Dretha M. Phillips. 2002. *The Mismeasure of Crime.* Thousand Oaks, CA: Sage.

Mullins, Carolyn J. 1977. *A Guide to Writing and Publishing in the Social and Behavioral Sciences.* New York: Wiley.

National Institute of Alcohol Abuse and Alcoholism. 1994. "Alcohol-Related Impairment." *Alcohol Alert* 25 (July): 1–5.

National Institute of Alcohol Abuse and Alcoholism. 1997. "Alcohol Metabolism." *Alcohol Alert* 35 (January): 1–4.

National Opinion Research Center (NORC). 1992. *The NORC General Social Survey: Questions and Answers.* Chicago: National Data Program for the Social Sciences.

National Victim Center and the Crime Victims Research and Treatment Center. 1992. *Rape in America: A Report to the Nation.* Arlington, VA: Author.

Neuendorf, Kimberly A. 2002. *The Content Analysis Guidebook.* Thousand Oaks, CA: Sage.

Newbury, D. 2005. Editorial: The Challenge of Visual Studies. *Visual Studies 20:* 1–3.

Newport, Frank. 2000. *Popular Vote in Presidential Race Too Close to Call.* Princeton, NJ: The Gallup Organization.

New York Times. 2009. "Binge Drinking on Campus." Editorial published on June 30, 2009, p. A32.

Nie, Norman H. and Lutz Erbring. 2000. *Internet and Society: A Preliminary Report.* Palo Alto, CA: Stanford Institute for the Quantitative Study of Society.

Novak, David. 2003. "The Evolution of Internet Research: Shifting Allegiances." *Online* 27: 21.

O'Dochartaigh, Niall. 2002. *The Internet Research Handbook: A Practical Guide for Students and Researchers in the Social Sciences.* Thousand Oaks, CA: Sage.

Orcutt, James D. and J. Blake Turner. 1993. "Shocking Numbers and Graphic Accounts: Quantified Images of Drug Problems in the Print Media." *Social Problems* 49 (May): 190–206.

Ousey, Graham C. and Matthew R. Lee. 2004. "Investigating the Connections Between Race, Illicit Drug Markets, and Legal Violence, 1984–1997." *Journal of Research in Crime and Delinquency* 41: 352–383.

Padilla, Felix M. 1992. *The Gang as an American Enterprise.* New Brunswick, NJ: Rutgers University Press.

Pager, D. 2007. *Marked: Race, Crime and Finding Work in an Era of Mass Incarceration.* Chicago: University of Chicago Press.

Papineau, David. 1978. *For Science in the Social Sciences.* London: Macmillan.

Parlett, Malcolm and David Hamilton. 1976. "Evaluation as Illumination: A New Approach to the Study of Innovative Programmes." Pp. 140–157 in *Evaluation Studies Review Annual,* vol. 1, edited by G. Glass. Beverly Hills, CA: Sage.

Pate, Anthony M. and Edwin E. Hamilton. 1992. "Formal and Informal Deterrents to Domestic Violence: The Dade County Spouse Assault Experiment." *American Sociological Review* 57: 691–697.

Paternoster, Raymond, Robert Brame, Ronet Bachman, and Lawrence W. Sherman. 1997. "Do Fair Procedures Matter? The Effect of Procedural Justice on Spouse Assault." *Law & Society Review* 31(1): 163–204.

Paternoster, R., L. E. Saltzman, G. P. Waldo, and T. G. Chiricos. 1983. "Perceived Risk and Social Control: Do Sanctions Really Deter?" *Law & Society Review* 17(3): 457–479.

Patton, Michael Quinn 1997. *Utilization Focused Evaluation: The New Century Text,* 3rd ed. Thousand Oaks, CA: Sage.

Patton, Michael Quinn. 2002. *Qualitative Research & Evaluation Methods,* 3rd ed. Thousand Oaks, CA: Sage.

Pepinsky, Harold E. 1980. "A Sociologist on Police Patrol." Pp. 223–234 in *Fieldwork Experience: Qualitative Approaches to Social Research,* edited by William B. Shaffir, Robert A. Stebbins, and Allan Turowetz. New York: St. Martin's Press.

Peterson, R. A. 2000. *Constructing Effective Questionnaires.* Thousand Oaks, CA: Sage.

Petrosino, A. and J. Lavenberg. 2007. "Systematic Reviews and Meta-Analyses: Best Evidence on 'What Works' for Criminal Justice Decision Makers." *Western Criminology Review* 8(1): 1–15.

Piliavin, Jane Allyn and Irvin M. Piliavin. 1972. "Effect of Blood on Reactions to a Victim." *Journal of Personality and Social Psychology* 23(3), 353–361.

Posavac, E. J. and R. G. Carey. 1997. *Program Evaluation: Methods and Case Studies.* Upper Saddle River, NJ: Prentice Hall.

Powell, Kenneth E., Lois Muir-McClain, and Lakshmi Halasyamani. 1995. "A Review of Selected School-Based Conflict Resolution and Peer Mediation Projects." *Journal of School Health* 65(10): 426–432.

Presley, Cheryl A., Philip W. Meilman, and Rob Lyerla. 1994. "Development of the Core Alcohol and Drug Survey: Initial Findings and Future Directions." *Journal of American College Health* 42: 248–255.

Price, Richard H., Michelle Van Ryn, and Amiram D. Vinokur. 1992. "Impact of a Preventive Job Search Intervention on the Likelihood of Depression Among the Unemployed." *Journal of Health and Social Behavior* 33: 158–167.

Punch, Maurice. 1994. "Politics and Ethics in Qualitative Research." Pp. 83–97 in *Handbook of Qualitative Research,* edited by Norman K. Denzin and Yvonna S. Lincoln. Thousand Oaks, CA: Sage.

Pyrczak, F. 2005. *Evaluating Research in Academic Journals: A Practical Guide to Realistic Evaluation,* 3rd ed. Glendale, CA: Pyrczak Publishing.

Ragin, Charles C. 1994. *Constructing Social Research.* Thousand Oaks, CA: Pine Forge Press.

Rashbaum, William K. 2002. "Reasons for Crime Drop in New York Elude Many." *New York Times,* November 29, p. A28.

Regoli, R. M. and J. D. Hewitt. 1994. *Delinquency in Society: A Child-Centered Approach.* New York: McGraw-Hill.

Reicher, Stephen and S. Alexander Haslam. 2006. "Rethinking the Psychology of Tyranny: The BBC Prison Study." *British Journal of Social Psychology* 45: 1–40.

Reiss, Albert J., Jr. 1971. *The Police and the Public.* New Haven, CT: Yale University Press.

Reiss, Albert J., Jr. and Jeffrey A. Roth. 1993. *Understanding and Preventing Violence.* Washington, DC: National Academy Press.

Reynolds, Paul D. 1979. *Ethical Dilemmas and Social Science Research.* San Francisco: Jossey-Bass.

Richards, Thomas J. and Lyn Richards. 1994. "Using Computers in Qualitative Research." Pp. 445–462 in *Handbook of Qualitative Research*, edited by Norman K. Denzin and Yvonna S. Lincoln. Thousand Oaks, CA: Sage.

Riedel, Marc. 2000. *Research Strategies for Secondary Data: A Perspective for Criminology and Criminal Justice.* Thousand Oaks, CA: Sage.

Ringwalt, Christopher L., Jody M. Greene, Susan T. Ennett, Ronaldo Iachan, Richard R. Clayton, and Carl G. Leukefeld. 1994. *Past and Future Directions of the D.A.R.E. Program: An Evaluation Review.* Research Triangle, NC: Research Triangle Institute.

Rise, Eric W. 1995. *The Martinsville Seven: Race, Rape, and Capital Punishment.* Charlottesville, VA: University Press of Virginia.

Rives, Norfleet W. Jr., and William J. Serow. 1988. *Introduction to Applied Demography: Data Sources and Estimation Techniques.* Sage University Paper Series on Quantitative Applications in the Social Sciences, series no. 07–039. Newbury Park, CA: Sage.

Rodríguez, Havidán, Joseph Trainor, and Enrico L. Quarantelli. 2006. "Rising to the Challenges of a Catastrophe: The Emergent and Prosocial Behavior Following Hurricane Katrina." *Annals of the American Academy of Political and Social Science* 604: 82–101.

Rosen, Lawrence. 1995. "The Creation of the Uniform Crime Report: The Role of Social Science." *Social Science History* 19: 215–238.

Rosenberg, Morris. 1968. *The Logic of Survey Analysis.* New York: Basic Books.

Rosenfeld, Richard, Timothy M. Bray, and Arlen Egley. 1999. "Facilitating Violence: A Comparison of Gang-Motivated, Gang-Affiliated, and Nongang Youth Homicides." *Journal of Quantitative Criminology* 15(4): 496–516.

Rossi, P. H. and H. E. Freeman. 1989. *Evaluation: A Systematic Approach*, 4th ed. Newbury Park, CA: Sage.

Rubin, Herbert J. and Irene S. Rubin. 1995. *Qualitative Interviewing: The Art of Hearing Data.* Thousand Oaks, CA: Sage.

Rueschemeyer, Dietrich, Evelyne Huber Stephens, and John D. Stephens. 1992. *Capitalist Development and Democracy.* Chicago: University of Chicago Press.

Sacks, T., McKendrick, K., DeLeon, G., French, M. T., and McCollister, K. E. 2002. "Benefit–Cost Analysis of a Modified Therapeutic Community for Mentally Ill Chemical Abusers." *Evaluation & Program Planning, 25,* 137–148.

Sampson, Robert J. and John H. Laub. 1990. "Crime and Deviance Over the Life Course: The Salience of Adult Social Bonds." *American Sociological Review* 55(October): 609–627.

Sampson, Robert J. and John H. Laub. 1993. Structural Variations in Juvenile Court Processing: Inequality, the Underclass, and Social Control." *Law & Society Review* 22(2): 285–311.

Sampson, Robert J. and Janet L. Lauritsen. 1994. "Violent Victimization and Offending: Individual-, Situational-, and Community-Level Risk Factors." Pp. 1–114 in *Understanding and Preventing Violence: Vol. 3, Social Influences*, edited by Albert J. Reiss, Jr. and Jeffrey A. Roth. Washington, DC: National Academies Press.

Sampson, Robert J. and Stephen W. Raudenbush. 1999. "Systematic Social Observation of Public Spaces: A New Look at Disorder in Urban Neighborhoods." *American Journal of Sociology* 105: 603–651.

Sampson, Robert J., Stephen W. Raudenbush, and Felton Earls. 1997. "Neighborhoods and Violent Crime: A Multilevel Study of Collective Efficacy." *Science* 277: 918–924.

Sanchez-Jankowski, Martin. 1991. *Islands in the Street.* Berkeley: University of California Press.

Savage, J., R. R. Bennett, and M. Danner. 2008. "Economic Assistance and Crime: A Cross-National Investigation." *European Journal of Criminology* 5: 217–238.

Savelsberg, Joachim L., Ryan King, and Lara Cleveland. 2002. "Politicized Scholarship? Science on Crime and the State." *Social Problems* 49: 327–348.

Savin, H. B. 1973. "Professors and Psychological Researchers: Conflicting Values in Conflicting Roles." *Cognition* 2: 147–149.

Schuman, Howard and Stanley Presser. 1981. *Questions and Answers in Attitude Surveys: Experiments on Question Form, Wording, and Context.* New York: Academic Press.

Sechrest, Lee and Souraya Sidani. 1995. "Quantitative and Qualitative Methods: Is There an Alternative?" *Evaluation and Program Planning* 18: 77–87.

Seltzer, Richard A. 1996. *Mistakes That Social Scientists Make: Error and Redemption in the Research Process.* New York: St. Martin's Press.

Shadish, William R. 1995. "Philosophy of Science and the Quantitative-Qualitative Debates: Thirteen Common Errors." *Evaluation and Program Planning* 18: 63–75.

Shadish, William R., Thomas D. Cook, and Laura C. Leviton, Eds. 1991. *Foundations of Program Evaluation: Theories of Practice.* Thousand Oaks, CA: Sage.

Shaw, Clifford R. and Henry D. McKay. 1942. *Juvenile Delinquency and Urban Areas.* Chicago: University of Chicago Press.

Shepherd, Jane, David Hill, Joel Bristor, and Pat Montalvan. 1996. "Converting an Ongoing Health Study to CAPI: Findings From the National Health and Nutrition Study." Pp. 159–164 in *Health Survey Research Methods Conference Proceedings*, edited by Richard B. Warnecke. Hyattsville, MD: U.S. Department of Health and Human Services.

Sherman, L. W. 1992. *Policing Domestic Violence: Experiments and Dilemmas.* New York: Free Press.

Sherman, L. W. and Richard A. Berk. 1984. "The Specific Deterrent Effects of Arrest for Domestic Assault." *American Sociological Review* 49: 261–272.

Sherman, L. W., P. Gartin, and M. Buerger. 1989. "Hot Spots of Predatory Crime: Routine Activities and the Criminology of Place." *Criminology* 27: 27–56.

Sherman, L. W., D. Gottfredson, D. MacKenzie, J. Eck, P. Reuter, and S. Bushway. 1997. "Preventing Crime: What Works, What Doesn't, What's Promising." Unpublished report by the Department of Criminology and Criminal Justice, University of Maryland.

Sherman, L. W., Douglas A. Smith, Janell D. Schmidt, and Dennis P. Rogan. 1992. "Crime, Punishment, and Stake in Conformity: Legal and Informal Control of Domestic Violence." *American Sociological Review* 57: 680–690.

Sieber, J. E. 1992. *Planning Ethically Responsible Research: A Guide for Students and International Review Boards.* Thousand Oaks, CA: Sage.

Sjoberg, Gideon, Ed. 1967. *Ethics, Politics, and Social Research.* Cambridge, MA: Schenkman.

Sjoberg, Gideon and Roger Nett. 1968. *A Methodology for Social Research.* New York: Harper & Row.

Skinner, Harvey A. and Wen-Jenn Sheu. 1982. "Reliability of Alcohol Use Indices: The Lifetime Drinking History and the MAST." *Journal of Studies on Alcohol* 43(11): 1157–1170.

Skocpol, Theda. 1984. "Emerging Agendas and Recurrent Strategies in Historical Sociology." Pp. 356–391 in *Vision and Method in Historical Sociology*, edited by Theda Skocpol. New York: Cambridge University Press.

Smith, J. 1991. A Methodology for Twenty-First Century Sociology. *Social Forces* 70: 1–17.

Sosin, Michael R., Paul Colson, and Susan Grossman. 1988. *Homelessness in Chicago: Poverty and Pathology, Social Institutions and Social Change.* Chicago: Chicago Community Trust.

St. Jean, Peter K. B. 2007. *Pockets of Crime: Broken Windows, Collective Efficacy, and the Criminal Point of View.* Chicago: University of Chicago Press.

Stake, Robert E. 1995. *The Art of Case Study Research.* Thousand Oaks, CA: Sage.

Straus, M. 1979. "Measuring Intrafamily Conflict and Violence: The Conflict Tactics (TC) Scale." *Journal of Marriage and the Family* 41: 75–88.

Straus, Murray A. and Richard J. Gelles. 1990. *Physical Violence in American Families: Risk Factors and Adaptations to Violence in 8,145 Families.* New Brunswick, NJ: Transaction Publishers.

Strunk, William, Jr., and E. B. White. 1979. *The Elements of Style*, 3rd ed. New York: Macmillan.

Sudman, Seymour. 1976. *Applied Sampling.* New York: Academic Press.

Tannenbaum, F. 1938. *Crime and the Community.* New York: Columbia University Press.

Thornberry, T. P., M. Krohn, A. Lizotte, and S. Bushway. 2008. "The Rochester Youth Development Survey." Albany, NY: Hindelang Criminal Justice Research Center, University of Albany.

Thorne, Barrie. 1993. *Gender Play: Girls and Boys in School.* New Brunswick, NJ: Rutgers University Press.

Thrasher, Frederic. 1927. *The Gang: A Study of 1,313 Gangs in Chicago.* Chicago: University of Chicago Press.

Tjaden, Patricia and Nancy Thoennes. 2000. "Extent, Nature, and Consequences of Intimate Partner Violence." In *Findings From the National Violence Against Women Survey*. Washington, DC: National Institute of Justice, U.S. Department of Justice.

Toby, Jackson. 1957. "Social Disorganization and Stake in Conformity: Complementary Factors in the Predatory Behavior of Hoodlums." *Journal of Criminal Law, Criminology and Police Science* 48: 12–17.

Tolan, P., D. Henry, M. Schoeny, and A. Bass. 2008. "Mentoring Interventions to Affect Juvenile Delinquency and Associated Problems." *Campbell Systematic Reviews* 2008(16). Retrieved November 15, 2009, from http://www .campbellcollaboration.org/library.php

Tonry, Michael and Mark H. Moore. 1998. *Youth Violence: Crime and Justice,* Vol. 24. Chicago: University of Chicago Press.

Torre, M. E. and M. Fine. 2005. "Bar None: Extending Affirmative Action to Higher Education in Prison." *Journal of Social Issues* 61(3): 569–594.

Tourangeau, R. and T. W. Smith. 1996. "Asking Sensitive Questions: The Impact of Data Collection Mode, Question Format, and Question Context." *Public Opinion Quarterly* 60: 275–301.

Turabian, Kate L. 1967. *A Manual for Writers of Term Papers, Theses, and Dissertations*, 3rd ed., rev. Chicago: University of Chicago Press.

Turner, C. F., L. Ku, S. M. Rogers, L. D. Lindberg, J. H. Pleck, and F. L. Sonenstein. 1998. "Adolescent Sexual Behavior, Drug Use, and Violence: Increased Reporting With Computer Survey Technology." *Science* 280: 867–873.

Turner, Charles F. and Elizabeth Martin, Eds. 1984. *Surveying Subjective Phenomena*, Vols. 1 and 2. New York: Russell Sage Foundation.

Tyler, T. 1990. *Why People Obey the Law.* New Haven, CT: Yale University Press.

U.S. Census Bureau. 2009. *Internet Use Triples in Decade, Census Bureau Reports.* Press release. Retrieved August 4, 2010, from http://www.census.gov/newsroom/releases/archives/communication_industries/cb09-84.html

van de Vijver, Fons and Kwok Leung. 1997. *Methods and Data Analysis for Cross-Cultural Research.* Thousand Oaks, CA: Sage.

Van Maanen, John. 1982. "Fieldwork on the Beat." Pp. 103–151 in *Varieties of Qualitative Research*, edited by John Van Maanen, James M. Dabbs, Jr., and Robert R. Faulkner. Beverly Hills, CA: Sage.

Van Maanen, John. 1995. "An End to Innocence: The Ethnography of Ethnography." Pp. 1–35 in *Representation in Ethnography,* edited by John Van Maanen. Thousand Oaks: CA: Sage.

Van Maanen, John. 2002. "The Fact of Fiction in Organizational Ethnography. Pp. 101–117 in *The Qualitative Researcher's Companion,* edited by A. M. Huberman and M. B. Miles. Thousand Oaks, CA: Sage.

Venkatesh, Sudhir Alladi. 1997. "The Social Organization of Street Gang Activity in an Urban Ghetto." *American Journal of Sociology* 103: 82–102.

Venkatesh, Sudhir Alladi. 2000. *American project: The Rise and Fall of a Modern Ghetto.* Cambridge, MA: Harvard University Press.

Vidich, Arthur J. and Stanford M. Lyman. 1994. "Qualitative Methods: Their History in Sociology Anthropology." Pp. 23–59 in *Handbook of Qualitative Research*, edited by Norman K. Denzin and Yvonna S. Lincoln. Thousand Oaks, CA: Sage.

Vigil, James Diego. 1988. *Barrio Gangs.* Austin: University of Texas Press.

Wallace, Walter L. 1983. *Principles of Scientific Sociology.* New York: Aldine.

Walters, Pamela Barnhouse, David R. James, and Holly J. McCammon. 1997. "Citizenship and Public Schools: Accounting for Racial Inequality in Education for the Pre-and Post-Disfranchisement South." *American Sociological Review* 62: 34–52.

Watson, Roy E. L. 1986. "The Effectiveness of Increased Police Enforcement as a General Deterrent." *Law & Society Review* 20(2): 293–299.

Webb, Eugene, Donald T. Campbell, Richard D. Schwartz, and Lee Sechrest. 1966. *Unobtrusive Measures: Nonreactive Research in the Social Sciences.* Chicago: Rand McNally.

Weber, Max. 1949. *The Methodology of the Social Sciences*, translated and edited by Edward A. Shils and Henry Finch. New York: Free Press.

Weber, Robert Philip. 1985. *Basic Content Analysis.* Beverly Hills, CA: Sage.

Wechsler, Henry, Andrea Davenport, George Dowdall, Barbara Moeykens, and Sonia Castillo. 1994. "Health and Behavioral Consequences of Binge Drinking in College: A National Survey of Students at 140 Campuses." *Journal of the American Medical Association* 272(21): 1672–1677.

Weisburd, D., L. Maher, and L. Sherman. 1992. "Contrasting Crime General and Crime Specific Theory: The Case of Hot Spots of Crime." *Advances in Criminological Theory* 4: 45–69.

Weisburd, David, Stanton Wheeler, Elin Waring, and Nancy Bode. 1991. *Crimes of the Middle Class: White-Collar Offenders in the Federal Courts.* New Haven, CT: Yale University Press.

Weiss, Carol H. 1993. "Where Politics and Evaluation Research Meet." *Evaluation Practice* 14: 93–106.

Whyte, William Foote. 1943. *Street Corner Society: The Social Structure of an Italian Slum.* Chicago: University of Chicago Press.

Whyte, William Foote. 1955. *Street Corner Society,* 2nd ed. Chicago: University of Chicago Press.

Whyte, William Foote. 1991. *Social Theory for Social Action: How Individuals and Organizations Learn to Change.* Newbury Park, CA: Sage.

Williams, B. N. and M. Stahl. 2008. "An Analysis of Police Traffic Stops and Searchers in Kentucky: A Mixed-Methods Approach Offering Heuristic and Practical Implications." *Policy Science* 41: 221–243.

Williams, Kirk R. and Richard Hawkins. 1986. "Perceptual Research on General Deterrence: A Critical Review." *Law & Society Review* 20: 545–572.

Wines, Michael. 2006. "To Fill Notebooks, and Then a Few Bellies." *New York Times,* August 27, Week in Review.

Wolcott, Harry F. 1995. *The Art of Fieldwork.* Walnut Creek, CA: AltaMira Press.

Wolf, N., C. L. Blitz, J. Shi, R. Bachman, and J. Siegel. 2006. "Sexual Violence Inside Prisons: Rates of Victimization." *Journal of Urban Health* 83: 835–846.

Wolfgang, Marvin E. and F. Ferracuti. 1967. *The Subculture of Violence.* London: Tavistock.

Wright, Richard and Scott Decker. 1994. *Burglars on the Job: Streetlife and Residential Break-ins.* Boston: Northeastern University Press.

Zaret, David. 1996. "Petitions and the 'Invention' of Public Opinion in the English Revolution." *American Journal of Sociology* 101: 1497–1555.

Zimbardo, Philip G. 1973. "On the Ethics of Intervention in Human Psychological Research: With Special Reference to the Stanford Prison Experiment." *Cognition* 2: 243–256.

Zimbardo, Philip G. 2004. "A Situationist Perspective on the Psychology of Evil: Understanding How Good People Are Transformed Into Perpetrators." Pp. 21–50 in *The Social Psychology of Good and Evil: Understanding Our Capacity for Kindness and Cruelty,* edited by Arthur G. Miller. New York: Guilford.

Zimbardo, Philip G. 2007. *The Lucifer Effect: Understanding How Good People Turn Evil.* New York: Random House.

Zimbardo, Philip G. 2008. *The Lucifer Effect: Understanding How Good People Turn Evil,* 2nd ed. New York: Random House.

Zimbardo, Philip G. 2009. "Revisiting the Stanford Prison Experiment: A Lesson in the Power of Situation." Retrieved July 2, 2009, from http://www.lucifer effect.com

Index

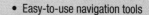